CULTS

CULTS

Inside the World's Most Notorious
Groups and Understanding
the People Who Joined Them

PARCAST'S
MAX CUTLER
WITH KEVIN CONLEY

BASED ON THE ACCLAIMED PODCAST

GALLERY BOOKS
NEW YORK   LONDON   TORONTO   SYDNEY   NEW DELHI

G

Gallery Books
An Imprint of Simon & Schuster, Inc.
1230 Avenue of the Americas
New York, NY 10020

First Gallery Books hardcover edition July 2022

GALLERY BOOKS and colophon are registered trademarks of Simon & Schuster, Inc.

For information about special discounts for bulk purchases,
please contact Simon & Schuster Special Sales at 1-866-506-1949 or
business@simonandschuster.com.

The Simon & Schuster Speakers Bureau can bring authors to your live event.
For more information or to book an event, contact the Simon & Schuster Speakers
Bureau at 1-866-248-3049 or visit our website at www.simonspeakers.com.

Interior design by Jaime Putorti

Manufactured in the United States of America

10 9 8 7 6 5 4 3 2 1

Library of Congress Cataloging-in-Publication Data is available.

ISBN 978-1-9821-3354-2
ISBN 978-1-9821-3356-6 (ebook)

CONTENTS

CULTS

INTRODUCTION

Everyone wants to believe in something or someone: a higher ideal, a god on Earth, a voice from heaven, an intelligence beyond our own. When this appetite for belief combines with the need to belong, great things can happen: nations are born, temples and cathedrals rise, astronauts land on the moon. The need to belong is a powerful instinct. It's part of our DNA as social creatures who depend on each other to survive, and the organizing principle that keeps religion and politics going. Belief and belonging can be intoxicating when acting in unison, along with the feelings they inspire when amplified by community.

But what about those rare moments when the dark side of human nature takes hold?

At Parcast, our focus from inception has been on the small subset of these close societies of dedicated believers known as cults and the frighteningly charismatic figures who lead them. We released our first *Cults* podcast in September 2017, and from that premiere episode—which debuted at number one on Apple's podcast charts—and every week since, we've been surprised by the intense response to these histories, with more than 55 million downloads over the past four years, with no sign of letting up. That outpouring of interest has kept us searching in the annals of extreme beliefs for the cults that will satisfy this fascination, week after week. It's not unusual, at the conclusion of one report, to think that we've finally discovered the worst that cults can offer, only to be rocked to our core by something far worse.

Thanks to our weekly podcasts, we have a catalog of case studies at our fingertips. From the beginning, we've not just looked at the raw data of cult leaders' lives and that of their followers but also examined their psychologies and motivations (although we are not psychologists). We take the time to step back and look at the types of manipulation they employed and pay close attention to the unconscious drives that have led so many to the outer limits of behavior, whether serial murder, sexual deviance, or mass suicide.

In the chapters that follow, readers will see similarities in the ways the cult leaders of every era have attracted and seduced their followers . . . how their near-total command over others drove them to test the limits of such control, and then—either out of boredom or sadistic curiosity, or because they, too, had begun to believe their own fantasies—to go beyond that to claim a godlike power over life and death.

The cult leaders detailed in this book would stand out in any lineup. Each has some trait that sets them apart: ruthlessness, childhood shame, repressed sexuality, a grandiose belief in personal genius, the sense of pleasure derived by inciting terror in their intimates. Almost all share three distinguishing traits—what is known as the dark triad of malevolent narcissism: lack of empathy, a manipulative attitude, and excessive self-love. In each case, it is impossible to say whether they arrived at these characteristics by nature or nurture. But nearly every figure highlights evidence of the forces that shut off their capacity for empathy.

Although the arc of their lives is known and the facts of their misdeeds are almost entirely settled, there is still a mystery in every one. The more closely readers look, the harder it is to settle this central question: Did these people, with their extraordinary capacities to charm, lie, manipulate, seduce, and fabricate alternate realities, come to their core malevolence at birth, or did the circumstances of their lives somehow turn them into monsters? Did they have a choice? If they did not feel regret about the worst of their choices, what *did* they actually feel?

We begin with **Charles Manson,** who in 1969 masterminded six murders in Hollywood from a distance, just weeks after Neil Armstrong first stepped foot on the moon. The Cuban American **Adolfo de Jesús Constanzo,** trained in the rituals of animal sacrifice, perverted those practices to serve his own needs, creating a campaign of terror, drug trafficking, and slaughter as the bloodthirsty head of the Narcosatanists in Mexico City.

Bhagwan Shree Rajneesh had undeniable gifts and spiritual insights, but used these talents as a smoke screen to hide his appetites for drugs and sex and multiple Rolls-Royces, and disguised his dark intentions, allowing his followers to release a biological agent on American soil in the 1980s. Nine years after Manson's "Helter Skelter" murder spree, **Jim Jones** shocked the world with the mass suicide that he oversaw in the jungle camp he called Jonestown in Guyana. **Claude Vorilhon,** or "**Raël,**" born in Vichy, France, after the Second World War, gave up a career as a café musician turned race car driver before finally settling on the role of founder of the UFO religion Raëlism, based on an alien visitation he claimed occurred in December 1973, expanding his space-based beliefs over the years to include lifetime sexual servitude.

Sexual deviance is a common thread, perhaps an inevitable by-product of the combination of ego, power, and lack of feeling that is the hallmark of cult leaders. **Roch Thériault,** the leader of a Canadian back-to-the-land cult, called himself Moses and fashioned himself as the prophet who could lead his followers, dubbed the Ant Hill Kids, into the wilderness, avoid the end of the world, and help them live in equality and happiness, free of sin. In practice, he inaugurated a reign of brutality that included beatings, surgery without anesthesia, toes amputated with wire cutters, starvation, sleep deprivation, slavery, sexual abuse, the torching of genitals, and other barbaric practices. **David Koresh** shared this mixture of megalomania and priapic appetites as he took over a sect of the Seventh-day Adventist Church called the Branch Davidians, establishing himself as a messianic figure and fathering children with multiple women in the sect before leading them all to their deaths in April 1993 after a fifty-one-day siege on their compound by the Bureau of Alcohol, Tobacco and Firearms.

Many of the life stories of cult leaders collected here also end all too predictably in a variety of violent deaths, but a few have passed on from natural causes, long after the dissolution of the cults that made them infamous. **Keith Raniere,** founder of NXIVM and the mastermind of a group of sex slaves who were branded with his initials, still survives in a federal penitentiary specializing in the incarceration of sex offenders and pedophiles, where the sixty-two-year-old will have plenty of time for remorse and introspection—120 years, to be precise.

When a leader dies with the rest of the cult, as Jim Jones did, it may seem like retroactive proof of sincerity. But in one of the deadliest tragedies on record, **Credonia Mwerinde,** the founder of the Movement for the Restoration of the Ten Commandments of God, did not appear among the bodies of the dead—close to a thousand in all. Most of the followers, who gave their worldly possessions to the Movement as soon as they joined, died after they were locked inside a wooden church. After the exits were nailed shut, the building was set on fire. Mwerinde, whose purported vision of the Virgin Mary inspired the Movement, disappeared, and neither she nor the money that the cult had amassed has ever been seen since.

More than once, the narcissism encountered in these cult leaders has grown beyond self-involvement to become a deadly force capable of overriding reality. Isolation makes this combination even more dangerous. In March 1997, in a gated community in Rancho Santa Fe, California, **Marshall Applewhite,** the founder of Heaven's Gate, set in motion an elaborate escape plan that would allow the group to board a UFO trailing Comet Hale-Bopp, leading them all to their new, next-level existence and leaving their bodies behind, in matching shirts, sweatpants, and Nike sneakers. In reality, it was a mass suicide that took the lives of thirty-nine members of Heaven's Gate, including Applewhite.

Looking closely at the lives of cult leaders chronicled here and the fates of the followers they inspired, you'll see the strange and often deadly symbiosis of belief and charisma and perversity. These cult figures may have left trails of bodies in their wakes, but that could never have happened without the misguided devotion of their acolytes— their eagerness to step beyond the rules of ordinary life and even the boundaries of common sense. The larger-than-life dominators who seized control of their small but often highly profitable bands of believers were gifted at gaining confidence and misdirecting it, but their devotees were willful and energetic in the execution of their faith. As seen in case after case throughout the following pages, it was the cult leaders who lit the fire, and the people trapped within their grip who tragically acted as the fuel.

SHAME

CHARLES MANSON
AND THE FAMILY

Over two nights in August 1969, Charles Manson and a group of his followers committed a series of murders so violent that the specter of cults began to haunt the nightmares of the entire nation. His highly publicized trial, complete with sensationalized coverage on the nightly news broadcasts, conjured images of a lost youth dedicated to free love, acid trips, race wars, and the random murder of movie stars and the Hollywood elite. Manson's own background in youth homes and prison equipped him with a nearly complete tool kit of criminal psychology: manipulation, a taste for unpredictable violence, and a deluded sense of his own importance. When the ex-con landed in California at the height of the 1960s counterculture movement, he turned a band of dropouts and runaways into a bloodthirsty cult whose murder spree signaled the end of the Flower Power era.

MURDER BY MIND CONTROL

More than any other cult leader, Charles Manson and the Manson Family is responsible for introducing the image of cults into the modern national consciousness. This isn't an exaggeration, like saying Al Gore invented the internet. Charles Manson and the nightmarish Tate-LaBianca murders that he masterminded mark the moment that everything changed on the American landscape.

How did Charles Manson achieve such notoriety? The 1960s were the television decade. There were only three broadcast networks, and every night a good part of the nation tuned in for the 6:00 p.m. news. One can point to TV becoming a transformative force in history when, on September 26, 1960, John F. Kennedy won the first-ever televised presidential debate. Radio listeners gave the victory to Kennedy's Republican rival, the sitting vice president, Richard Nixon. But those following on TV witnessed an entirely different event: Nixon, sweating due to nervousness and a low-grade fever, facing a dashing rival who grew more confident and commanding as the hour-long debate progressed.

The Kennedys' romance with television and vice versa continued after they took office, when the glamorous Jackie Kennedy gave the nation a televised tour of the White House. Then, tragically and indelibly, the TV cameras again brought the First Lady into American homes when they captured her in a bloody dress during the immediate aftermath of her husband's assassination. Three days later, the state funeral was broadcast live for seven hours straight. Ninety-three percent of the television sets in the entire country were tuned to the event.

For the rest of the turbulent decade, TV continued to shape the issues as protests and social unrest swept through the United States. The Vietnam War was dubbed the "living room war" as nightly news programs beamed in footage of American bombing raids, executions of civilians, and Vietnamese monks setting themselves on fire. President Lyndon Johnson, who sensed that the war would be his political undoing, even claimed that CBS and NBC were controlled by the Viet Cong.

In 1965, state and local police routed civil rights marchers in Birmingham, Alabama, and ABC News broke into the network's scheduled broadcast with shocking coverage of law enforcement trampling, clubbing, and tear-gassing six hundred civilians—a turning point that would lead to the Johnson administration passing the Voting Rights Act five months later. When large-scale riots gripped the crowded inner cities of Detroit and Newark in 1967 and Miami, Chicago, Watts, and Washington, DC, in 1968, the footage showed cities in flames.

On July 20, 1969, an estimated 530 million people watched live as Neil Armstrong and his fellow astronauts on the *Apollo 11* mission orbited the moon, successfully landed a lunar module, and exited down the ladder, stepping foot for the first time on Earth's only natural satellite. The inspirational event was heralded as the greatest proof of what humanity could accomplish.

Then, only a few weeks after this achievement, on August 9 and 10, TV showed humanity's dark side emerging as the evening news reported the murders of seven people in Los Angeles, brutally executed on consecutive nights.

It wasn't until two months later, on the night of October 12, that the police finally arrested Charles Manson. He was a small man, barely five-foot-three and 130 pounds at the time, but he nevertheless had an electrifying effect on those who gathered around him. The murders that he ordered his followers to commit—first of movie star Sharon Tate and four others staying with her at 10050 Cielo Drive in Beverly Hills, and then of married couple Leno and Rosemary LaBianca the following night at 3301 Waverly Drive in Los Feliz—sent the area into an immediate panic.

In Manson's misguided imagination, he hoped the fear those killings inspired would plunge the country into a race war. The apocalyptic conflict he was counting on never materialized, but the random nature of the crime and the brutal details of the killings—closely followed as news of the investigations reached the public through sensational nightly TV coverage—shocked America to its core.

It gives Charles Manson too much credit to think that this effect was intentional. But he was hungry for attention. At the time of the murders, he had spent the better half of his life in either reform school or jail. His uncanny ability to draw the spotlight to himself and to use it to get what he wanted was the one trait that his prison counselors and psychologists noted in nearly all their reports. When he was released on good behavior in 1967 from San Francisco's Terminal Island after serving six and a half years of a ten-year sentence for forgery at McNeil Island federal penitentiary in Washington State, he emerged into a country that was dividing sharply along generational lines over issues like women's liberation, civil rights, and the Vietnam War. Just a few years earlier, students in the Free Speech Movement at the University of California, Berkeley, had been warning their peers not to trust anyone over thirty. Although Manson was thirty-four in 1969, nearly all the members of his "Family" were in their teens and early twenties.

The Manson murders showed the nation how quickly all those youthful impulses could go wrong. The members of the Manson Family were all from the baby boom generation, the over 76 million children born between 1946 and 1964, and who came into their prime years of rebellion and experimentation en masse. They proved to be highly susceptible to Manson's mix of LSD and psychological manipulation. Manson himself was never present when his victims were killed, but he didn't have to be. Even without raising a finger, the slayings had his unmistakable signature on them.

Manson exerted a near-absolute control over the Family, and he used this power with the same intent as if he himself had wielded the murder weapons: the bayonet, the kitchen knife, and the .22-caliber Hi Standard Longhorn revolver, or "Buntline Special." This was his modus operandi—murder by proxy. Over two nights he demonstrated how easy it was to turn orphans, runaways, and college dropouts into highly motivated killers. And his hold on his Family continued even after he was caught. A gauntlet of young women in peasant dresses knelt on the ground outside the courthouse, telling any reporter who asked that they were holding a vigil, "waiting for our father to be free." Inside the courtroom, Charles Manson and his co-conspirators invented new disruptions every day, singing, laughing maniacally, or chanting during the proceedings, even rushing the presiding judge, Charles H. Older, as Manson did at one point, yelling, "In the name of Christian justice, someone should cut your head off!"

Thanks to the circus atmosphere of the murder trial, millions of gullible teenagers and young adults who wanted to "turn on, tune in, and drop out" started to look like threats. In the months that followed the murders, the term "cult" quickly took on a new and terrifying meaning, in part because the horrific nature of the crimes seemed to require a whole new vocabulary. Up until that point, "cult" usually referred to a religious sect whose belief system differed from those of traditional religions, even if its inception and practices could be traced in part to one or more of those same traditional religions. There had long been cults that splintered off from Buddhism, Judaism, Islam, and Christianity, and most were not viewed as inherently dangerous or malevolent. For sects like those, experts prefer the term "new religious movement," or NRM.

Before Manson, "cult" was often applied loosely to elements of popular culture, describing die-hard fans of a singer or a television show. But in the years that followed, the word came to refer to what psychiatrist Robert Jay Lifton calls "destructive" cults—the groups that systematically harm and kill others or themselves. There had certainly been dangerous cult leaders before Charles Manson, but these figures didn't start fascinating the American public until the Tate-LaBianca murders. According to Lifton, one can recognize destructive cults because they generally have three distinct features: a charismatic leader who becomes an object of worship; a shift in attitude that allows that cult leader to take advantage of group members for sex and/or financial gain; and near-total control that can be traced to the cult leader's ability to exert something Lifton calls "thought reform"—or, as it's colloquially known, mind control.

TROUBLE IN THE HEARTLAND

Charles Milles Manson's grandmother, Nancy Maddox, a fundamentalist Christian and the widow of a Chesapeake & Ohio Railroad conductor, had five children to raise on her own—Glenna, Aileene, Luther, Dorothy, and her youngest, Ada Kathleen—in the hardscrabble eastern Kentucky town of Ashland. Nancy was strict, but she hoped that her brand of Golden Rule discipline would help her kids beat the odds and grow up to be moral and pious. But Ada Kathleen wanted to have fun like other girls and at age fifteen began sneaking over the state line, across the Ironton Bridge, and into the dance clubs on the opposite side of the Ohio River. She started keeping company with a man eight years older—the handsome Colonel Walker Henderson Scott—and hid any evidence of the relationship from her mother. Scott had a secret too: he was a married man. But, married or not, as soon as he discovered that Ada Kathleen was pregnant, he skipped town.

Nancy sent Ada Kathleen to Cincinnati to have the baby, where the teen birth would not inspire so much local gossip. Left on her own, Ada Kathleen proved to be resourceful. She convinced another man, twenty-five-year-old William Manson, to marry her despite her pregnancy, and on November 12, 1934, at the age of sixteen, she gave birth to a boy, Charles.

But motherhood didn't settle Ada Kathleen. Her family, including her son, later told stories about her wild-child teenage years, which included one particularly outrageous incident in which the young mother carted her baby out to the bar with her and traded the boy for a pitcher of beer. In 1987, Al Schottelkotte, a news anchor at Cincinnati's WCPO-TV, unearthed a version as part of a feature on Manson: Supposedly, a waitress in the bar where Ada Kathleen was drinking had confessed how much she wanted a baby herself, and Kathleen offered the trade. The waitress, thinking Ada Kathleen was joking, brought the beer anyway. Later she was surprised to discover that her customer had not only finished off the pitcher but had actually left the bar without her baby. It took Ada Kathleen's brother, Luther, several days—a mysterious detail that suggests the waitress might have decided to make the best of her newfound maternity—to locate the bar and the waitress and recover the boy.

Ada Kathleen soon began leaving Charles with relatives so she could go out and party, disappearing for days with Luther. But her husband, William, who at first had been happy enough to help Ada Kathleen raise another man's child, quickly grew sick of these disappearances and divorced her in 1937. Ada Kathleen couldn't have cared less. She was busy taking Colonel Scott to court, trying to force him to pay child support. She won her lawsuit, but all she ever recovered from the boy's biological father was $25.

Did Charles inherit his mother's ill will and grow up to resent his biological father for abandoning him? There is little evidence one way or the other. But there is a thriving network of amateur detectives researching nearly every aspect of Charles's life and connections, no matter how obscure. And many in this community connect Manson to an unsolved murder in his hometown of Ashland four months before the Tate-LaBianca killings: Darwin Scott—Colonel Scott's brother and Charles Manson's uncle—was discovered in his home, stabbed nineteen times, a butcher knife sticking out of his body. The similarity of the crimes in Beverly Hills and Los Feliz has led many to attribute to Manson the same murderous feelings of resentment and desire for revenge in all three cases. But Kentucky detectives came to the more reasonable conclusion that Darwin Scott had a long rap sheet, a history of lengthy prison stays, and an unfortunate habit of running up astronomical gambling debts to shady underworld figures.

THE CHILDHOOD SHAME
OF A YOUNG PSYCHOPATH

What can be verified is that, long before Charles Manson became the deeply disturbed and vengeful leader of the Manson Family, he'd had a remarkably troubled childhood. A rough upbringing is a common feature among violent cult leaders, and most share a history of abuse, neglect, and criminality. (It's not a rule, though, and several whom we will look at appear to have grown up with loving and supportive families and had privileged educations.) But even among cult leaders, Manson's childhood stands out for its lovelessness: scarred by frequent run-ins with the law, subject to reluctant care from a rotating cast of relatives, visits that were sandwiched between his own frequent stays in reform schools and homes for wayward boys. And these troubles started early, in August 1939, when he was only four years old and his mother and uncle teamed up to rob a man named Frank Martin.

After a night of drinking, the siblings lured Martin to a gas station, then assaulted him and stole his money, sticking a ketchup bottle in their victim's back to make him think they had a gun. They did a terrible job of disguising their identities, and the police found and arrested them the next day. Charles may even have been watching as his mother was led away. A few weeks later a judge sentenced Ada Kathleen to five years in prison for her role in what the local media called the Ketchup Bottle Robbery.

With his mother locked up, Charles's closest relatives had to decide on the proper family member to take care of the boy. The best candidate seemed to be his mother's sister Glenna, who had a husband, Bill Thomas, and an eight-year-old daughter, Jo Ann. They lived the closest to where Ada Kathleen was serving her sentence, and that's where he was sent: the small middle-class town of McMechen, West Virginia, where almost everyone worked in the mines or for the railroad.

It wasn't long before Charles began creating problems for his new family. He was smaller than the other boys at school but always wanted to be the center of attention. Whenever people ignored him, he would act out impulsively. The standard punishment of the era—a whipping for bad behavior—didn't have any effect on him. And he didn't seem worried about getting beaten up at school either. He talked back to the bullies no matter how large they were. Jeff Guinn, in his expansive biography, *Manson: The Life and Times of Charles Manson*, tells how Charles's cousin Jo Ann was instructed to keep an eye on him—which was why, when Charles got in an argument with a larger boy on the playground, she rushed to the young Manson's defense, biting the bigger boy's finger to scare him away.

Jo Ann's behavior surprised the teachers, who didn't expect to see the mild-mannered girl getting into fights. She explained that her cousin had been harassed and she'd only tried to defend him. But when confirmation of the story was attempted with Charles, he simply said that he wasn't involved. It didn't matter. The teachers already considered Charles a habitual liar: they'd previously witnessed him recruiting classmates, especially girls, to attack other students he didn't like. And whenever they'd questioned Charles about these early efforts in mind control, he claimed innocence, saying that the girls had only done what they themselves had wanted to do. So when it came to his word against Jo Ann's, the teachers had no choice but to believe her.

Jo Ann now saw her cousin for what he really was: a gifted con artist with no sense of loyalty, ready to lay the blame for his mischief on anyone but himself. But Jo Ann also came face-to-face with her cousin's deeper pathological level of violence.

When she was ten and Charles was seven, an especially terrifying incident took place. Jo Ann's parents had left for the day, and she was charged with babysitting and doing the housework. Charles refused to help with the chores—not an unusual position for a young boy. But he didn't stop at that. He went out to the yard, found a sickle, and came back inside to frustrate her own attempts at her duties. When he refused to stop, Jo Ann kicked Charles outside and locked the screen door.

Charles screamed and slashed the door with the sickle blade. The look in his eyes terrified her, and Jo Ann was convinced that he planned to use the tool on her when he got back inside. Luckily, her parents pulled up at just that moment and he dropped the sickle before anything worse could happen.

These traits that Charles Manson exhibited as a boy could be considered consistent with recognized elements of psychopathy, a common condition in cult leaders, typified by amoral and antisocial behavior, the inability to love, and a host of other traits. The clinical psychologist Robert D. Hare developed a checklist that helps therapists to identify potential psychopaths. What could one infer that he might check off for the young Manson? Pathological lying? The tendency to manipulate others for personal gain? Lack of empathy? Glibness and superficial charm? Even though there is a hesitation among psychiatrists to put such a freighted label on one so young, these are all signs of what Hare classifies as both "factor 1" on his psychopathy scale—the most unequivocal diagnosis, typified by "selfish, callous, and remorseless use of others"—and "aggressive narcissism."

Would this mean that, at such an early age, Charles Manson was already a psychopath suffering from a recognizable mental illness? Not necessarily. Although his behavior clearly aligned with the early warning signs, these same traits (including a natural facility for lying) also have positive correlations associated with highly intelligent, extroverted people. Dr. Hare warns that these so-called core traits of the psychopath can prove to be useful, earning the person who displays them attention, rewards, and popularity. It may seem like a dangerous contradiction, but one of the greatest weapons in the arsenal of the psychopath is that, on a good day, people tend to enjoy being in their company.

But how did Manson pick up these traits in the first place? For example, it's believed that a child can become insensitive and unemotional through either nature or nurture. Some children are born empathetic, but if they grow up with abusive parents in an unstable home, that empathy can disappear in self-defense and as a reflection of their environment. Kids raised this way are the most treatable and likely to be able to lead normal, productive lives—if therapists are able to help them in time.

The more dangerous children are those from loving homes and safe neighborhoods but who still exhibit the same traits as the ones who grow up in a directly opposite environment. According to authorities on psychopathy—from Hervey M. Cleckley in his seminal 1941 book, *The Mask of Sanity: An Attempt to Clarify Some Issues on the So-Called Psychopathic Personality*, to Robert Hare, who developed the Hare Psychopathy Checklist—there is widespread agreement that some children have a genetic predisposition to psychopathy. Even as toddlers, they crave stimulation, they lie constantly, and they're heartless (or, as they're categorized in the clinical literature, "callous and unemotional," or "CU"). If they seem like they're being sweet or empathetic, it's only because they want something from a person—thus, Cleckley's "mask of sanity." This condition is not uncommon; Robert Hare suggests that it afflicts about 1 percent of children, or roughly as many as those exhibiting symptoms of autism or bipolar disorder.

If untreated, it is expected that the psychopathic child will be committing violence against others by the age of eight or nine and engaging in criminal acts by fourteen to sixteen. One way to help prevent the condition from getting worse is constant attention and timely positive intervention—a loving family does have a protective but still not foolproof effect. And that kind of familial environment was precisely what was missing in Charles Manson's childhood.

Manson experienced many traumatic events at a young age. Growing up with a mother who left him behind to party could have made it difficult for Charles to form a proper attachment bond with her as an infant. Watching his mother get arrested and visiting her in prison was almost certainly traumatic. Those were the chronic conditions that could have altered his nature. But Manson also suffered some distinctly hellish experiences that could have warped the way he looked at himself and the world. When Charles was five years old and living with his aunt and uncle, he attended first grade with Mrs. Varner, who was infamous in McMechen for verbally abusing and terrorizing her students.

Mrs. Varner spent Charles's first day at school relentlessly mocking him for having a mother in prison. He ran home crying, a sign of weakness in the eyes of his disgusted uncle Bill. The next day Bill forced Charles to wear one of Jo Ann's dresses to school, allegedly so his nephew could profit from the experience, toughen up, and learn how to be a man. Decades later, Charles still vividly remembered the humiliation.

According to Harold Koplewicz of the Child Mind Institute in New York City, in the right supportive situation, cross-dressing can be a positive and beneficial form of expression for children who want to explore their gender identity. But those who've been forced to cross-dress against their will by parental figures can be severely traumatized by the experience. In fact, while we can't say for certain that this single event can be the turning point in an already deeply troubled childhood, it's significant that several different serial killers, all of them with a gruesome trail of criminal behavior, went through the same kind of experience. Henry Lee Lucas, a pathological liar who confessed to killing first sixty, then a hundred, and later three thousand people, was made to dress as a girl by his prostitute mother, who also made him watch her having sex with clients. She was the first person he was proven to have murdered, in 1960. Ottis Toole, also forced to cross-dress by his mother (who called him Susan), was raped at the age of five by his father's friend, had a reported IQ of 75, and killed seemingly at random—ranging from a six-year-old boy to an eighteen-year-old male hitchhiker to a sixty-year-old man to a twenty-year-old woman he abducted from a nightclub in Tallahassee, Florida. Doil Lane, dressed in girl's clothing as a child, was as an adult convicted of killing two girls, ages eight and nine, and admitted that he liked girls' panties. Charles Albright, the "Texas Eyeball Killer," was dressed as a girl by his mother, who also gave him a doll and helped him learn taxidermy, although she would not allow him to buy the expensive glass eyes sold in taxidermy shops. He later killed three prostitutes, murders that were linked by one common trait: all three had had their eyeballs removed with surgical skill.

Apart from these links, recent research has further associated an acute sense of shame as a result of a specific incident of humiliation with future psychopathic behavior. For many people, the reaction is internal, and the shame can lead to a variety of negative outcomes, from saying demeaning things about oneself to self-harm, even suicide. For others—and it seems true of Charles Manson—the sense of shame can lead to aggression. Often this can set off a cycle of behavior with a dangerous dynamic: the source of shame remains hidden even while it repeatedly acts as the trigger for incidents of inexplicable rage. While the incident in the first grade is unconfirmed as the precipitating source of Manson's shame, his elaborate schemes of revenge and his unstable nature—uncontrollable rage welling up from unacknowledged stigma—may sound familiar to those who study the patterns of cults.

CRIMINAL FAILURE

In the late 1930s and early 1940s, Manson lived with the Thomases for two and a half years, and during that stay he developed three interests that remained with him for the rest of his life: a love of music (the family had a piano and, in their happiest moments, played and sang together), knives, and guns. Around the time of his eighth birthday in late 1942, his mother, Ada Kathleen, was paroled, and Charles went to live with her. At first he was thrilled to be back with his real mother instead of his strict relatives. Later in life, he told Nuel Emmons, for the book *Manson in His Own Words*, that the hug Ada Kathleen gave him when she first got out of prison was the only happy memory he had from childhood.

For eight weeks Ada Kathleen and her son stayed in McMechen while she worked as a barmaid, but then they moved south to Charleston, West Virginia, where Ada Kathleen found a job as a cashier in Van's Never Closed Market. It didn't take very long for her to notice her son's disturbing behavior, such as constantly skipping school and spending most of his time trying to sweet-talk women into giving him money for candy. When he started stealing things and blaming others for the crimes, she turned to her mother, Nancy, for help in teaching Charles right from wrong. But the lectures on morality had no more impact on her grandson than they'd had on her own daughter.

In the end, Ada Kathleen had no idea how to get through to her child. It probably didn't help that she'd gone back to carousing at the ends of her shifts, leaving Charles in the care of a series of not-entirely-trustworthy babysitters. Finally, as a last resort, she decided to see if an institution for troubled boys might be able to instill some discipline and moral fortitude. So, in 1947, when Charles was twelve years old, she sent him to the Gibault School for Boys in Terre Haute, Indiana, run by the Brothers of Holy Cross.

Suddenly, a tormented boyhood turned into an adolescence filled with petty and ineffective criminal behavior. At the first Christmas break, Charles was allowed to spend the holidays with his aunt and uncle and his forgiving cousin Jo Ann, who had encouraged the invitation. But Charles was quick to take advantage of the Thomases' hospitality. With the adults away at church, he tried to steal his uncle's gun, running the shower to mask the noise he made rummaging in the gun case. Jo Ann, who was afraid of Charles at this point, did nothing to stop him, but when her parents returned home and asked her why the water was running, she told them to go and ask her cousin. When they did, they caught him red-handed with the weapon.

A few months after returning to school, Charles ran away and began robbing local stores. But the now thirteen-year-old didn't have the patience to be careful or the keen awareness necessary to make a clean getaway. Soon he was nabbed again. In 1948 a judge, who assumed that Charles was Catholic because he'd been sent to the Gibault School, sent him to Boys Town, Nebraska, to the home for wayward boys that had inspired the Spencer Tracy movie a decade earlier. A feature in the *Indianapolis News* at the time had a picture of Manson, who, the paper reported, had told the court, "I think I could be happy working around cows and horses. I like animals."

Charles didn't stay there long. Within four days of arriving, he and another youth named Blackie Nielson stole a car and drove to Illinois. Somehow the two managed to get a gun somewhere, which they promptly employed in a pair of armed robberies. Then they tried to continue their criminal apprenticeship, eking out a living working for Blackie's uncle, himself a professional thief.

In early 1949 the police apprehended Charles once more. This time he was sent to the Indiana Boys School in Plainfield, a much harsher institution. Now fourteen, he had to survive in the company of a frightening array of individuals who had committed everything from robbery and assault to manslaughter. The staffers and older occupants regularly abused smaller, younger boys like Manson. And according to Charles, not long after his arrival, he was brutally raped.

Manson's later description of the event could serve as a textbook example of what psychologists call dissociation: "You know, getting raped, they can just wipe that off . . . I don't feel that someone got violated and that's a terrible thing. I just thought, 'Clean it off, and that's all that is.'" This kind of distancing mechanism in extreme cases can lead to multiple personality disorder, but it probably helped Charles cope with the memory of the trauma and his surroundings. It also provides early evidence of a troubling trait: his ability to numb himself to pain and disengage from objective reality. Manson later explained that this was the time that he first developed what he called the "insane game." Since he was too small to intimidate other students, he tried to scare them into believing he was crazy by flapping his arms and shrieking and making terrifying faces, a skill that he later displayed for television reporters who came to interview the famous cult leader in prison.

There can be little doubt that Charles was suffering at the Indiana Boys School. He lived in constant fear of being physically and sexually abused, and attempted to run away four times in 1949 alone. In October of that year, he and six other boys initiated the largest mass escape in the school's history, but police quickly caught Charles trying to break into a gas station. Two years later, Charles and two other boys fled again, this time getting as far as Beaver, Utah—1,600 miles from Indiana—in their stolen car, provisioning themselves along the way with supplies stolen from gas stations. But despite this successful breakout and the long joyride that followed, an arrest came after only a few days.

Charles was then sent to the National Training School for Boys in Washington, DC, where he was given a battery of tests that found him to be functionally illiterate. But they also showed that he had an IQ slightly above normal at 109. He certainly proved that he could manipulate the staff psychologists. Soon, Charles had one of them believing that the only thing he needed to turn his life around was a confidence boost. His potential would be optimized by a transfer to the Natural Bridge Honor Camp, a minimum-security prison in Rockbridge County, Virginia. There the Thomases reentered his life, assuring administrators that, if Charles were released early, they would house him and help him find employment. His parole hearing was set for February 1952; all Charles had to do in the meantime was keep a low profile and follow the rules. Instead, one month before the hearing, he was caught sodomizing another inmate while holding a razor to his throat. He was then transferred to the Federal Reformatory in Petersburg, Virginia, where he continued to be cited for "eight serious disciplinary offenses, three involving homosexual acts."

HONING HIS PRISON SKILLS

By this point, after five years, Charles Manson had become the kind of prisoner considered a danger to the general population. He landed next at Chillicothe, a maximum-security reformatory, with no hope of parole until his twenty-first birthday: November 12, 1955.

Surprisingly, though Chillicothe authorities called him "grossly unsuited" for rehabilitation even there, this is when Charles finally made a concerted effort to change his behavior. He learned to read at a seventh-grade level, became a model prisoner, put in some dedicated work at the facility's automotive shop, and, after earning a commendation for meritorious service, was finally released. By the age of nineteen, he'd effectively spent the past seven years in six different reform schools.

While he endured this long detention, various instructors, caseworkers, and prison psychiatrists regularly assessed him. Their insights provide the best sense of Charles Manson at the time, as they spotted the first glimmers of the master manipulator that he would soon become. At his first stop in the Gibault School for Boys, one instructor described him as a middling student, a likable boy, moody, with a bit of a persecution complex. By the time he got to the Indiana Boys School, which took in "incorrigibles," the teachers were growing more skeptical, complaining that Charles "did good work only for those from whom he figured he could obtain something." At the National Training School for Boys, he got more mixed results, convincing one caseworker that he was aggressively antisocial, a trait attributed to his "unfavorable family life, if it can be called family life at all." Another caseworker viewed him with even less patience, saying, "This boy tries to give the impression that he is trying hard to adjust although he actually is not putting forth any effort." Still, the same observer did detect his will to power, saying, "I feel in time he will try to be a big wheel in the cottage." Manson's skills at deceiving seemed to be proven by the last report from the Natural Bridge Honor Camp, where one gullible psychiatrist wrote that "one is left with the feeling that behind all this lies an extremely sensitive boy who has not yet given up in terms of securing some kind of love and affection from the world." It is hard to look through this file and not see the mind games and calculations that were Manson's primary means of self-defense.

After he was paroled in April 1954, Charles went from Chillicothe, Ohio, back to West Virginia, where he moved from home to home, first at the Thomases', then to Ada Kathleen's in Wheeling, and finally to his favorite place of all, with his grandmother, Nancy Maddox, who doted on him. But there was one condition Nancy laid down if Charles hoped to remain with her: he had to attend regular Sunday services with her at the Church of the Nazarene across the street. So Charles dressed up and listened to the sermons, absorbing some of the biblical strictures he would one day impose on his own followers, such as the idea that women should obey men, and the admonition to abandon one's own identity to serve a higher power.

It's no surprise that Charles didn't fit into this sanctified circle. He tried to make friends with the other Sunday school kids but soon alienated them with talk of the violence of his reform school days and the drugs he claimed to have done. He found it hard to showboat when the people he was trying to impress had no idea what "shooting up" meant. Then, on a visit to his cousin Jo Ann—who was now married to a local minister—she noticed him buttering up a teenage girl who had come to their home for counseling. Charles showered the girl with compliments, and Jo Ann quickly realized her cousin was trying to seduce the vulnerable guest. As a result, Jo Ann made the girl immediately leave his company and her house.

Still, by other measures, Charles seemed to be making a sincere effort to live a normal, middle-class life. He met a divorced dad, Charlie Willis, at Wheeling Downs, a local horse track, and Willis introduced him to his youngest daughter, a popular girl named Rosalie. The match seemed improbable when they were dating, and when they got married, on January 13, 1955, many speculated that the girl had to be pregnant. But if she was, she never had the child. Charles got a job, made some friends, turned to music—as he often did when he was trying to be on his best behavior—and began learning chords on the guitar. But his attempt to lead a stable life did not last long. When Rosalie did become pregnant a few months into their marriage, Charles started stealing cars for extra money. In the summer of 1955, he decided to take Rosalie and leave McMechen to visit his mother, who was now living in Los Angeles. Unfortunately, the couple was apprehended there, having driven cross-country in a stolen car across state lines—a federal crime.

Before sentencing, the judge had psychiatrist Edwin McNeil examine Charles. Manson claimed that he didn't know how to live a productive life due to growing up in reform schools. Dr. McNeil suggested leniency, since Charles was married with a child on the way. The judge took McNeil's recommendation and sentenced Charles to five years' probation. However, Charles, facing another court date in February 1956, decided to skip town with Rosalie.

He didn't evade police for long. On April 23, 1956, not long after the birth of his son, Charles Manson Jr., the twenty-one-year-old father was sent to San Pedro's Terminal Island penitentiary. Once in prison, Charles continued his real education. He learned from pimps how to single out vulnerable girls who lacked strong parental figures and take advantage of their psychological weak points. They taught him techniques employed by domestic violence abusers: isolate the woman, convince her you're the only one who truly loves her, then beat her to keep her fearful and subservient.

Charles mixed these prison-yard lessons with an official prison course created by Dale Carnegie, author of *How to Win Friends and Influence People*. Courses of instruction, sometimes for college credit or as a constructive use of time, are standard in prison systems. But this was the first class in Charles's life to gain his undivided interest. In his cell, he practiced lines that Carnegie recommended putting to use. Many of the ideas outlined in the book echoed Manson's own manipulative tendencies. And there was one piece of advice that he committed to heart: "Let the other fellow feel the idea is his."

Eventually, when Charles got out of prison on September 30, 1958, Rosalie and their son were living with another man, so Charles moved back in with his mother. He didn't stay out of jail for long.

Manson applied the darker lessons he'd absorbed at Terminal Island, and by mid-1959 he was pimping out a young woman named Leona (who'd already successfully pleaded with a judge to let Charles off for forging a signature on a stolen Social Security check he'd tried to cash at a Ralph's supermarket). To add to his revenue, he stole credit cards and cars, again driving them north across state lines, this time with Leona and one of her friends for the purposes of prostitution—a violation of the Mann Act, which, by June 1961, landed the twenty-

six-year-old in prison once again, this time at Washington State's
McNeil Island Corrections Center.

During this stint, Charles started studying Scientology for additional pointers in manipulation. He thought that Scientology's belief
in past lives and immortal souls could help him target troubled women,
allowing him to personally offer a way to let go of their traumatic
backgrounds. He also improved his guitar playing, feeding a passion
for music he'd first picked up in his time with the Thomases. He discovered the Beatles, who were so popular by then that they could easily be heard even in a federal penitentiary. Despite his petty rap sheet
and personal history, Charles still harbored delusions of being adored
and beloved by the entire world, just like the Fab Four. He began writing songs and planning a career as a famous musician, combining a
sturdy baritone and a feel for rhythm and blues with a talent for song-
writing. Even the prison staff grew hopeful that Charles could secure
work as a musician after his release.

By the time Charles was up for parole in 1967, the thirty-two-year-
old had spent half his life in prison. But, much to the surprise of the
authorities, he requested permission to stay in. Did he already have
an intuition of what he would become? It's impossible to know but
also easy to see why he wanted to remain. Prison is a world of rules,
a world he knew how to survive and thrive in. As Manson had admitted years earlier to psychiatrist Edwin McNeil, he had no idea how
to manage outside of prison. Asking to continue his life inside actually represented an uncustomary amount of self-awareness on Charles
Manson's part.

A FREE MAN LANDS IN THE SUMMER OF LOVE

The United States prison system is not designed to accommodate
requests of any kind, let alone one for continuing room and board at
taxpayer expense. Charles Manson was paroled in 1967 with permission to relocate to San Francisco. It was the Summer of Love, and a

hundred thousand young men and women were converging on the city. Between a life of incarceration and his isolated small-town childhood, Charles was doubly unprepared for the rapidly changing world he entered. War protesters and throngs of hippies were everywhere, and a prominent group known as the Black Panthers, which had its national headquarters across the bay in Oakland, had become a highly visible presence on the San Francisco streets. After years of negotiating the strict racial segregation of the prison yard, he was intimidated by these newly assertive and outspoken Black men and women ready to fight for their rights.

Still, in San Francisco's anti-authoritarian atmosphere, Charles's prison experience gave him street cred, and he relished the positive reception, which differed so sharply from the rejection he had experienced back home in McMechen. He spent a few days blending in with the protesters and hippies on the University of California, Berkeley, campus, studying the young people and learning to mimic them. He quickly realized that among the counterculture he could repurpose his long rap sheet as a badge of courage, a sign of his independence and irrepressible revolutionary nature. Charles sensed this profound shift in attitudes and realized, through no effort of his own, that he'd actually come up in the world.

Using all these newfound wiles, he charmed Mary Brunner, a young woman he met at Berkeley, pretending that he shared her idealism and social views, and quickly manipulated Mary into sleeping with him and giving him a place to live. Charles convinced her that he was the only person who could make her feel listened to, valued, special, and beautiful, and then he plied her with his interpretation of the newfound concept of "free love" that he'd picked up from the hippies in Haight-Ashbury. While Mary worked at the Berkeley library, Charles stood on the street corners, piecing together the best lines from the various gurus on the scene, playing a little guitar, charming the vulnerable sorts who'd come to San Francisco to be part of the scene.

One of them lent him a car and he drove down to LA, where he met Lynette Fromme, a runaway child of divorce who fell hard for

Charles's patter and came back with him to Haight-Ashbury. "They call me the Gardener," Charles told her, "because I tend to all the flower children." Charles put his views on free love immediately into practice, having sex with Lynette while Mary watched, then having sex with Mary while Lynette watched. A few weeks later he added a third convert when he was invited to dinner by a man who'd picked him up while he was hitchhiking: his teenage daughter, Ruth Ann Moorehouse, fell for him, and Charles even managed to come away with an old piano that he traded for a VW bus, which now meant he could travel with his growing flock.

His growth strategy worked like a standard Ponzi scheme. Manson's come-on wasn't all that different from the pitches of many others of the era: he told people to abandon their inhibitions along with their possessions and love everybody, tossing together bits of Scientology and Dale Carnegie with Beatles lyrics and Bible verses. But even though the content of his pitches was standard fare, his manner during these impromptu performances was charismatic and unpredictable: he sang and whispered and preached and seduced by turns, mesmerizing in a crowd and in an intimate one-on-one. The style won him followers whose devotion he tested by getting them to go out in turn and bring in more people to join their band. Manson soon had a large group of devoted female followers, even though one of his teachings was that women were subservient to men and had to do their bidding. Within months he could order anyone in his hippie harem to sleep with anybody, and began calling his followers the "Family."

Charles Manson then started expanding his reach beyond San Francisco, traveling around in their rainbow-painted bus, recruiting more women to join his cult, a lot of them teens who'd come to San Francisco as soon as school let out. In fall 1967 he moved his growing Family to Los Angeles. Manson soon found that it wasn't easy to feed such a large group, and they had to resort to foraging in dumpsters to survive. A few months later, in 1968, he made an arrangement with an old blind man named George Spahn for the Family to stay, for free, on the five-hundred-acre Spahn Ranch—or Spahn Movie Ranch, as it was also called—in the Santa Susana Mountains, north of LA, in exchange for doing chores and helping with horse rides through the old movie sets.

Although the free-love communal vibe helped the group fit right into the spirit of the sixties, the fact that there wasn't much beyond a belief in Manson and his words and impulses holding the rootless group together meant that they were passing an invisible line that separated a commune from a cult. For instance, one of the shadowy bonding and seemingly harmless but highly illegal activities he convinced them to do was dubbed "creepy crawling": it involved breaking into people's houses in the middle of the night and rearranging things, a profoundly random intrusion that grew even more troubling when the homeowners discovered that nothing at all had been taken. But delinquency, adventurism, and strange beliefs weren't all that exceptional in those days, as baby boomers turned flower children all over the country were banding together in social experiments that often turned sour—though none quite so spectacularly as the Family's did.

In Los Angeles, the unsuspecting cult started to grow exponentially larger. Manson had a knack for discovering troubled young people with malleable personalities and convincing them that he was the answer to all their problems in life. And it didn't hurt that one of the constant rituals on the farm was group LSD trips, during which Charles wove their trippy perceptions into his growing body of personal revelations. One of his most well-known followers, Linda Kasabian, a key figure in his murder trial (who was granted immunity and not charged with a crime), would later comment that, when she first met Manson, she thought, "This is what I've been looking for." And Manson was incredibly skillful, able to appear as whatever the potential Family member wanted him to be, with his cryptic sayings open to almost any interpretation. (He told Lynette "Squeaky" Fromme, for instance, that "the way out of the room is not through the door; just don't want out and you're free.") He was so successful at recruitment that he soon began teaching male followers, like Charles "Tex" Watson, how to bring others into the cult. At its peak, the Family could count more than a hundred people among its devotees.

A FAILED MUSICIAN FORESEES
THE APOCALYPSE

Manson still hoped to gain worldwide fame through his music, and he thought he'd finally gotten his chance in the spring of 1968 when Dennis Wilson, drummer for the Beach Boys, picked up two hitchhiking Family members. Charles used this opportunity to introduce himself to the musician, ply him with drugs, and compel the women in the Family to have sex with him. Soon he'd played on Wilson's musical insecurities and gotten him to buy the rights to the Manson-penned song "Cease to Exist," which Wilson later produced with the Beach Boys. It was through Wilson that Manson met Terry Melcher, the son of actress Doris Day, and a powerful record producer. The three met regularly at Melcher's home: 10050 Cielo Drive, the future site of Manson's most horrific murders.

Terry Melcher had a lot of hits under his belt, producing albums for the Byrds and the Beach Boys. Charles hoped that Melcher could perform the same magic for him, securing his fame and helping him with the musical career he'd set his heart on. But things didn't work out that way. After seeing Manson get into a violent brawl with a stuntman at Spahn Movie Ranch, Melcher flatly refused to sign Charles to any recording deal.

Then the Beach Boys' version of "Cease to Exist" came out on December 2, 1968, as the B side to "Bluebirds over the Mountain" and as a cut on their album *20/20*. Wilson had made several alterations that enraged Manson, changing the title to "Never Learn Not to Love," revising some of the lyrics—rewriting the darkly spiritual invitation "cease to exist" to the more standard Beach Boys seduction ploy "cease to resist."

On top of that, Wilson hadn't given Charles a writing credit. Wilson felt entitled to the sole credit, partly to recoup some of the expenses he'd racked up having Manson and the Family mooching off him and having his Ferrari totaled at Spahn Ranch. Wilson says he did pay Manson $100,000 and had given him a motorcycle for his part in the song. But what may have ticked Charles off more than anything was that the single failed to sell, and the release that he'd hoped would be his big break fizzled out as the B side of a song that stalled at no. 61 on the charts, an ignominy that ended Manson's professional music career before it really started.

Wilson had no idea how dangerous it was to make Manson angry. When Manson found out that he didn't have a writing credit on the song, he threatened to murder Wilson. Now it was Wilson's turn to cut ties with Manson. After this fiasco, Manson no longer had any contacts in the music industry and his hopes for stardom were gone. All he had now was the undying loyalty of his cult, the Family.

He began prophesying a strange fantasy for them, an apocalyptic future that would follow the bloody race war he was sure was coming, pitting African American militants and their white liberal supporters against the racists who resisted civil rights. He predicted that the few white people to survive this war would promptly be slaughtered in turn by the militants. According to Manson, the Family would find safety during this uprising by fleeing to a "bottomless pit" in Death Valley that would lead them to a secret underground city where they could live in peace while the battle raged above them. Once the dust had settled, Manson's Family would emerge from Death Valley, the only white people left in America. With the old, corrupt civilization purged in the uprising, Manson's Family would rule over the African Americans, whom Manson considered unable to govern themselves. In a last leap of illogic, he somehow thought that the militant victors of the race war would actually welcome Manson's rule.

After the Beatles' "White Album" dropped on November 22, 1968, Manson became convinced that the iconic record somehow offered mystical signs of the coming race war. He began calling it "Helter Skelter" after the Beatles' song of the same name. In Manson's twisted mind, the Beatles also knew about the approaching end times; Manson persuaded his followers that he might be the only one who'd received their true message. This was, of course, nonsense: the Beatles had named the song after an amusement park ride beloved by British children.

Manson's outrageous scenario is clearly so delusional that it has led some observers to claim it as evidence of paranoid schizophrenia. At least one member of a parole board that Manson faced endorsed this theory even though an FBI agent who interviewed him in prison found him to be sane—albeit clever, callous, unemotional, manipulative, and a pathological liar. This was an unstable mix of characteristics to start with. But now add to this his free-floating desire for revenge, the recent triggers for his rage, his near-absolute control over a large group of drug-addled followers who all thought that he was blessed with prophetic powers, and it wouldn't take much for this combustible mixture to ignite.

This is the state of mind that Charles Manson was in on a hot and muggy August 9, 1969, at Spahn Ranch. But Manson had more than just the heat to deal with. One of his followers, Bobby Beausoleil, a devilishly handsome young actor from the Haight-Ashbury crowd, had been arrested for killing a music teacher and drug dealer named Gary Hinman. The longer Beausoleil sat in jail, the likelier it was that he would talk to the police, and that was what worried Manson.

Only two weeks earlier, on July 25, Manson had been at Hinman's home with Beausoleil, demanding that he give them their money back after a drug deal gone bad. When Hinman didn't comply, Manson cut off his ear with a sword. That clearly turned Hinman into a risk, and he could easily lead the police to the Family. Manson told Beausoleil: "You know what to do."

Was Manson like a mob boss, or was he acting on one of Dale Carnegie's principles? Either way, it was a rule he seemed to live by: Let the other person feel the idea is theirs. He never needed to directly order a follower to commit murder. And sure enough, two days later, on July 27, Beausoleil stabbed Hinman with the help of two of Manson's most devoted cultists, Susan Atkins and Mary Brunner, who took turns holding a pillow over Hinman's face. Beausoleil wrote the words "political piggy" and stamped a paw print—the symbol of the Black Panthers—on the wall using the dying man's blood. The Family members intended to mislead the authorities, hoping they would assess the crime scene evidence and blame the Black Panthers instead.

But Beausoleil left fingerprints at the scene, and on August 6, police discovered him sleeping on the side of the road in the murdered man's car. Once they had him in custody, they discovered that Beausoleil's prints matched the ones found at Hinman's residence. It wouldn't be the last time that somebody in the Manson Family got sloppy and careless.

With Beausoleil in prison, Manson now decided he needed to create a series of random copycat murders to distract the police. Someone needed to die, someone rich and famous whose brutal murder would make headlines. It wasn't just the prospect of returning to prison that troubled him. He also needed to maintain control over his followers, the people who believed he was a higher being, equal parts Jesus—after all, as he frequently told his followers, his name was "Manson," or "Son of Man"—and the devil.

The psychologist Robert Lifton pointed out this particular maneuver in cult leaders, who often position themselves as powerful spiritual figures to their followers, elevated above the rest of mankind. He called the technique "mystical manipulation." According to Lifton, this is one of the key steps in thought reform (or mind control). Another aspect of this brand of mystical manipulation involves a cult leader pretending to look into the future, setting himself up as a prophet to his followers. To pull this off, a cult leader tries to reframe everyday coincidences to appear as the fulfillment of prophecies. This is what Manson was attempting to do by turning a fairly commonplace event in the late sixties—the release of a new album by the Beatles—into a sign of the coming apocalyptic race war.

The Manson Family already believed their leader was a kind of modern prophet. But as the summer was coming to an end, the Black population still had not risen up against the white oppressors. Manson couldn't let his followers think that he was wrong—that he was some-how less than a divine being. So while simultaneously trying to distract the police from his connections to the murder of Gary Hinman, he was also putting a scheme in place that would instigate the race war: the Manson Family would commit a new series of murders meant to implicate the Black Panthers again.

This all depended on a chain of events that would have African Americans, facing racist reprisals in the aftermath of these murders, rising up as one to rebel—a situation of such violence and mayhem that the police would have to abandon their investigation of the death of Gary Hinman. In the chaos, the Manson Family would rescue Bobby Beausoleil, Manson would avoid another prison sentence, and all of them would retreat to the promised underground sanctuary in Death Valley some 250 miles away. Like so many of Manson's plans, this was all a fantasy, based partly on the actual network of ghost towns and abandoned mines in and around the area and partly on his delusional interpretations of the Beatles' White Album, which suppos-edly predicted race war ("Blackbird") and revolution, and the book of Revelation, in which the Family members believed Manson appeared as the prophesied Christ.

Given the outlandish nature of this prophecy, it's hard to attribute the hold that Manson exerted over his followers solely to his powers of mystical manipulation. Clearly the hundreds of LSD trips that the Family members had taken together played a part in their belief that a race war was inevitable and that soon this tiny band of hippies and dropouts who could scarcely feed themselves would begin to rule the world. But no matter how they arrived at this absurd conclusion, by the night of August 9, 1969, the faithful members of the Manson Family stood ready to answer his every command.

THE DEVIL'S BUSINESS

Manson chose Tex Watson to act as the leader on the fateful mission. Watson got his nickname because he was in fact from a small Texas town, where he'd once seemed destined for a promising future: a track athlete and football star voted Class Favorite, an honor roll student, and "yell leader"—a prestigious position designated to rile up the student body. Watson, despite all his LSD trips, still saw himself as a natural leader, maybe even a rival to Manson himself. And Manson played on this ambition to stir Watson's addled mind into action.

Manson also reminded Watson of his personal responsibility: in June 1969, Manson had shot a drug dealer, Bernard "Lotsapoppa" Crowe, after Tex mishandled a swindle designed to get the Family $2,500 that they'd need to move to Death Valley. Lotsapoppa survived, but never went to the police. Still, Charles had proven that he was willing to kill to defend Watson. Could Watson really say the same?

To kick off the race war scheme, Manson didn't think he needed to murder anyone in particular; he just had to find somebody rich and famous enough so that the shock alone would set things in motion. So he dipped into his deep well of resentment and pulled up the address of Terry Melcher, the record producer who'd refused to give him a deal. He knew that Melcher no longer lived at 10050 Cielo Drive in Beverly Hills—but whoever was there now would surely be just as well-off. After Manson put this idea in Watson's head, Watson proposed that he would, in fact, go to Terry Melcher's former residence. Manson's ability to manipulate Watson was so powerful that even when Watson was interviewed years later by the FBI, he still believed the brutal killings were his own idea.

Manson wanted three female followers to accompany Watson. In the Manson Family, women were supposed to do what men told them to do without question—an article of faith that he'd picked up back at the Church of the Nazarene and twisted to his own purpose. Manson didn't tell them about the planned murders that night, knowing that they would do anything Watson commanded.

To assist in the murders, Manson selected one of his first cultists, Patricia Krenwinkel. At first glance, this sweet churchgoing middle-class girl might not seem to fit in with the Family, but her parents had separated when she was fifteen, and she'd switched high schools three times. As a result, Patricia grew up feeling isolated. Her older half sister introduced her to LSD, and both girls later tried, separately, to kill themselves. When she met Charles Manson, he immediately noticed the nineteen-year-old's loneliness and lack of self-confidence. Krenwinkel was an ideal candidate for the Family—cracked but not broken—and even though Manson was thirteen years older, he proceeded to seduce Krenwinkel and make her believe that he was her soul mate. He could offer her all the love and attention she needed. He could give her a sense of purpose. By the time she realized that Manson wasn't who he claimed to be, he'd already made sure that she was too terrified to leave. He would make Krenwinkel stand still so he could throw knives at her. He shamed her in front of the other women, placing her naked in the middle of the other followers and calling her ugly and stupid. He made her life hell and yet gave her just enough attention that she felt she could never flee.

Susan Atkins was another accomplice in the slayings and one of the first women Manson had met after he was paroled in 1967. Atkins's mother died of cancer when she was only fifteen, and she'd spent the rest of her teen years cycling through abusive boyfriends, drinking, and taking drugs. She'd already attempted suicide, spent a few months in prison for robbery, and worked as a topless "vampire" dancer for a group of Satanists. Once she saw Charles Manson playing guitar, she was easy prey. When she and Manson had sex, he spotted her insecurity and ordered her to pretend that she was being intimate with her own father. His skillful mind control had a powerful effect: Atkins had already helped Bobby Beausoleil kill Gary Hinman, and Manson knew he could rely on her once again when the time came.

Manson also needed a getaway driver. Linda Kasabian, a recently divorced woman who'd left the American Psychedelic Circus commune, had slept with Tex Watson, and had come to Spahn Ranch to join the Family, bringing $5,000 that she'd stolen from one of her ex-husband's friends. Unlike most of Manson's followers, Kasabian had a valid California driver's license, which was the reason Manson had wanted her, over the objections of other Family members, to join the group in the first place.

On August 8, 1969, Watson took the wheel of a yellow 1959 Ford, since he was the only one who knew where the four of them were heading. He brought with him a length of rope, a knife, and a .22-caliber Hi Standard "Buntline Special" revolver. As the vehicle wound its way through Benedict Canyon to 10050 Cielo Drive, the three women wondered aloud what they'd be doing that night. Would they would be stealing cars or heading off for another round of "creepy crawling"? They had no idea that they were about to go on one of the most notorious murder sprees in American history.

Watson stopped the car at the front gate of the residence. No one could see the main house from there, but the fence was decorated with the twinkling Christmas tree lights that Terry Melcher's girlfriend, actress Candice Bergen, had put up before the two of them moved out, not long before director Roman Polanski rented the place in mid-February 1969. Watson cut the phone lines at the house with bolt cutters, then backed the Ford down the hill and parked it out of sight.

The four scaled the fence as Watson explained they were now going to go into the house and murder everyone inside. But before they could do so, a car came down the driveway and pulled up to the gate. They hid in the bushes and saw behind the wheel eighteen-year-old Steven Parent, who'd just dropped in on his friend William Garretson, the young caretaker staying in the guesthouse on the Cielo Drive property.

As Parent rolled down the window to open the electronic gate, Watson walked out of the bushes and slashed him with his knife. Parent begged for his life, but Watson then shot him four times at close range. The canyons swallowed the sound, making the nearby shots appear to come from far away. No one in the main house noticed, and Garretson had already turned up his own music in the caretaker's cottage and didn't hear a thing.

The Family members now made their way to the main residence. Watson sent Kasabian to check for a way in through the windows, then noticed a hall window that was already halfway open. He cut through the screen, pulled up the window, and sent Kasabian back to the gate to act as lookout. Watson, Atkins, and Krenwinkel then entered the home.

The residence was sprawling and occupied that night by four people: Abigail Folger, a social worker and heir to the Folger's Coffee fortune; Wojciech Frykowski, an actor from Poland and Folger's boyfriend; the movie star Sharon Tate, who was eight months pregnant with husband Roman Polanski's child; and Hollywood hairstylist Jay Sebring, an ex-boyfriend of Tate's who'd remained a close friend. They'd all just come back from dinner and were settling in for the night. Tate had spoken earlier with Polanski, who'd called to say he'd just finished the screenplay for *The Day of the Dolphin*, the next movie he hoped to direct, and would be home in a couple of days. As long as her husband was away, Tate liked having people over to keep her company.

Tate was a fashion model turned actress, who'd gone from bit roles in TV series like *Mister Ed* and *The Man from U.N.C.L.E.* to starring roles in such films as *The Fearless Vampire Killers*, where she'd met Polanski, and 1967's *The Valley of the Dolls*, for which she'd received a Golden Globe nomination. Nobody in the Manson Family was aware of who was living in the home on Cielo Drive, but they had just landed by chance on exactly the kind of celebrity whose death would shock the entire country.

A little after midnight, the residents all started turning in for the evening. Folger settled down in the guest bedroom to read, Frykowski fell asleep on the living room couch, and Sebring and Tate were deep in conversation in the master bedroom.

The first person the Family members spotted was Frykowski. Watson told Atkins to check around for any others, and his voice woke

Frykowski up. Watson kicked him in the head, saying, "I'm the devil, here to do the devil's business," and warned Frykowski that he'd be a dead man if he tried to warn the others or called for help.

Atkins passed the open door of Folger's room and waved at her; Folger was used to people dropping in on Tate at all hours and waved back, then returned to her book. Down the hall, Atkins spotted Tate and Sebring talking, but they didn't even notice her.

Meanwhile, Krenwinkel realized that she'd forgotten her knife in the car and ran back to the gate to borrow one from Kasabian, who wouldn't need it on lookout duty.

After getting the report from Atkins, Watson ordered Atkins and Krenwinkel to bring everyone into the living room, which they did, at knifepoint. Watson tied Sebring's hands, then put a rope around his neck, looped it over a ceiling beam, and tied the other end around Tate's neck. Tate started to cry while Sebring complained about their rough treatment of a pregnant woman. Watson replied by shooting him in the stomach. The hairstylist collapsed, bleeding onto the living room carpet.

Watson demanded money, but nobody had much, except for the $70 in Folger's purse. Watson had hoped to walk out of there with a huge haul for the Family's relocation fund and was incensed at how badly things had gone south—after all, here was an extravagant house with a movie star in it, and nobody had much more on them than he did.

The slaughter that followed the first stage of the attack was ugly, violent, and unpredictable. But even though the victims were defenseless and their killers relentless, brainwashed, and acting without conscience, the slayings still didn't prove to be easy. Watson and Atkins had both taken acid and meth earlier in the day, which added a further level of incoherence to the ensuing bloodbath.

Watson began stabbing Jay Sebring repeatedly. As Sebring lay on the floor dying, Frykowski struggled to free himself from his restraints. Atkins tried to stab him, but once Frykowski got free and they wrestled on the floor, most of her blows landed on his thighs and shins. His screams drew Kasabian up from the gate. She arrived just in time to see Frykowski stagger out of the front door and collapse in the bushes. Kasabian tried to apologize to Frykowski but was interrupted when Watson followed him outside. Kasabian then watched Watson leave Frykowski for dead on the lawn; the coroner later reported that he'd been shot twice, stabbed fifty-one times, and bludgeoned over the head with the butt of the Buntline Special revolver.

Kasabian—the only one of the four to betray any moral compunction during the killing spree—was horrified and yelled into house that people were coming, a lie she hoped would frighten the other Family members and bring the grisly events to an end. She was ignored.

Folger tried to make a break for it out the front door, but Krenwinkel followed, slammed her to the ground, and stabbed her repeatedly, drenching Folger's white nightgown in blood. Perhaps in shock at what she'd just done, she told Watson that she wasn't sure if Folger was dead. He came over to help. While he finished her off, he instructed Krenwinkel to check if there was anyone else they could kill in the guesthouse.

Krenwinkel was torn. She was terrified of disobeying a direct order, but she also didn't want to round up more people to add to the slayings. So she walked toward the guesthouse until Watson couldn't see her, waited a minute, and then returned, telling him there was nobody else on the property—the only reason caretaker William Garretson survived the massacre.

By this point, Sharon Tate was the last one left alive. She begged and pleaded with the killers to save her child's life. They could take her hostage, wait two weeks for her baby to be born, and then do whatever they wanted. But Atkins and Watson were high on drugs, drunk on bloodlust, and too indoctrinated in the Manson Family's beliefs to care about the welfare of an unborn child. Atkins stabbed Sharon Tate sixteen times, telling her, as Atkins herself later testified in court, "Woman, I have no mercy for you!" while Tate cried for her mother.

In a little under half an hour, everyone who'd been staying at the main house at 10050 Cielo Drive lay dead.

Afterward, Atkins remembered that Charles Manson wanted them to do something "witchy" at the crime scene, so she took the towel that had been used to tie Frykowski's hands and scrawled "PIG" on the front door in blood, mimicking what she'd seen Beausoleil write on the wall after killing Gary Hinman. Then Watson, Atkins, and Krenwinkel left the crime scene and walked down the driveway to Kasabian, who was now waiting for them by the yellow Ford. They retrieved the spare clothing they'd brought along, and everyone except Kasabian, who'd waited by the car and hadn't gotten bloodied, changed into clean clothes.

On the drive back to Spahn Ranch, Kasabian bundled up the bloody clothes and threw them all down a steep hill on Watson's command. A little farther down the same road, they got rid of the weapons as well. Taking a detour down a side street, they spotted a garden hose on a lawn, and turned it on to wash the blood off their hands and faces. The homeowner came out to stop them, but they jumped in the car and raced away—just not fast enough before he got their license plate number.

When they made it back to Spahn Ranch, Manson was deeply unhappy. They'd barely retrieved any money, and as far as he could tell from their ensuing descriptions, they hadn't created a dramatic enough crime scene. He then drove back to 10050 Cielo Drive himself to wipe down their fingerprints and spread an American flag on the couch near Sharon Tate's corpse, hoping that in this era when young people were burning the flag to protest the Vietnam War, the juxtaposition of the flag and a dead pregnant woman would get significant attention. But even though Sharon Tate's death was all over the media by August 10, Charles Manson wasn't satisfied. From what he could gather, the police hadn't picked up any of the clues connecting this crime scene to the Black Panthers and Gary Hinman's murder. It was clear that these killings simply weren't going to be enough to start the race war he'd prophesied. He needed more people to die.

HELTER SKELTER

On the evening of August 10, Manson gathered Watson, Atkins, Krenwinkel, Kasabian, and two additional devoted followers, Steve "Clem" Grogan and Leslie Van Houten. At nineteen years old, Van Houten was the youngest of the group, the product of a middle-class family in the LA suburb of Monrovia. But after her parents divorced five years earlier, she began using drugs and running away from home. She met Manson the year before through Bob Beausoleil. Van Houten ended up eager to please Manson any way she could, her key function in the Family being the transcriber of Manson's improvised song lyrics in shorthand. But that night Charles had far bigger plans for her.

Manson explained that since all concerned had effectively bungled the murders in the early morning hours of August 9, he wanted at least two more copycat killings and was going to ride along to make sure things went well. He directed the car crammed with seven people to the house of Leno and Rosemary LaBianca on Waverly Drive in Los Feliz. Manson, who'd attended parties next door, believed that everybody on Waverly Drive was rich enough to have their murders cause a sensation. He had no idea that his intended victims only owned a grocery store, and Rosemary also had partial interest in a boutique.

The LaBiancas' back door was unlocked. Manson and Watson found Leno sleeping on the couch and roused him at gunpoint. Manson, who always wanted to be liked, even by the people he intended to kill, assured Leno that this was just a robbery and asked who else was in the house. Leno directed them to his wife in the bedroom. Manson brought Rosemary out to the living room, took her wallet, and then brought Krenwinkel and Leslie Van Houten into the house. Manson ordered them to put Rosemary back in the bedroom and make sure that "everybody did something" so they would all bear equal responsibility. Then he went back to the car with Kasabian, Atkins, and Grogan and drove away, on the lookout for another murder target.

Meanwhile, Watson put a pillowcase over Leno's head, gagged him, and tied him up with lamp cords. Then he did the same thing to Rosemary, who was still in the bedroom. Krenwinkel grabbed a kitchen knife to take care of Rosemary. After killing Abigail Folger the night before, she didn't want any more blood on her hands, but disobeying Manson was a more terrifying prospect. Krenwinkel and Van Houten waited in the bedroom while Watson stabbed Leno to death with a bayonet given to him by Manson. When Rosemary heard her husband's cries and put up a struggle, Krenwinkel began stabbing her. Watson then came into the bedroom and finished Rosemary off, dealing the final blow.

This time the Family was careful to give Charles Manson the dramatic scene he'd demanded. Watson carved the word "WAR" into Leno's abdomen. Krenwinkel, getting over her initial hesitation, stuck a fork into Leno's stomach and a knife in his throat. Van Houten wrote "DEATH TO PIGS" and "RISE" on the walls in the LaBiancas' blood. Van Houten hadn't done much to participate in the actual murders at this point, so Watson made her pull up Rosemary's dress and stab her even though she was already dead. Leslie spotted a bag of change and grabbed it. Then, with the couple dead, the trio realized they were hungry and looked in the refrigerator, partaking of the watermelon and chocolate milk they found there. After their post-murder snack, they neatly placed the watermelon rinds in the sink while Krenwinkel wrote the words "HELTER SKELTER" in blood on the refrigerator door.

It was those two fateful words, taken from the Beatles' White Album, that would be the key to unlocking the secrets of the Family and securing Charles Manson's eventual conviction for murder. Manson had thought the police would see the writing on the wall—literally—and blame the African American community for a series of copycat murders. Yet initially the police had no idea that the murders of Gary Hinman, Sharon Tate and her friends, and the LaBiancas were part of a pattern. In fact, on August 12, authorities told reporters that there was no connection between the Tate and the

LaBianca murders; they truly thought they had unrelated cases on their hands.

Manson had failed to start "Helter Skelter." And it also seemed as if he were going to get away with the slayings even though the police were busy investigating him for car theft. The Family had been stealing vehicles and transforming them into dune buggies for their underground city while waiting out the race war. And that was why the cops finally came to the Spahn Ranch on August 16: to make arrests for the lesser crimes. Manson and twenty-five of his followers were rounded up and taken into custody. That included Susan Atkins, who craved attention and approval, a key reason she belonged to the Manson Family in the first place. Once she was locked up, she started bragging to her cellmate Virginia Graham about her part in the previous week's killings. When Graham asked how she felt about it, Atkins said that in murdering the pregnant Sharon Tate she had been killing a part of herself and that now she felt tired, elated, and at peace, because she knew this was the beginning of "Helter Skelter."

That was the break that investigators needed to connect the Tate and LaBianca killings to a single group, and it wouldn't be the Black Panthers. Charles Manson, Tex Watson, Susan Atkins, Leslie Van Houten, and Patricia Krenwinkel were all charged with murder. Linda Kasabian, hesitant to participate in the killing spree in the first place and horrified by the murders, had left Spahn Ranch in the Family station wagon and, when Manson thought she was off on an errand, fled instead to New Mexico and offered to turn state's evidence. In return for her freely offering her testimony, the prosecution granted her immunity, although she never asked for it. She was on the witness stand for seventeen days, and prosecuting attorney Vincent Bugliosi credited her unwavering testimony with securing guilty verdicts for all involved.

Charles Manson had just been caught in a web of his own making. As the number of his followers grew, he had to rely on more than just his abilities to spot hidden character weaknesses to exploit for personal gain. He fell into the trap—one that repeatedly befalls cult leaders—of building himself into a godlike figure, one capable of prophesying what was to come. He never suspected that he'd cornered himself, that his improvised promise of a race war, an underground sanctuary, and a future in which his band of misfits would rule the country, if not the world, was just a maneuver to buy time. He'd forgotten his own hapless history of crime: the failed escapes from reform school, the careless break-ins, the stolen check he'd tried cashing at Ralph's supermarket, a pimping career that led him back to prison. His genius for exploiting insecurities didn't help him when it came to orchestrating a horrific crime and the blunders that led to hard evidence: Susan Atkins inexplicably leaving her knife under a couch cushion on Cielo Drive; Tex Watson beating Wojciech Frykowski so hard with the butt of his Buntline revolver that the cheap gun's grip broke and left traceable fragments around the corpse; Watson pressing the button of the electronic gate with a bloody finger. As a criminal enterprise, the Manson Family had all the skills one might expect from a random collection of unemployed acidheads from broken homes. For all his loyal following and his messianic ambitions, Manson's grandest scheme had led him right back to the place he'd spent most of his life—prison—and, despite the notoriety he'd gained, to that same primal shame that had been his lot nearly from birth.

LOCKING THE FAMILY AWAY

Charles Manson's trial began on June 15, 1970, and it quickly turned into a circus that captivated America, with the proceedings featured every night on television. Manson treated each court appearance like a performance. He constantly misbehaved. He attacked the judge by rushing at him, armed with a pencil, while screaming, "Someone should cut your head off, old man!" He gave Atkins, Krenwinkel, and Van Houten specific instructions on how to join in the disruptions. One day the women sang in court, the next day he had them screaming nonsense or shaving their heads. He carved an X into his forehead and in a speech to the cameras, in which those present can make out a haunting mixture of truth, incoherence, self-pity, and manipulation, he said, "I am what you are making me. I was good and now I know none. For you as a group of people have shown me no mercy. The mark on my head simulates the deadhead black stamp of rejection, anti-church, falling cross, devil sign, death, terror, fear. I wanted to be a good guy, but you didn't let me."

Many of Manson's female followers who weren't on trial for murder spent their time camped out just outside the courthouse, dressed like flower children, giving interviews to the press. Some of them tried to threaten and even poison witnesses. Barbara Hoyt, a Family member who'd agreed to talk to the prosecution, was offered a trip to Hawaii instead by several of Manson's followers in exchange for refusing to testify. Ruth Ann Moorehouse and Barbara Hoyt traveled together to Hawaii, and just before she left, Ruth Ann tricked Barbara into consuming a potentially lethal ten hits of LSD she'd hidden inside a hamburger. Barbara survived and became an even more eager witness for the prosecution.

As his ultimate gambit, Manson tried to get his codefendants to announce to the court that they'd committed the murders themselves without any involvement from him. But Van Houten's defense lawyer, Ronald Hughes, recognized that Manson was manipulating his client. The attorney may have been too perceptive about Charles Manson for his own good: before closing arguments, Hughes disappeared while on a weekend camping trip. His body was found the same day that every single defendant received the death penalty.

Although the cause of Ronald Hughes's death has never been definitively solved, an anonymous Manson Family member contacted lead prosecutor Vincent Bugliosi—who, in his closing argument, had described Charles Manson as "the dictatorial master of a tribe of boot-licking slaves"—and told him that the Family was responsible. Even with their leader behind bars, the Family was willing to kill for him.

Despite the prison sentence, none of the Manson Family members remained on death row for long. In February 1972, after California abolished the death penalty, Manson, Watson, Krenwinkel, Atkins, and Van Houten—along with every other convicted killer in the California system (including Sirhan Sirhan, who'd assassinated Robert F. Kennedy)—had their sentences commuted to life in prison with the possibility of parole.

Once Manson's followers were locked up and safe from his influence, they finally began to think for themselves. Many tried to take on new identities. Tex Watson converted to Christianity and became a popular jailhouse minister, although an FBI agent who interviewed him was skeptical about his sincerity and believed the principal killer was just angling to get out on parole. Despite all of Watson's efforts to reform, the California parole board still considers him a risk to society, denying his freedom as recently as October 2021.

Susan Atkins became a born-again Christian also, trading one form of devotion for another. She died of cancer in 2009, setting a state record for the longest time incarcerated by a woman—one that Krenwinkel and Van Houten have now surpassed.

Bobby Beausoleil also exchanged one type of fanaticism for another, joining the white supremacist Aryan Brotherhood. He, too, was denied parole, in 2022.

Patricia Krenwinkel began thinking on her own once she landed on death row: learning that Charles Manson had sold her to another prisoner in a card game certainly provided a jolt in that direction. She claims to have regained her sense of self and, with it, all the remorse she initially couldn't allow herself to feel. She is now a model prisoner and a mentor for several prison groups. However, despite her claims of breaking away from Manson's influence, in 2017 she was denied parole for the fourteenth time. She is eligible for reconsideration once again, in 2022.

Leslie Van Houten, the youngest of the convicted murderers, has also become a model prisoner and openly expressed remorse for the Manson Family killings. As a child of a bitter divorce that led to her dropping acid repeatedly at age fourteen, she credits her father for coming back into her life and helping her regain both her grip on reality and her own moral code. Her lawyer pointed out at her 2013 parole hearing that her value system has been completely transformed since falling under Manson's sway back in 1969. She was twice recommended for parole, in 2016 and in 2017, but both times her release was blocked by Governor Jerry Brown, honoring the request of the victims' family members, who still consider her to be an unrepentant killer. Her latest appeal for parole was denied by the California Supreme Court in February 2022.

For some, Charles Manson's mind control proved too powerful to overcome. Mary Brunner, his first follower, who only missed participating in the murders because she was in prison for credit card fraud at the time, felt guilty about testifying against the Manson Family at the explosive murder trial. She and several other Family members were later sent to prison for stealing guns, which they'd hoped to use as part of a 1971 plane hijacking to free Manson. She was released in 1977 and then disappeared from the public eye.

Lynette "Squeaky" Fromme went to jail in 1975 after attempting to assassinate President Gerald Ford. But life in prison wasn't enough to shake her devotion. She was locked up alongside fellow Family member Sandra Good, and the two referred to themselves as "sisters in the church of Charles Manson." Fromme's dedication to Manson was so unwavering that she broke out on December 23, 1987, to see him after hearing that he had been diagnosed with cancer. She was recaptured and finally released on parole in December 2009. In an interview with ABC for a television special called *Manson Girls*, Fromme confessed that she was still in love with Charles fifty years after the brutal murders. "I feel honored to have met him," she said. "And I know how that sounds to people who think he's the epitome of evil."

Linda Kasabian, whose seventeen days of testimony against her fellow Manson Family members sent them all to death row, vanished into a life of obscurity. When last sighted, she was living in low-income housing under her second assumed name in Tacoma, Washington, not far from the home of the youngest of her four children. In the years since those convictions, she has struggled with her own guilt, and with drugs and alcoholism, and has said that she thinks about the senseless murders every day. Her arrest record attests to her problems with self-control in the intervening years: in 1976 she was fined $100 for disorderly conduct when she tried to prevent firefighters from putting out a bonfire in Nashua, New Hampshire; in 1982 she was charged with indecent exposure for flashing her breasts at a biker rally in Laconia, New Hampshire; in 1987 she was charged with a DUI in Cape Canaveral, Florida; and on her last arrest in 1996, during what she describes as a "period of drugs and alcohol and self-destruction," she was arrested for possession of rock cocaine and methamphetamine. She told the *Daily Mail* in an interview soon after Manson died that, to this day, she can still hear the screams of the victims "if I let myself go there."

SHAME

ADOLFO DE JESÚS CONSTANZO
AND THE NARCOSATANISTS

Adolfo de Jesús Constanzo, a Miami native and the American son of a Cuban refugee, is arguably the most sadistic and systematically bloodthirsty of all the cult leaders depicted in these pages. During his brief reign of terror in the late 1980s, from Mexico City to the border towns near Brownsville, Texas, Constanzo was responsible for the ritual murders of at least sixteen people that can be verified, although his insatiable appetite for killing, cruelty, and intimidation suggests there are likely more. Adolfo grew up in a home filled with animal filth and the rotting remains of amateur sacrifices, leaving him with an indelible sense of shame that fueled lifelong ruthlessness. One of the few sources of order in Constanzo's life came from his training in a dark branch of Santería known as Palo Mayombe, where he learned to shed blood and disregard the pain of living creatures offered up in rituals. After his own elaborate initiation in Miami, he set up shop in Mexico and quickly transformed from a fortune-teller into El Padrino, the mastermind of the Narcosatanists, a violent criminal enterprise and cult that operated under the supernatural protection of his regular bloodthirsty human sacrifices of astonishing brutality, during which he would skin victims alive, mutilate them piece by piece, organ by organ, or kill them with a swift blow of a machete to the skull or the slice of his knife on the neck.

DESTINED TO KILL

What could make a boy born to a fifteen-year-old single mother grow into the young man who calmly drained blood, severed genitals, and cut out the brains of his victims to add to his *nganga*, or mystical cauldron? What could possibly have happened in his childhood that turned him into such a pitiless and systematic killer?

Delia Aurora Gonzalez del Valle gave birth to Adolfo de Jesús Constanzo on November 1, 1962, in the Little Havana section of Miami. Teenage Delia had recently fled post-revolution Cuba. There are very few details of Adolfo's upbringing: his surviving family has remained understandably publicity-shy in the aftermath of his trail of murders. What we know of the boy and his early life comes from the testimony of his followers, one of whom was Delia's friend during his childhood.

According to those sources, Delia was a devout believer in Santería, a religion that developed in Cuba over four hundred years ago among the descendants of West and Central Africans forced to live as slaves. The purest forms of Santería are based on Yoruba customs—trances, ritual drumming, animal sacrifice, mystical communication with ancestors—and those who refined the practice in Cuba hid the true nature of their worship by imbuing the Roman Catholic saints with the supernatural abilities of the gods they had worshipped in their homeland. It was a simple disguise that allowed them to continue to practice their ancestral rites almost in the open.

Delia once claimed that she had always been a practicing Catholic and never had anything to do with Santería. (This is impossible to verify: soon after she claimed the body of her son in May 1989, she disappeared from public view entirely and has never been heard from again.) Her claims were contradicted by statements from Adolfo's followers and Delia's former neighbors. The Miami police also gathered extensive evidence of her involvement in both Santería and Palo Mayombe, the principal Cuban and Haitian religion that Adolfo and the Narcosatanists, as they would later be called, claimed to practice. These accounts form the basis for a more comprehensive understanding of Adolfo's early life.

One big distinction between Santería and most other Abrahamic religions—principally Judaism, Christianity, and Islam—is that Santería has no absolute commandments. In Santería, magic can be used for good or evil; spells can be beneficial or malicious. Whether they help or hurt people is up to whoever casts the spell. Today, Santería is practiced by people of all walks of life throughout the Caribbean and Latin America. Like many Cuban refugees, Adolfo's mother brought this tradition with her to the United States.

Adolfo's father abandoned the family shortly after the boy's birth, and there is no evidence that Adolfo ever knew the man. Delia married at least three other men over the years, but the most influential male figure in Adolfo's life was the one who taught him the ways of Palo Mayombe.

Palo Mayombe is another Cuban religion similar in many ways to Santería, combining Catholicism with religious practices transported from West Africa along with the people forced into slavery, in this case those from the banks of the Congo River. Mayombe is the region of Africa where the religion originated, and *palo* is Spanish for "stick" or "branch," used to stir the cauldron before casting spells.

Although there is no formal connection between Santería and Palo Mayombe, there is significant overlap in the beliefs and believers of both. Instead of asking the gods for help, adherents of Palo Mayombe seek to control the spirits of the deceased through their spells. Like Santería, these can be used for good or evil. Palo Mayombe is often portrayed as a morbid cousin of Santería due to its association with the dead, but it's important to note that there is nothing inherently evil about it.

When Adolfo was six months old, Delia brought him before a Haitian *palero*, the equivalent of a priest in Palo Mayombe. Delia hoped the man could provide guidance in raising her son. The palero examined the baby and proclaimed him a chosen one, predicting that he would go on to do great things, and even offered to become Adolfo's spiritual teacher, his *padrino* or "godfather," a move that Delia graciously accepted.

RAISED IN SQUALOR

But before this apprenticeship could even begin, Delia moved from Miami to San Juan, Puerto Rico, while Adolfo was still a toddler, to follow a man she soon married. Little is known about the family's many years in Puerto Rico or about this first of Adolfo's three stepfathers. According to Delia, her son was a model child, an altar boy in the local Catholic church who also excelled at tennis.

But even while Adolfo was leading a seemingly exemplary life in public, he was plunged into a very different sort of existence at home. There were two key formative circumstances from his childhood that seem to foretell the violence and notorious cruelty that would later be routinely visited upon strangers, enemies, and close associates: the squalor of his surroundings and his early education in animal sacrifice.

Growing up in an unsanitary environment of near-perpetual disorder seems to have deeply affected Adolfo. Delia was a hoarder, nearly incapable of throwing anything away. This compulsion quickly turned anyplace they lived into chaos. And, to make matters worse, the home soon became mired in filth and animal remains, evidence of her eager if amateur attempts to practice Santería.

Priests of Santería, or *santeros*, often entreat the gods through sacrificial offerings. For minor problems, the sacrifice is typically something small, like food or flowers. While animal sacrifices are not uncommon, the shedding of blood is taken quite seriously. Only a situation of great importance would call for a killing. And even when an animal is sacrificed, it's common practice to accompany the ritual slaughter with prayers, and participants in the ceremony then cook and share the meat of the sacrifice at its conclusion.

But Delia seemed to live in a nearly constant state of emergency and alarm. Perhaps as a defense against imagined threats, she also hoarded large groups of animals to sacrifice at the slightest opportunity. Neighbors reported finding decapitated chickens on their doorsteps. One claimed to have watched Delia depositing the headless corpse of a goat right in the street. Although these incidents were reported to the authorities, no charges were ever made.

Almost certainly as a reaction to the mess he saw around him, Adolfo developed an unusual trait at a young age: he became obsessively neat. Around when he was capable of dressing himself, he began carefully laying out his clothes every night before bed and kept his room—and anything else he could identify as his own—spotlessly clean.

Like Charles Manson, Adolfo Constanzo seems to have fought against a profound sense of shame from the most impressionable age. While Manson's humiliation seemed to have grown out of specific incidents—seeing his mother arrested and sent to jail, being forced to attend grade school dressed as a girl—Adolfo's shame came as a result of persistent squalor at home. Neighbors in Miami regarded his family with suspicion, and those with small children didn't invite Adolfo over for playdates.

Delia got a local reputation for never answering the door, something corroborated in police reports. This refusal may have been connected to a common behavior in hoarders informally known as "doorbell dread." Some people allow their living spaces to degrade to such a degree that they avoid ever letting nonfamily members into their residence, aware of the immediate disapproval regarding their living conditions. This often sets off a spiral of unhealthy outcomes, like profound social alienation. This set of behaviors, sometimes referred to as Diogenes syndrome, is often associated with senile dementia, but any wider distribution in the general population is hard to verify, since nearly half of hoarders are highly intelligent people who successfully evade detection, avoiding all but the most minimal interactions with the outside world. It's therefore not surprising that Delia was able to disappear after her son's death: she'd been practicing such a trick for his entire life.

The shame that Adolfo internalized growing up in these squalid surroundings goes by many names—toxic shame, core shame—but such persistent feelings, no matter how repressed, can lead to the same dynamic that seemed to trigger Charles Manson's dangerous rages. Perhaps Adolfo thought that his own compulsion—his obsession with maintaining order over everything within control—was proof that he was free from the chaos that ruled his mother's sphere. But it is not hard to trace the link from Delia's seeming preference for domestic anarchy to the boy's uncontrollable cleanliness that followed him into adulthood, which then transformed into not just an insistence on spotlessness in all his surroundings but a need for order so extreme that he decreed blood oaths of total obedience from his followers on pain of death. Palo Mayombe helped nourish this frenzy, for it divided the world into believers and nonbelievers. And, like his *padrino*, Adolfo Constanzo came to believe that as a *palero*—a priest of Palo Mayombe—he owed nothing to nonbelievers. They all deserved to die.

APPRENTICESHIP IN MURDER

The Costanzos lived in San Juan until 1972, when Delia's husband was diagnosed with cancer. Like so much about Adolfo's mother, it is impossible to know now why she chose to move back to Miami at this time, but nevertheless her spouse stayed behind in San Juan, passing away the following year.

The return to Miami reunited ten-year-old Adolfo with his Haitian *padrino*, the one who had examined him as a baby and considered him marked by destiny. Little is known about this man, and the few details that exist are based on secondhand statements of Adolfo's followers. But reports agree that he owed his steady income to the Palo Mayombe spells he performed for underworld figures in the Miami drug trade.

There are two branches of Palo Mayombe, known as Palo Cristiano and Palo Judio. So-called Christian *paleros* work in concert with God and spurn evil spirits. In the other branch—called "Judio" not through any association with Judaism but only because these adherents refused to follow the tenets of the religion of those who had enslaved them—the *paleros want* to work with evil spirits. This branch identifies with a being they call Kadiempembe, the "devourer of souls"—a rough analogue to the Western conception of the devil. Adolfo's *padrino* was a *palero* in this very tradition, revering Kadiempembe's power.

Adolfo was only eleven when he first stood in the presence of his *padrino*'s *nganga*—a Kongo word that, in a larger sense, denotes the dead or supernatural forces. In Palo Mayombe, the word also refers to the cauldron, the main tool through which a *palero* interacts with the spirit world. The *nganga* is the source of a *palero*'s power and is unique to Palo Mayombe.

The *nganga* is meant to be filled with the carcasses of sacrificed animals, sacred herbs, insects, and an array of branches or *palos*. But the key ingredient is human remains. The *nganga* requires the skull, brain, and several bones of the same individual to properly represent the spirit of the deceased. When the remains are properly placed in the *nganga*, the spirit will carry out the orders of the *palero*.

Paleros believe a *nganga* will obey its owner with unquestionable loyalty. The remains of violent criminals and the insane are prized by *paleros* who work with evil spirits, as they believe these entities will not hesitate to commit any act, no matter how depraved. The belief is that it requires no sacrifice beforehand, although a *palero* will reward it with the blood of a rooster after it carries out orders.

The study of Palo Mayombe was the closest that Adolfo Constanzo came to a real education. At home he participated in his mother's amateur bloodletting, and under the supervision of his *padrino* he learned the intricacies of sophisticated death rites. This is the second formative influence that helps account for his notorious cruelty: his systematic introduction to killing.

This is a critical development. Since 1970, as reported via FBI profilers, one consistently observed trait of serial killers that the most heartless seemed to share is the near-universal engagement during childhood in some form of intentional animal torture and malice. Adolfo's *padrino* provided him with a master class in exactly this sort of behavior, training the boy to believe that, for a powerful *palero*, even the murder of another person—especially a nonbeliever—could be justified. Step by step, ritual by ritual, Adolfo became initiated into the belief that any systematic killing could be justified if a *palero* decreed it.

If heartless murder was the goal, this was an unusually rigorous, structured, and effective training ground, and whether it was done intentionally or not, it served as the perfect means to instill in Adolfo Costanzo what psychologists refer to as the "dark triad" of personality traits: psychopathy, or lack of remorse; malignant narcissism, or sadistic grandiosity; and Machiavellianism, or self-interested exploitation of others.

FEEDING THE *NGANGA*

Adolfo's *padrino* kept his *nganga* in a small, windowless garden shed. He made Adolfo wear a blindfold while in this location, claiming his *nganga* could kill a person who wasn't ready to see it. The *padrino* insisted on this protocol throughout Adolfo's training and beat him when he attempted to peek out from under the blindfold.

The *padrino* taught him how to cast protective spells for drug dealers—a steady clientele who paid well. He made clear that the relationship was strictly business. The *padrino* held the dealers themselves in disdain. It made no difference if nonbelievers wanted to destroy themselves with drugs. Like Delia, the *padrino* placed little value on the lives of those who didn't subscribe to Santería and Palo Mayombe. Dr. Robert Lifton calls this attitude the "dispensing of existence." This concept explains behavior common among cult members, who believe themselves alone in their knowledge of higher truth, and their possession of this truth means that people without it, even family members, live outside the sacred circle. This is a key belief that cult members use to justify all sorts of crimes against outsiders—i.e., nonbelievers— including murder.

One of the rules that the *padrino* imparted to Adolfo was absti- nence from all drug use. He told him that if a spirit ever took posses- sion of Adolfo's body and found it polluted with illicit substances, the entity would kill him. Adolfo heeded this advice for the rest of his life.

In 1977, at the age of fourteen, Adolfo began to claim that he had psychic powers—a skill that became the foundation of his cult, a crucial element of his illicit business, and a key factor in his eventual undoing. The first evidence of his abilities seemed aimed at his mother, a fan of Marilyn Monroe. Adolfo told Delia that he'd learned in a dream that the iconic movie star did not commit suicide, as many sus- pected, an alternate ending that pleased his mother. Three years later his mother swore that Adolfo had predicted the assassination attempt on Ronald Reagan. Other members of the local Santería community dismissed her boasting. Ernesto Pichardo, a former landlord and a prominent Miami *santero*, remarked, "You listen to [Delia], you'd think [Adolfo] was another messiah."

The sense of self-importance and entitlement so common among cult leaders had to come from somewhere. Delia's and his *padrino*'s treatment of Adolfo as a "chosen one" taught him that he was bet- ter than other people. He was certainly not another messiah to his teachers. In 1981, Adolfo graduated high school with poor grades. He attended one semester at a local community college but dropped out. He was subsequently a complete failure as a shoplifter and appre- hended first for stealing clothing and later a chain saw.

PICKING LOYAL FOLLOWERS

In early 1983, Adolfo's *padrino* urged him to move to Mexico City to start a business in spellcraft. Santería and Palo Mayombe were not commonly practiced in Mexico, but another brand of folk magic called Curanderismo, involving spiritual healing with herbs, was rather popular. Adolfo and his *padrino* thought that patrons of one brand of folk magic might be susceptible to another. Adolfo soon began regular trips to Mexico City with his mother, who introduced him to María del Rocío Cuevas Guerra, an acquaintance who became an early client and provided most of the details of Adolfo's mysterious childhood to the authorities after his death.

In Mexico City, Adolfo set up shop in a Zona Rosa sidewalk café among the fortune-tellers in this premier tourist district and began reading cards for customers there. His childhood apprenticeship made him very good at performing seemingly magical spells for clients. It was there in April 1983 that Adolfo met a young business student named Martin Quintana Rodriguez, newly single after leaving a serious relationship, a fact Adolfo ostensibly figured out without Martin telling him. The two began a romantic relationship of their own, with Adolfo introducing Martin to acquaintances as his bodyguard. The title was more than just a cover story: Martin was stocky and muscular, an intimidating presence at Adolfo's side.

Within weeks of arrival, Adolfo gained renown as a startlingly accurate fortune-teller. How he achieved this reputation for clairvoyance is unknown, but he seemed to have a gift, one that could not always be explained away as manipulation. And he was not shy about using it whenever he needed to increase his following or add to his bottom line.

Jorge Montes and Omar Orea Ochoa found Adolfo at his card-reading table just a few weeks after he met Martin. Jorge was a fifty-year-old former model and a card reader himself, performing his own readings in Zona Rosa's gay bars. That was the scene where he had met Omar, an eighteen-year-old journalism student obsessed with the supernatural since a fortune-teller told him he would one day meet a powerful man who would change his life. So when Jorge reported the local rumors of an incredible new card reader, Omar was eager to meet him in person.

Nearly as soon as the two men sat down for a reading, Adolfo told Omar he was about to fulfill a prophecy from his youth, claiming that he was indeed the powerful man from Omar's reading years earlier. Omar was immediately taken with Adolfo.

After the card reading, Jorge, Omar, and Adolfo chatted for hours. Adolfo told them that he was a *santero* and bragged about the power of his religion. When Adolfo mentioned that he planned to move to Mexico City permanently, Jorge offered to find him modeling work: Adolfo was handsome, and Jorge said he could use connections from his own career to help him. He also said he could spread the word about Adolfo's card-reading services.

Adolfo had planned to spend two more weeks in Mexico City before returning to Miami, but after the meeting, he spent most of this time with Omar, explaining the religions of Santería and Palo Mayombe and the different magic he could perform with them. He threw cowrie shells, a common technique that *santeros* use to forecast the future, and told Omar that the shells predicted a successful life ahead. He again seemed to know things he'd never been told, revealing the names of Omar's brothers and sisters to him as proof of his abilities.

Adolfo began seducing Omar, buying him meals in the Zona Rosa and expensive gifts, and the campaign was successful. The two slept together within days of their first encounter. And almost immediately Adolfo began setting the parameters of what soon became an abusive relationship, letting Omar know that Martin was also Adolfo's lover. He intended for Martin to be his "man," while Omar would fill the role of being his "woman." Omar did not like sharing Adolfo, but he agreed to the setup.

The patterns of emotional manipulation emerged early on. Adolfo withheld simple things, such as refusing to perform any magic beyond simple tricks—like throwing the cowrie shells—even though Omar begged him. Then he withheld affection. He'd be generous with Omar but also distant. Adolfo never seemed satisfied or happy even though both Omar and Martin only ever did what he wanted. This system of "intermittent reward"—long periods of withholding affection or emotional acknowledgment, followed by brief interludes of passion— is a hallmark of an abusive relationship, and it only increased Omar's desire to please Adolfo, who soon established emotional control over Omar. That paved the way for more overt and violent forms of exploitation.

RITUAL POSSESSION

Adolfo traveled back and forth from Miami to Mexico City many times in 1983, building a reputation in the Zona Rosa and reporting on his prospects to his *padrino*. Finally, near the end of that year, after such a long time spent learning from and assisting his *padrino*, the twenty-one-year-old Adolfo was ready for initiation into Palo Mayombe. He was to be what practitioners call *rayado en palo*, or "cut into Palo."

The account of his initiation is, to the best of our knowledge, based on statements from several of his followers, all of whom participated alongside Adolfo in ceremonies he said were patterned on his own experience. And their accounts are consistent with scholarly descriptions of Palo Mayombe initiation rituals.

Adolfo's preparation began weeks before the ceremony. He slept seven nights under a ceiba (kapok) tree, sacred to Palo Mayombe and native to the Caribbean, tropical and subtropical areas of the Americas, and parts of West Africa. The ceiba is a stately tree with a disturbing appearance, featuring a large, spreading canopy and buttress roots that can be taller than a person and can easily shelter a *santero* overnight. Adolfo then took a set of new clothes to a cemetery, buried them in a grave, and left them for three Fridays. During that period he took a series of purifying baths with sacred herbs and made daily offerings to Kadiempembe. Just like his *padrino*, Adolfo had selected him as his own personal guiding spirit.

On the day of the ceremony, Adolfo unearthed his buried clothes from the cemetery. He put them on and went to the shed where his *padrino* kept the *nganga*. Inside the shed, the *padrino* blindfolded him, then asked a series of questions to confirm that Adolfo had performed each ritual preparation correctly. *Paleros* believe that spirits possess a person's body during a religious rite; therefore, if the body isn't prepared properly, this process can become dangerous.

For the final question in the ritual, the *padrino* asked Adolfo if he truly wanted to go through with the ceremony. Once this ritual was complete, the *padrino* explained, Adolfo's soul would perish; there was no going back. Adolfo responded that his soul was already dead and that he had no god. The *padrino* then brushed him with the branches of a ceiba tree and ran a live chicken up and down his body. According to Palo Mayombe doctrine, the chicken was intended to draw anything out of him that didn't belong, to purify his body for possession by spirits.

After this act, the *padrino* slit the chicken's throat and poured the blood into the *nganga*. He then burned a mound of gunpowder on a knife and began carving a series of symbols into Adolfo's shoulders. This is the *rayado*, or "cut," for which the ceremony is named. The symbols were unique to Adolfo and served as his identifying mark to set him apart from other *paleros*.

Once the *padrino* finished marking Adolfo, he removed the blindfold. The room was lit by candles now. For the first time after a decade of training, Adolfo saw the illuminated *nganga*, filled with blood, animal remains, and a human skull. The *padrino* presented him with a black bag made of cloth. Inside it was what *paleros* call a *kisengue*: a human tibia bone. This macabre diploma was a scepter for the new initiate to stir the contents of the *nganga* and summon the dead to work his magic. Adolfo left his initiation believing that he could now command that power on his own—a *palero* in his own right.

LOVER, ABUSER, GOD ON EARTH

Adolfo de Jesús Constanzo permanently relocated to Mexico City in 1984, renting an apartment in the Zona Rosa. Jorge came through with his promise to help him in his career, recommending his services as a psychic and healer and even getting him some modeling gigs. By the end of that year, both Omar and Martin had moved in with Adolfo, although neither of their families approved of the arrangement. Adolfo's reactions foreshadowed the violence to come: when Omar's sister tried to have Adolfo arrested for corrupting a minor—even though Omar was a legal adult—Adolfo threatened to kill her. Martin's brother Alfredo quietly pulled Adolfo aside at a family gathering to register his own objections, and Adolfo whispered that he would cut Alfredo's heart out if he came between him and Martin.

This protectiveness of his new polyamorous relationship did not stop Adolfo from being abusive toward his two lovers after they moved in. Adolfo made Martin and Omar shine his shoes, lay out his clothes for him, and act as general servants around the residence. He sometimes insisted they dress in women's clothing. The headstrong Martin was more of a target: Adolfo would beat him and Martin accepted this outburst without retaliation even though he was a physically imposing man. Whenever this occurred, Omar would hide.

Martin regularly became fed up enough and went to stay with Alfredo. Adolfo would then drive over to Alfredo's house and scream to Martin that he loved him, that he needed him back, and that he would kill himself or both of them. This vicious cycle repeated every few months.

Abuse specialist Vera E. Mouradian has compiled extensive lists of violent behavior, and, while she never commented directly on this case, Adolfo did exhibit many classic examples of the manipulations she catalogs, such as withholding affection, treating a partner like a servant, and making a partner perform demeaning things. It may seem strange that the two men stayed, but this is common in abusive relationships. Abusers often display a charming side, keeping their victims in constant hope for an end to a harrowing cycle that never comes. Researcher Zlatka Rakovec-Felser writes that this "honeymoon phase" typically sees an abuser apologize, ask for forgiveness, and minimize the abuse. Adolfo, the principal breadwinner of the three, spent large sums of money on Martin and Omar and used his financial resources to regain their trust and loyalty, taking them on shopping sprees and buying them a car.

While Adolfo's home life was overwhelmed by his own domineering behavior, his business was doing quite well. His good looks and uncanny psychic readings were a hit in the Zona Rosa, and he made good money. Jorge, Omar, and Martin assisted him with his growing clientele, and Adolfo began to feel the need to formalize his relationship with his three assistants. He decided to initiate them into Palo Mayombe, as his *padrino* had done with Adolfo. He took over a spare room in Jorge's apartment and darkened the windows, building a shrine to Santería and Palo Mayombe. He led Omar, Martin, and Jorge in one by one. For each, he sacrificed a chicken and carved a unique series of symbols into each man's back. The men were *rayado* now—"cut in." Each pledged to obey Adolfo, the oath of loyalty being Adolfo's own addition to the ceremony. There is no evidence Adolfo's *padrino* had made any similar demands.

These initiations were hasty, and people with knowledge of the traditions of Santería and Palo Mayombe have cast doubts on Adolfo's standing. Less than a year after his own initiation, he would not be considered experienced enough; his own training, by comparison, had lasted nearly a decade. But Adolfo wasn't interested in doing things the traditional way; he wanted it *his* way, fast. By quickly gathering followers pledged to carry out his wishes, Adolfo was creating his own form of religion centered on himself, taking a significant step beyond Palo Mayombe and toward the formation of a cult.

PROOF OF SUPERNATURAL POWER

In 1985, Adolfo's reputation began to grow, thanks to a series of incidents that burnished his reputation for otherworldly mystical powers. Word of the first incident came from María del Rocío Cuevas Guerra, the friend of Adolfo's mother he met when he first visited Mexico.

María claimed that she saw Adolfo on a rainy day for a psychic reading. Adolfo excused himself from the apartment to get some air—and stepped off his third-floor balcony.

María rushed to the lobby in a panic but found Adolfo walking back into the building unharmed. Passersby gathered in the street around a damaged car with the roof caved in. They claimed that a man had landed on it and survived without a scratch on him.

Adolfo laughed at this story whenever anyone brought it up, but he never denied it happened. María's insistence that Adolfo survived a potentially fatal fall unscathed is consistent with mystical manipulation. One of its hallmarks is so-called planned spontaneity, when the manipulator casts prearranged events as the manifestation of a higher power. It's hard to say which aspects of María's story are true, if any. Adolfo may have set up this event to convince her of his magical prowess, hoping a local legend would grow from there. Or perhaps he fell by accident and was simply lucky.

Soon after this occurrence, in mid-1985, a down-on-his-luck real estate broker named Francisco asked Adolfo for assistance. His business was failing and he didn't know where to turn. Adolfo agreed to help and charged $4,500. After consulting the cowrie shells and performing a *limpia*, or ritual cleansing, Adolfo told the man to buy a piece of dilapidated real estate in downtown Mexico City. Francisco sank all his money into it, spending $20,000.

On September 19, 1985, Mexico City was hit by an 8.1 magnitude earthquake—the worst in the city's history. Thousands died. But Francisco was able to sell his property for $250,000 in the rebuilding effort. A natural and unforeseeable event made it appear as if Adolfo had really given Francisco critical, prophetic advice based on his own mystical foreknowledge.

The next artful coincidence gave Adolfo his first association with death and mystical power, and Adolfo welcomed this addition to his carefully cultivated legend. It began when a singer in the Zona Rosa approached him about an unsettled debt. A nightclub owner had refused to pay wages the singer was owed and had the bouncer rough him up. The singer wanted revenge and hoped Adolfo could help. Adolfo performed a ritual with a doll doused in chicken blood, then told the singer to place the doll on a fresh grave.

The singer followed Adolfo's instructions. Adolfo then left the dead chicken on the nightclub owner's doorstep and sent him a series of threatening letters, also doused in blood. The club owner believed in the occult and took the threats seriously. He began drinking heavily and died of a heart attack a month later.

Until this point, Adolfo's spells had consisted of cleansings and psychic readings. But now a man was dead. As far as Omar, Jorge, and Martin were concerned, they'd all had a hand in it. They expressed trepidation and remorse over the incident, but Adolfo assured them that what they had done could not have been wrong, since the gods always seek justice. If a higher power gave this man a heart attack, it was because he deserved it.

This psychological manipulation worked. Adolfo had introduced his trio of followers to the concept of the dispensing of existence, in which cult members have the right to determine who may live based on their interpretation of divine whim. Adolfo was carefully constructing an environment where Omar, Martin, and Jorge could feel justified committing murder on his behalf.

The death of the nightclub owner represented an ambitious direction, and Adolfo took the next logical step in the effort to create his cult of Palo Mayombe. He and his new *paleros* set about building their own *nganga*. The recounting of this process is based on later statements of Adolfo's followers.

One night in 1985, Adolfo convinced Omar, Jorge, and Martin to descend on a cemetery. At a previously selected grave, they dug until they found the coffin. From the corpse inside, they took the skull, tibias, ribs, fingers, and toes. These parts were not randomly selected. Each corresponded to the abilities of the spirit once it was under a *palero*'s control. The skull and ribs housed the soul and allowed the spirit to think, the tibias and toes allowed it to walk, and the fingers allowed it to use its hands.

It's likely Adolfo and the others knew the identity of the corpse and that it was a relatively fresh grave. As *paleros*, they wanted a skull with an intact brain, believing it would make the spirit smarter. They brought the remains back to Jorge's apartment, and the ritual to determine the spirit's suitability began. After laying the remains on a makeshift altar, Adolfo reclined on the floor and was covered by a sheet. Seven mounds of gunpowder were placed on a knife, which was held over a lighted candle. Soon Adolfo began seizing up and contorting his facial muscles into terrifying expressions.

Adolfo's mimicry of a Palo Mayombe spiritual possession is another example of mystical manipulation. Those present genuinely believed that this was a sign the spirit was taking over Adolfo's body, rather than it being merely playacting. Omar asked if the entity would serve Adolfo; speaking as the spirit, Adolfo replied that it would. The gunpowder on the knife having burned, the ritual was complete. If the alleged spirit had refused to serve them, or the mounds of gunpowder had not ignited at the same time, they would have reburied the remains and started over again with a new skull and bones.

The four placed the skull and bones in the cauldron. In with the human remains went the bodies and blood of various animals, as well as insects, coins, deer antlers, railroad spikes, herbs, and tree branches—all part of the ritual. After the *nganga* was prepared, Adolfo told his three followers that they were a family now. He implored the *nganga* to protect his family from harm, to make them rich, and to bring them new believers.

FIRST BLOOD AND A NEW BUSINESS

Adolfo's operation continued to grow. His business records from the mid-1980s show thirty-one regular clients, many of whom were paying him thousands of dollars at a time. One drug trafficker gave $40,000 over three years. Adolfo's services became so popular that he even made a price list to pass around to his clientele.

Around the time he made his *nganga*, Adolfo met Florentino Ventura Gutierrez. Of all the clients found in Adolfo's ledger, Ventura was perhaps the most shocking: he had been the director of the Mexican Federal Judicial Police, Mexico's equivalent of the FBI, and became the head of the Mexican branch of Interpol soon after that.

Ventura, one of the most powerful lawmen in the country, was secretly very superstitious. As a top police officer during the rise of the drug cartels, he had countless enemies and sought magical protection from them. He eventually heard of Adolfo de Jesús Constanzo and would pay this local celebrity a small fortune for his aid. Federico Ponce Rojas, the assistant attorney general in Mexico City, suspected that Ventura also provided inside information about drug enforcement to Adolfo. DEA agents who worked with Ventura doubted these allegations, but Adolfo entered the narcotics business at the same time he became close to Ventura and even occasionally introduced himself as Ventura's nephew to prospective clients.

Ventura wasn't Adolfo's only connection in the police. In 1985, Jorge introduced him to Salvador Vidal García Alarcón, a narcotics officer who'd been scarred down the middle of his face by a knife attack. The cruel wound made him look different from every angle. Jorge told Adolfo that Vidal had come to believe his three "faces"—left side, right side, and head-on—were possessed by three different entities: a Sioux Native American, a Cuban drug dealer, and an African witch. Knowing the potential benefits of having a narcotics officer in his debt, Adolfo eagerly told Jorge to set up a meeting. After making a show of studying thrown cowrie shells, Adolfo repeated the information Jorge had provided about the three entities supposedly possessing Vidal. Once again, Adolfo was making use of mystical manipulation to deceive a client.

Salvador Vidal's anguish over the spirits he believed controlled him made the man a perfect target. Adolfo, the experienced fortune-teller, knew how to exploit Vidal's weaknesses, and Vidal soon joined Adolfo's growing cult.

Vidal's addition was pivotal to Adolfo's ambitions. He was not just a police officer but also large and intimidating. During his initiation,

Adolfo informed Vidal that he was to be the enforcer of the group. When Adolfo ordered Vidal to do something on behalf of the cult, he needed to obey without question. Vidal accepted the terms.

By making such a radical request, Adolfo may have actually increased Vidal's commitment. Psychologist Nigel Barber writes that cults last longer the more they demand of their members. This does not hold true for secular groups, but followers of strict religions are more likely to stay faithful. Believers are willing to tolerate great personal sacrifice in the name of a higher purpose.

In a study of eighty-three religious communes that existed in the nineteenth century, sociologists Richard Sosis and Eric R. Bressler found that communes with only two costly requirements—such as celibacy or the surrendering of possessions—lasted an average of less than ten years. Communes with six to eight requirements lasted for fifty years, and those with more than eleven requirements lasted for sixty years. The more they demanded of followers, the longer they existed.

With a narcotics officer now firmly in his inner circle, Adolfo gained access to both sides of the drug war. Vidal was reportedly already corrupt and connected to many underworld figures, and he began introducing Adolfo to entire families made up of superstitious drug smugglers. Like his *padrino* before him, Adolfo began advising the smugglers on when to move shipments. And with Vidal in the fold, he could tell a smuggler to continue running drugs and then instruct Vidal to ensure the narcotics were left alone. This way Adolfo turned a bribe—a fairly common cost of doing business in the drug trade—into full-on spiritual protection.

In taking over this key role that corrupt police once served, Adolfo began amassing previously unimaginable sums of money. But his new business endeavor also set him and his followers on the path to wanton murder. In the fall of 1986, Adolfo met cocaine smuggler Guillermo Calzada and began advising him on when to ship his drugs. Salvador Vidal made sure the police left Calzada's shipments untouched, which helped his profits increase. By early 1987, Adolfo was making tens of thousands of dollars through drug trafficking, and it was then that his followers noticed a change: he became obsessive in his quest for money and grew increasingly ruthless.

According to Sheri Johnson, a psychology professor at the University of California, Berkeley, narcissists are often compulsive in the search for power and wealth. While Adolfo de Jesús Constanzo cannot be diagnosed in a clinical sense, it's clear that his lack of empathy, his eagerness to exploit others, and his inflated sense of self-importance are classic markers of narcissism—traits he often exhibited, based on the testimony of his followers.

Guillermo Calzada paid Adolfo several thousand dollars a month for his services. But as Adolfo learned more about the drug business, he tried to charge more. He griped to Omar and Martin that his magic and connections were making Calzada's profits possible. He deserved half the money, he said. They of course agreed. In a meeting at Calzada's house in April 1987, Adolfo dared to propose an even split. Calzada rejected the proposal. Adolfo flew into a rage and Calzada ordered him off the premises.

Adolfo was furious. But he apologized to Calzada several days later, blaming his behavior on an evil spell. As a token of his remorse, Adolfo insisted on a free ceremony for Calzada's entire family.

On April 30, 1987, Adolfo arrived at the Calzada home. Present for the ritual were Calzada himself, along with his wife, his mother, his maid, his business partner, his secretary, and his personal bodyguard.

Adolfo began his Palo Mayombe chants. Then two men burst in with guns drawn. One was Martin. Followers claim the other gunman was Salvador Vidal, although he was never charged. The two of them slaughtered Calzada and his entire inner circle. They removed various body parts, including fingers, vertebrae, hearts, sexual organs, and even the brains of two victims. Then they dumped the corpses in a nearby river. When police found the bodies a week later, only three could be identified at the time; the other four were too mutilated to match any known records.

According to Omar, Martin refused to speak any further of the incident. But Adolfo recounted the murders for his followers, saying the body parts recovered from the crime scene would live on in the *nganga*. By describing the horrific events to them in detail, Adolfo had arguably made his followers accessories to the murders, but they were all too loyal to him to leave the cult.

Forensic psychology professor Katherine Ramsland writes that killers who seek partners in crime are notably adept at vetting and grooming people who are likely to participate with them. Al Carlisle, a former prison psychologist, describes the relationship as such: "The dominant person needs the follower's total loyalty in order to validate him- or herself. The subservient follower needs the power and authority of the dominant person, so he or she attempts to become that person's shadow and to mirror the dominant person's beliefs and ethics. Each receives justification from the other." It seems that Adolfo and his followers were well down this path by the time of the Calzada murders.

In June 1987, a month after the brutal killings, Salvador Vidal transferred to the city of Matamoros, just south of the Texas border. Adolfo seized on this opportunity to expand his operation and told Vidal to find a local partner. Not content with his takeover of the Calzada drug operation, Adolfo was relentlessly expanding his influence.

SEDUCING A *MADRINA*

Salvador Vidal García Alarcón connected with a local drug smuggler named Elio Hernández in mid-July 1987. Elio was in his twenties and had been the leader of his family's business for only seven months; one of Elio's brothers, who'd previously headed the business, had been gunned down outside a restaurant six months earlier. Elio was violent and impulsive, and his leadership was untested. His business sense was not much better. The Hernándezes were desperate, which made them ideal candidates for Adolfo's services.

Adolfo hatched a very roundabout plan to get inside the Hernández world. It started with Elio's ex-girlfriend, twenty-two-year-old Sara

Aldrete. Vidal told Adolfo that Elio still carried a torch for Sara, even though he was now married. That made Sara, by Adolfo's twisted way of thinking, his ticket in.

On July 30, 1987, Adolfo and Martin cut Sara off in traffic and stopped in front of her, refusing to move. With cars piling up behind them, Adolfo came up to her vehicle and insisted on meeting her. Sara just wanted him to get out of her way, but she eventually relented, either due to exasperation or fear.

Adolfo told Sara he was a lawyer from Miami. She asked about the beaded necklace he wore. "It's part of my religion," he said, but would say no more. Preying on her curiosity, he suggested they meet again the next day for lunch. Throughout August, Adolfo began drawing Sara in. He told her about Santería and Palo Mayombe—although he left out any mention of his human sacrifices. He claimed he was a "Santero Cristiano," or Christian Santero, presumably so as not to scare her off. When he told Sara he could divine the future by reading cards, she asked him for her own reading. Adolfo refused, claiming she wasn't ready.

While Adolfo pursued her, Sara was still dating another man. But that August the other beau received an anonymous phone call telling him that Sara was cheating on him. This led to a fight and breakup. The next time he spoke to Sara, Adolfo claimed that he had foreseen the breakup. He then agreed to finally read the cards for her and made three predictions: she would get money from her school for the next semester, she would receive a phone call from an old friend, and someone she once dated would come to her with a problem.

As he had with so many others, Adolfo then reeled off accurate details about Sara's life. Although his three predictions, and all the details of her background, were based on the detective work of Salvador Vidal, to Sara it felt like magic. The first two foretellings quickly came true: Sara received a scholarship from her school, and an old friend did call her. When she told Adolfo, he reacted as if he expected nothing less. His confident and accurate prophecies convinced Sara that he really could see the future. She became a believer and, soon after, his girlfriend. Adolfo's plan to get close to Elio was playing out just as he'd hoped.

Adolfo maintained the same kind of relationship with Sara that he had with Omar and Martin—generous but unaffectionate. That October, when he finally told her he was bisexual, she was angry but didn't leave him. Beyond her connection to the Hernández family, Adolfo had no interest in Sara but continued to manipulate her into staying by his side as he waited and hoped for Elio to find her. To Adolfo, she was merely a resource to exploit. His unyielding quest for power dictated his every decision, even in his intimate relationships.

By November, the time and money he'd spent on Sara paid off.

She was at a taco stand when she heard a man call her name. She turned to see Elio Hernández running toward her from across the street. Elio told her that his family was down on its luck. His brother had been killed ten months earlier, and Elio feared for his own life. The tension and the responsibilities of running a drug operation were getting to him. Sara told him about a man who could help. Adolfo's third prediction about Sara came true, and the next piece of his plan had now fallen into place.

Like many of the quasi-mystical events that happened in Adolfo's orbit, this encounter seems hard to believe. We can't establish now whether he helped arrange this meeting—he could be patient, but he rarely left things to chance—although he certainly had identified Elio as a prime target for mystical manipulation. The combined stress of leadership, his fear of rival drug dealers, and the plight of his family after his brother's death made Elio vulnerable, which was exactly what Adolfo needed. Sara was vital to the plan: Elio's continuing attraction to her was a weakness that Adolfo could exploit. He planned to initiate Elio into the cult, then use Sara to control him.

But first he needed to initiate Sara herself as a way to establish her at the top of the cult's hierarchy. He wanted her to be *La Madrina*—the godmother—the way he was *El Padrino*—the godfather. On March 23, 1988, Sara traveled to Mexico City for her own initiation; it was where

Adolfo was spending the winter. That night Omar blindfolded Sara and led her into a darkened room. Adolfo began chanting in the hissing voice he used when supposedly possessed by the spirit of his mystical cauldron—the *nganga*. Someone ran a chicken along Sara's body before cutting its head off, as in the initiation ceremonies of Adolfo and the others. A larger animal brushed against her. She realized it was a goat after she heard it bleating. Someone beheaded the animal, and Sara felt the blood spray onto her. Adolfo tore her shirt off and carved several symbols into her back, as he had for all his initiates. He answered that her soul was dead and that the other followers were her family now. She was their godmother—their *madrina*—and they would obey her. From this time forward, she was *rayada*.

Sara could now serve as a lieutenant for Adolfo in his operation in Matamoros. Followers were to report to her in his absence, and it was up to Sara to inform Adolfo if anyone broke the rules. Adolfo had three principal edicts for his followers. First, obey his orders absolutely. The gods had no mercy, he said, and neither did he. Second, they had to accept the gods and spirits of the dead, particularly Kadiempembe, the devourer of souls. He reminded them they could not attend church, as Christians were animals. And third, Adolfo forbade any drug use, just as his own *padrino* had done. If they did not remain pure, he told them, they would surely die.

The very next day Adolfo initiated Elio in his own *rayado* ceremony. After the ceremony, Adolfo proposed a business deal. He would receive half of what Elio's family made, but he offered a money-back guarantee: he would take nothing if their profits didn't increase. Such an arrangement may have seemed generous to Elio, but to Adolfo he was simply another pawn to exploit in his selfish pursuit of control. Adolfo offered the deal because he was confident he could deliver on it.

Adolfo attributed the increase in profits to his powerful magic, but the new business owed more to straightforward networking. The Hernández family had lost important connections after Elio's brother was killed. Salvador Vidal could use his corrupt police contacts to reestablish those ties. As usual, Adolfo's magic owed more to muscle and tip-offs supplied by dirty cops than to the supernatural.

THE BODY COUNT GROWS

Once they were back in Matamoros a few weeks later, Adolfo asked Elio to gather his most loyal men. Elio chose five employees. Alvaro Darío de Léon Valdés, known as El Duby, was a ruthless enforcer and known for getting into bar gunfights. Carlos de la Llata made money selling cocaine to tourists. Aurelio Chavez was the foreman of Rancho Santa Elena, the Hernández base of operations. Sergio Martínez Salinas was Elio's cousin and had experience running drug shipments. Finally there was Malio Fabio Ponce Torres, a college student from a wealthy family. Adolfo saw the potential to make this one a leader within the business. These five men formed the core of Adolfo's cult in Matamoros. During the first half of April 1988, Adolfo and Sara taught them the ways of Santería and Palo Mayombe in Sara's living room. Three weeks after Sara and Elio had been initiated, the five newcomers were brought into the cult themselves. Adolfo now had loyal foot soldiers to use however he saw fit.

Meanwhile, Salvador Vidal saw to it that the Hernández business thrived again. Shortly after the initiation of the new members, he arranged for one ton of federally seized marijuana to fall into Elio's hands. Adolfo's rituals ensured his mysticism got the credit for their success, telling Elio the name of a buyer he claimed to have identified through cowrie shells. The drugs brought a $200,000 profit.

The crew continued to make similar deals between April and May of 1988. Adolfo and Vidal secured the transactions through business channels, but Adolfo presented them to Elio as the result of black magic. The Hernández family was making more money than ever, but it wasn't enough to satisfy Adolfo. In late May, he proposed to Elio that they expand their scope by stealing drugs from rival smugglers.

New recruit Aurelio learned of small-time drug trafficker Hector de la Fuente, who stored his marijuana at a farm next to Aurelio's house. Aurelio informed Adolfo and, on May 28, the gang went after de la Fuente, finding him in town, kidnapping him, and forcing him to lead them to his stash. The five new initiates and their captive, as well as Adolfo and Martin, arrived at the farm to find Moises Castillo, the fifty-two-year-old son of the farmer who owned the land, there to help his elderly father. Adolfo's people took the marijuana, as well as trafficker de la Fuente and Castillo, and they drove back to Rancho Santa Elena.

They hid the drugs, then brought the two kidnapped men to a nearby orchard. With gun in hand, Adolfo asked de la Fuente and Castillo if they were good Christians. De la Fuente remained silent, but Castillo answered in the affirmative. Adolfo then reminded his men that Christians were animals, and animals were meant to be sacrificed. He shot both de la Fuente and Castillo in the head. Despite all their experience in the drug trade, his men were utterly shocked. Adolfo likely welcomed this: his actions made clear that he was willing to go to any lengths to achieve his own ends. Adolfo's casual executions may have disturbed his acolytes, but it also gained him some admirers in this world's violent culture, and the ranks of his cult swelled. In June 1988, he initiated Elio's nephew, Serafin Hernández, dubbed "Little Serafin," to distinguish him from his father and Elio's brother, referred to as "Old Serafin."

As Elio's nephew, Little Serafin was not considered competent, but he had one quality that made him a valuable member of the cult: he was an American citizen and could cross the border much more easily than Adolfo's other followers. Little Serafin took to his cult member status with enthusiasm, quickly developing a swagger and attitude that drew attention in the Matamoros bar and club scene. He became a useful recruiting agent, helping the Matamoros chapter of the cult increase in size from seven to twelve followers by mid-June of 1988. At the same time, Salvador Vidal continued to arrange lucrative drug deals, and Adolfo didn't hesitate to take credit for the success. His rituals moved from Sara's apartment to a shack on the ranch, and he then decided it was time to make an official Rancho Santa Elena *nganga*. He began compiling the ingredients for the cauldron.

Meanwhile, in early July 1988, Adolfo and Martin returned to Mexico City, where Sara joined them. They hadn't been there long before follower Jorge Montes came to Adolfo with a problem: Jorge wanted to get rid of his roommate, Ramón Paz Esquivel, an antiques salesman who also performed in Mexico City's red-light district as a character called "La Claudia." Ramón was Jorge's former lover. Although they still lived together, their relationship had deteriorated.

Ramón frequently came home drunk with younger men, raising a ruckus in the building. He also occasionally refused to let Jorge's card-reading clients into the apartment. Recently, Ramón had accused Jorge of stealing one of his antiques. He stormed through the house, upending furniture. It was the last straw when he kicked one of Jorge's beloved pet poodles. Adolfo agreed to help.

On the night of July 16, 1988, Adolfo, Jorge, and other followers, including Martin and Omar, waited in Jorge's apartment for Ramón. When the man entered, the group dragged him into the bathtub. Martin bound his hands and covered his mouth with duct tape. Adolfo then shocked everyone once again, cutting off Ramón's toes, fingers, and genitals while he was still alive. Jorge and Omar fled the room: Adolfo had sacrificed many animals in front of his followers, but never anything on the level of this brutality. Adolfo then partially skinned Ramón before finally killing him. He collected the dead man's blood in a container, took several bones, and finally removed Ramón's brain from his skull. Adolfo now had the human soul he needed for Rancho Santa Elena's *nganga*.

Adolfo believed sacrificial victims would better serve his *nganga* if they died in immense pain and fear. Santería and Palo Mayombe scholar Migene González-Wippler writes that some *paleros* torture and boil a black cat to place in the *nganga*. According to González-Wippler, this type of cauldron is designed exclusively for evil deeds.

It seems Adolfo applied this philosophy to his human victims. He created his own religion, in which such cruelty and murder were not only tolerated but integral to the practice of it.

Adolfo was becoming increasingly ruthless in both his murderous habits and his business dealings. In August 1988, Adolfo and Salvador Vidal set up their biggest score yet. Vidal had seized 75 kilograms of cocaine. They planned to offer the drugs for $800,000 to a buyer named "El Gancho." Elio and his brother Ovidio had set up the deal, as El Gancho was the brother of one of their in-laws. He and the Hernándezes had done smaller deals before, but Adolfo had no plans to give El Gancho the drugs; he intended to steal his money and keep the coke. Elio and Ovidio didn't want to betray a relative, but Adolfo was insistent. As always, the feelings of his followers was secondary to his pursuit of wealth.

When El Gancho arrived, an apologetic Elio and Ovidio took the money at gunpoint. El Gancho claimed that he himself would be in trouble, that his boss would kill him for this insult. They ignored his warning, and, three days after the robbery, El Gancho kidnapped Ovidio and his two-year-old son. He made Ovidio call Elio to tell him he and his boy were dead if the money wasn't returned the following day. But Elio knew Adolfo would never relent. In desperation, Elio and his brother Old Serafin turned to the police, who refused to help unless the siblings admitted that the kidnapping was the result of a drug deal gone bad.

With nowhere else to turn, Elio sought Adolfo's advice. In response, Adolfo ordered Elio to find a ritual victim. Elio drove around the area until he saw a drifter and offered the man a ride. The stranger accepted. Elio drove back to Rancho Santa Elena, where the cult hauled the drifter into the shack with the *nganga*. There Adolfo sent everyone out except Elio, who stayed behind to assist. Adolfo began cutting the man up while still alive, depositing various body parts in the *nganga* and requesting protection for Ovidio before killing the drifter. After Adolfo placed the victim's brain in the *nganga*, he made Elio cut the man's heart out.

The next day Ovidio and his son safely returned home. In the subsequent investigation, police never determined why. But as far as the cult was concerned, it was the direct result of Adolfo's ceremony.

THE FATAL MISTAKE

Adolfo's growing preoccupation with murder fit a common pattern among serial killers. In his book *The Psychopathology of Serial Murder: A Theory of Violence*, criminologist Stephen J. Giannangelo described how killers become more dangerous over time. If someone gets away with murder, their confidence grows. If murder excites a perpetrator, their confidence leads to additional murders. Soon the killer becomes comfortable with the act, even desperate for it.

This pattern is similar to Adolfo's. He had waited a year after the Calzada murders before doing it again. But once he began killing on a regular basis, he wanted it more and more. Adolfo's ruthlessness had inspired fear and tightened his grip on the cult, and he used this capacity for intimidation to manipulate his followers into doing whatever he asked. When Elio complained that Sara would not sleep with him, Adolfo ordered her to do so. She protested, but he countered that once she did so, her control over Elio would be even greater than before. She eventually relented.

Sara was demonstrating a common characteristic for a victim of mystical manipulation. Robert Lifton maintains that people who have been successfully manipulated will merge their own psychology with that of the leader, even to the point where they will start engaging in their own manipulation of others. Sara was doing just that to Elio through having sex with him, even though she was reluctant.

From late 1988 through early 1989, Adolfo picked up the pace of his killings. In November, he murdered one of his own followers for cocaine use, which violated his ban on recreational drugs. In December he executed Salvador Vidal's two police assistants because Vidal didn't trust them anymore. In February 1989 alone, the cult did away with five people. One of the victims was a fourteen-year-old boy whom Adolfo made Elio kill after several other cult members noticed the teenager walking past the ranch. It was only later that Elio realized the boy was actually his second cousin.

Adolfo had no sympathy. He wanted his followers to slay without hesitation, to see people the way he saw them: as a means to an end. The February murder spree didn't satisfy Adolfo, though, and he craved more victims. But in mid-March, he performed a sacrifice that he interpreted as a bad omen. He wasn't necessarily incorrect: that heinous act would eventually lead to the downfall of the Narcosatanist cult.

By this time, Adolfo de Jesús Constanzo had successfully established his extensive drug-smuggling operation in the border city of Matamoros, Mexico. He had also cemented his place at the head of a brutal, murderous cult. His followers soon noticed he was becoming less interested in the magical side of his rituals and seemed increasingly fixated on just the killings, which were now being committed on a weekly basis.

On March 13, 1989, Adolfo demanded yet another victim. His gang found a dealer selling cocaine in a bar within the limits of what they considered their territory and hauled him back to the ranch. Adolfo began his horrific routine, cutting and skinning the dealer while he was still alive. But miraculously the man would not scream; Adolfo couldn't elicit a sound from him and therefore could not bring the man's pain and fear to the surface. Adolfo considered a sacrifice without visible expressions of agony a failure. An alternate plan was concocted: he needed to kill someone softer. The ideal target was younger, like a college student, a typical gringo, Adolfo said. Conveniently, spring break was in full swing in Matamoros.

The next night, March 14, 1989, Narcosatanist followers Malio and Little Serafin set out in Serafin's pickup truck to do as Adolfo had demanded. At 2:00 a.m., as college students streamed across the bridge from Matamoros on the Mexican side to Brownsville on the Texas side, the cult members saw a blond twenty-one-year-old named

Mark Kilroy straggling and alone, and they wrestled him into the truck. They drove their prize back to Rancho Santa Elena and handcuffed him, then left him in the back of the truck for the night.

The next morning, Domingo Reyes, the ranch caretaker, found Kilroy. He brought him some eggs for breakfast. The caretaker felt sorry for the boy, but he knew better than to offer anything else. Reyes retreated to his residence before any Narcosatanist followers found him helping their intended victim.

At noon on March 15, 1989, the Narcosatanist cult convened on the ranch at the *nganga* shack. While they waited outside the shack, Adolfo tortured, raped, and murdered Mark Kilroy. He made El Duby, one of the original five Matamoros followers, cut the young man's heart out. Kilroy's brain was placed in the *nganga*, with Adolfo stating that an educated person would make it smarter, better able to carry out complex tasks.

But now the cult's violent beliefs had crossed an international border. There would be much scrutiny: Mark Kilroy's friends were already frantically looking for him, and the police were investigating his disappearance. Kilroy's father became a daily fixture at the bridge between Brownsville and Matamoros, handing out missing person flyers with his son's picture on them. The probable crime had occurred on Mexican soil and thus was legally the jurisdiction of that country's authorities. But Kilroy's uncle, a US Customs supervisor, pushed for an investigation to take place stateside as well.

Mexican police also had great incentive to solve the case. The negative publicity could cripple tourism, which many local communities relied on, including Matamoros. But for the last two weeks of March, neither side made headway. Kilroy had vanished late at night while the streets of Matamoros were crowded with drunken college students. It was well-nigh impossible to find reliable leads.

A break came on April 1, 1989, although authorities didn't know it at the time. A red pickup truck drove through a drug checkpoint of the Mexican Federal Police without even slowing down. The driver was none other than Little Serafin Hernández. Officers on the scene found Serafin's behavior suspicious, so they tailed him without alerting him to their presence. Serafin wouldn't have cared even if he'd known about it. He accelerated through the checkpoint because, as he later told authorities, he believed his cult's magic made him literally invisible to the police.

The officers followed him to Rancho Santa Elena, then staked out the premises. Once Serafin left, they looked around and concluded the ranch was likely a stopping point for drug shipments, then began to monitor the Hernándezes. Their hunch paid off: a week later, on April 8, the Narcosatanist cult went through with a $300,000 drug deal. The Federal Police were watching the entire transaction, listening to their conversation via tapped cell phones. They arrested Elio, Little Serafin, and two other cult members on drug-trafficking charges the very next day.

The Hernándezes were not afraid to speak to the police and, according to the officers who apprehended them, seemed strangely unconcerned with their arrest; they almost seemed amused by it. The authorities couldn't understand why these men were so convinced they were safe, but the Hernándezes believed the spirits—and their *padrino*—were protecting them from certain harm.

Then the police arrested Domingo, the caretaker, who was neither a dealer nor a cult member. He was quickly intimidated into talking, admitting that the family was involved in the drug trade but also stating that people sometimes came to the ranch and never left. One of them had been a blond American. The officers immediately became much more interested. Domingo was then shown a picture of Mark Kilroy and readily confirmed the young man as the missing youth.

The same day the Federal Police arrested Elio and Little Serafin, Ovidio Hernández called Adolfo and informed him that his followers were in police custody. Consequently, Adolfo, Martin, El Duby, and Sara fled to Mexico City in the early morning hours of April 10 and met up with Omar.

On April 11, Little Serafin directed the police to several bodies buried at Rancho Santa Elena. There they found the remains of Mark Kilroy as well as numerous unidentified mutilated corpses that were all missing fingers, ears, toes, hearts, genitals, and brains.

Some of the graves, including Kilroy's, were marked by pieces of wire protruding from the ground. Serafin explained to the police that the wire was wrapped around the spine of each corpse. Once a body was sufficiently decomposed, they could use the wire to pull the spinal column from the ground, a horrific practice that Adolfo had learned from his own *padrino*. The victim's vertebrae could then be made into a necklace, which Adolfo had told them would bring luck to the wearer.

Serafin and the other arrested cult members freely told authorities about Adolfo and all his savage methods. They believed the police could do nothing either way, since Adolfo's magic protected them. The followers' confidence that the authorities held no power over them was the result of Adolfo's perfectly executed mystical manipulation. The Narcosatanist cult got away with its heinous crimes for as long as possible mainly due to the corrupt police work of Salvador Vidal. But through numerous ceremonies and sacrifices, Adolfo had fooled them all into thinking that his magic was responsible for their continued success. He was so effective that, even after his followers confessed, they had more faith in Adolfo's magic than in the law's ability to prosecute them.

THE BLOODY END OF A KILLER

After the discovery of the bodies at Rancho Santa Elena, the manhunt for Adolfo and his remaining followers was on. While holed up in one of the cult's condos, Adolfo, Martin, Sara, Omar, and El Duby watched the case unfold on television. The news reports were accompanied by a photo of Adolfo. As a result, the five fugitives cut and dyed their hair to make themselves less recognizable, preparing to live a life on the run.

The group remained indoors as much as possible, spending several days in one location, then moving on to the next. Adolfo became tyrannical during this period, particularly toward Sara. Meanwhile, she was growing increasingly unstable by the day. She became listless and begged to go home to her parents. Adolfo, worried that she would betray them all to the police, informed her that she could never leave.

He was still convinced they could escape, thinking his mystical manipulation and cunning would see them through the crisis. He called Salvador Vidal and ordered him to steal a cocaine shipment in Guadalajara. This would provide the money for the fugitive group to bribe their way out of Mexico. In a sign of his increasingly frantic behavior, he got in touch with María del Rocío Cuevas Guerra, his mother's old friend and witness to his miraculous three-story drop, hoping that she could help arrange for counterfeit passports. He also demanded that she find a plastic surgeon to alter their looks.

The Narcosatanists bounced between hiding places throughout that April while police remained a step behind. But time was running out. Investigators noticed similarities between the Calzada murders, the slaying of Jorge's roommate Ramón, and the bodies at Rancho Santa Elena. On the recommendation of two Palo Mayombe experts flown in from Miami, the police burned the *nganga* shed at Rancho Santa Elena to the ground on April 22, 1989, in the hope of riling Adolfo so badly that he might make a mistake. This would be a game-changing strategy: the cultists were at a remote cabin when they saw the news report of the burning shed and *nganga*. Adolfo shot the TV with a machine gun, then trashed the cabin in a screaming rage for over an hour.

By late April the manhunt for Adolfo was closing in. Salvador Vidal informed him by phone that he had witnessed the destruction of the *nganga*. He now believed Adolfo's magic was gone, and Vidal would no longer help them. The cultists now had no source of income for their escape. Once a loyal partner, Vidal ended up distancing himself from Adolfo.

Adolfo saw the end coming and made his loyalists agree to a suicide pact. If confrontation with the authorities became inevitable, Omar was to kill Adolfo and Martin, then the others, then himself. Adolfo then announced they would return to Mexico City, where they arrived on April 27, holing up in a dingy apartment that María had found. Five days later, Adolfo sent Sara out to call the plastic surgeon he hoped would alter their looks enough for them to flee the country. She made contact, but the surgeon refused to help them.

She also telephoned her parents' neighbor during this outing to check on her family. She relayed the message that Adolfo had kidnapped her and that she wanted to escape. On May 6, authorities investigating an unrelated case arrived outside the apartment where the cult was hiding out. But when Adolfo spotted the police car, he yelled to the others that the chase was over. As they armed themselves, he opened the window and aimed his submachine gun at an officer. According to Sara and El Duby, Adolfo cried, "Mother, this is it!" and opened fire.

A vicious gun battle ensued. Adolfo threw wads of their dwindling cash out the window, hoping to cause enough mayhem among bystanders that he could escape. When that didn't work, he trained his gunfire on a nearby propane tank, hoping to blow it up and cause a diversion. That failed as well. Sensing it was all over, Adolfo ordered Omar to burn the several thousand dollars of their remaining money. If he couldn't have it, neither would anyone else. El Duby handed Adolfo the last two magazines of bullets left, and he finally snapped.

Adolfo demanded that the Narcosatanists immediately carry out the suicide pact. But Omar refused to kill Adolfo and Martin. Adolfo ordered El Duby to take the initiative, to no avail. Adolfo assured El Duby he would be back from the dead. With Sara now screaming in agreement, El Duby reluctantly carried out this final task. While Adolfo and Martin stood in the bedroom closet, El Duby emptied the gun's magazine into them. He didn't kill anyone else. All at once, the nightmare had ended.

Sara ran to the police, claiming to be a hostage. El Duby came out soon after and was apprehended. Police stormed the building and found Omar hiding under a bed. In the confusion at the scene, the police, who'd been engaging in an on-and-off gunfight with the trapped Narcosatanists, initially reported killing Adolfo themselves. But ballistic evidence uncovered later proved that El Duby had shot his *padrino*, as he soon confessed.

Police questioned all three soon after, and much of the public knowledge of the Narcosatanist cult's crimes comes from these detailed interrogations. Sara maintained her innocence, stating that she originally left Matamoros for Mexico City on a vacation with Adolfo. But she did not pack a bag, and her parents knew nothing of any such plans. She couldn't explain why she didn't take off while outside the apartment, making phone calls.

She also knew too much about Adolfo's drug deals and murder sprees to be credibly innocent. Sara insisted she knew only a little about Adolfo's darker side through the bits and pieces he told her. Nevertheless, she recounted many of his brutal crimes, and her status quickly went from that of a key witness to a major suspect.

El Duby was also forthcoming in his confession. He was initially horrified by his role in killing his *padrino*. But he soon regained the swagger he'd experienced in the cult, telling police that nothing they did could affect him. He still seemed to believe Adolfo would return from the dead and deliver him from their custody. Even after his death, Adolfo's mystical manipulation was largely intact.

Omar was not so willing to admit to anything. He insisted he had nothing to do with any of the cult murders and was merely Adolfo's lover and housekeeper. This was true, in part: Omar was not as involved with the Narcosatanists cult activities. And he lived in Mexico City, several hundred miles from Matamoros. But eventually he acknowledged his presence at the sacrificial murder of Jorge Montes's roommate, Ramón.

El Duby was convicted of murder for killing Adolfo and Martin and sentenced to thirty years in prison, and Jorge Montes received a thirty-five-year sentence for the murder of Ramón, a discrepancy in sentencing that may be attributable to the fact that Montes was not honoring a request but murdered Ramón outright.

Sara was found innocent in the killing of Adolfo and Martin but guilty of criminal association. She was sentenced to six years in jail. In 1994 she was subsequently found guilty of multiple counts of murder for the cult's sacrifices and received a sixty-two-year sentence. At the same time, Elio, Little Serafin, Sergio, and a follower named David Serna each received sixty-seven-year sentences.

Omar never made it that far. Once in custody, his health began to severely falter. Less than a year after his arrest, in February 1990, he died of a heart attack at twenty-four years old due to complications from AIDS. Two other followers were charged but did not stand trial: Malio Fabio Ponce Torres, another of the original five Matamoros initiates, and Ovidio Hernández, Elio's brother; both disappeared and were never apprehended.

Salvador Vidal was charged with possession and sale of cocaine, but his crimes did not extend to murder. Authorities claimed he was a good police officer who had been corrupted by drug money and his belief in witchcraft. They also insisted that no other police were involved in Adolfo's cult. Vidal faced seven to twenty-five years in prison for the drug charges, but there is no evidence he ever served any time.

Rancho Santa Elena became the property of the Mexican government. It stood idle after the killings, since no one was willing to work there. Occasional nighttime digging of the ground, likely by magic practitioners looking for body parts, gave rise to rumors that the Narcosatanist cult had not disbanded, but there was little local activity to suggest that was true.

Adolfo de Jesús Constanzo did leave behind one mystery that suggests the story is not over, though. When officers searched his condo in Calle Pomona, Mexico City, they found a room with an altar in which many of the cult's Mexico City rituals and initiations were held.

Among the putrefying blood and animal carcasses on the floor was a large, clean circle where none of the filth had accumulated. Something had been there and removed shortly before the police search: the *nganga*. Adolfo and the Narcosatanists had taken it when they escaped, but they did not have it with them on the run.

After all is said and done, Adolfo's original *nganga* is still out there. It has never been found.

EXPLOITATION

BHAGWAN SHREE RAJNEESH

Bhagwan Shree Rajneesh was a witty professor of philosophy who rebranded himself as a charismatic guru. His ashrams, first in India in the 1970s and then in Oregon in the 1980s, attracted a huge following of mostly Americans and Europeans with a gospel of free love, capitalism, and enlightenment through dancing. But while Rajneesh spiraled into drug use, huffing nitrous oxide and trading blessings for expensive gifts—at his peak he owned ninety-three Rolls-Royces, including one with tear-gas guns hidden in the fenders—his followers pulled off a biological attack, lacing the salad bars in Oregon restaurants with salmonella, in order to rig a local election and take over the nearby town. Eventually they seized control of the rural community, legalizing public nudity and harassing any residents who objected. But once the government built a case against them, their fate was sealed: Rajneesh was deported to India, his devotees sent to prison, and the numerous Rolls-Royces auctioned for $7 million.

MATERIAL GURU

Nobody played the part of enlightened guru better than Bhagwan Shree Rajneesh. With his flowing robes, long, white beard, mischievous eyes, and regular talks to his orange-clad devotees, he inspired tremendous devotion. In his sessions of *darshan*—a Sanskrit word meaning the opportunity to behold the deity and receive spiritual blessing—Rajneesh gave his followers their new names as sannyasins, or renunciants who'd turned away from the world. He assumed a throne-like chair in the center of his ashram, or monastic community, and gave spontaneous talks full of mysterious, sunny, permissive sayings such as "God is not serious, otherwise he cannot create such a beautiful world with so much music and delight in it, with so much love in it."

In the 1970s, as thousands of those seeking spiritual renewal flocked to India, Rajneesh built a fanatical following made up mostly of Westerners, who swarmed into his ashram to learn his peculiar brand of "dynamic meditation," a pogoing, wild-eyed dance style/meditation that the guru passed off as a path to enlightenment. Under the guidance of Rajneesh, baby boomers who might not have had the patience or stamina for more traditional forms of seated meditation were free to practice this new high-energy brand of Eastern spirituality. To prove their devotion, many renounced their earthly possessions, giving Rajneesh elaborate gifts and large and regular donations that allowed the holy one to live in tremendous splendor. "Capitalism is a state of freedom," he told his devotees. "That's exactly why I am in support of it. It allows you all kinds of freedom."[1]

But while the guru was living the high life, his followers were working for twelve hours at a stretch for him, making his extravagant lifestyle possible. In the 1980s, when health problems and concerns about persecution led him to abandon India, he charged his most devoted follower, Ma Anand Sheela, a tough and charismatic leader in her own right, with establishing a new ashram in America. She threw herself into the task, buying a 64,000-acre estate outside Antelope,

Oregon. Within months, under her leadership, the devotees turned it into a self-sustaining community, with buildings and sewers and a power plant, and thousands of acres for growing the food the community needed to live on.

But when sannyasins by the thousands started to descend on Antelope and the new settlement, now called Rajneeshpuram, they soon found themselves at odds with the surrounding communities. The locals objected to the flood of new inhabitants in the remote valley and their strange ways, which included wandering about without clothes on and loud bouts of sex at all hours. When the town threatened to change the laws that allowed Rajneeshpuram to operate, Sheela mobilized, bringing in homeless people and housing them on the premises so that they could establish residency and vote down any measure. The ashram began buying up properties in Antelope proper and taking over the local businesses. And when state and local authorities continued to investigate, Sheela turned violent, plotting murder and even biological warfare.

Meanwhile, Rajneesh found a Hollywood-based dentist who could supply him with drugs—his favorite was nitrous oxide—and began to withdraw into a life of self-indulgence. He established regular sessions of drive-by *darshan*: adoring followers would line the roads of Rajneeshpuram, throwing flowers while he slowly rolled by in one of his Rolls-Royces. But by then the authorities were closing in, and in 1985 they raided the settlement, discovering enough evidence to file charges for attempted murder, wiretapping, and conspiracy to defraud the government. Within months the Oregon ashram was a ghost town. Sheela pleaded guilty, but served only thirty-nine months. She was released and deported, and then claimed she was innocent.

A DEVILISH CHILD WITH A CURSE ON HIS HEAD

The man who inspired all this mayhem was born on December 11, 1931, at his grandparents' home in Kuchwada, India, to Jain parents, who named the boy Mohan Chandra Jain. Jainism is an ancient

Indian religion that believes in nonviolence, truthfulness, chastity, and a life without possessions. Its adherents believe above all in the pursuit of higher spiritual levels, with the goal of destroying karma and perfecting life from one incarnation to the next. This is a philosophy that informed a great deal of Rajneesh's teachings, although he clearly did not aspire to a life without possessions.

At the time of Rajneesh's birth, the infant was the subject of a troubling prediction. His grandfather had commissioned a leading astrologer to draw up Rajneesh's birth chart, which mapped the alignment of the planets at the exact instant he was born. These charts, and the resulting geometry of the planetary alignments, are believed to hold the key to one's personality and future, although they are subject to individual interpretation. And because this astrologer didn't believe Rajneesh would survive the first seven years of his life, he refused to complete the boy's chart until he reached that age. As a result, the threat of death threw a pall over Rajneesh's early childhood. And to put his family even more on edge, the prediction seemed plausible, since he suffered from chronic asthma and contracted a case of smallpox that nearly took his life.

Rajneesh's parents, who lived in Gadarwara, were extraordinarily busy: they had eleven children and carried the additional responsibility of managing a business inherited from Rajneesh's paternal grandmother. To ease their burdens, Rajneesh's parents sent him to live with his maternal grandparents. His grandmother soon established herself as the most influential person in his formative years; she raised him with absolute freedom and imposed no restrictions.

But alongside this free-spirited independence, there lived a darkness inside Rajneesh, and he grew to obsess over death and the occult. In 1938, after Rajneesh managed to survive his first seven years, the astrologer fulfilled his promise and finally made the boy's chart. But his interpretation had not improved with age: now the prediction was that Rajneesh would not survive past age twenty-one, a prophecy that would haunt the child for the remainder of his youth.

This dire reading coincided with the death of Rajneesh's maternal grandfather that same year, which had a great impact on the boy. He referred to this loss as "the death of all attachments." Soon he began withdrawing from those around him, perhaps as a way of protecting himself from the pain and grief, or because, after his grandfather's death, he and his grandmother moved back to the bustling home of his parents in Gadarwara.

There, Rajneesh began formal schooling and proved adept in his studies but was contentious with his teachers, whose authority he constantly challenged. He refused to adapt to expectations and frequently got in trouble for his rebellious behavior. According to his own account as well as those who knew him, he was a daredevil and a prankster. Not only did he delight in breaking rules; he liked to test his own physical limitations, as if to mock the specter of death that loomed over his young life.

OUTLIVING DEATH

When Rajneesh was fourteen, he decided that if a cruel fate was his destiny, then he would face it head-on. "If death is going to occur as the astrologer has said, then it is better to be prepared . . . ," he stated. "Why should I not go and meet it halfway? If I am going to die, then it is better to die consciously."[2] So he went to an old temple at the outskirts of Gadarwara and meditated there among the ruins for seven days. He arranged to have his food and water delivered every day, but otherwise he remained alone, waiting for death.

That this could happen at all is not an indictment of young Rajneesh's parents, as it might possibly seem to a Western sensibility. It should be seen instead as a testament to the spirituality of both India, where such an observant child might not only be recognized but encouraged, and also as a sign of the young boy's fierce dedication. Even at his young age he showed the stamina and persistence that eluded so many aspirants. In this way Rajneesh stands apart from many cult leaders in the authenticity of the spiritual gifts he later leveraged for his own self-indulgence.

"For seven days I waited . . . ," he said. "Death never came . . . Strange, weird feelings happened . . . [I]f you are feeling like you are going to die, you become calm and silent. Nothing creates any worry then, because all worries are concerned with life."[3] By convincing himself that he was about to pass on, Rajneesh seemed to have created the ideal circumstances to go through a near-death experience that many interpret as spiritual or religious. Researchers believe that this state induces heightened brain activity and that it shares many of the signature characteristics of mystical experience, such as separation from the body, transcendence of time and space, a sense of cosmic unity or oneness, a deeply felt positive mood, a sense of sacredness, and intuitive illumination. Some describe such experiences of being on the brink of death as peaceful and calming, while others recount visions of divine beings from an afterlife. These phenomena could account for what Rajneesh described after surviving the seven days in the temple.

Rajneesh, of course, did not die, but according to Bruce Greyson, formerly of the University of Virginia and one of the leading researchers on near-death experiences, these events can launch a person in an entirely new direction in life. This is especially common for those whose lives have been marked by struggle, doubt, or fear, as Rajneesh's had clearly been.

But even if he had outpaced the predictions of his own death, as he now believed, he was still haunted by its presence. When he was fifteen, his girlfriend Shashi Sharma died of typhoid, but in keeping with the Jain belief in reincarnation, she'd promised to come back to him in her next life. (Twenty-two years later, Rajneesh would remember that promise when an Englishwoman, Christine Wolf Smith, born a year after Sharma died, came to a meditation camp where new followers were learning his dynamic meditation. Under his tutelage, Christine came to remember her previous incarnation, and she became his constant companion.)

Rajneesh was on the cusp of a personal revelation, though. At nineteen he left home for Hitkarini College in Jabalpur, about ninety miles from his parents. Then in 1953, seven years after his experience in the ruins of the temple, he marked his twenty-first birthday and survival of yet another seven-year cycle by declaring enlightenment.

The term means different things for different religions, but in the Jain tradition there are broader and more expansive implications. Usually enlightenment is thought of as a peaceful state of being in which the soul has transcended ordinary worries and concerns of day-to-day human life. But in Jainism, enlightenment is referred to as *kevala jnana* and signifies a broader claim to supreme wisdom, even omniscience. Of course, it is not unusual for college students like Rajneesh to believe they know everything, but in this case he was fully aware that his claims were not ordinary. He was taking his first steps to set himself apart and even convincing himself that he was now operating on a higher spiritual plane than the rest of humanity.

As part of his schooling in higher consciousness, Rajneesh had become enthralled by the teachings of George Gurdjieff, a Greek Armenian spiritual philosopher. Gurdjieff claimed that most humans experience a disconnect between their emotions and bodies and therefore live in a hypnotic state of semiconsciousness. However, this "waking sleep," as he called it, could be overcome and transcended on the way to achieving one's maximum potential of higher consciousness and inner growth. One particularly appealing aspect—which later became central to the runaway growth of Rajneesh's cult—was that Gurdjieff believed the enlightened teacher could see the individual needs of the disciple and helpfully point out the tasks that disciple needed to perform to reach higher consciousness. This became an especially useful principle that helped Rajneesh exploit his thousands of devotees, who would happily commit to unpaid labor in Rajneesh-puram, thinking that they were ascending to a higher plane by digging latrines or washing bean sprouts or incubating salmonella.

CHALLENGING AUTHORITY

Perhaps because he was already enlightened, or maybe because he was clever and combative prior to attaining omniscience, Rajneesh felt no qualms about taking on his teachers during class. He loved to derail the lessons of the day, questioning the reasoning and authority of his professors and generally acting disruptive to such a degree that he was finally asked to leave the school. He transferred to D.N. Jain College, also in Jabalpur, and earned a BA in philosophy by 1955.

At his new school, Rajneesh didn't soften his argumentative approach, but the faculty came up with an ingenious solution: they exempted him from class so his shenanigans couldn't disrupt his peers. He only needed to attend when a test was scheduled. And he was finally rewarded for his incessant arguing when he joined the school's debate club and became a national champion.

Immediately after he graduated college, Rajneesh entered the University of Sagar to earn a master's degree in philosophy. From there he joined Raipur Sanskrit College as a lecturer. But according to Anil Kumar Mysore Nagaraj, a psychiatrist who investigated Rajneesh's philosophies, the Raipur Sanskrit College administration worried that Rajneesh would be a negative influence on the students and a danger to their morality and character, so he was quickly removed from his post. At his next stop, Jabalpur University, Rajneesh became a lecturer, and in 1960, at the age of twenty-nine, he was made a professor of philosophy.

He started speaking at the annual Sarva Dharma Sammelan—the meeting of all faiths—held annually at Jabalpur. The transcripts of Rajneesh's lectures there produced over four hundred books of musings on topics as wide-ranging as Christianity and Hasidism, yoga and Zen, even Sigmund Freud and Henry Ford. He borrowed from many different philosophies, picking and choosing the tidbits that appealed to him, and subsequently created his own belief system.

By 1962, the main pillars of Rajneesh's teachings were nearly fully formed, and he started opening camps where he could lead

three- to ten-day retreats dedicated to his own brand of meditation, which he called "dynamic meditation." This unique technique
combined movement and stillness. According to his instructions, the
meditation required ten minutes of vigorous and irregular breathing followed by ten minutes of explosive and again irregular movement. ("Go totally mad," he advised. "Scream, shout, cry, jump,
kick, shake, dance, sing, laugh; throw yourself around. Hold nothing back; keep your whole body moving."[4]) In the third ten-minute
segment, he ordered his disciples to jump up and down with their
arms over their heads, repeating "Hoo! Hoo! Hoo!" to the point of
exhaustion. The fourth stage of dynamic meditation lasted fifteen
minutes: the disciples would simply freeze in place. ("The fourth
stage comes of its own accord," he explained. "Then something
happens that is not your doing. It comes as a grace: you have become
a vacuum, an emptiness, and something fills you. Something spiritual pours into you when you are not. You are not there because
there is no doing; the ego disappears when there is no doer."[5]) In
the fifth stage, also fifteen minutes, the disciples would celebrate and
indulge themselves.

This was clearly a ritual that did not take much discipline. In most
meditations, students are instructed to sit and empty their minds of
thought, but in Rajneesh's teachings they are told to go through a state
of nervousness, to exhaust themselves in an attempt to shut off their
minds through pure frenzy. It's a perfect boredom-free form of meditation for hyperactive Westerners with no prior training or inclination
to sit in silence, and from the start it gained adherents.

At the same time that Rajneesh was inventing this part workout/
part meditation, he went on lecture circuits, criticizing orthodox Indian
religions and praising capitalism, an approach that won the enmity of
religious authorities but gained him the love—and support—of several wealthy Indian businessmen who, in 1965, collaborated to create
Jeevan Jagruti Kendra, or the Life Awakening Center, a group that
financed Rajneesh's travels and lectures and freed him from the need
to work in academia.

His philosophy about capitalism was later recorded and can be found in the book *Come, Come, Yet Again Come*, in which he wrote: "Capitalism is not an ideology; it is not imposed on the society, it is a natural growth. It is not like communism, or fascism, or socialism—these are ideologies; they have to be imposed. Capitalism is a state of freedom; that's exactly why I am in support of it."[6]

SEX AND CHARISMA

In 1968, when Rajneesh was thirty-seven years old, his talks started to focus even more on the acceptance of sex and sexuality. These lectures were eventually published under the title *From Sex to Superconsciousness*, earning him the reputation in Indian media as a "sex guru." His teachings received a great deal of backlash from the scandalized conservative community, but it was also a savvy marketing tool for someone who had already realized that a high percentage of his most generous supporters came from the West, where the sexual revolution was starting to take hold. He was intentionally sparking outrage, and even mixing hypnosis into his lectures like a magician, to draw attention to himself wherever he went.

In his talks on the sacredness of sexuality, Rajneesh claimed that such vigorous expression was a vital part of achieving spiritual growth and a higher consciousness. He believed that religion and social norms restricted sexual expression in all its forms by associating it with shame and embarrassment. He insisted that such negative connotations prevented children from getting the proper education they needed to understand their own desires. This viewpoint clashed with that of conservative leaders, who were upset over the public discourse of such matters that they felt should be spoken of—and practiced—privately.

Rajneesh wanted none of that. Too many religions, he said, focused on the rewards of the afterlife while ignoring the beauty, joys, and sacredness in the here and now. He taught that love in general and sex in particular was the way to enlightenment. And he advocated releasing love—which is often trapped inside—through sexual expression. "Man's whole society is sick and wretched," he said. "And if this cancerous society is to be changed, it is essential to accept that the energy of sex is divine, that the attraction for sex is essentially religious."

This was timely talk for Westerners: same-sex liberation and feminism joined open marriages and no-fault divorces in overturning long-standing social norms and encouraging sexual expression in all its forms. It was a movement that aligned perfectly with Rajneesh's philosophical teachings. Hugh B. Urban's book *Zorba the Buddha: Sex, Spirituality, and Capitalism in the Global Osho Movement* discusses the ways in which the formation of Rajneesh's movement conveniently coincided with second-wave feminism. Rajneesh believed in the superiority of women, claiming that their ability to have multiple orgasms was proof that they were in possession of a greater sexual energy. This instilled a certain fear in men, who proceeded to oppress and dominate women for centuries. According to Susan Jean Palmer, who wrote about the role of women in religious cults, this was an attractive message, especially to upper-middle-class thirty- and fortysomethings, who would travel to India and later to Oregon and become his disciples.

Rajneesh believed he could offer these women a path to freedom and enlightenment that no other feminist movement could. "My own vision is that the coming age will be the age of woman. Man has tried for five thousand years and failed. It is enough! Now feminine energies have to be released . . . ," he said. "The freedom of women cannot come through stupid movements like women's liberation. . . . If we create a few woman buddhas in the world, then woman will be freed from all the chains and fetters."[7]

It's at this critical turning point, from the late 1960s through the 1970s, when Rajneesh began to transform into what sociologists call a charismatic leader, a term that political economist and sociologist Max Weber applied to many cult figures. Weber's work in political sociology names three types of authority: charismatic, traditional, and legal. By his definitions, rational-legal authority and traditional authority are more common and conventional. Rational-legal authorities are legitimized by complex rules and regulated by government laws. Traditional authority refers to power that typically passes from one generation to the next.

But charismatic leaders are set apart and treated as though they have intrinsic superhuman powers or qualities. This definitely applied to Rajneesh, who claimed he was an enlightened being and, as such, had recently anointed himself "Bhagwan," or "Blessed One." This started to play out right away in Bombay, where he established his headquarters from 1969 to 1974, living in expensive apartments funded by his lectures and meditation camps.

While residing in Bombay, Rajneesh surrounded himself with adoring followers who believed that his philosophy could save humankind. And among these devotees, his advocacy of sexual awakening was not purely theoretical. Many female followers in the early 1970s spoke of having been fondled by the guru. And he used "private *darshan*" sessions to have intercourse with disciples: after a session with one woman that stretched until midnight, he would sleep until 4:00 a.m., and then conduct another session with a different woman. Sometimes he would ask disciples to strip for him or have sex right in front of him so he could "heal their energy."

During this five-year period, we begin to see two key elements of Rajneesh's philosophy start to merge. The first was his great disdain for institutionalized authority and rules of society, and the second was his desire to build a Buddhafield—a promised land where his "New Man" could live peacefully. His devotees believed that Rajneesh alone could deliver on this promise of salvation for all humanity.

This corresponds to Max Weber's final qualification for a charismatic leader, who appears to his followers as a "revolutionary force," meant to "result in a radical alteration of the central system of attitudes . . . toward . . . the 'world.'"[8] Rajneesh's Buddhafield evoked these notions of a new world that offered enlightenment and salvation as never experienced before. Over the course of two decades, Rajneesh established himself as a being of higher power and recruited people who would worship him and validate that power. He built a community based on freeing his followers from the restrictions and obligations of society. The lure of his promised benefits—such as sex and enlightenment—secured their absolute devotion, and convinced many ardent disciples that Rajneesh was the one guru who could lead them to the promised land.

A DEVOTEE ENABLER

In the early 1970s, followers were flocking to Bombay (now called Mumbai), and soon Rajneesh was swarmed everywhere he went. "Now, he was no more a private person, but a man of public interest. He was talked about as a saint, a holy man, a guru,"[9] his devotee Ma Anand Sheela wrote in her book about Rajneesh and the critical— and often illegal—role she played in the expansion of his cult.

She was born Sheela Ambalal Patel in 1949. In the late sixties, at the age of seventeen, she left her privileged middle-class family in Baroda to travel overseas and study at Montclair College in New Jersey. While she was there, she fell in love with wealthy student Marc Silverman, who'd been diagnosed with Hodgkin's lymphoma at the age of eighteen. He was hesitant to marry, since his doctors told him he had only two years to live. But Sheela was young and wanted to be with Marc no matter what fate might bring. "We decided to defy logic and spend what little time we had joyfully," she wrote. "We wanted to feel love and not give up on life, even if it was limited."[10] So, in 1968, despite Marc's terminal illness, the couple married, and Marc outlived the predictions by a full eleven years.

In 1972, when Sheela was twenty-two, she received word that her mother was having eye surgery. Sheela returned to her hometown to be with her, with the plan that Marc would follow once he completed his courses. After visiting her mother in the hospital, Sheela and her father took a spur-of-the-moment trip to Bombay to visit a cousin. They were staying in an apartment just blocks away from the popular Rajneesh, so they went to see him on a whim. Quite unexpectedly, Rajneesh's personal secretary, Ma Yoga Laxmi, who was dressed in the orange garb of a sannyasin—a title that Rajneesh bestowed on nearly anyone who agreed to work for him—let them in and led them directly to Rajneesh. Right away, Rajneesh held Sheela to his chest and, as she later wrote, she "looked at him with a completely dissolved heart."

Overcome with this new emotion, Sheela signed up for Rajneesh's meditation camp and quickly took the given name of Ma Anand Sheela. "Ma" was the title Rajneesh gave to all women who followed him, as it meant "mother." "Anand" meant "joy" and "Sheela," already part of her name, meant "one with a strong character." She immediately became a sannyasin. "I have left everything to my master. When he says, 'Wear orange,' then I will wear orange. When he says, 'Walk naked in the street,' then I will walk naked in the street," she wrote. "I know no other reason for what I do. To find out why I do what I do, you must ask my master, because he has become my absolute guide."

When her husband, Marc, finally joined her in India, he was skeptical at first, but soon he too became a sannyasin. Rajneesh, eager to test the limits of their devotion, sent them for three weeks to the mountains of Pahalgam, Kashmir, in the middle of winter to meditate in the bitter cold. They accepted this mission and spent the time there without heat and little food. "We came back feeling superb—we had passed his litmus test with flying colors," Sheela wrote.

This is an example of what psychologist Robert Jay Lifton in *Thought Reform and the Psychology of Totalism: A Study of "Brainwashing" in China*, his book on mind control, calls "self-sanctification through purity."[11] Tests like this—one could even call them trials—are often designed to be so difficult that failure is inevitable. That failure then goads the devotee to try harder and take on even more impossible tasks in the hope of pleasing the master. Of course, in the rare cases when one does succeed in performing the impossible or uncomfortable or humiliating task assigned, the guru now knows the lengths his devotees are willing to go to please him.

After Sheela and Marc passed this hurdle, Rajneesh asked that they fly back to America and put their affairs in order. In her book, Sheela didn't explain what this entailed, but their return and the news of their recent conversions put them at odds with their families, especially Marc's. Sheela wrote of Marc's father, "He would have preferred a criminal son to a son walking around in an orange sarong." This is another example of the thought-control techniques that Lifton laid out, something he called "milieu reform," which involved cutting off communication with the outside world. This creates a dependency on the cult leader.

But these mind-control tricks could scarcely compare to the next wave of requests that Rajneesh made. In 1974 he grew tired of Bombay altogether, blaming the city for the return of his childhood asthma. But beyond such pretexts, there were practical concerns as well: his followers were growing so numerous that he needed a larger piece of property to allow his membership to really take off. With the help of his secretary Laxmi, he purchased land in Pune, located outside Bombay, for an ashram, a spiritual monastery that became the headquarters for all operations until 1980. This ashram was also incorporated as a nonprofit charity called the Rajneesh Foundation, which would lead to financial chicanery.

POWER LADIES

The Pune ashram ran on donations from Rajneesh's followers, and status within the ashram rose in proportion to the wealth of the sannyasin and the size of their donation. According to Sheela, the sannyasin could earmark their donations for Rajneesh himself as a way of getting his attention. "Some people were more willing to donate money for his personal needs than for the organization," she wrote, as they were hoping to finagle a closer connection to the guru. Thanks to the generosity of his disciples, Rajneesh began to indulge his appetite for luxury, and Rolls-Royce automobiles in particular, which in India were associated with the extravagances of the maharajahs. The materialism on his part drew widespread criticism. "True spiritual leaders are not expected to lead a luxurious life. Spirituality in popular consciousness means material poverty," Sheela wrote, in a tone of admiration, as if Rajneesh were a clever but mischievous child. "His lifestyle drove many traditional religious people crazy."

Between 1974 and 1980, the ashram in Pune rapidly expanded, with as many as six thousand sannyasins living on and around the commune, attending therapy sessions, lectures, and meditation workshops, sometimes in states of semi- or complete nudity. Some of these workshops were called encounter groups, intensive group therapy sessions that encouraged sexual exploration, supposedly to help push sannyasins out of their psychological and spiritual comfort zones. Others simply thought that Rajneesh had a taste for voyeurism.

As part of the power structure, Sheela came to realize how far Rajneesh was willing to go in exploiting his devotees. He began charging fees for group therapy participation, meditation sessions, and access to the ashram. On this change in the financial structure in Pune, Sheela wrote, "Everyone was so crazy for enlightenment and so zealously anxious to be without ego and to be meditative that they could do anything for it. The *sannyasins* emptied their pockets, and proved their devotion by expensive gifts. This exploitation was dirty, ugly and repulsive." Rajneesh was beginning to assert his power more aggressively. "He let everyone know clearly who the master was."

The guru was very aware of his inconsistencies and once said, "[Consistency] is impossible for me. I live in the moment and whatsoever I am saying right now is true only for this moment. I have no references with my past and I don't think of the future at all." But this wasn't entirely true. He clearly always had an eye on how he could get more out of his hordes of followers. To help him achieve this goal, he deputized a circle of women in the ashram and invested them with the authority to take control of the operations and keep the ashram running smoothly.

Susan Jean Palmer, the Canadian sociologist and author of the book *Moon Sisters, Krishna Mothers, Rajneesh Lovers: Women's Roles in New Religions*, studied the dynamics between Rajneesh and his followers and wrote about this central core group of women in high-level positions at the commune in Pune. They became known as the "power ladies." Many of them were allowed unusual access to Rajneesh himself, filling roles ranging from personal secretary to personal nurse. But they also managed the day-to-day operations and often took charge of major decision-making.

However, Rajneesh subverted this empowerment by encouraging competition and infighting, leaving the women prey to feelings of insecurity about their relative positions in the group. "Rajneesh had set it up to let conflicts arise. Conflicts were considered a good tool to go deeper inside," Sheela wrote. "According to him, conflicts should become visible and tangible and not be suppressed or pushed under the surface. Only thus can they serve inner growth."

Supposedly, Rajneesh preferred to work with women because he felt they were less aggressive and more receptive and open to his energy. For him, receptivity was a key element of reaching enlightenment. On the other hand, it was an elusive concept, defined by an openness only Rajneesh himself could identify. While it was considered a great compliment and sign of merit if the guru deemed one more receptive than others, in practice this meant that he had successfully surrounded himself with anxious people, mostly women, each trying to outdo each other with acts that would prove themselves to him.

His own comments about Ma Yoga Laxmi, the power lady who served as one of his early personal secretaries, illustrates the ways he delegated to these women in one breath and discredited them in the next. "Always remember that Laxmi never does anything on her own. She is the perfect vehicle and that is why she is chosen for this work . . . ," he noted. "Whatsoever is said, she does."[12] Here one can see the two conflicting ideas that helped Rajneesh maintain control over his devotees. Laxmi performed based on the guidelines that only

Rajneesh knew. But she was not so powerful that she acted on her own ideas. Everything she did was guided by Rajneesh.

THE GOD HAS FLED

Due to a general absence of rules and regulations, behavior at the ashram often threatened to spiral out of control. In 1979 a German sannyasin named Wolfgang Dobrowolny visited the ashram and made a film called *Ashram in Poona* that featured a fifteen-minute sequence of uninhibited brutality that broke out at one of the nude encounter group therapy sessions when a group pillow fight meant to release violent impulses got out of hand. The film made it all the way to the United States, with the *Los Angeles Times* reporting that the path to enlightenment involved some "broken bones, and black eyes"[13] along the way. This kind of chaos is typical of organizations that operate at the whims of a charismatic authority. This is due to charismatic leaders rejecting the norms that come with more highly organized forms of governance.

The thirty-year-old Sheela was going through her own personal upheaval during this time as well. In 1980, at the age of thirty-three, her husband Marc passed away from his long battle with Hodgkin's lymphoma. "When he died, [Rajneesh's] teachings gave me the strength to accept the loss," Sheela wrote. After Marc's death, she devoted herself to Rajneesh and the ashram with a fierce dedication. But when violence escalated among the communal ranks, it became clear that the stability she had hoped to find by disappearing into the details of governance would be hard to come by. Additional incidents of mental breakdowns, injuries, and sexual assault occurred on the property. Nearly every violation was overlooked, as disciples were urged to see the encounter groups and anger therapy as part of a necessary process to help them overcome their inhibitions, an approach that fared well with Westerners. At the same time, Rajneesh's relationship with the surrounding community grew hostile as overcrowding at his compound became a serious issue. It was clear that Rajneesh needed to do something to keep his devoted followers together and united, and at the same time lower the profile of the ashram.

Although the exact timing of this is uncertain, another pivotal change took place in early 1981, according to Win McCormack's timeline of the movement. Rajneesh took a vow of silence, withdrawing from public speaking engagements. He conferred only with his top aides. His followers called this the "ultimate phase" of his work, which was meant to "deepen his communion" with his devotees. Sheela claimed that she was dismayed by the news of Rajneesh's vow. "I couldn't believe my ears," she wrote. "It meant the end of the man I loved. I could not understand why he was doing it."

Maybe Sheela truly worried about the growing violence and the potential collapse of their movement in the wake of Rajneesh going mute. Or perhaps she was excited by the newly created power vacuum. Whatever her intentions were at the time, the silence of the guru gave her the opportunity she needed for a power grab.

After his vow had been taken, Rajneesh's personal secretary, Laxmi, was tasked with finding new land for the sannyasins, something large enough for the movement's six thousand followers. Rajneesh also believed that moving away from Pune would allow them the freedom to practice their religion free from the persecution of fundamentalist Hindus. On top of that, Indian prime minister Indira Gandhi viewed Rajneesh and his followers as a threat to society. In *Wild Wild Country*, the 2018 Netflix docuseries directed by Chapman Way and Maclain Way, Sheela states that this prevailing prejudice resulted in a "gridlock" and made finding new land next to impossible within India.

Sheela was homesick for her years spent in the United States, but she was also thinking like a Rajneeshee. She believed that, thanks to the protections for religious freedom in the US Constitution, her adopted community could live there without persecution from Hindu traditionalists. So in the spring of 1981, when she suggested that

Rajneesh move his commune to America, he eagerly agreed. "Let it suffice that his delicate health, overcrowding in the ashram, and the growing clashes with Orthodox Hindus ultimately led to his decision to move out of [Pune]," she wrote. That could be historical revisionism on her part, as many news reports suggested that tax flight was the real reason for this sudden relocation.

Because so many in Pune seemed to depend on the knowledge that Rajneesh was nearby, all the arrangements for his departure had to be handled with the utmost secrecy.

On June 1, 1981, with everything finally coordinated, Rajneesh, Sheela, and a handful of confidants got into one of Rajneesh's Rolls-Royces and left the commune without a word to anyone else. A BBC One headline announced: "The God Has Fled." The report offered few explanatory details. "Without warning and without saying goodbye, his followers have been given no idea of his whereabouts."

The devotees were devastated to be deprived of their charismatic leader. "I had taken my children, my husband and gone to India to live with [Rajneesh]. Everything I had known, my whole world, was taken apart," Jane Stork writes in her book *Breaking the Spell: My Life as a Rajneeshee, and the Long Journey Back to Freedom*. Rajneesh pulled up to the ashram gates and then simply drove away, leaving Stork to ponder her fate alone. "If he didn't come back," she wrote, "what was I going to do?" The community was in a panic, with Jane Stork not the only one who wondered what would happen next.

But Rajneesh had a specific message delivered to those he left behind: "Everyone has to go back to his or her hometown for some time and put my teaching into practice in normal life. Everyone has to live in his old environment in a meditative way. They can come back when the new commune is ready, when they are invited to live within a Buddhafield." This "Buddhafield" was the promised land that Rajneesh described as being free from societal restrictions, where one could embrace life and laughter and truly become an enlightened new person. The Buddhafield (and Rajneesh's well-being) were now Sheela's only concerns.

Rajneesh clearly offered meaning to his followers, but whatever gifts he had for spiritual insight were offset by his talents at exploitation. As noted earlier, he was incredibly adept at leveraging the admiration of his followers to feed an extravagant lifestyle. But when it came to Sheela, such exploitation was subtler. He took a woman of superhuman dedication—something he knew quite well, since he had sent her to meditate in the extreme cold of a Kashmir mountaintop— and utilized that level of devotion at precisely the moment when she was most vulnerable. As Margaret Singer, an expert in the study of brainwashing, says, "Almost anyone who is in a period of loneliness is in a vulnerable period in which he or she might get taken in by the flattery and deceptive lures that cults use to recruit new members."[14] Rajneesh chose Sheela out of hundreds of followers to be his secretary, and the attention she received from the guru and the work she did likely filled the lonely space she was experiencing after the loss of her husband, Marc.

Sheela recalled in her memoir, "The fear of failure was overpowering. It was not easy to work for him. He drove me to the brink of madness." She traveled around the United States looking at properties in Tennessee, Colorado, and Arizona, writing, "From being desperate, I slowly began to feel discouraged. I felt I would never be able to find the land that I had promised [Rajneesh]." Eventually, she called her brother Bipin, who'd been living in the States for many years and was, according to Sheela, extremely well-connected. To her relief, instead of simply offering advice, Bipin told her that he would arrange for her to be taken to Oregon to view a property that he believed would suit her every need.

Sheela arrived in Oregon, her sights set on Big Muddy Ranch, a 64,000-acre-plus piece of desert land about four hours from Portland. The size and remoteness of the property made it extremely attractive and fit right into Sheela's vision for the future of the movement.

"It was June 11, 1981. The first death anniversary of [my late husband, Marc]. For me these connections were important," Sheela wrote. "I told the man that I would like to buy the land." She presented herself to the townspeople and the owners as a soft-spoken, sweet young woman. To blend in even more, she used her legal name, Sheela Silverman, rather than the one that Rajneesh had given her. She immediately began to charm the local officials and ranchers in the area, doing everything she could think of to win their favor. She even hosted a dance party and purchased cattle for the ranch, although Rajneesh's community was vegetarian.

FREE LOVE IN THE BUDDAHFIELD

Rajneesh could be unreasonable about practicalities, such as how long it took to build fifty A-frame homes to house his disciples, but Sheela tried to anticipate his demands. It wasn't enough just to push his followers. As the work on the commune began, she went to the legal limits to suit her needs and to fulfill the orders from Rajneesh. For example, Sheela had been informed of and promptly disregarded the local zoning laws, which mandated that only about 150 people could inhabit the ranch land.

Sheela either was given more responsibility or, with Rajneesh's deadline as a pretext, took it further and began to assume command. With this shift in power, Rajneeshpuram commenced the transition from charismatic leadership to one of traditional authority. To paraphrase Weber, in traditional authority structures, the obligation to follow orders comes from a sense of personal loyalty, which is "essentially unlimited." Adrian Greek, codirector of the Positive Action Center, a cult counseling center in Portland, Oregon, examined the role that guilt can play as an instrument to seize control. In an interview with the *New Republic*, he pointed out that cult leaders—in particular Rajneesh and Sheela—like to "induce guilt by setting up a perfect standard for you to follow, one that is humanly impossible to attain. Then, if you feel bad, it's your own fault." This creates a cycle in which, to rid themselves of this guilt, the follower strives to be even more devoted, leaving them open to a cult leader's machinations. And when failure occurs, it's an even harder landing. Greek says, "You always feel pressure to change—and guilt—because you always fall short of 'enlightenment.'"[15]

This twisted dynamic helped Sheela organize her crew of Rajneeshees into an extremely productive labor force. They began farming thousands of acres and even built a medical facility and a public transportation system. They often worked up to twelve hours a day to build Rajneeshpuram. And they did so because, as Sheela explained, this retreat would be their promised land, and all their efforts were laying the foundation for the entire community to live a spiritual life—or at least the one that Rajneesh outlined, with its frenzied meditation and easy access to sexual partners.

As more sannyasins arrived, the work crew soon totaled over one hundred. They used prefabricated houses and precut building materials to complete their task even faster. They constructed new offices and a home for Rajneesh himself, and quickly blew past their limited number of building permits just by putting up the A-frame homes for the workers on the ranch and those soon to arrive.

In only a few months, Rajneeshpuram was thriving. The sannyasins' farmland sustained its residents; their electric grid supplied power to hundreds of homes; they built plumbing, infrastructure, and roads; they implemented a banking operation, established a meditation hall, and even constructed their own private airport, as well as purchased a hotel in Portland where arriving sannyasins could stay before making their way to the ranch. There was even a shopping complex, complete with a pizzeria and its own boutique of red and orange clothes.

On August 29, 1981, barely eighty days after the purchase of the property, Rajneesh landed in Oregon and set foot in his new promised land for the first time. He was greeted by hundreds of sannyasins who'd already moved to the Buddhafield. Although the commune continued to expand over the next four years, Sheela and her team had raced against the clock over the previous two months, creating everything Rajneesh required to join his devotees and worship there with them.

Sheela described his arrival: "He . . . went into his new house. He looked golden in his happiness. The *sannyasins* were euphoric. I was drowning in my love for him. I had created a new home . . . where he could build a commune of the grandest vision."

But while Sheela could behave serenely around the guru, she proved to be vengeful with nearly everyone else. When she suspected a disciple named Veena was taking advantage of her position as the personal seamstress to Rajneesh, she moved the woman's living quarters to one of the makeshift shelters and made her tend to the commune's bean sprouts. And when Sheela heard that Veena was enjoying her new setup and even seemed to be thriving there, Sheela relocated her to an even more remote and poorly insulated cabin shared with seven other devotees.

This kind of petty revenge was tolerated because Sheela was so effective. And the followers were pouring into the remote retreat. There, far from the prying eyes of the locals in nearby Antelope, and hours away from the big cities closer to the coast, they began leading the kind of permissive lifestyle that had earned Rajneesh his reputation as the "sex guru." Women and men lived in separate dormitories, but sexual expression in private huts was encouraged. One man, Noa Maxwell, whose parents joined the cult when he was just six, told the *Guardian* that he remembers walking through the ashram and "you could hear people having orgasmic sex all the time. All night . . ."[16]

Who was paying the price for all this free love? Women, it seemed. Despite Rajneesh's supposed support of feminine energy, the atmosphere could be particularly poisonous. Onetime devotee Roselyn Smith told Win McCormack in his book *The Rajneesh Chronicles* about the sexual exploitation that she witnessed. "I think Bhagwan attracts a lot of men to him because of this. People have been very impressed by the quality of the men he attracts; he has doctors, and lawyers, lots of professionals. One of his main hookers [*sic*] is sex. People heard that if you went to Pune, if you went to Oregon, there was lots of sex, the women were really open, and you could get all you wanted . . . You could pick up anybody. You could walk up to anybody and say,

'You want to get it on? You want to go home with me?' If they say no, there's loads of other people you could ask. I think he attracts a lot of men because of this. Because men can't find that anywhere else."[17]

Meanwhile anti-Rajneesh sentiment was growing in Antelope. Shortly after Rajneesh arrived in 1981, the leading state environmental group 1000 Friends of Oregon began a fight against the sannyasins, petitioning to have the buildings removed from the ranch, citing land-use violations that they claimed the newcomers had committed. The Rajneeshees needed more buildings, but they'd already far exceeded the number of structures that local building permits allowed. So the Rajneeshees came up with a clever solution that infuriated their neighbors.

At the time, Oregon law stated that any group of at least 150 people had the right to assemble a city by a vote of incorporation, which is just what the sannyasins did. In October 1981 they voted unanimously to incorporate their ranch into the city that became known as Rajneeshpuram. Sheela told reporters soon after: "It's a very beautiful city . . . one which has never existed in the universe. Where people live in harmony, people live in love . . . An example to the universe." Dashiell Edward Paulson, who wrote about the cult in "The Routinization of Rajneeshpuram: Charisma and Authority in the Rajneesh Movement, 1981–1985," his doctoral thesis at the University of Oregon, applies Weber's theories to Sheela's behavior on the ranch. "Sheela quickly consolidated her power after her appointment,"[18] Paulson noted.

Sheela's position was never questioned by the followers, since traditionally Rajneesh's secretary was always the second most powerful position in the commune. Paulson described Sheela as "a traditional ruler with traditional means. But she also built a large, pyramided [sic] shaped bureaucracy in order to handle the complex, demanding, and expensive development of the commune." Weber calls this pyramid a "bureaucratic administrative organ," which Paulson said "bolstered her power, meshing her autocracy with an efficient means for action."

GUN-TOTING DEVOTEES

Sheela dismissed the backlash in Antelope as evidence of ignorant prejudices. There was a subsequent media frenzy. She made appearances on *The Merv Griffin Show*, *Donahue*, and *Crossfire*, as well as a number of other news and talk shows, unapologetically declaring time and again that Rajneeshpuram was there to stay. She was fearless, aggressive, and provocative, and seemed to love every minute of the media attention.

Smaller versions of the Oregon commune were established in Italy, Germany, the United Kingdom, India, Australia, and Japan. Each of these centers supported themselves by forming a variety of businesses. Some offered construction services, while others opened restaurants or dance clubs. But one thing all Rajneesh centers had in common was that each of them would fly members into Oregon for the aptly named World Festival, a five-day celebration that culminated in Master's Day, a special time set aside to honor Rajneesh himself. As many as ten thousand sannyasins from all over the globe spent World Festival dancing, eating, sunbathing, and meditating. The celebration was meant to raise morale, but it also served to rake in a great deal of money for the ranch.

Sheela believed that the number of working sannyasins was thirty thousand worldwide and that the number of disciples who had not yet taken sannyas, the vow of surrender to Rajneesh, numbered as high as five hundred thousand, a dubious claim but typical of Sheela's confident presentation. After the successful bid to incorporate, which made the commune a legal independent city, Rajneeshpuram elected sannyasins to the former Antelope City Council, and by January 1983 they held six of the seven seats. But despite Sheela's apparent triumph, her troubles with the outside world were only just beginning.

In July 1983, Sheela received an overnight phone call: the Rajneesh hotel in Portland had been bombed. The attack inflicted $200,000 worth of damage. The *Los Angeles Times* reported that the bomber,

Stephen P. Paster, did not present a motive but that he "belonged to a militant, fundamentalist Muslim organization."[19] The Rajneesh community immediately blamed the bombing on the bigoted and hateful communities in Oregon. In her memoir, Sheela wrote, "We understood that the police and the courts were not on our side . . . [T]he state did not only do nothing to protect our rights, it even deliberately violated them." She believed that if she "did not take drastic measures to protect" Rajneeshpuram, no one else would.

In response to these threats, real and imagined, Sheela and the sannyasins decided to take up arms, purchasing a cache of weapons and training themselves in their proper use. And as an incorporated city, Rajneeshpuram created its own law enforcement, which they called the Peace Force. Antelope residents said they were anything but peaceful, as the group employed intimidation tactics and harassed the townies, patrolling at night and flashing bright lights into homes. They even arrested a local Antelope picketer for "menacing," charges that Wasco County immediately dropped. The tension and distrust between the two communities escalated rapidly.

These aggressive tactics were one of the main reasons that the city of Rajneeshpuram came under scrutiny in 1983. Dave Frohnmayer, the attorney general of the state of Oregon, grew up near Antelope and was still close to several of its residents, who had a direct pipeline to him. They argued that Rajneeshpuram was not an agricultural group as claimed but a religious organization. This drew concern over whether the new city was honoring the constitutional separation of church and state derived from the establishment clause laid out in the First Amendment of the US Constitution and echoed in the Oregon State Constitution, as well as the belief that their Peace Force was not loyal to the state laws but only to their spiritual master.

In October 1983 the attorney general ruled that Rajneeshpuram was to be nullified as a city, since it violated the separation of church and state. The decision was met by the Rajneeshees with outcries of bigotry and religious persecution. But Sheela would not be swayed from her course. "How can we solve the problem?" she asked in *Wild*

Wild Country. "The more creative we were, the more destructive the politicians were against us. It was their hate that forced us to take these steps for self-preservation, self-protection, self-survival."

"The people of Oregon knew then that we were armed, that we could use our weapons well and that we were prepared to use those weapons if push came to shove," Jane Stork told *Wild Wild Country*. Jane, who was living in India when Rajneesh fled the ashram in Pune, eventually made the move to the ranch and was noted by Sheela as a particularly skilled marksman. This could be one of the reasons why Jane was pulled into Sheela's tight-knit circle, a group that Jane described as Sheela's lieutenants. They frequently met in Sheela's home, a complex of bungalows on the ranch that was referred to as Jesus Grove. All-out war between the Rajneeshees and their neighbors had now begun.

VOTER SUPPRESSION
AND BIOLOGICAL ATTACKS

The buses started arriving at Rajneeshpuram in September 1984, dropping off thousands of potential new residents, just two months before the Wasco County November election. This program, dubbed the "Share-a-Home" initiative, was Sheela's brainchild, and it was clearly designed to support the two Rajneeshees running in the local election as write-in candidates. This influx of people, nearly all drawn from the ranks of the homeless in the state's biggest cities and towns, at first seemed to take great joy in their new surroundings. And the only thing they had to do to stay within the confines of Rajneeshpuram was register to vote and then cast their ballots for whichever candidate they were told to write in.

But this swarm of new voters from the ranch did not go unnoticed. Before long, Norma Paulus, the secretary of state in Oregon, halted the registration process. The ruling applied to all new voters, but it was clearly aimed at preventing what Oregon considered a high "probability of election fraud" perpetrated by the religious cult. This led to predictable troubles. One formerly homeless man skipped his medications in his new environment, then grew furious that he'd been denied the right to register and attacked Sheela, grabbing her by the throat and lifting her off the ground. She and a few other sannyasins managed to deescalate the confrontation, and the man was driven off the ranch and left on a park bench some miles away. Soon, even more of the new residents began behaving erratically and even violently—by attempting to swell the voter rolls, Sheela had unwittingly imported many of the medical problems and social dysfunctions that had precipitated the homeless condition of those people in the first place—and it became obvious that the Share-a-Home project was an utter failure. Sheela had barely escaped with her life, and after the harrowing encounter, the sedative Haldol was added to all the beer on the ranch without anyone's knowledge.

Even more ominously, soon after the Share-a-Home initiative began, Ma Anand Puja, a nurse at the Rajneesh Medical Center, bought a number of vials of *Salmonella* Typhimurium from a medical supply company in Seattle, then oversaw the culturing of the bacteria in labs at Rajneeshpuram. According to Win McCormack, based on information eventually provided to authorities by those who worked under Puja, she and Sheela had deliberated over the right pathogen to bring onto the ranch. They finally settled on the salmonella, a common agent in food poisoning, in the mistaken belief that an outbreak might debilitate enough people to affect the outcome of the vote but still be small enough in number that it would escape the notice of authorities.

Once the vials arrived, they began cultivating the salmonella on the premises, hoping to unleash it in salad bars across Wasco County. *Time* magazine's Philip Elmer-DeWitt, in his reporting years after the event, claimed that the Rajneeshees had "put it in blue-cheese dressing, table-top coffee creamers and potato salads at ten local restaurants and at supermarkets"[20]—all with the intention of incapacitating voters, allowing the Rajneeshees to gain control of the county.

Sheela later claimed that she had nothing to do with the salmonella poisoning.

When the outbreak did occur, the locals suspected the Rajneeshees right from the start. The effects were widespread: 751 people exhibited some signs of gastroenteritis, and more than 150 people became violently ill, from a newborn infected while still in the womb to an eighty-seven-year-old. Jim Weaver, the congressman for Oregon's Fourth District, directly accused the cultists of planting the bacteria, and he did so on the floor of the US House of Representatives. As he later explained to McCormack, "It is impossible for salmonella bacteria to spread throughout so many different restaurants that have no common linkage, except by deliberate human agency." Despite that it took months to definitively establish the connection, from the beginning Weaver was convinced that the Rajneeshees had poisoned his constituents.

The initial response to these accusations at Rajneeshpuram was to laugh it off as a wild fantasy. In a press conference soon after the outbreak, Jane Stork took to the podium to defend her community. "We're going to infect the world," she said, "with joy and laughter of epidemic proportions." As far as affecting the vote, the biological attack was a complete disaster, since the outbreak galvanized voters in the community, who turned out in such numbers that the Rajneeshees did not win a single seat at the polls.

DRUGS, SUICIDE, AND MURDER

Everything that Sheela had worked so hard for was beginning to unravel with frightening speed. To add to the legal jeopardy, Sheela learned of troubling behavior that originated with a group from Los Angeles, nicknamed the Hollywood Crowd, lured to Oregon by Rajneesh's teachings. Ma Anand Hasya, the former wife of Albert S. Ruddy, the producer of *The Godfather*, was a particular point of contention for Sheela. Hasya and Ruddy gave Rajneesh hundreds of thousands of dollars and diamond watches. Soon Hasya gained the guru's favor, spending more and more time in his home—without Sheela.

Many sannyasins have described Sheela as bitterly jealous, and Jane Stork recounted in *Wild Wild Country* that Sheela soon learned the Hollywood Crowd was plying Rajneesh with drugs, particularly nitrous oxide and Valium. Sheela was mortified and betrayed by this news: her master, this man to whom she had dedicated so much of herself and for whom she had done so much work, was not even following his own teachings to live life purely. And he'd lied to her about it. She angrily confronted Rajneesh, begging him to stop, to think of his teachings, his followers. But Rajneesh simply told Sheela to stay out of it. This infuriated her, as illegal drug use added to Rajneesh's precarious position with the law. His visa status had already come under scrutiny, and Oregon officials were mounting an investigation over charges of immigration fraud stemming from the sham marriages believed to be taking place within the community.

As a result of these cases, Charles Turner, the US attorney for the District of Oregon, became Sheela's number one enemy, since he was the person who could make or break Rajneesh's case. According to a 2005 press release from the Department of Justice, "in May 1985, Sheela called a meeting of her closest subordinates and initiated a conspiracy to kill the US Attorney. At this meeting, Jane Stork agreed to join the conspiracy and subsequently performed several acts in furtherance of it, including volunteering to be the actual killer, buying weapons, and surveilling what was thought to be Mr. Turner's workplace garage."

Between his vows of silence, his preference for secluding himself, and his increasing drug use, Rajneesh remained out of touch in regard to these plots. That doesn't mean he was guiltless: he had created this system whereby his devotees, especially those closest to him, were encouraged to go to extremes to compete for his attention, and he also cultivated among his followers the goal of getting past inhibitions of any form, whether sexual, psychological, or societal, and the combination of these circumstances led to a sense that anything done on his behalf, even the most outrageous deeds, was justified as an act of devotion. This precipitated the chain of events that led to mass poisoning and attempted murder.

But murdering a government official wasn't the only felony on Sheela's mind. According to Jane, Sheela—who'd now taken to wiretapping Rajneesh's quarters as a means of getting the jump on the Hollywood Crowd—overheard Rajneesh asking his doctor, Swami Devaraj (also known as Dr. George Meredith), how he could induce a painless, dignified death. Devaraj described a cocktail of chemicals that would do the job, and Rajneesh ordered him to acquire them.

Shortly thereafter, Rajneesh told Sheela that he was planning his own death for July 6, 1985—Master's Day, the biggest time of celebration at the World Festival. Jane remembered the meeting that took place in Jesus Grove when Sheela relayed this information to her close inner circle. To save their guru's life, Sheela told them, they needed to kill Devaraj. Jane described a heavy silence; no one volunteered until Jane herself raised her hand.

Sheela provided the murder weapon: a poison-laden syringe. Jane described the day during the World Festival in 1985 that this took place: "I approached Devaraj . . . and as he leaned towards me, I pushed the syringe [into him]. . . . [T]here was a bit of a struggle, I got it out again and threw it away. . . . As he staggered away from me, I turned and walked away. . . . I wanted to be alone. There was the part of me who felt I had saved [Rajneesh's] life, I had done what I had to do. But deep inside of me, I was shattered. I had grown up clearly understanding that thou shalt not kill. And now I had tried to kill somebody." Nevertheless, Devaraj survived the assassination attempt.

PARADISE LOST

In September 1985, Sheela left the commune with Jane Stork and a few other close confidants in tow. They flew to Germany, where they stayed in a local Rajneesh center, but their welcome was brief. Rajneesh broke his silence that same month and set out to destroy Sheela, perhaps because it was clear the authorities were closing in and he wanted to distance himself from the deeds committed on his behalf. He smeared her name, accusing her of atrocious and criminal behavior, including attempted murder and the poisonings that took place on and off the ranch. Sheela responded by calling Rajneesh a con man who exploited and manipulated his followers. He shot back, "Either she will kill herself out of the very burden of all the crimes that she has done, or she will have to suffer her whole life in imprisonment."[21]

Many sannyasins described this spectacle as a shock, like seeing one's parents argue in public, and they spoke to the reporters who started inundating the complex about their feelings of depression, betrayal, confusion, and pain. As a result of Rajneesh's accusations, the federal authorities now had grounds to enter the commune with search warrants, and in October they raided the ranch. In Sheela's rush to leave Rajneeshpuram, the usually meticulous private secretary had been careless: government agents collected evidence of elaborate wiretappings, illegal drugs, and an on-site laboratory that tied the salmonella poisonings to Rajneeshpuram. They found plans to assassinate US Attorney Turner and elaborate schemes for arranged marriages that precipitated charges of "conspiracy to defraud the government."

Despite Rajneesh's claims that this had all been Sheela's doing and that no one else had knowledge of any unlawful activity, the federal and state governments built airtight cases against Rajneesh and his top advisors. Charges included first-degree assault, attempted murder, illegal wiretapping, and thirty-five counts of defrauding the United States. Soon, Sheela, Jane Stork, and Ma Anand Puja were arrested in Germany and extradited back to the United States, where they were all found guilty. Ma Anand Sheela was sentenced to three terms of twenty years for her involvement in the mass poisonings and wiretappings, but was paroled after twenty-nine months for good behavior.

Ma Anand Puja spent thirty-nine months in jail. Jane Stork served almost three years for her role in the cult's various crimes.

In October 1985, Rajneesh himself was arrested and charged with immigration violations and conspiracy. In his resulting deal with the prosecution, he pleaded guilty to two counts of making false statements to immigration authorities, was fined $400,000, and was forced to leave the United States. The Rolls-Royces and other property on the ranch were sold to cover legal fees as the community began to disband. By the end of 1986, eighteen other Rajneeshees had also been convicted of state crimes.

Yet despite the rampant violence, malfeasance, and dysfunction, there are those disciples who remember their time at the ranch as the best years of their lives and still consider Rajneesh's teachings revolutionary and enlightening. Their master, they claim, had been misunderstood. Many continue to follow his teachings to this day.

Rajneesh himself called the Antelope Valley commune "a beautiful experiment that failed." He eventually returned to his ashram in Pune, India, where he remained until his death of heart failure in 1990 at the age of fifty-eight. In the aftermath of his passing, Swami Amrito, a.k.a. Dr. George Meredith, a.k.a. Swami Devaraj, read a message that the guru had prepared for his followers: "I am leaving this tortured body because it has become hell for me. Don't cry for me. My presence will be always with you."[22]

The ashram in Pune continues to accept visitors to this day under the name Osho International Meditation Resort, or, as it is sometimes known, Club Meditation. The ashram boasts a "Basho Spa," with tennis, pool, sauna, and other "facilities for spiritual growth." Many firsthand accounts of visits in online forums emphasize the beauty and youth of visitors, as if the free love that Rajneesh once preached was still part of the spa agenda. Between the beauty and the other inducements, and incidental charges for daytime and nighttime meditation robes, the ashram is a big money earner, and two factions of devotees, the Osho Friends Foundation and the Osho International Foundation, are in court fighting for control of the property and its assets. There are classes at the resort's "Multiversity" in subjects like "Osho No-Mind," in which the student learns to speak gibberish as a way of cleaning the mind, and "Inner Tantra Taster,"[23] where the classes of both men and women are instructed to "feel the energy at the tip of your sex." It is hard to know if this is what Rajneesh himself meant when, in his last words on this earthly plane, he stated, "I leave you my dream."

EXPLOITATION

JIM JONES AND
THE PEOPLES TEMPLE

Jim Jones was the slipperiest cult leader, charismatic and compassionate in the spotlight and sadistic and manipulative in the shadows. He built up the membership of his church, the Peoples Temple of the Disciples of Christ, with a signature blend of faith healing and political activism, capitalizing on the mid-twentieth century's growing Civil Rights Movement to bring in followers from poor and African American communities. He treated his devoted followers like a combination money machine and sexual playground, clearing upward of $30,000 a week in services in Los Angeles and San Francisco and being sexually active with any follower, male or female, who needed "healing." As his power grew, he became a political force in California politics. But when a congressional investigation of the church began closing in, he and nearly a thousand of his followers fled the country. Jones had promised them a socialist paradise, but once they were isolated from society and he was in total control, his paranoia and addiction took over and he delivered a nightmare to them and the world.

DEATH ON THE EQUATOR

On November 18, 1978, in the dense jungles of Guyana, situated in a remote clearing of three thousand acres known as the Peoples Temple Agricultural Project, or Jonestown, 908 American citizens died together. The carnage took little more than four hours from the first passing to the last. The Peoples Temple's longtime leader, Jim Jones, the man they all called "Father" or "Daddy," took his own life alongside them, part of the largest mass suicide in modern history. Nearly all the faithful seemed to have died by their own hand or, in the case of three hundred infants and children under the age of ten, as a result of their parents.

Thanks to recordings made on-site—known through the FBI as the "death tape"—the world has a clear account of what happened that day. Nearly all of those who perished ingested a mixture of Flavor Aid (a South American version of Kool-Aid) and cyanide. On the tape, Jim Jones—who'd founded the Peoples Temple twenty-four years earlier, starting with a small church in the poorest section of Indianapolis—can be heard exhorting his followers to drink up. "It's simple, it's simple. There's no convulsions with it," he says, in the singsong cadence of the revival preacher. "It's just simple. Just please get it before it's too late."

Everyone could see that the drink caused convulsions. The children took the poison first. Some infants who were too young or afraid to drink it on their own had to have it squirted into their open mouths by nurses armed with syringes of the deadly concoction. They died quickly, often within minutes. Adults took longer—twenty minutes or more. Cyanide poisoning does not bring about a peaceful death. Some victims vomited or foamed at the mouth, while others spat up blood. Despite this display, there were still followers who cheered, thanking Daddy repeatedly over the wails of the children.

The process was carried out under the supervision of armed guards, who surrounded the pavilion where the poisoned mixture was being handed out. They kept the people in line and saw to it that no one ran off into the wilderness. After the guards had watched all the members of the Peoples Temple camp take their portions, they drank their own cups. Only two of the dead did not perish from cyanide poisoning: Jones himself and one of his mistresses, Annie Moore. Both died from what are presumed to be self-inflicted gun-shot wounds.

In the local region's heat, the bodies decayed with astonishing speed. By the time the scene was discovered the next morning by members of the Guyana Defense Force and local teenage conscripts guiding them to the camp, many of the corpses had grown mis-shapen, been half eaten by animals, or were distended. Some were found to have abscesses, probably formed around injection sites, a fate most likely reserved for those who wouldn't drink the poison on their own. Jones did not want any survivors; he believed that their actions that day would go down in history as bravery. "This is not a self-destructive act," he intoned on the tape. "This is a revolutionary act." In his vision, this communal death would seem noble—on a par with the historic mass suicide of Jews at Masada, who burned their homes and killed themselves rather than surrender to Roman forces. To achieve such a historic impact, Jim Jones wanted all his followers to die together.

Despite his efforts, there were still several who made it through the horror. When the members of the Guyana Defense Force arrived, a seventy-six-year-old African American woman, Hyacinth Thrash, who'd hidden under her bed when the followers were all called to the pavilion to drink the cyanide mixture, came out of the building where she slept, wandering through the grounds, looking in vain for her sister, Zipporah Edwards. She cried out, "Oh, God, they came and they killed them all and I's the onliest one alive!" Two visiting lawyers, Mark Lane and Charles Garry, who were defending the Peo-ples Temple in lawsuits that had been brought against Jones and the Peoples Temple back in the States, had miraculously managed to talk their way past the guards. They then circled through the jungle, sticking to the outskirts of the camp, until finding the road to the nearest town, thirteen miles away.

Another follower, Grover Davis, a seventy-eight-year-old African American man, had walked up to a guard, who said, "Where do you think you're going?" When Davis simply replied, "I don't want to die," the guard let him walk out into the jungle, remarking, "Have a nice life." Davis hid in a ditch until he heard nothing from the camp.

How did one man attract so many followers who believed in him so blindly and passionately that they would take their own lives? How did so few people pick up on the dangers he posed until it was far too late? In the gallery of cult leaders, Jim Jones represents an extreme—and not just in body count. He excelled at every item on Robert Lifton's checklist of mind control, or "thought reform": mystical manipulation, milieu control, dispensing with existence, and more. This was the work of a lifetime. But from the beginning Jones learned to hide his appetites and instinct for power in a showy brand of kindness, righteousness, and revolution.

THE BARNYARD PREACHER

On May 13, 1931, near the rock bottom of the Great Depression, James "Jimmy" Jones was born to Lynetta and James Thurman Jones in rural Crete, Indiana. The month before, there'd been food riots in Minneapolis. National unemployment had climbed to 16 percent and restless mobs threw bricks in grocery store windows, hoping to grab enough and feed their families for a night or two. In some parts of the country, subsistence farmers were abandoning their land, and these "Dust Bowl" émigrés took to the road, lured by rumors of work, settling in makeshift encampments known as Hoovervilles. It was an ironic legacy for then-president Herbert Hoover, the once-successful businessman who'd run for the Oval Office in 1928 with a promise to "put a chicken in every pot and a car in every garage."

By the time Jimmy arrived on the scene, there were very few comforts in the Jones household. The family was prominent in their part of eastern Indiana: the young boy's grandfather, John Henry Jones, owned large tracts of farmland in rural Randolph County and was a formidable figure in local politics. He had also laid out the down payment on a small farm in Crete—population 28—for his son, James T., and his bride, Lynetta. She was headstrong; this was Lynetta's third marriage, and her second one had lasted only three days. She was also ambitious, and had attended agricultural and business college in an era when few women did. It wasn't an easy time for a woman with independent ideas, and with this marriage to a man some fifteen years her senior, she'd thought she'd finally found security.

But James T. Jones was not a healthy man. He'd never been reliable even before he enlisted in the First World War, and he returned home broken, haunted by battle and suffering from persistent respiratory problems caused by a mustard gas attack. These injuries left him useless for the hard labor it took to make a living on the land. Soon the family was driven from a hardscrabble life in the country to the rough part of the town of Lynn, Indiana, population 950.

There the Joneses rented a house not far from the train yards, furnished with whatever they salvaged from the farm, and they kept a hand-me-down car in a combination garage and hayloft behind the domicile. James worked on road crews, but the lingering effects of his war wounds, coupled with a heavy smoking habit, made it nearly impossible for him to hold a job. Lynetta earned most of the money to support the family by working at a nearby glass factory, while her husband played cards and gambled away his disability checks at local clubs.

Lynetta toiled for long hours at the factory, smoking and talking politics and cursing up a storm. James T. Jones was also an absentee parent, splitting his days between custodial work and the card tables. Thanks to an unusual rule that Lynetta strictly enforced—her boy could not stay in the house unless she was home (perhaps because she didn't want him to be alone with his father if she wasn't there to protect him)—Jimmy spent most of his childhood wandering the streets of Lynn.

The setup wasn't quite as cruel as it sounds: the Joneses had a roster of relatives in and around town who took turns keeping an eye on the child. Still, the harshness of the edict played a formative role in the boy's character. More often than not, he had to fend for himself for hours at a time and days in a row. On one level, he learned to connect with strangers, intuit what they wanted, and reshape his own behavior to appeal to their tastes.

Jim Jones became the neighborhood waif, roaming about Lynn with a red toy wagon, corralling stray animals and bringing them back to the hayloft. He gained local notoriety for the gang of wild dogs that began to follow him around. He soon realized the power of his little pack: with the dogs at his side, his parents found it hard to discipline him.

Many neighborhood ladies took pity on the child, inviting him in for a meal, and little Jimmy became adept at finding out their interests and sharing their fascinations. He struck up many friendships with this approach, perhaps none more influential than with Myrtle Kennedy, the pastor's wife at the Church of the Nazarene. Myrtle was tall—six two and rail thin—and compassionate. She was famous among the hobos who passed through town hopping on and off freight trains, baking the men dozens of pies and setting out servings on her windowsill for them to eat when they walked by the house.

Soon Myrtle was taking young Jimmy along to church. The boy had a knack for committing long Bible passages to memory. He took to putting on robes and preaching to the menagerie of animals he kept in his garage: chickens, goats, cats, lizards, snakes, the strays that followed him. He ended up loving church so much that one service was not enough. After attending with Myrtle, he visited other houses of worship, working his way week after week through all the churches in town: the Methodists, the Quakers, the Disciples of Christ.

But despite all this Christian fellowship, he came to resent the tenderness he wasn't getting at home. It was clear that his parents didn't love each other. In a tape recording made late one night in Jonestown about a year before the mass suicide, he remembered the era: "I was ready to kill by the end of the third grade. I was so fucking aggressive and hostile. Nobody gave me any love, any understanding. In those days, a parent was supposed to go with a child to school functions. If your parent didn't go, you were an outcast. I was a fairly good singer. There was some kind of school performance and everybody's fucking parent was there but mine. I'm standing alone, always alone. Everybody else'd have their families, their cousins, their aunts and uncles—not Jones."

He was a good-looking boy, but with his dark hair, dark eyes, broad face, and strong features, Jimmy didn't look like the other local blond, blue-eyed Midwesterners. However, after school, when the children were free to run around and form groups, he discovered his talent for organizing, gathering neighborhood kids together the way he once did with his pack of strays. He even managed to start a baseball league, forming and managing teams, recruiting others from nearby towns, creating the scheduling. On that same late night in Jonestown when he was caught on tape looking back on his childhood, he said:

> I was always the guy who got the kid[s] together, and I didn't like it because I had to assume so much of the planning. So I died [*sic*] very early to the need for reinforcement from people. I can't even remember when I had a real need for people.
>
> . . . It wasn't a matter of whether people appreciated it or whether, when they got through with you they tossed you aside like an orange with all the juice squeezed out. I expected that, but I thought, "I may not be a person of great talent, but one thing I could give was loyalty."[1]

He would continue to sound this theme of heroic self-sacrifice until his final day on Earth.

Jones would take groups into the barn where he kept his stock of animals, trying out preachy exhortations and lecturing the gang on morality, religion, and science. He put on his robes, and decorated the barn with candles and stacks of books. In the hot summer months, he made lemonade to lure the boys into his makeshift temple, and in the cool autumn months, his lectures and lessons could span six hours a day.

Jones raised carrier pigeons, and in front of his improvised congregation he liked to send the birds out of the barn with mysterious messages tied to their legs. He never told the boys what the messages were, and he noticed that their interest only grew the more he played up the enigma. These early signs of the Svengali-like control that he would come to exert as a leader of the Peoples Temple grew more frequent. As Jeff Guinn noted in his acclaimed book *The Road to Jonestown: Jim Jones and the Peoples Temple*, the young man showed troubling tendencies early. At one point, as Jones was leading the boys in walking over the rafters in his garage—a treacherous passage where a single beam crossed over a ten-foot drop—one of them grew frightened and tried to retreat to safety, only to find Jones refusing to let him by. "I can't move," Jones proclaimed. "The Angel of Death is holding me." He finally gave way, but, as one of the childhood friends who witnessed the moment later admitted to Guinn, "Even at the age of six or whatever, I thought that was nuts."

Jones had an undeniably devious streak. Townspeople thought he got it from his mother's influence whenever she was around. One of the ways Jim liked to entertain himself was gathering his cousins or peers and teaching them the facts of life in explicit detail. He also could be cruel, at one point throwing a puppy from the ten-foot drop in his garage onto the floor in front of his friends. Later he experimented with improvised surgical procedures on his menagerie, a display of callousness that is one of the classic early warning signs of a psychopath.

His obsession with death blossomed. He led his gang to break into a local casket company, then made them lie down inside the coffins so they could all feel what being dead was like. In similar macabre entertainments, he performed mock funeral services for roadkill. Sometimes he didn't even bother with an audience, leading the services alone in a playground as other kids watched from a distance. When World War II began, he became infatuated with the Nazis, their uniforms, and goose-stepping. He studied Hitler and admired the way this man could hold a crowd, and later, when the dictator committed suicide in his bunker, the bravado impressed Jones.

Myrtle Kennedy was devoted to the Church of the Nazarene, and Jones continued his regular attendance there with her. But he also kept sampling other houses of worship, confessing that he liked to see the areas where they departed from the true belief, a justification that satisfied her. When a storefront Apostolic church opened at the outskirts of town and began aggressively recruiting converts, Jones became fascinated with the loose format of their Saturday night services with all its Holy Roller theatrics, the speaking in tongues, the swooning and jumping and shouting. He started attending tent revivals whenever he got a chance, soaking in the freewheeling exuberance, the music, and the charismatic preaching style. Soon he was carrying a Bible everywhere he went, going so far as to take it from class to class in high school.

His enthusiasm for the sensationalistic aspects of worship did bring him one moment of public glory and popularity. When a team at his high school was preparing for a big game, his classmates asked him to conduct a mock funeral for the opponents during a school pep rally. He really threw himself into it, putting his deep knowledge of the preacher's stagecraft on display, bringing the assembled students to their feet as he laid the members of the rival team to rest in a mass grave amid the wild cheers of the student body. According to Jeff Guinn, one classmate who attended the rally said, "He had a flair for the dramatic."

THE BIRTH OF A SOCIALIST

Just after World War II ended, Lynetta Jones got a divorce, so the year after Jim's triumph at the pep rally, as he was entering his senior year of high school, mother and son moved from Lynn to Richmond, Indiana, a small Ohio border city with a population of around 42,000. The move came at a cost: without her husband's disability checks and the occasional support from her now ex-husband's family, money for Lynetta as a single mother was tight. Jim, who did well enough in the new school to graduate a semester early, took a job at nearby Reid Memorial Hospital, starting as a night orderly.

In the hospital, young Jim thrived. Where his boyhood in Lynn provided plenty of evidence of his manipulative and dangerous side, in his new setting he took full advantage of his talent for intuiting people's needs and interests. He remembered everyone's name and went out of his way to bring the patients and their families anything they needed. He took on tough and unpleasant jobs—giving sponge baths and cleaning up the incontinent—and turned them into playful and friendly encounters. He worked long hours overnight when he had the run of the place, and he used his growing knowledge of the hospital's inner workings to make sure that poor people in the charity wards had access to the same medicines as the wealthy patients on the paying floors.

Compared to his previous life, Richmond was the largest city Jones had ever lived in . . . and there was another major difference. Crete and Lynn had both been almost entirely white towns. Ku Klux Klansmen operated out in the open as if they were just another social group or civic organization. At one point in the 1930s, nearly a third of all white men in Indiana belonged to the Klan. That never sat well with Lynetta, who was outspoken about poverty and injustice and labor unions and discrimination. Her son carried on her vocal commitment to social issues. On weekends he took to visiting poor neighborhoods in the north side of Richmond to preach on street corners, drawing a crowd among the mostly Black residents, who weren't used to hearing a stocky, clean-cut white man advocating for racial equality.

This was the central paradox for the rest of Jim Jones's career: his devotion to social issues, especially campaigning against racism and for civil rights, seemed to be sincere, even inspiring. It convinced people from the ranks of both the oppressed and the powerful to join forces with him. As he took on the mantle of social activist, his pioneering politics became his primary source of credibility over the next several decades of racial turmoil. As someone who grew up with little in the way of love, approval, or worldly advantages, the war between the haves and the have-nots spoke to Jones, and he became an unapologetic Socialist.

In his sermonizing, he combined this stance as a political firebrand and community organizer with a wild evangelical streak picked up from the Holy Rollers. Offstage, when it came to practical matters, he followed the grounded, commonsense perspective of Lynetta Jones. Social justice was the link, and socialism was the marketing strategy. It became the bedrock of Jim Jones's proselytizing until the very end.

With most cult leaders, politics can feel irrelevant: when one encounters a devious, even murderous psychopath who demands total devotion, the first question is rarely *What political party does he belong to?* The cult leader's fundamental motivation is self-gratification on a grandiose scale. Whatever brand of politics, religion, or ethics they preach, no matter how passionate they sound, it's all just a means to an end. Charismatic cult leaders abandon core principles when it suits them. At the heart of it all, they follow just one rule: *Whatever I want, I take, no matter what I have to say to get it.*

But for Jones, ideas about politics drove his recruitment, inspired his members, and fueled his appeal. In addition, his mule-headedness, his sadism, his disregard for any law except the one he laid down came out in ugly flashes throughout his life. For instance, when he left Lynn, after a farewell dinner with his best friend, Don Foreman, Jones pulled out a gun in response to Foreman wanting to leave and shot at him as he was walking away. Another time, at college, his roommate, who was asleep in the bunk above him, felt a sharp jab and looked down to find Jones reaching up and forcing a hat pin through the mattress. His cruelty was real, but it took place in the shadows.

But Jones declared his devotion to racial justice and economic equality loudly in the light of day. In fact, it was his seriousness on this issue that attracted the attention of Marceline Baldwin, a kindhearted and beautiful Christian woman five years his senior, who lived in a dormitory on the Reid Memorial campus reserved for the nurses. When Jones told her that he'd quit his high school basketball team because his coach was racist, it won her over, even though the story was a complete fabrication. Jim Jones, with his instinct for saying exactly what people wanted to hear, kept at it, telling Marceline that he'd walked out of a barbershop when his haircut was still only halfway done after the barber said something disparaging about Black people. Soon, Marceline was telling her roommate she thought she was in love with this intense and handsome younger man.

At the hospital, administrators and colleagues knew nothing of the orderly's street preaching or his politics. There he was viewed as polite and energetic, kind to the point of saintliness with the patients. He earned the respect of the doctors with his seriousness and growing knowledge of medical procedures, and he gained the trust of the nurses with his eagerness to lend a hand. He stayed up late with older residents, reading to them and pulling long hours doing dirty work, even as he continued his high school studies.

The work ethic and ambition of the young man won over Marceline's parents, and in 1949 the two were married. Jim Jones was eighteen and Marceline twenty-three. Jones then began his studies at Indiana University, uncertain whether he should be a doctor or a lawyer or a teacher. The first days of their marriage were fraught with tension, as he unexpectedly fought with Marceline's family over their entitlement and privilege, and he bitterly told her that he no longer believed in God—that if God were real, there would not be so much suffering in this world.

This troubled Marceline, but she tried to find a way to make her marriage work, with the advice of her parents. Then, in 1952, the couple stumbled across a new social creed from the Methodist Federation for Social Action, which was posted on a bulletin board at a church they visited. It was the kind of manifesto that Jones could believe in, laying out, as it did, that the church should pledge to work for "the abatement of poverty; security for the aged; collective bargaining; free speech; prison reform; and the rights of racial groups." As usual, Jim acted quickly, telling his in-laws he now intended to be a full-time preacher. By 1953 the couple had

moved to Indianapolis and Jones took a job as a student minister
at Somerset Methodist Church in a poor part of town while taking
classes at Butler University. He'd now found a vocation that could
make use of all his passions: public speaking, political action, and
bringing people together.

SELLING MONKEYS FOR THE PEOPLES TEMPLE

Jones began hopscotching from one pastoral position to the next,
expanding his congregation and building his reputation at each stop,
picking off parishioners from other churches, thanks to his moon-
lighting as a guest preacher. He seemed to change denominations as
often as his clothing. Initially, Jim's vision was straightforward and
idealistic: he wanted to create the first fully integrated Methodist
congregation in Indianapolis. But soon he abandoned the strictures
of any specific sect, choosing instead to ally himself with—or at least
draw followers from—a freewheeling, even fanatical branch of Pen-
tecostalism and faith healing that was known then as the New Order
of the Latter Rain.

He rented a storefront in a poor neighborhood and called his
small church Community Unity. The precise brand of religion he
chose to preach didn't matter to him: what he really wanted people
to pay attention to was him as a preacher. As he'd proven before at
the hospital, he didn't mind working hard to get ahead. It was this
ethic and not his proselytizing that first got him on the front page of
the *Indianapolis Star* on April 10, 1954. He'd begun selling monkeys
door-to-door, riding around town with them on a bicycle, charging
$29 apiece, and often preaching a little bit of the Gospel in the bar-
gain. This grew from a neighborhood spectacle into a news item, at
least to the *Star* editors, when Jones refused to pay for a shipment from
India because most of the animals had died in transit.

Thanks to his occasional appearances at revival meetings, his reputation grew as a charismatic presence in the pulpit. Among the Latter

Rain circuit, preachers were part entertainer, part mind reader, and part charlatan, guessing names and license plates and Social Security numbers of people in the crowd with whom they supposedly had no prior acquaintance. Jones, who'd studied the Holy Rollers in Lynn and Richmond, thought he could do better.

The first time Marceline witnessed Jim in this role, she was afraid he'd freeze in front of the crowd. But once he closed his eyes and overcame his initial anxiety, he entered what can only be described as a trance state. Speaking at full speed, nonstop, for almost an hour, he held an entire convention of Pentecostals mesmerized. He quoted biblical passages seemingly at random. He called up members of the audience. People fell to the ground under his touch. Marceline couldn't believe the magnetic effect he had.

A local reverend, Russell Winberg, from the Laurel Street Tabernacle, also saw the performance and gave Jones a recurring guest spot in his pulpit. There, Jones began to perform faith healings on a regular basis. He would call for a volunteer stricken with some disease and cure them onstage in front of everyone. Jones brought a new level of theatrics and "reality" to this brand of faith healing—if a congregant was suffering from cancer, Jones would stand close to them and, utilizing sleight of hand and animal organs, pull out a fleshy, bloody mass. Jones and his miracle cures became a hot property on the Latter Rain circuit, where pastors traded appearances and built their reputations both locally and at national conventions.

Of course, his cures were just an extension of his barnyard preaching; he kept the "malignant tumors" in jars backstage. Whether or not there was any medical benefit, his healing succeeded on one level: Jones began to choose a corps of fiercely loyal adherents from the Tabernacle congregation. He soon organized his own massive convention, headlined by the nationally famous preacher William Branham, who appeared in stadiums and welcomed people of all races. When Jones combined the money collected at that event with the savings he'd stashed away from selling monkeys, he had enough to buy his own church in a racially mixed Indianapolis neighborhood. The new building, with its steeple and stained glass, was a big step up. Its official name was Wings of Deliverance, but almost immediately he took to calling it the Peoples Temple.

His new parishioners from this era included some who would eventually follow him all the way to Guyana, like construction worker Jack Arnold Beam, the lively and gossipy Patty Cartmell, and Jim Cobb, an African American youth seemingly healed under the Reverend Jones's touch. Jones prophesied that Cobb would be a great leader within the church one day, sealing the boy's fate with a few encouraging words.

Perhaps the most important convert he picked up at the Wings of Deliverance was Archie Ijames, a Black man who'd attended the joint Jones-Branham conference to see the legendary Branham. Instead, he came away impressed with Jones's dedication to social justice. In Jim Jones, Ijames saw a kindred spirit. Jones, in turn, told Ijames that he was destined for the ministry. In truth, Jones needed a Black leader for his church to prove to people that he really did practice what he preached.

Having a dedicated space changed everything. Instead of losing donations to the controllers of venues like the Laurel Street Tabernacle, Jones was able to directly accept every penny given by his followers. While the congregation only numbered about a hundred by 1958, Jones had also gained enough traction to be recognized by the city as a social justice leader. He opened a soup kitchen as well as two nursing homes. These functioned in two ways: first, it helped solidify the mission of the Peoples Temple in the eyes of the public, and second, it gave Jones prime recruiting grounds for desperate and lonely souls.

Jim Jones wanted the makeup of his own family to reflect his social mission, while Marceline desperately just wanted a family of her own. They started by adopting a ten-year-old girl named Agnes, abandoned at the Temple by her own mother. Next, Marceline and Jim adopted two Korean children, naming them Stephanie and Lew. Within two years Stephanie died in a car accident, and Jones and Marceline reached out to the orphanage in Korea, bringing Stephanie's friend

Suzanne into their lives. In 1959, Marceline gave birth to her one and only natural-born child, Stephan Gandhi Jones. They simultaneously adopted an orphaned Black child and named him Jim Jones Jr. Stephan and Jim were to be raised like twin brothers, a metaphor for the greater mission of the Peoples Temple.

LOOKING FOR THE PROMISED LAND

By the beginning of the sixties, Jones began to align himself with the wildly popular and fabulously wealthy Father Divine, a Harlem preacher who claimed to be God himself or the Second Coming. Like Jones, Father Divine used his ministry to campaign for civil rights, the rights of women, and desegregation. Taking a page from Divine's success, Jones began preaching a doctrine of anti-materialism, encouraging his followers to give up all their earthly attachments and dedicate themselves fully to serving in the Temple's various social wings. Divine had people working for him, feeding the hungry and staffing his headquarters. Jones made frequent visits to Harlem and later to Philadelphia when the eighty-year-old Divine moved his headquarters there due to tax issues, with an eye to taking over the elder's Peace Mission movement upon his eventual passing.

Whether or not he was inspired by Divine's example, Jones began moving closer to assuming divinity himself. It was about this time that his followers began referring to Jones himself as "Father." And he began orchestrating events so that people could assume he had mystical abilities, that he, too, was some sort of earthbound deity. If it alienated some, Jones didn't care: he only wanted the followers who would buy into his cult of personality. With the help of Patty Cartmell, who acted as a spy within the congregation, Jones began pretending to read minds and predicting futures in his high-energy sermons. He tried to know everything he could about his congregation so that he could play on their fears. He would craft personal prophecies of doom for those whose belief seemed to be wavering—and reward those firmly in his ranks with visions of their own success.

While he built up his devoted following, he made sure that the good works continued. The Peoples Temple continued to offer food, clothing, and care for the aged in the community. Its membership swelled with nearly equal numbers of Black and white disciples. At the urging of an idealistic young minister, Jones savvily affiliated his church with a new denomination, the Disciples of Christ, a move that gave him legitimacy (as well as a slew of tax exemptions) for a minimal number of annual dues. On top of that, the Disciples of Christ granted its congregations a tremendous amount of freedom.

The newfound and nearly mainstream status of the Peoples Temple—along with Jones's growing reputation for social justice—caught the attention of the Democratic mayor of Indianapolis, Charles H. Boswell. In recognition, Boswell, who was himself promoting new construction in poor neighborhoods, appointed Jim Jones to what had previously been a largely ceremonial position: the director of the Indianapolis Human Rights Commission. But Jim Jones took it seriously and started a citywide campaign to integrate restaurants. He'd arrive with Black guests in his party and be told that he didn't have a reservation, although he'd never needed one before. Then he'd return, sometimes on multiple occasions, to speak politely with the owner, explaining how the new customers would be good for business and how he really didn't want the alternative: staging a protest outside the establishment with all his parishioners, Black and white.

One after another, local restaurants buckled under his threats. For his part, Jones proved as good as his word, filling the places that surrendered to his pressure campaign with his rainbow coalition of parishioners. They arrived during quiet times of the day so the restaurant could still put up a facade during prime dining hours. The meals were all paid for by the Peoples Temple, so there were always members eager to join in.

Jones expanded his outreach, working to integrate the Indianapolis Police Department. He started an employment service to supply businesses with qualified applicants, cautioning his parishioners to be ideal employees, since it was his reputation and that of the Temple that was on the line.

When severe abdominal pain sent Jones to Indiana University Health Methodist Hospital—bleeding ulcers were the eventual diagnosis—he refused to be treated despite his clear distress until the hospital integrated and Black patients were resettled in the wings reserved for white people. As a result of his efforts, which didn't let up even after he was discharged, the facility joined the list of places he had integrated. These were solid civic accomplishments that Jim Jones pulled off in a hurry and earned him entry into activist circles for the rest of the decade and well into the next.

But these efforts did not sit well with everyone. This was a time in America when advocating for integration could get one labeled as a Communist. The mayor urged Jones to take a lower profile, which he refused to do, even when some angry elements painted swastikas on the Peoples Temple building and planted a stick of dynamite in the coal pile on the grounds. Jones subsequently pulled off a couple of publicity stunts, approaching both the Nation of Islam and the Ku Klux Klan and getting roundly rejected by both. He printed the letters he got from them and passed them around City Hall as if to say, *See how moderate I am? Both extremes have rejected me.*

The only thing that finally made him back down from this aggressive schedule of political action was his own fear. After President John F. Kennedy gave an address warning about the dangers of nuclear war, Jones—who was already in the prophesying business—foretold a coming disaster: he didn't know when, as the full vision had not yet been granted to him, but it would happen at 3:09; whether a.m. or p.m., he couldn't say. Following his hospital stay, his doctor had sternly told him he needed to take a sabbatical. So he combined two bits of urgent business, telling the Peoples Temple that he was going to scout a safe place somewhere they could all retreat to, far from the coming apocalypse. The January 1962 issue of *Esquire* featured the article

"9 Places in the World to Hide," and Jones was determined to visit as many as he could and find the best.

He then took an extended trip with his family to Brazil, British Guiana (the country gained its independence in 1966 and became Guyana), and Hawaii, investigating which place would be most receptive within their borders to a large congregation with socialist principles. He stayed away from the mainland United States for more than a year, with very little financial support from the Temple, trying to survive by teaching English or finding work at the better-funded missionary institutions.

While he was in Rio de Janeiro, he was supposedly approached by a diplomat's wife. It was a story he told often to his followers in later years, although its veracity cannot be confirmed. At the time, the Joneses were trying to raise money for one of the local orphanages, and this woman offered to donate $5,000 in exchange for sex. This put him in a moral quandary, as Jones framed it; after all, it seemed selfish to hold his own morality in higher regard than the clear need of the orphans. He approached Marceline for advice, and she agreed that the orphans' need was greater than any personal considerations. It made for an exciting and unusual sermon, but the underlying message had nothing to do with sexuality: for Jones, the end justified the means, and he expected nothing less from his followers.

Jones had put Russell Winberg in charge of the Peoples Temple while he was away, but Archie Ijames informed him that Winberg seemed to be leading the church in a different direction, trying to install himself as the chief and downplaying the activism that had brought in so many. Parishioners were losing interest and the proceeds from the church activities were no longer enough to fund the good works that the Peoples Temple had become locally famous for. Jones convinced the Reverend Edward Malmin, an older missionary whom he'd met in Brazil, to return in his stead and put the Temple's finances in order. But by the time he got there, Winberg was in open rebellion and Ijames warned Jones that he would lose his entire operation if he didn't immediately come back to lead again. Jones and his family arrived in haste, soon after the assassination of President Kennedy, and Winberg left, taking dozens of older white Temple members with him.

GOD IS ONE OF US

By the end of 1964, Jim Jones told his Indianapolis congregants that he had a new prophecy: the year 1967 would bring atomic destruction to Indianapolis. And they had to get out before it happened. The Peoples Temple then packed up and resettled in Redwood Valley, California, outside Ukiah, 130 miles north of San Francisco. Jones said the place was chosen because it was a safe distance from nuclear fallout. Many congregants in Indiana didn't buy into the prophecy and stayed put—and those lucky skeptics would avoid a real-life apocalypse in Jonestown fourteen years later.

But 140 of Jones's followers did make the move to California. This represented a dramatic change in lifestyle for members of the Peoples Temple. Families now lived in large groups within rugged commune housing. Material amenities were forbidden. Animals and children roamed freely in the yards. In the new setup, Jones had greater responsibilities, but he remained at every stage an efficient organizer, and with Marceline's help he found work for many congregants at the nearby Mendocino State Hospital. Then he set to work opening two nursing facilities, a soup kitchen, a drug treatment center, and three college-style dormitories, hoping to expand the model he'd pioneered in Indianapolis.

He also successfully campaigned for legitimacy in more direct ways. The Temple applied to become and was accepted as a full participant in the national framework of the Disciples of Christ, the mainstream reformed Protestant denomination now known as the Christian Church. From that point on, the Peoples Temple had an official stamp of approval that other new religious movements lacked. But it came at a cost: the Temple had to pay hefty annual dues, which made the Disciples' leadership happy, since Temple membership had grown to three hundred by 1969, then three thousand by 1973, by which time they were paying more than $15,000 a year to the Disciples network.

Much of this growth was fueled by Jim Jones's outreach in Black neighborhoods throughout San Francisco and Los Angeles. By 1970 he was holding services at a new branch of the Peoples Temple in San Francisco, with another opening in LA two years later. At their peak in the seventies, Temple membership was 80 percent Black. Jones soon began translating the devotion of his following into political muscle, becoming a powerful force in California politics, thanks to his ability to deliver votes for the liberal politicians of his choice. In a tight 1975 San Francisco mayoral election that was decided by less than five thousand votes, for example, voter drives led by the Peoples Temple almost certainly sealed the victory for the eventual winner, George Moscone. In key precincts where Jones and his followers went door-to-door, Moscone won by a margin of 12 to 1.

The grateful Moscone appointed Jones the chairman of the San Francisco Housing Authority. Jones was a rising power broker, and national figures in Democratic politics like First Lady Rosalynn Carter and Vice President Walter Mondale treated him as if he were a respectable mainstream pol.

Jones deployed his Temple forces in other ways, baking cakes for local power players and police chiefs and writing fan letters to politicians from both sides of the aisle, praising conservatives for their law-and-order agenda and liberals for their opposition to the war, according to Tim Reiterman in *Raven: The Untold Story of the Rev. Jim Jones and His People*. Dutiful responses from law enforcement figures and elected officials like Ronald Reagan and J. Edgar Hoover would be printed in Temple newsletters.

One key Temple member in the political outreach was Timothy Stoen. He was the most traditionally successful participant, with a degree from Stanford Law School and a flourishing practice. He and his wife, Grace, were granted favored status and allowed the kind of conventional middle-class amenities (record players, dishwashers, televisions) in their private apartment that other members had to give up. Stoen was well-to-do and traditional in his habits, but he soon made himself indispensable, closing his private practice to work in the local district attorney's office, running interference and fixing legal problems before they arose. His wife was less enthusiastic about the arrangement, but she loved Tim and went along for his sake.

At the same time that Jim Jones was burnishing his reputation through public engagement, he was accelerating his highly manipulative faith healings, planting loyal members of the Temple in the crowd who were in on the big con. They put on old-age makeup, even blackface, and pretended to have seizures or die. The faithful had already absorbed Jones's message that the end justified the means, and with their well-timed performances they felt they were saving lives by bringing more people into the fold.

Meanwhile, Jones solidified his iron grip on his followers. Most worked long hours and gave 10 to 25 percent of their earnings over to the church. Within the community, he established a so-called Planning Commission, a name taken from Soviet government structures and inspired by its hierarchy. It was ostensibly a leadership council, but the initial group quickly ballooned in size, encompassing over half of the Temple membership. So Jones kept dividing and breaking down the greater Planning Commission into smaller and more elite agencies, creating a tiered reward system, and turning Temple members against one another as they all competed to impress Jones and win a place closer to his side.

In 1971, during an infamous sermon that subtly blended politics, personal history, and brazen grandiosity, Jim Jones took the greatest liberty of all, declaring with a self-assurance typical of the malignant narcissist that he was the God Socialist. "No more poverty!" he announced, launching into a theme of great promise to his audience. "I'm here to show you as a sample and example that you can bring yourself up with your own bootstraps. And you can become your own God! Not in condescension but in resurrection and upliftment from whatever economic condition, injustice or racism or servitude which you have had to endure. Within you rest the keys of deliverance!" It was in many ways a typical power-of-positive-thinking message with a left-wing spin. But not too much later the power seemed to shift to him as the raven-tressed object of worship, a new Christ on Earth, as foretold in the Old Testament. "I have taken myself a body, the same one that walked on the plains . . . of whom Solomon said his hair was as black as a raven, and he would shave as Isaiah said, 7:20, with a razor. I come shaved with a razor! I come with the black hair of a raven! I come as God socialist!"

By 1972, the combined offerings from the Los Angeles and San Francisco Temples surpassed $30,000 a week. Jones took some of those funds and invested in eleven tour buses, selecting an honored group of followers to join his evangelizing tour, stopping in Denver, Houston, New York, Washington, DC—all the while selling as much promotional material like healing oils (really just cheap olive oil) or scraps of his old robes (thrift store purchases cut into shreds). Most egregiously, new believers were upcharged on small photos of Jim Jones himself.

On the way back to California, Jones thought it would be an excellent idea to swing by his Indiana hometown. When the lead tour bus pulled over, asking for directions to their prophet's old home, by sheer chance the man they stopped was Don Foreman, the childhood friend whom Jones had shot at once. Don asked the name of their prophet, and when he heard it was Jim Jones, Foreman wasn't even surprised. He laughed, shook his head, and pointed them down an old dusty road.

Jones's mentor Myrtle Kennedy was more pleased to see her old religious charge return home. He had his tour buses stay in Lynn overnight in order to show the entire town how far the local boy had come.

SEX, DRUGS, AND SOCIALISM

Back in California, though, success was proving hard to hold on to. The settlement in Redwood Valley was coming under scrutiny by local officials. Although Temple children were allowed to attend public elementary school, teachers were growing suspicious. The kids were precocious, speaking out in class about Marxism and dialectical materialism. One teacher discovered a group of Temple kids comparing bruises. In a group setting, they all claimed to have been hurt playing over the weekend, but when the concerned teacher spoke to each of them alone, they admitted that Temple leadership had forced them all on a brutal unsupervised hike into the mountains.

Before heading west, Marceline had suspected her husband of having several affairs, but once back in California he no longer tried to hide it. Jones encouraged more openness in congregants' relationships, and as the concepts of free love and wife-swapping took over the national imagination during the seventies, sexual sharing became a core feature of the Peoples Temple, fitting neatly into Jones's haphazard communalist manifesto. Jones treated sex, with both men and women, as an extension of ministering to his flock. He helped men finally overcome repression of their innate homosexual urges and aided troubled women who, he could see, needed to experience a relationship based on respect.

He had many casual encounters. Frustrated by the frequent requests for sex from his parishioners, he once announced that he was available for anyone who wanted him, and tallied upward of sixteen sex acts, with both women and men. He had many short-term mistresses and maintained a long-term open relationship with Carolyn Layton, whose husband was also a Temple member. Layton, who viewed the affair as a blessing, as if she'd been selected by God, fell deeply in love with him and didn't bother to hide their relationship from anyone, including Jones's children. She became pregnant, and Jim Jon, also known as Kimo, was born in 1973.

Between the constant affairs and his growing drug use—with Quaaludes and injectable Valium competing as his favorite—Jones was beginning to lose control of himself. This may have had something to do with his increasingly wild attempts to assert control in other arenas. Reacting to imaginary assassination attempts, he beefed up his personal security detail, providing guns to the most physically intimidating followers, who shadowed his movements and patrolled the compound. In this mania for control, he took one step that later came back to haunt him—and 908 others in Jonestown. In 1972, Tim and Grace Stoen had a son, John Victor Stoen. But without Grace's knowledge, Jones got Tim to sign an affidavit proclaiming that Jim Jones was actually the child's true father. This of course was a lie, but Jones knew that this token of loyalty could be used as leverage later on if the couple ever wavered in their commitment to him.

Jones's dangerous hold on his followers now started to attract the attention of the press. After his homecoming antics in Lynn, journalists at the *Indianapolis Star*, who remembered the Peoples Temple as a faith-healing stunt church from the sixties, passed word to the *San Francisco Examiner* and religion editor Lester Kinsolving. He began collaborating with *Indianapolis Star* lead journalist Carolyn Pickering. They staked out the Redwood Valley compound and began interviewing locals, collecting stories of alleged child abuse and other rumors. They went to Temple services and witnessed the armed patrols.

As their newspaper series began to appear, San Franciscans read about the absurd claims (Jones was supposed to have raised forty people from the dead), the carnival-like healings at the Temple, and his half-hearted denials when someone called him God. ("If you say, 'He is God,' some people will think you are nuts. They can't relate. I'm glad you were healed, but I'm really only a messenger of God . . . I have a paranormal ability in healing.") One article revealed how a teenage girl was married off to another Temple member, entered into the Mendocino welfare rolls, and then was forced to sign her checks over to the Temple.

Jones reacted by sending his faithful to picket the *Examiner* headquarters. When the paper tried to interview Jones himself, he showed up in a limo, sat the reporter in the back seat next to an armed member of his security patrol, and, according to Reiterman, drove the newspaperman around the dicey parts of town past the empty Embarcadero docks. Tim Stoen sat in the front seat and, without identifying himself, threatened legal action. The *Examiner* killed the remaining pieces in the series.

In 1973, eight Temple youth leaders, including Jim Cobb, one of the loyalists from the Wings of Deliverance days, defected. These apostates, known afterward as the "Eight Revolutionaries," were the first to stand up to Jim Jones, going so far as to hold him at gunpoint in one of the Temple communes. They wanted Jones to let them go and not punish their remaining family members. Under such circumstances, Jones agreed. In exchange, they left Jones and the Temple to continue in peace.

Then, on December 13 of that year, while Jones was in LA to give a few sermons, he dropped into a theater off MacArthur Park that was showing the Clint Eastwood movie *Dirty Harry*. The nearby park was known as a gay cruising area, and undercover cops were working the theater. So when Jones propositioned a young man and then exposed himself and began masturbating, he was hauled in. Tim Stoen fabricated a preposterous cover story, complete with a doctor's note, saying that Jones had recent urinary surgery and needed to regularly stimulate his member. The LAPD let Jones go but opened up a file on him and began monitoring the Temple.

Jones realized that he was exhausting the goodwill of his political connections and called together the top leaders of the Temple: Marceline, Ijames, Beam, and Cartmell. The time had come, he said, to find their safe haven. Beam and Ijames flew to Guyana—chosen because it had no extradition treaty with the United States—where they lubricated the wheels of local government with a promised $2 million gift to the development committee in the capital city of Georgetown. They bought a 3,200-acre plot of land, and by the end of 1974, construction of their socialist utopia was underway.

DEATH AND SUSPICION

Bob Houston, a musician fresh out of Berkeley, joined the Peoples Temple along with his wife, Phyllis, back in 1969. In the communal setting, Bob and Phyllis grew apart, and during one of the Temple's "catharsis" or criticism sessions, the couple was questioned by the group about their sex life. In the candid spirit of the era that Jones seemed to delight in, they were brutally honest: they hadn't had sex in more than a year. Jones asked them if they would each like to see other people, and Phyllis replied that she didn't care, as long as it was discreet. Jones then gave Bob permission to start a relationship with Joyce Shaw, another recent arrival at the Redwood Valley commune.

Joyce and Bob worked together on the Temple magazine, the *Living Word*, but as soon as they began to be intimate, Jones ordered Bob back to Phyllis. It was the kind of arbitrary exercising of power in which he frequently indulged. It enforced obedience and stripped away ego. However, Jones soon relented and allowed Joyce and Bob to get back together. They were even granted permission to take jobs outside the Temple and rent an apartment in San Francisco. And they were both made members of the Planning Commission, part of a group of those in the inner circle who ran Temple business. They enjoyed the freedom and responsibility that came with the elite position, even though they had to work hard and house other members in their San Francisco home.

Bob almost always had two jobs, as a music therapist or teacher or counselor, along with a steady union job as a night switchman in San Francisco's Southern Pacific train yards. He was thoughtful and studious—his nickname was the "Little Professor"—and he took the politics of the Temple seriously, studying Marxism and world events. During services, when Jones asked if anyone had any questions, Bob mistook it as a sincere request and asked probing queries about current events about which Jones didn't know the answer. Soon, Bob was being ridiculed for his fancy vocabulary and bourgeois intellectualism, something that could never have happened without Jones's encouragement.

Meanwhile, Joyce was growing disaffected and wanted to leave. The Temple, under increasing scrutiny in the aftermath of the MacArthur Park incident, had begun demanding members give their entire paychecks to the church. Jones was planning to move everyone to Guyana as soon as they could arrange it. People were given small allowances to cover expenses. Meals were communal and served at Temple facilities. Despite the severe rationing, Joyce managed to set aside enough for a bus ticket back to her parents. Although she still loved Bob, one night after work, without telling anyone, she simply left and returned to Ohio.

There were plenty of reasons to abandon the Temple. Jones had instituted corporal punishment, spankings that were administered with a wooden "Board of Education," and even boxing matches. Those getting punished were paired with stronger opponents. If they somehow managed to defend themselves and avoid a beating, they were forced to fight again with somebody even stronger. Jones justified the brutality because the world was a cruel place. The Temple, Jones told them, was always loving, and its corrections were always merciful. The outside world would not be so kind.

On top of that, there were even more devious and extreme methods to guarantee control. Parents were made to sign confessions that they'd had sex with their children, documents that would then be kept in church files in case anyone ever tried to leave or speak with the press. Sometimes Temple members were simply made to sign blank pages, with contents to be typed in at a later date. It was this menu of rough treatment and mental cruelty that had prompted the Eight Revolutionaries to defect, and Joyce started calling Bob long distance to convince him to leave as well.

Bob was a true believer, but he did take her calls. On October 4, 1976, he mailed her some clothes she'd asked for in their last conversation, then went to the first of his jobs that day, as a probation counselor at a juvenile hall. While at his second job, he was crushed to death in the train yards. The trains there moved at a walking pace and Bob was a meticulous man who'd been working there for years. Joyce believed that there was no way he could have made a fatal mistake, much less, as the Temple was saying, committed suicide. Their conversations had been hopeful, although Bob had been noncommittal over the Temple phones. Joyce suspected that he'd been murdered by Jones's enforcers, either forced to lie on the tracks or knocked unconscious and placed in harms's way.

Joyce sent Bob's parents letters, explaining her suspicions. For years she'd been caring for Bob's two young children from his previous marriage to Phyllis and she still loved them (the couple had married at the request of Jones and a group of the Planning Commission). She warned that their grandchildren should never be allowed to go to Guyana. People were being tortured there, she said, and life was harsh. At one recent gathering in San Francisco, Jones announced that he'd poisoned the drinks, and while parishioners planted in the crowd pretended to gag and die, he merely watched the reactions. When he revealed that, in fact, they hadn't been poisoned, he congratulated those who hadn't panicked, who'd been ready to commit what he'd called "revolutionary suicide"—these events perhaps being rehearsals for future emergency measures in Guyana.

In the aftermath of Bob's death, the Temple said that he had typed out his letter of resignation that morning and submitted it to Jim Jones. In her correspondence to Bob's parents, Joyce explained why that was a lie: her husband never typed anything. The letter was clearly a warning to other Temple members. For those who believed that Jones was God, it was evidence of the harsh fate that could befall traitors. For those who were losing faith and beginning to question the path the Temple was now on, the warning was even clearer: it showed the violent lengths that Jones would go in order to punish anyone who left.

Bob's father, Sam Houston, was a photographer at the San Francisco branch of the Associated Press, and he brought Joyce's letters to Tim Reiterman, one of the *San Francisco Examiner*'s best investigative reporters. Not long after that, Joyce returned to California and began talking to Reiterman as well. And Bob's father didn't stop there: he got in touch with US congressman Leo Ryan, an unusual figure who liked to throw himself into the issues he cared about. After the Watts riots of 1965, he took a job as a substitute teacher to understand what life was like there. As a California state assemblyman in charge of a committee on prison reform, Ryan got himself incarcerated anonymously to investigate prison conditions firsthand. Some thought these were all publicity stunts, but the coalition of journalists and congressional investigators that Ryan was starting to put together could bring a lot of unwanted attention to the Peoples Temple.

Amazingly, in Jim Jones's eyes, this event was secondary to a much bigger crisis: in 1976, Grace Stoen, the wife of Jones's political proxy, defected from the Peoples Temple. But because Tim had signed a document stating that Jones was really the father of their child, John Victor Stoen was now legally the son of Grace and Jim Jones, even though the two had never shared a bed. When Grace took off, she had to leave John Victor behind. Knowing that her son would be turned against her, she sued for custody. In the process, she threatened to spill all of the Temple secrets—and as the wife of the Temple's legal fixer, she knew pretty much everything.

Late in 1976, *San Francisco Chronicle* reporter Marshall Kilduff started covering Jim Jones and the Housing Authority. Something was off about the minister who arrived at the sleepy bureaucratic hearings with a squad of armed security. Thinking Jones was a colorful figure, Kilduff arranged to visit Redwood Valley and was given a tour with a group of other visitors. Halfway through, he realized that everyone around him was a plant; they were only there to ask questions that allowed the tour guide to talk about the wonders of the Peoples Temple, its geriatric homes and youth homes and drug rehabilitation center. Kilduff talked to his editors about doing a story, but they discouraged him. The topic had already been covered a few years before by Lester Kinsolving, and it hadn't amounted to much.

Kilduff was not deterred. He decided to pitch it around as a freelance piece, and *New West*, a sister publication of *New York* magazine, jumped at the chance. Armed with the assignment for the hard-hitting weekly, Kilduff started digging deeper. It took him months to find the sources he used in the story: most of the Eight Revolutionaries and a handful of other defectors such as Grace Stoen. And when the story finally came out in the last week of July 1977, the report was devastating. *New West* detailed a wide range of abuses firsthand. Elmer Mertle recalled the day his daughter was whipped with a belt seventy-five times. "She was beaten so severely," Elmer told Kilduff, "that the kids said her butt looked like hamburger." Birdie Marable detailed the overcrowded bus trips back east where people were forced to stay in the aisles, the luggage rack, sometimes even in the compartments underneath the bus. Wayne Pietila and Jim Cobb talked about guarding the chicken gizzards that were supposed to be the "cancer" that Jim Jones extracted as part of his fraudulent faith healing. Walt Jones (no relation to Jim) revealed the running of a home for emotionally disturbed boys and having to sign over to the Temple more than 50 percent of the money that the state paid them to take care of the kids. Micki Touchette recounted taking in $15,000 or more at every Los Angeles and San Francisco service. It was a shocking piece that helped spur Congressman Leo Ryan to fully investigate the Peoples Temple.

Just before the *New West* story came out, Jim Jones—whose spy network had already obtained copies of the story—called Cecil Williams, the minister of Glide Memorial United Methodist Church in San Francisco. He asked his friend and supporter about his chances if there were legal proceedings, telling the pastor that he was at Los Angeles International Airport, getting ready to go to Guyana. Williams was a fighter—one of the first African American ministers to get involved with the struggle for gay and lesbian rights—and he urged Jones to stay and stand up for himself and the Peoples Temple. Leaving would only be taken as an admission of guilt.

But Jim Jones didn't heed his friend's advice. He left that day for Guyana and never set foot in the United States again.

THE HEART OF DARKNESS

In the chronicle of every cult, especially the ones that end in outright violence, there's always a point when the organization crosses the line to inhumanity. In some cases the shift from charismatic leader to murderous lunatic is so gradual that it's hard to pinpoint exactly when it happened. In Redwood Valley, Jim Jones had already begun to institute all the classic techniques of mind control: separating people from their families, punishing dissent, dictating behavior (like arranging marriages and separating parents and children), rationing precious resources such as food and money and sleep, and creating an us-versus-them mindset that further divided true believers from the rest of the world. But once he arrived in Jonestown, all of these traits grew more pronounced, more violent, more unhinged. The Peoples Temple's stay in paradise was brief: from the day he arrived in Guyana to that of the mass suicide was little more than a year and four months.

Back in San Francisco, Jones's supporters were confounded. Mayor George Moscone felt betrayed but supported him publicly, continuing to believe what he'd been told—that his housing commissioner would soon return—until Jim Jones dictated his resignation letter over the radio on August 2, 1977. The mass migration of his followers to Guyana—forty to fifty arrived at a time on charter flights—taxed the immigration authorities there, as they were more accustomed to people fleeing their country. Many Temple members left their families without a word and under the cover of night; others took off first to the East Coast, where they hoped to disguise their tracks with an elaborate series of short flights to Guyana. By September, nearly a thousand people had come to the makeshift jungle commune.

As they made their way over the broken road from Port Kaituma to the gates of Jonestown, the first thing followers saw was the sign hanging from a wood gantry over the entrance that declared:

GREETINGS
Peoples Temple
Agricultural Project

Next, they passed by a security checkpoint. Weapons had been smuggled into Guyana via false-bottom boxes originally used to ship machinery. Jones ordered more for his arsenal over the radio using code words such as "Bible" for guns. In *Raven*, Tim Reiterman quotes one such transmission: "I want you to go to the Bible Exchange at Second and Mission," Jones stated, indicating the San Francisco Gun Exchange, which was located at that intersection. "They have a flashlight, the kind with black metal and it's twenty-four inches long. Do you copy?"

Finally, the new arrivals would reach a clearing where the complete vista of Jonestown came into view. There were acres of plantain groves and fields for farming. The compound began with a large building, the mess hall. There were showers next to that, and a path leading to the most active part of the encampment: the pavilion, a huge gathering space covered by a metal rain guard. There were five dormitories, segregated by gender, along with clusters of village homes for communal families, as well as a nursery, a school, and a radio room. Behind all of the living quarters lay a vast recreation area. The two most upscale buildings, relatively speaking—it was the middle of the jungle, after all—were the East House, designed for dignitaries and overnight visitors, and the West House, where Jim Jones and his family lived. But even Jones's accommodations, the most private and least communal, were sparse by US standards, more of a rugged cabin than a plush retreat. The one feature that separated his accommodations from all the others was a stockpile of drugs, stored in cabinets and drawers beneath his bed: heavy tranquilizers like Demerol, Quaaludes, and an assortment of amphetamines to counteract that drugged-out state, to help him become presentable again whenever he had to meet visitors.

In Guyana, Jim Jones was no longer able to maintain the fictions that made him into a godlike figure. It was more than just that there was little privacy in Jonestown; there were no secrets. The elderly slept in a dormitory within view of Jones's cabin, which meant his affairs, his special treatment, his long stretches of stoned inactivity, were all on display. Followers could look out from their quarters, hungry, tired from forced labor, and see him having long and lavish meals being served by women in bikinis. His extended drug-induced stupors didn't keep him from getting on the loudspeaker, slurred speech and all, and indulging in paranoid fantasies about the enemies who threatened their socialist paradise. Jones, who was used to talking for hours on end, persisted in his lifelong habit, still holding forth even when he'd long since stopped making sense. One time when he was particularly incoherent, camp headquarters cut the mike, and everyone working in the fields enjoyed the blessed silence. Sometimes his top lieutenants would take over, interpreting Jones's intentions.

Public enemy number one in Jones's harangues, though, was Tim Stoen, who'd come to visit early in 1977 and help ease political tensions between the Temple and the national government in Georgetown—and also to see his son, John Victor. Ever since Grace's defection, Jones had been cutting Tim out of meetings, and Tim suspected that Jones planned to turn John Victor against both of his parents. Tim Stoen knew he was under constant surveillance and tried not to act too suspiciously. He had no plans to steal his son away in the night, but John Victor's closeness to Jim Jones bothered him. And although Tim and Grace had divorced a few years earlier, he still felt as if he'd betrayed her.

Soon after he left, Tim joined Grace in a California lawsuit seeking custody of John Victor. On September 7, 1977, Jim Jones announced this act of betrayal to the camp, telling everyone that the Stoens had sent a legal authority to arrest him and reclaim John Victor. That evening he pulled an old trick out of his hat: staging an attack on the West House. Jones, who had been sick nearly constantly as a result of his drug use, announced that he had healed his grievous injuries, but there was no denying the truth—Jonestown was under siege. For the next six days he allowed no rest for his followers, declaring that a covert American strike force had been sent to Jonestown with the purpose of either capturing Jones or killing everyone there.

In the midst of this supposed war, Jones pulled the Temple members together in the pavilion. With sadness in his voice, he told them all they were reaching a tipping point. Those who had been in San Francisco that terrible night a few years earlier might have recognized where this was heading: Jones was publicly returning to his idea of revolutionary suicide. Stephan, Jim Jones's only biological child, was eventually able to calm his father down and make him forget the imaginary siege of September 1977. But Jim Jones's calls for mass suicide would not end.

Every time the PA system would crackle to life, the cult would gather in the pavilion. Jones would harangue them about the potential and power of killing themselves for the cause. Followers would ask questions, and Jones would charismatically bend their will, telling them that there was no greater gesture than coordinated suicide. These were the events known within Jonestown as "White Nights." For hours at a time, deep into the evening, Jones would terrify his followers into thinking they were moments away from death. But every time, the White Night ended, just like the imaginary siege. Jones would send his followers back to their everyday lives in Jonestown, even giving them a day off to recover.

After a White Night, Jones would commend his loyalists for exercising their strength of will, for it was only by virtue of loyalty that they would be able to defeat the forces gathering against them. These deadly training sessions are now widely cited in psychology classes as an extreme example of operant conditioning, as Jim Jones gradually normalized through repetition and reward what was inhuman. In this way, the unnatural idea of revolutionary suicide became normal, even routine behavior.

THE INVESTIGATION CLOSES IN

Back in the United States, Tim Reiterman met with Temple defector Leon Broussard, who'd been living on the streets when Jones promised him freedom from want in Jonestown. But once Broussard arrived in Guyana, he was put to work nonstop, cutting the grass or carrying wood from the sawmill to construction sites. The labor was backbreaking, and those who couldn't keep up were publicly flogged and deprived of food. When Broussard developed a sore on his shoulder from hefting so much lumber, he asked for a break, first from the camp security and then, when singled out for punishment, from Jones himself.

Jones threatened to put him in a pit nine feet deep by nine feet square, where, as Broussard had already seen, followers who allegedly didn't work hard enough were forced to mindlessly dig all day. He subsequently escaped the compound and made his way to Port Kaituma, where his complaints about his mistreatment caught the attention of the US embassy. To avoid unwanted attention, the Peoples Temple paid for Broussard to fly home, exactly as he'd asked. But the interaction meant that Jonestown was now officially under wary observation by the US government, an outcome that fed Jones's paranoid prophesies of impending attack.

Leon Broussard's account could not be verified, but it added to the damaging material that Tim Reiterman's investigative team was gathering from concerned relatives and from their own research. Congressman Leo Ryan's office was becoming increasingly convinced of foul play in Guyana, and Ryan began looking into his options. His first instinct was always to find a way to intervene firsthand, and he began laying the groundwork to lead an official visit to Jonestown itself.

Meanwhile, now divorced from civilization, Jim Jones began to act as if Jonestown were a sovereign nation. He invited delegations from communist bloc countries like Cuba and Yugoslavia, and even North Korea. He had an 8,500-word letter marked "URGENT URGENT URGENT" sent to President Jimmy Carter, cc'ing Secretary of State

Cyrus Vance and the US embassy in Guyana, explaining the ways that the Peoples Temple—which had done so much to turn the drug-addicted and hard-core unemployed into upstanding citizens—were being mistreated by the United States (such as by not forwarding the Social Security checks of its members to Guyana). The missive read very much like the ranting of a drug-addled man that was then cleaned up by well-paid legal consultants—which is exactly what it was.

Many in Jonestown were learning Russian, as Jones had floated the idea that if they couldn't establish their socialist paradise in Guyana, they could move again—this time to the USSR. Feodor Timofeyev of the Soviet embassy in Guyana even paid a visit to Jonestown, where he was serenaded with communist anthems. Timofeyev made approving noises during his visit about the Peoples Temple relocating to his country, but when the word got back to the American embassy, and the US consul, Richard McCoy, teased him about the prospect, Timofeyev confirmed that no such move was in the works or ever would be.

Meanwhile, Jones was having trouble controlling all his followers all the time, so he established the "Extended Care Unit," which was part infirmary, part psych ward, part punishment. In the ECU, Jones and his doctor, Larry Schacht, stored a hoard of powerful drugs: more than 10,000 injectable doses of the antipsychotic Thorazine, along with another thousand pills. The facility also held 20,000 doses of the painkiller Demerol and 5,000 doses of Valium. It had caches of morphine, Quaaludes, addictive sleeping pills, and surgical tranquilizers. Jones and Schacht dosed the disagreeable and the dangerous, essentially turning loyal followers into living zombies.

When Jones's son Stephan realized what was really going on inside the ECU, he was ready to commit patricide. Jonestown had given him purpose for a while, but his father's personality had only degraded further, and Stephan now believed his mania for control of every aspect of Jonestown life had escalated into full-on psychosis. But a violent coup was the last thing Jonestown needed. Stephan put his hopes on outlasting his father, who seemed sicker by the day. His drug use was out of control, and, partly to mask that reality, a rumor was spread around the camp that he had cancer. In fact, Dr. Carlton Goodlett had diagnosed him with a lung infection—and he later told a newspaper that Jones was in such bad shape that if he hadn't died with his followers, he probably wouldn't have survived more than a few weeks on his own.

Carolyn Layton, Jones's mistress, who lived with the family in the West House, even told Stephan she would back him as leader when Jim's final day arrived. Stephan occupied his time trying to keep others happy and healthy, including his younger half brother Jim. They formed a basketball squad, which was eventually accepted into a tournament in Georgetown. Jim Jones didn't want them to go, but Marceline managed to convince him to let his sons participate, citing that Stephan needed some time off. So, in early November 1978, Stephan and the team packed up and left Jonestown, intending to never return.

Meanwhile, preparations had begun for the first and only official expedition into Jonestown. In response to the complaints of constituents, Congressman Leo Ryan had organized a fact-finding mission to Guyana as a welfare check on the Americans now living there. Jim Jones realized there was no real way to keep Ryan out of Jonestown unless he was willing to physically resist. Ryan was backed by the US government, and the people of Jonestown were still American citizens. Jones told his followers this was another test of faith, hoping to keep as many as possible from defecting.

Accompanying the congressman was a team of reporters, including Tim Reiterman and an NBC news crew. Also on the trip was a small group of concerned relatives, including members of Bob Houston's family, who were hoping to check on his granddaughters, and former Temple youth leader Jim Cobb. Even Tim Stoen was coming—although he would remain in Georgetown, far from the wrath of Jim Jones.

Their plane touched down in Georgetown on November 15. Two days later, on the evening of November 17, they flew into Port Kaituma and were escorted by a Temple convoy into the Peoples Temple Agricultural Project itself. There were no weapons in sight at the guard booth. They would later discover that Jones had ordered all guns to be locked away.

The visitors were greeted by a party in the pavilion, complete with food and music. Even Jim Jones attended, watching as his people danced and sang, the exact opposite of a White Night. A banner above the pavilion read: THOSE WHO DO NOT REMEMBER THE PAST ARE CONDEMNED TO REPEAT IT.

Congressman Ryan and the reporters were surrounded by Temple members extolling the praises of Jonestown and their beloved leader. When Ryan stood before the group to give a speech, even he had to admit this wasn't what he'd expected. He told them that it seemed like Jonestown had been a very positive experience for many of them, and he was happy for that. Tim Reiterman and his fellow journalists weren't as convinced. They took the chance to corner Jim Jones for an impromptu interview in front of everyone, where he couldn't get too defensive. When pressed on how Jonestown represented socialist values, Jones admitted: "It's a reflection of what I thought was best."

Jones then brought out young John Victor to tell everyone that he was happy there and that he didn't want to go home and back to Grace and Tim Stoen. Jones could only shrug and express his regrets that the US mission had been a such a waste of time and taxpayer dollars, as Jonestown was a peaceful place. But when Congressman Ryan's party asked if they could spend the night instead of making the long drive back to Port Kaituma, Jones refused, telling them there wasn't enough room. Even when they persisted, saying they could sleep in the pavilion, he remained staunch: it was clear they were no longer welcome in Jonestown.

The party boarded their vehicles and their convoy began the return trip to Port Kaituma. When they were safely out of the area, NBC reporter Don Harris huddled close to Tim Reiterman and showed him a slip of paper that had been passed to him during the celebration. It was a message: *Vernon Gosney and Monica Bagby. Please help us get out of Jonestown.* This was the first sign during the entire trip that things weren't so perfect after all. As it turned out, more than a dozen people had covertly approached different members of their team throughout the night. Ryan was now reenergized.

The group returned on the morning of November 18, and Congressman Ryan let Jim Jones know that his mission would be taking at least a dozen defectors out of Jonestown. Sadly, this didn't include Bob Houston's two daughters: they took a smiling picture with Ryan and their family members but intended to stay in Guyana. During his final interviews, Jim Jones seemed drained of energy and enthusiasm. He tried to play it cool, telling the defectors they would always have a place in Jonestown if they chose to return.

Tim Reiterman and the others noticed Jones whispering to top lieutenants like Jack Beam and Patty Cartmell throughout the afternoon while Ryan collected the defectors for departure. Then Cartmell delivered a fiery statement of her own: "No one has ever left. Jim Jones has never expressed anything but love. I've been with him twenty-one years. I've been here eighteen months. This is the whole world to me. He represents all that is kind and loving. He has one fault: his heart is too big."

Jones's last words to the media present carried an undercurrent of unease: "I feel sorry that we are being destroyed from within. All we want is to be left in peace. I will continue to try. Time will tell whether I will succeed." The defectors were then led toward the fact-finding mission's convoy. Congressman Ryan took a final spin through the pavilion, full of confidence, hoping to pick up any stragglers, as Jim Jones watched him from a distance.

Suddenly, Temple member Don Sly rushed through the crowd, a homemade blade drawn. He got behind Ryan, slicing open the congressman's shirt and putting the blade to his throat. As Ryan's allies ran to the pavilion, calmer Temple followers managed to drag Sly off the politician. But in the pavilion Jim Jones had witnessed the entire event while remaining motionless, calm, and silent.

Ryan ordered the team to board the convoy with the defectors they already had. Jones quietly assured Ryan that Sly would be sent to the Guyanese authorities as punishment. At this point the team just wanted to get the defectors out of there. Some of them cried, pointing back toward Jonestown, claiming there were others who wanted to leave but were too afraid to speak up. At the last minute, follower Larry Layton, Carolyn's ex-husband, jumped aboard the truck, telling them he wanted to leave too. Jim Cobb softly informed Reiterman that Layton was an intense loyalist who would never defect from the Peoples Temple. The two then braced themselves: something was wrong. It clearly felt like a trap.

PARADISE LOST

Stephan Jones woke up late in the Temple's Georgetown headquarters. The Jonestown team had lost the basketball game, although they lied and reported that they'd won. Then all hell broke loose. The lead operator of the Peoples Temple's Georgetown office, Sharon Amos, took a coded message from Jonestown: they were to collect as many weapons as possible and "get revenge on the enemies." Amos and others took this as a directive to find and kill Tim Stoen at his Georgetown hotel.

Sharon was ready to act, but Stephan told her to stop. Jim Jones had given drastic orders before, as he did during the White Nights. Stephan wanted instead to investigate what was going on with the US fact-finding mission before they did anything.

Meanwhile, the congressional mission was still in Port Kaituma. They had called a second plane in to deal with their increased numbers. When it finally arrived, the party split into two smaller groups for boarding. The atmosphere was charged, the mood tense. Larry Layton's shifty behavior continued, and the Temple guards who drove their convoys to the airstrip glared at the defectors. As they were preparing to board, two more trucks appeared on the horizon, heading for the airstrip. One of the reporters noticed the newcomers were carrying weapons.

After acting for months like the leader of his own country, Jim

Jones now took the ultimate step: he was committing a coordinated act of war.

The Temple trucks opened fire and Larry Layton simultaneously lunged for the pilot of the second plane, trying to overpower him. Jim Jones did not mean for any of them to leave alive. Congressman Leo Ryan, reporter Don Harris, cameraman Bob Brown, photographer Greg Robinson, and defector Patricia Parks were all killed within moments. Nearly everyone else, including Tim Reiterman, sustained injuries; panicked, they ran into the tall grasses and boggy marsh surrounding the airstrip, while another reporter, Steve Sung, played dead by one of the airplanes.

After a few minutes the shooting ceased, the Temple trucks fleeing as Guyanese police forces pulled up. Larry Layton was left behind, unconscious after the pilot fought back. The survivors crawled out of hiding to a scene of utter carnage. Port Kaituma locals questioned Reiterman and those still able to talk while the wounded were patched up as best as possible. The mission's survivors promised the Guyanese they weren't CIA spies, as the Temple had warned. Already suspicious of Jim Jones and his cult, it didn't take much to convince the locals that the Peoples Temple was the real threat there. At considerable risk to their own lives, the locals took the survivors into hiding in Port Kaituma.

Back in Jonestown, the nightmare had just begun. The familiar siren from the PA system echoed across the compound. Jim Jones came straight from a private meeting with Peoples Temple leaders, including Jack Beam, Patty Cartmell, Carolyn Layton, and Marceline Jones, where he claimed that he'd had a vision of violent action, even now recasting his morally bankrupt schemes behind a cloak of supernatural power. He informed them that Temple members, acting on their own initiative, had armed themselves and gone after Congressman Ryan. Jones claimed that Larry Layton planned to hijack one of the planes and bring it down in the jungle—which might well have been the plan that Jones had set in motion before the pilot foiled that plot by fighting back.

It was at this moment, as the cult members still in Jonestown gathered in the pavilion for the final time, that the radio message went out to the Peoples Temple headquarters in Georgetown to put them on high alert. As Jim Jones began to address the assembled in Jonestown, Sharon Amos in Georgetown grew tired of the delays. The orders had come through: White Night protocol. She believed that the faithful were already in the process of "going to meet 'Mrs. Frazier,'" the Temple's radio code word for death. Revolutionary suicide had begun. Sharon grabbed her three children, Christa, Martin, and Liane, wrangling them into the bathroom. Once inside, Sharon cut Christa's throat first, then Martin's. Finally, she asked her eldest daughter, Liane, to kill her, and as Liane had trouble pushing in the knife, Sharon finished the job herself. Then Liane cut her own throat. These were the first suicides in the Jonestown carnage.

Lee Ingram, a member of the basketball team, was in the living room downstairs. Upon hearing the commotion, he ran upstairs to discover the bodies as Christa was still in her death throes. Then Stephan Jones returned from his drive to Georgetown and witnessed the violent scene. Ingram quickly called San Francisco and told them to ignore the earlier radio messages. Stephan tried to reach Jonestown, but there was no response. It was already too late.

In Jonestown, Jim Jones had taken the stage. He seemed to have regained some of his old energy, speaking clearly and walking without any help. He appeared almost relieved, recounting what he had told the camp leaders, expressing his conviction that they had reached the end of the road. He told them explicitly, "If we can't live in peace, we can die in peace." The comment was met with cheers. One can't tell from the tapes whether this was out of sincere excitement or the expectation that this, too, was a rehearsal and they'd be judged by their reactions. Either way, the White Nights had their effect: his followers knew exactly what to do.

As for the more than three hundred children present, Jones spoke gently: if their parents didn't spare them now, they would be butchered by the American government. Once the word got out about what happened to Congressman Ryan, and what Jones believed was now happening to Timothy Stoen, no one in Jonestown would be spared. It would be a blessing for the children to go quietly with their parents by their side. On the surviving recording of this horrific day, though, the reality is easier to hear: children openly weeping in terror throughout the entire afternoon.

Jim Jones framed everything he said in those final moments as if to absolve himself of blame. He wasn't killing them; he was still their father, tucking them all in for the long night. Only one follower, Christine Miller, spoke up when Jones asked for dissenting opinions, saying if the group could manage the transfer en masse to Guyana, they could do it again: "Well, I say let's make an airlift to Russia, that's what I say. I don't think nothing is impossible, if you believe it." But Jones shot that down: "Do you think Russia's going to want us with all this stigma?" he asked, pointing out that they'd lost any value they might once have had.

"Well, I don't see it like that," Christine replied. "I feel like as long as there's life, there's hope. That's my faith."

Jones's answer offered little comfort. "Well, someday we're gonna die, some place that hope runs out. Because everybody dies." There was kindness in his voice as Jones told Christine it wasn't worth living like this, in fear. And in front of the crowd, who were all on their leader's side, Christine backed down.

While this conversation was going on, Dr. Schacht led a team out of the ECU with vats of liquid containing Flavor Aid mixed with potassium cyanide smuggled into Jonestown as early as 1976. They set up a station by the stage. They had cups. They also had syringes so Schacht's nurses could spray the solution into the mouths of those who were too fearful to drink. Jim Jones then told people to line up, ordered that the deadly cocktail be administered to their children first, and the procession began. He oversaw a somber celebration of sorts, inviting supporters and believers onstage to speak and override the challenge of Christine Miller.

One by one, Jones's followers thanked or blessed him. They

encouraged everyone to stand in unity as the children, who were the first to receive the poison, began to cough and choke. As they died, the speeches praising Jim Jones continued. Adults told the older children to help comfort the younger ones. Some could be heard claiming that the poison didn't hurt; it just tasted strange.

Far from the pavilion, Maria Katsaris, one of Jones's mistresses, handed a suitcase to Michael Prokes and two other men who were brothers. It contained nearly $700,000 in mixed currencies, along with letters to Feodor Timofeyev arranging for the transfer of nearly $10 million in offshore accounts to the Soviet Union. They were ordered to take the suitcase to the Russian embassy in Georgetown. In reality, they traveled about a mile, then buried most of the money, ditched the suitcase, and walked away with $48,000 in their pockets. They were all later arrested by the Guyanese police.

Jim Jones's lawyers, Mark Lane and Charles Garry, fled into the jungle, promising the guards that they would tell the Peoples Temple's final story to the world. One follower, Stanley Clayton, pretended he was heading out to check on something at the guard post, but instead hid in fear in the plantain fields. As he was leaving, he saw one area surrounded by armed security where those who resisted taking the poison—Christine Miller among them—were being forcibly injected via syringe.

Even as the deaths began in plain sight, the testimonials praising Jim Jones continued. Men and women began to fall over. Some cried out or screamed. Dr. Schacht stood onstage and told those present that they were stepping over to the other side: it was a new beginning, not an end. Halfway through the hour-long mass killing, Jones received word that Congressman Ryan was dead. He told his followers: "It's all over. It's all over. What a legacy." He urged them to hurry up. There wasn't much time. The enemy was coming.

Hours later, night fell over Jonestown with none of the sounds that nine hundred residents usually made. In the middle of that silence, Stanley Clayton heard gunshots and then ventured out of hiding. The pavilion was quiet. He walked through the crowd, the heaps of bodies lying in the pavilion, lining the walkways, crowded together by the vats of liquid. Everyone was dead: Jack Beam. Patty Cartmell. Marceline Jones. Right onstage, just below the chair where he'd lectured for hours, lay Jim Jones, dead from a gunshot wound to the head. Later, an autopsy revealed high levels of pentobarbital—lethal levels in his liver, but less than that in his brain, a distinction that made it clear that Jones had tranquilized himself that afternoon and that he had a barbiturate addiction that made him tolerant of the drug in massive doses.

There were thirteen more bodies inside the West House, including those of John Victor Stoen and Carolyn Layton. Annie Moore, Carolyn's sister, had died by gunshot, the only other person besides Jones to die in that fashion. Her diary, one that wistfully looked back on her earlier experience in Guyana, lay on the ground beside her. "It seems that everything good in this world is under constant attack," she had written. Her last line, in a different-color ink, read: "We died because you would not let us live."

THE REVOLUTION WILL NOT BE TELEVISED

Jim Jones wasn't wrong: the Peoples Temple left an indelible legacy. But his revolutionary suicide failed to gain any sympathy. No one today thinks of Jim Jones as any kind of visionary. In the immediate aftermath, Larry Layton was the only Temple member to be prosecuted in a court of law, on the charge of conspiracy to kill a United States congressman.

The few survivors went in many different directions. Grover Davis, who was seventy-eight at the time of the mass suicides, went back to the States and lived off his Social Security checks until his death in 1993. Hyacinth Thrash moved back to Indianapolis, where she collaborated on a book, *The Onliest One Alive: Surviving Jonestown, Guyana*, with local author Marian K. Towne. She died in 1995.

Longtime Temple press agent Michael Prokes, who'd been sent out of Jonestown with the suitcase of money, called a press conference when he returned to the States, promising big headlines. During the event he praised Jim Jones, then went into the bathroom and shot himself in the head.

There were those who found solace in one another. Archie Ijames remained a committed universalist and often reached out to former members, trying to create a coalition of survivors. Tim Reiterman went on to publish the most authoritative historical profile of the Peoples Temple. Jonestown became lodged in history and memorialized in language: "drinking the Kool-Aid" has become synonymous with blind, unquestioning loyalty.

Years later Stephan Jones made an uneasy peace with his father's legacy. He moved past his rage simply because he had to as a means of enduring the rest of his own life. His brothers Jim Jr. and Timothy, who were both members of the Jonestown basketball team, survived, as did their Korean American sister, Suzanne, whom Jim Jones had also adopted. Suzanne had married Mike Cartmell, the son of Temple leader Patty Cartmell, and the two defected before anyone began leaving for Guyana. Lew and Agnes, the other two children Jones adopted with Marceline, and Kimo, his son with Carolyn Layton, all perished at Jonestown with their family.

Moving more than nine hundred bodies from Jonestown, along with the dead from the Georgetown headquarters and the Port Kaituma airstrip, proved to be a logistical nightmare. The Oakland Army base would have been the logical first choice for reentry, since most of the deceased still had family in Northern California, but, as Erika Mailman reported in *Rolling Stone*, the officials there didn't want to deal with grief-stricken crowds, so the bodies were transported to Dover Air Force Base in Delaware. After an initial rush, more than four hundred were left unclaimed, either because they had no family or the cost of the trip was too expensive; throughout his life, Jim Jones purposefully drew his followers from the poor and the oppressed. At least half of the unclaimed were children, their name tags washed out in the rain, too young to have ever had any identifying features recorded, such as fingerprints or dental impressions.

Evergreen Cemetery in Oakland, California, volunteered to give these lost souls a final resting place. The owner, Buck Kamphausen, thought the dead deserved a proper burial. He had a hill that would allow him to inter them efficiently, in stair-step formation. Thanks to funds raised by Jim Jr. and Stephan, Kamphausen was able to install a small memorial there, four granite slabs with the names of the identifiable dead.

The official opening was held up for years in court, as some families didn't want Jim Jones included in the list. But, in the end, his name appeared there, too, in alphabetical order. Every year now, on November 18, a mix of survivors and bereaved family members still gather at this site to say a few prayers and remember the lives that were lost on that fateful day.

PATHOLOGICAL LYING

CLAUDE VORILHON
AND RAËLISM

Claude Vorilhon is a failed French pop star turned failed race car driver turned failed journalist who finally found his niche when he invented a UFO. In 1973 he went out hiking and met a little alien in a green suit who gave him the name Raël. When Raël (née Vorilhon) appeared on French television to talk about the experience, the studio audience laughed at him. But enough of the viewers responded for him to start a cult based on sensual meditation, open relationships, intelligent design, and the promise of eternal life as a clone on another planet. Despite the absurdity of his claims and his complete lack of proof, "Raëlism" kept growing, fueled by a doctrine of sexual permissiveness, attracting upward of fifty thousand members worldwide at its peak, with healthy donations pouring in from those interested in cloning themselves. But today, as Raël reaches his mid-seventies, the advocate of free love is growing paranoid and his alien intelligence cult has started rapidly shedding followers.

THE PERVERT IN THE WHITE SPACE SUIT

The messenger from a race of highly advanced extraterrestrial beings wears an all-white outfit with exaggerated shoulder padding, like a *Star Trek* costume or an 1980s-era power suit. He refers to himself as Raël, a name that he claims he received from Yahweh, a visitor from an alien species called the Elohim. According to Raël, Yahweh's people are 25,000 years more advanced in their technology, and, as the Elohim leader, he makes regular excursions to Earth and checks on the intellectual progress and spiritual condition of humans. The Elohim created life on Earth, genetically engineering animals and, through these regular visits, providing humanity with enlightened spiritual representatives, like Abraham, Buddha, Jesus, and, as later discovered, Raël himself. According to no other witnesses, Raël was brought to Earth by Yahweh through the same kind of virgin birth that he had used with the Virgin Mary and Jesus.

Raël cannot furnish any proof of these claims. To start with, on December 13, 1974, the day that he was out walking among the dormant volcanoes in the Auvergne region of France, he did not remember to take his camera, so he couldn't photograph the humanoid being in the vivid green space suit. But in their brief conversations beside the blinking cake-shaped spaceship of the Elohim, Yahweh was able to convey enough material over the next two days that Raël was able to write a three-hundred-page book called *The Book Which Tells the Truth: Beings from Outer Space Took Me to Their Planet; the Two Messages Which They Gave Me*, based on the message from Yahweh.

The man who calls himself Raël, the head of the Raëlian cult, or *secte*, as they are called in French, was born as Claude Vorilhon, in Vichy, France, on September 30, 1946. His mother, Colette Vorilhon, was a fifteen-year-old farm girl, and according to his aunt Thérèse, who raised him, his father, Marcel, was a Jewish refugee. After his father's death, teenager Claude capitalized on his ability to mimic the popular French café singer Jacques Brel and recorded a minor hit record, "Le miel et la cannelle," or "The Honey and the Cinnamon."

With the proceeds of that brush with fame, Claude launched into a short-lived career as a race car driver. When that, too, ended in failure, he started a small publication devoted to race car driving, which allowed him to follow the circuit. While he was still trying to make it as a publisher, he had his alien encounter, wrote a book about it, and appeared on French television. Finally, Claude had found his calling as the prophet of a cult based on the teachings he'd absorbed during that experience.

From that point on, Raëlism took off, claiming some fifty thousand baptized members throughout the world at its peak in the mid- to late nineties. Vorilhon fashioned a version of intelligent design—the idea that life on Earth had been seeded by visitors from a superior planet who provided the genetic material for life as well as the intellectual foundation for our technology. He mixed the message of his religion, atheist in its godlessness, with a constantly expanding version of seventies-style free love. He also quietly selected a harem of his six most beautiful female followers, dubbed the Pink Angels, who would abstain from sexual relations with human beings, as they were being groomed for pleasing the Elohim once they arrived. In the meantime, they could practice pleasing the only descendant of the Elohim present: Raël himself.

When Vorilhon inaugurated his cult, he was still married. Presumably he had only submitted to the arrangement to appease his in-laws; however, his wedding vows to nurse Marie-Paul did not stop him from bringing home women at any time, having sex with them in front of his wife, and then making her clean up after these escapades. Marie-Paul, who hoped that her husband would someday set aside his alien persona and go back to being just Claude, said she put up with it for the sake of the children, Aurore and Ramuel, who both grew up being told that their father was descended from an alien god.

As the cult grew, many were smitten with its steamier side, which often had new initiates practice "sensual meditation" in large groups together. In his writings, Raël presented the session as a way of harmonizing one's mind and body by exciting all the senses along with one's own sexuality. But, in practice, the sessions often devolved into mass masturbation.

The Raëlism cult is certainly unusual: it has endured, though not without controversy, escaping the most damaging legal actions, despite a fairly well-established record of offenses. But the longer it survived, the more Raël's claims have been exposed as fiction. Investigative journalists have infiltrated the services, publicizing the tawdry practices that go on inside the cult. And the internet, with its nearly unlimited access to information, has exposed many alleged acts of plagiarism that Raël perpetrated during the course of writing his ten books.

At present, the septuagenarian is in retreat. His cult has lost members, and nearly all its sources of revenue—from new devotees and those willing to pay $200,000 for its suspect cloning procedures—have dried up. Dwindling numbers still do show up to see the "Last Prophet," the "Prophet Well-Loved," the "Gardener of Our Consciousness," the "Messenger of Infinity," and the "Guide of Guides"—to name just a few of the grandiloquent titles with which he allows his followers to honor him. But year by year, as the messenger grows bald and frail and the Pink Angels desert him, the appeal is quickly vanishing, like a fugitive UFO in the night sky.

AN ALIEN PROPHET LANDS IN FRANCE

Colette Vorilhon, Claude's mother, came from a strong Catholic household, a circumstance that made Claude's birth scandalous at the time. To make matters worse, his father Marcel (whose last name has not been recorded in any accounts of Claude's birth) didn't leave his marriage for Colette, even though the boy's parents continued to see each other on clandestine trips. Around 1949, when Claude was three years old, Colette and Claude moved in with Colette's sister Thérèse and their mother, as Thérèse was frequently helping to look after the boy.

In an interview for the French newspaper *Le Journal du Dimanche*, reporter Emmanuelle Chantepie asked Aunt Thérèse about Claude's home life, which she described as unstable. She said Claude and his mother bickered constantly, always finding the other one at fault. It was turbulent at best. She also said that from a young age Claude had a fierce belief in himself that could be described as arrogance.

Growing up, Claude wanted to be either a pop singer or a race car driver. Not everyone pursuing fame and fortune is a narcissist, but the need for fame combined with combative arrogance is a basic recipe for megalomania. Claude's behavior may have contributed to the fighting between mother and son, which got so heated that Colette began sending Claude off to boarding schools—most likely paid for by the absent Marcel.

The distance may have improved their relationship temporarily, but every time Claude returned home, the quarreling would start right back up again. To compound matters, Claude suffered the effects of an absent parent. He sought constant attention and approval from his elders and peers.

The desire for this adoration is another early seed of narcissism. Both *Psychology Today* and the Mayo Clinic have listed parental neglect as a cause of narcissistic behavior. If parents aren't there to instill a realistic sense of self, they leave a vacuum in place of gentle reinforcement. In that vacuum, the neglected child will often develop an overinflated sense of importance, a continual need to be admired and placed upon a pedestal. Often they will take this task upon themselves, building even the smallest of accomplishments into feats of mythic wonder.

Claude's aunt Thérèse, who harbored tender feelings for the boy long after he became the figurehead of an alien religion, said that he suffered terribly from boarding school, likely due to strict conformity. Claude seemed much more interested in writing pop songs than learning school rules.

As an illegitimate child of a teenage mother, he almost certainly felt the distance between himself and his peers. On top of that, he had not even absorbed the rudiments of faith from Colette, even though she was raised as Catholic. Claude was unconcerned about following orders, violating a sacrament by taking Communion even though he wasn't baptized. To the church, this was scandalous. But Claude seemed blissfully unaware of how disrespectful his actions were. He has stated in interviews that he found the priests' agitation to be more amusing than anything, as he never took the rituals and ceremony of religion seriously. Even at his own ceremonies, Raël can often be seen winking and smiling mischievously like a naughty child.

Like his mother, Claude didn't follow Catholicism's stricture about maintaining chastity until marriage either. In interviews Claude claimed that he lost his virginity at the age of fourteen to a twenty-year-old waitress. Although he wears that like a badge of honor, the age difference between Claude and the woman was not only illegal but also wasn't the healthiest way for a teenager to be introduced to sexuality. It's important to remember that Colette was only fifteen when she became pregnant, and this experience likely colored his views on the subject.

In 1962, when Claude was fifteen, he lost any chance of a reunion with his father when Marcel passed away. Claude told Susan J. Palmer, the author of *Aliens Adored: Raël's UFO Religion*, that his father died brutally, but didn't say anything more about it. One strong indication that Marcel had been supporting his young mistress financially is that right after Marcel's death, Colette withdrew her son from Catholic school. This was a dream come true for Claude, who took his guitar and hitchhiked to Paris with little more than the fantasies of stardom and a few spare francs.

THE COLLAPSE OF THE FANTASY LIFE

Claude's dreams of fame collided with reality on the road to Paris. He was broke and hungry . . . but, in his telling, just when he thought of giving up, a car came along and a somewhat famous race car driver whom Claude idolized actually picked him up. It was an event that would change the course of his life. The name of the driver is unknown and, like much of Claude's life story, the validity of the recollection is debatable. The encounter is only one of a series of occasions when fortuitous intervention at just the right moment suddenly saved him. And the sheer volume of these magical meetings contributes to the impression that Claude is, at best, an unreliable narrator. In classical theater, such miraculous turns in the plot were given the term "deus ex machina": in the middle of a complicated drama, a god would arrive onstage, literally flying in on some cumbersome bit of stage machinery, to solve all the conflict and provide a happy ending. The fact that Claude constantly resorts to such visitations in his own life story reveals not just his delusions of grandeur but also his fundamental insecurity. He believes he's so important that heroes, both here on Earth and from all over the universe, are always on call to swoop in for the rescue. He also allegedly possesses an emptiness in his life so monumental that he feels the universe actually owes him something.

En route to Paris, the unnamed race car driver brought Claude to a café, where they met a pair of hostesses (in other accounts, prostitutes) who had just finished their shifts. According to Claude, he sang songs for them and overwhelmed both women with his remarkable talent, putting them in such a receptive mood that both he and the celebrity driver then took one of them to bed.

Claude spent the rest of his teenage years in Paris, one of Europe's most liberal cities. It was the swinging sixties, and free love was all around him—a complete turnaround from the strict Catholic boarding school he'd just escaped from. Again, according to his own accounts of the era, he passed his nights charming women and singing in cafés, relying on a musical talent that was eventually discovered by radio program director Lucien Morisse, who marketed the young chanteur under the stage name Claude Celler, achieving a taste of fame with the song "Le miel et la cannelle."

In later years, Claude would be very proud of the silly erotic ditties he recorded, claiming they were emblematic of his sensuality. But his music career proved to be short-lived. Lucien Morisse had a brief, troubled marriage to the French singer/actress Dalida, who was most famous for her number one hit recording of "Itsi Bitsi, Petit Bikini." In 1970, Morisse shot himself, the first of three of Dalida's ex-lovers to commit suicide in the aftermath of their affairs. And without a promoter to shepherd him, Claude's musical career came to a screeching halt.

But with a narcissist's admirable resilience, Claude simply switched careers to his second choice: race car driving. He loved the combination of speed and danger and adrenaline, envying the machismo of its participants—quite the contrast to the café life he'd abandoned. Before he could hit the track, though, he experienced another major life change: falling in love with a beautiful nurse, Marie-Paul Cristini. They married, but, according to Claude, only to appease her deeply traditional parents.

In his memoir *Intelligent Design: Message from the Designers*, Claude wrote that his mother became excited about the prospect of becoming a grandmother, so he wanted to move closer to her, although this may have been just a pretext to convince Marie-Paul of relocation to the town of Clermont-Ferrand, 260 miles south of Paris, and near his own family.

Once they settled in, Claude had to face the fact that he was never going to be good enough at the expensive sport of auto racing to support a wife and family, so he took a back road into the sport: journalism. He launched his own racing magazine called *Auto Pop*, putting him right back in the heart of the action. He even got the chance to race several cars himself. It's possible that Claude used the leverage his magazine afforded to talk his way behind the wheel of race cars. He had no problem resorting to manipulation to live out his dream; in fact, competing in the races was almost certainly more important to him than the success of the magazine itself.

Thanks to *Auto Pop*, Claude raced for the next several years and even won a few trophies. He has told reporters that the high-octane sport fascinated him because the discipline and reflexes needed were almost spiritual. *Auto Pop* also gave Claude a firsthand look at mass media. As a publisher, he saw how a common interest could draw people together. He learned tricks of the trade when it came to marketing and appealing to a large number of people with a singular message. It's likely that it was this experience that reshaped Claude Vorilhon into one of modern history's most media-savvy cult leaders.

In the meantime, he and Marie-Paul now had two infant children. He was his own boss in a field for which he had a great passion. On the surface, all the elements of his life were in place. But his wife later revealed that the reporter persona was just a handy guise to continue sleeping around on the racing circuit while she stayed at home taking care of their children. However, this was exactly the life Claude had grown up with: his own mother would leave him to be raised by his aunt and grandmother while Colette went off to live as Marcel's young mistress. To Claude, it must have felt very familiar to do the same.

Then, on November 30, 1973, Claude's cushy arrangement was thrown into turmoil when French prime minister Pierre Messmer dealt the sport a crushing blow, forcing through new laws decreasing speed limits and making some of the most high-risk, exciting courses illegal. Because those same courses were the biggest draw and its financial backbone, Messmer had basically shut down the entire French racing industry.

It seemed as if Claude had lost his livelihood, his childhood dream, and his sexual outlet all at once. Circumstances were conspiring to force his return home. But just when it appeared he'd have to lead a more restrained life, divine intervention would touch down in a national park just miles from his house and reveal his true calling.

MAKING CONTACT WITH
A SUPERIOR INTELLIGENCE

On the morning of December 13, 1973, twenty-seven-year-old Claude Vorilhon felt compelled, he later claimed, to head some twelve miles out of town into an area of inactive volcanoes—all part of a national regional park, the quiet section known as the Puy de Lassolas. By his account, when he arrived, an aircraft that was not of earthly origin broke through the clouds.

Claude described the craft as the size of a small bus, flat on one side, conical on the other, with several blinking lights, a flashing white one above and a red one below. The craft landed silently right in front of him and a four-foot-tall humanoid being emerged. He described the childlike creature as giving him a look of pure love. The alien began to speak—in French—and later he learned that the creature could speak with the same fluency in any of the languages spoken on Earth. The visitor introduced himself as Yahweh, from a race known as the Elohim. He wore a vivid green space suit that earned the Elohim the playful and new iconic nickname "little green men."

In his writings, Claude gives a fanciful etymology of "Elohim": those who come from the sky. But he fails to back this up with any persuasive evidence. It seems designed to suit the myth that he began to fashion that day. In the same way, he offers a key and seemingly human moment from that first contact: Yahweh teased Raël about not having his camera to take a picture. The former café singer said he instantly regretted not having a photograph to substantiate his account.

But Yahweh said this was not the time; the alien promised to provide mankind with incontestable proof. But first Claude had to complete a mission: he was ordered to tell humanity about this meeting and to convince people without using any scientific backing. The people of Earth would be judged based upon their reaction.

This is a clever strategy, a narrative justification for the complete absence of logic to Claude's story and his utter lack of physical evidence. The newly anointed Raël was setting up a movement comprising fervent believers reliant solely on his testimony. And these believers would separate themselves from a society of skeptics who would be condemned by their failure to believe.

The visitor claimed that the Elohim had been watching Claude and his progress for some time and had chosen him because he was not a scientist and could explain things simply to laypeople around the world. They also picked him because he was born after the bombing of Hiroshima and Nagasaki. According to Claude, the advent of nuclear war worried the Elohim, enough for them to want a messenger of peace to lead the planet away from the coming horrors.

Yahweh told him that they had used telepathy to compel Claude to their landing spot on the volcano. But before Claude was allowed to spread the word, he was ordered to keep silent and come back the next day with a Bible. If he violated any of these commands, the Elohim would not return.

Notice the role that Claude is being told to play by the alien: he becomes the hero to save mankind. By his own admission, Claude was the only person on the entire planet worthy of carrying this message—a rather clear indication of full-fledged narcissism. Still, there are inconsistencies during Claude's supposed encounter. In his foundational treatise, *The Book Which Tells the Truth*, Claude claims he was just out on a leisurely hike when he felt an attraction toward the volcanoes. In later interviews he would state that he was going to his office for an assignment. Either way, he returned the next day with a Bible as instructed. Yahweh of the Elohim was back at the landing area, pleased that their meeting had been kept a secret.

According to Claude, the Elohim are an advanced race responsible for the creation of all life on Earth. Yahweh pointed out passages in the Bible that showed their work in genetically engineering every animal and plant species. But since the ancient people were too primitive to understand the alien science or even the idea of the Elohim as another species, they considered them deities. So their names—both Yahweh and Elohim—came to mean "God."

In *The Book Which Tells the Truth*, Claude emphasizes the scientific aspect of the Elohim, working hard to demystify them. He refers to the Elohim often as both "the designers" and "the scientists." They are, he claims, "25,000 years ahead of our current technology." This is, of course, nonsense from a scientific standpoint, as the Elohim would have needed to arrive on Earth hundreds of millions of years ago.

If they came only when *Homo sapiens* first appeared, that would have been about two hundred thousand years ago. And if they appeared only within the span of history covered by the Torah, then the naming of the animals happened some thousand years before Moses received the law on Mount Sinai.

It's also inaccurate as scripture and history, but Raël glosses over the logical inconsistencies by claiming that the Elohim are the intelligent designers of the entire variety of life on Earth. According to Claude, the Elohim can manipulate DNA, and the virgin birth of Jesus as depicted in the Bible was their handiwork. He claims Jesus was their creation with the purpose of spreading the truth of the scriptures throughout the world.

The Elohim not only designed humanity, according to this story, but are also guiding our development by introducing concepts of spirituality to one generation and spoon-feeding tidbits of their superior science to future generations. And now, Claude learned on Puy de Lassolas, they had chosen their next prophet to spread their message. Yahweh told Claude Vorilhon he was henceforth to be known as Raël, or "light of God," or "light of Elohim." His mission was to make people understand peace and steer humanity away from the path of nuclear weapons and world wars. His message was to be one of pure love. In practice, it would eventually lead to making videos of women in sheer tops dancing for him or pretending to perform sex acts while he held a yard-long balloon in front of his genital area.

For years Claude answered to both his birth name and his given alien name. The choice of the name Raël is odd: it does not mean "light of God" in Hebrew, as he likes his followers to believe. If anything, it appears to be a clipped version of "Israel." This would fit with Claude's contention that the Jewish people were direct descendants of the Elohim. It would also fit with the wish-fulfillment fantasies of a lonely boy, abandoned by his Jewish father, whose grasp of theology had always been limited to a few of the most basic terms.

In keeping with this pseudo-religious theme, Claude said that the Elohim wanted him to build an official embassy for them in the Holy

Land. Once he did this, they would arrive on Earth for all of mankind to witness. Of course, even when Raëlism was attracting its greatest number of followers, and money was flowing in from all the gullible people who hoped to clone themselves using the movement's extra-terrestrial technology, no real or convincing effort was ever made to build such an embassy. The reason for this inaction is evident: if he ever did complete it, and the Elohim failed to arrive as promised, his mission would be shown to be a total fabrication, a product of fervent daydreams and delusions of grandeur.

THE PR BLITZ FOR FREE LOVE
AND ALIEN WORSHIP

By the end of December 1973, Claude had set his plan in motion. He started by confiding in his wife about the extraterrestrial rendezvous in the local volcano range. Their accounts of this differ: in his memoir he contends that Marie-Paul believed him and dedicated herself to the cause; Marie-Paul, though, said in an interview that she acknowl-edged *he* believed it but never conceded that *she* did. After letting his wife in on the game—or the otherworldly mission, depending on one's interpretation—"Raël" put together a manuscript in remarkably short order and based it on his encounter with the Elohim. He then sent it off to a Parisian publisher, who found it bizarre but highly marketable.

The publisher had some editorial suggestions, but Claude refused to make any changes, claiming it would dilute the purity of the extra-terrestrial message. The publisher seemed to have made a calculation that the potential sales of this unverifiable memoir might be worth putting up with an author's otherworldly ego. As preparation was underway for publication that year, the publisher sent the manuscript to the host of a French talk show, *Le grand échiquier* (*The Great Chess-board*), who booked Claude, thinking the tale so outlandish that the author would make a great guest.

On March 13, 1974, Raël appeared on TV, all in black, with a neatly trimmed beard. He came off as unassuming, charming, dead-pan. Jacques Chancel, the host, would say in a later interview that he couldn't tell if Raël really believed the tale he was peddling. People backstage were laughing audibly, but Raël was unflappable in his con-viction. When he was asked point-blank if he had made the whole thing up, the response was "I just did the work of a messenger. And as such, I believe that what I'm saying is good. And if we think that what I say is false, I have such a fantastic imagination that I also deserve respect as a science fiction author."

After his appearance on TV, Vorilhon was flooded with letters from people who seemed to be waiting for someone with a message like his. They believed in UFOs and they had always known that for centuries humanity had been manipulated by aliens. He was validat-ing beliefs that a huge swath of the population already held. It's hard to know if this is what he'd counted on, but it quickly became appar-ent that he'd stumbled into the beginnings of a movement. So many yearned for the verification that we are not alone in the universe. And just like that, Claude Vorilhon had stepped in and appointed himself their leader.

His new work, simply called *The Book That Tells the Truth*, was pub-lished in late 1974. It turned out to be a perfect moment for his other-worldly message. In the 1960s and '70s, a new generation was eager to discard the organized religions they'd grown up with and were ripe for even the most outlandish visions of a new utopia. UFOs were part of the zeitgeist; David Bowie was dressing much like Raël in his Ziggy Stardust outfits. Pink Floyd was singing about the dark side of the moon; Led Zeppelin was rhapsodizing about a stairway to heaven.

And there was even pseudointellectual support for these ideas in popular books, like *Chariots of the Gods?*, a 1968 publication by Swiss author Erich von Däniken, which popularized the notion that human civilizations had always been guided by extraterrestrial intervention. A little further afield, there was the "flying saucer" mania left over from the 1950s, with mysterious craft supposedly sighted with some frequency around Roswell, New Mexico. There were movies such as

2001: A Space Odyssey. Aliens were everywhere, it seemed. They certainly could generate publicity, and, as Claude knew, publicity was capable of subsequently generating income and fame—a combination he'd been chasing all his life.

Raël jumped on this wave, and the audiences he commanded made it possible for him to book appearances both in person and over the airwaves. His ideas were subject to ridicule, but his rising public profile stimulated sales, which in turn brought even more believers to the Raëlian message. On September 14, 1974, Raël tested the waters at a public conference in Paris and drew more than two thousand attendees.

During his live appearances, Raël played the charming gentleman who was humble in the face of a great responsibility. He also began to fashion his own religious set of ethics, heavy on the brand of peace and love that was already popular in the turbulent 1970s. Sensing an opportunity on many levels—financial, spiritual, sexual—he began to try to package his message into some semblance of organization. His first attempt was MADECH, a French acronym that translates to "Movement for Welcoming the Creators of Humanity," which his grandmother joined. She contributed a revelation that became part of the Raëlian mythology, telling him that in 1947 she saw a strange spacecraft fly by her house, reinforcing the notion that the Elohim had been watching him for quite some time.

According to early members, Raël would bring believers to Puy de Lassolas, the volcano region where he first met Yahweh. They would sing and pray, trying to summon the Elohim to return. Their failure to show didn't deter many would-be recruits. These people saw Raël, the man who met an alien, as their closest bridge to the stars. By 1975, MADECH grew to a membership of seven hundred. But just as he had with his books, Raël wanted complete control of the message, and some of the new followers wanted to dilute his doctrinaire take on the Elohim specifically by extending their welcome to any extraterrestrials. Halfway through 1975, Raël resigned as MADECH's leader.

Luckily, just when he needed something to jump-start the next phase of his not-so-secret campaign to become the leader of his own organization, the Elohim returned on October 11, 1975. He said he felt guided by some unseen force to an area nearby surrounded by forest, where once again Yahweh appeared in a small spacecraft and this time invited Raël aboard. He was treated as if he were arriving at a spa, given a luxurious bath, and offered a delicious potion tasting of almonds. He was also given his own loose-fitting white bodysuit, and then somehow he emerged from the spacecraft, welcomed into a domed hall filled with lush plants and exquisite art. He'd arrived on the planet of the Elohim, and they ordered him to form a new kind of government called "geniocracy," where the greatest power would reside with those possessing the greatest capacity for intelligence and compassion.

Raël was then ushered into a dining room area where he met the other saviors whom the Elohim had anointed to lead humankind: Jesus, Buddha, Elijah, Muhammad. Raël felt completely accepted; in fact, he felt like one of them, with no need for extra acts of reverence for these principal figures in Earth's religions. It's hard to come up with a self-image that's more deluded and grandiose than Claude Vorilhon breaking alien bread with the most enlightened people in history.

Then, before he left the distant planet, Raël was taken to a machine that created a "biological robot," a living, breathing, perfect copy of him—i.e., a clone. This was the Elohim's version of immortality, and Raël would one day turn his followers' hopes of signing up for this service into one of the biggest money earners for his cult.

Upon his return from beyond, he published another account of his alien encounter, this one called *Extraterrestrials Took Me to Their Planet*. Following its publication, membership in Raël's newly minted religion took off. He'd jettisoned God but kept the part about eternal life (thanks to the alien technology of "biological robots"). He created a symbol for his new religion, an extremely strange combination of the swastika and the Star of David. He also invented an update on baptism that he called "transmission of the cellular plan": basically, if he dunked you in water, your genetic material would be telepathically beamed to a nearby Elohim spaceship for storage. He performed the first such transmission on August 6, 1976, the thirty-first anniversary of the bombing of Hiroshima, a historic event that was Raël's mission to ensure would never happen again.

By 1979, Raëlism had three thousand adherents, and membership was rising quickly. He wrote his next book, *Let's Welcome the Extra-Terrestrials: They Genetically Engineered All Life on Earth—Including Us*, setting out one new startling claim: Yahweh had told him while he was on the Elohim planet that he, like Jesus, had been born of a virgin when his mother was abducted and impregnated by Yahweh without her knowledge. Behind this outrageous statement that put him on the level of Jesus, it also revealed Claude Vorilhon's degradation of women: his own mother was nothing more than a vessel to carry the seed of the master race, and women in general were objects to be used for sex, with or without their consent. This is one of the most damning exhibits in his psychological portrait; a stunning lack of empathy is one of the telltale signs of the most virulent strain of narcissism. His own mother, though, played along. When asked years later whether this could have been possible, she laughed it off, admitting that she did sleep by an open window, so "Why not?"

Apart from this typically grandiose declaration, the latest book set out the organization for Raël's religion and one of the cornerstones of the new faith: sex. Raëlism championed sex in all its forms: masturbation, homosexuality, bisexuality, a whole menu of activities that other religions scorned or prohibited—all celebrated by Raël, as long as everyone involved was a willing participant.

This wasn't just scripture; Raël put it into practice. His wife, Marie-Paul, later told of her husband coming home with multiple women, flagrantly indulging himself right in their home, and not stopping even when she walked in on them. She put up with this horrific treatment, she later explained, for the sake of their daughter, Aurore, and their son, Ramuel. But her two young children would also become ardent believers, taking their father at his word that he was the messenger from an alien race.

But outside of their dysfunctional home, the message of sexual liberation sold, drawing in the curious and sometimes luring in the innocent, and Raëlism grew throughout the 1980s. In an interview on a Quebec TV news show, one former member, Dominique Saint-Hilaire, explained the appeal, coming to believe the stories of an alien intelligence and feeling a connection to Raël. And when she attended a gathering to further investigate, she was drawn to the company of the sexually curious, eager to experiment. Campsites and communes were established where Raëlians could worship the Elohim in private, practicing sensual mediation and various sexual activities away from a society they felt was too conservative.

TV BITES BACK

When examining the nature and magnitude of Raël's lies, it is important to look closely at his manner. Pathological lying—the territory of the true narcissist—can be distinguished from pseudologia fantastica, the kind of nervous, habitual, compulsive lying of con artists, people who fabricate lie after lie even when they don't need to. People with this psychological condition, it has been shown, betray telltale signs of nervousness when they lie: they sweat, their blood pressure and heart rates rise, their eyes dilate. Narcissists, however, exhibit no such signs or alteration and appear to be entirely untroubled by their claims, especially if it helps them acquire something they want and feel entitled to—and there is very little that a narcissist doesn't feel entitled to.

One distinguishing factor of Claude Vorilhon's falsehoods is that they have been closer to a lifelong performance—one that has proved, for the most part, wildly successful. Despite the obvious inventions of his imagination, he has had to endure very few consequences thanks to behaving in ways that one often associates with honesty and conviction. He smiles, he speaks quietly and modestly, and he even seems to laughingly acknowledge the absurdity of the stories he tells. He charms his audiences, conspiring with them while sporting a lively and mischievous grin. He looks comfortable in the spotlight, utterly at ease. These are the behaviors that most viewers associate with sincerity.

Take his appearance in 1988 on *The Late Show*, an Irish talk show featuring the popular host Gay Byrne. Raël came in wearing the big-shouldered, long white robes that he'd first worn as a visitor on the home planet of the Elohim. He communicated his story in a gentle tone, emphasizing his essential message: love. The mocking laughter of the studio audience could be heard throughout, but Raël plowed on, smiling over the snickering. This level of self-possession appealed to certain viewers who, like Raël, spoke to nonbelievers about UFOs and alien abductions and superior intelligence. His grace in dealing with such scorn was a big draw. Raël even laughed along with them, telling the audience he knew his tale sounded crazy, but still he never flinched in his veracity. He came across as a man who utterly believed in what he was saying.

Contrast that smooth appearance with one in October 1992 on *Ciel mon mardi!*, hosted by Christophe Dechavanne. It was a raucous airing, with multiple panelists, like a French version of *The Jerry Springer Show*. Raël was scheduled to appear with a priest, a psychologist, and a social worker to discuss the sexual practices of Raëlism. This was the setup, and it's a testament to Vorilhon's complete confidence in himself that he didn't hesitate for a moment to take on the assembled intellectual firepower in a debate.

But there was a surprise guest: Jean Parraga, a former Raëlian who'd been convicted of smuggling hashish in a stolen car. Raël had intervened in the case, paying for his legal defense and helping him earn a lighter sentence. But upon his release, Parraga became enraged to learn that his wife and children were now living with a Raëlian guide. He even tried to ambush Raël, but was thwarted by the henchmen whom Raël had begun to surround himself with.

But none of this backstory was mentioned on *Ciel mon mardi!* Parraga was allowed to paint Raël as the kidnapper of his family. He even suggested that the death of an eleven-year-old boy at a Raëlian camp the previous year—a child had fallen off his bicycle into an empty swimming pool and died of his injuries—was not at all what it seemed . . . That it was instead some sort of ritual sacrifice to the Elohim.

After the broadcast, the popularity of Raëlism in France plummeted. He went from a quirky hippie talking to aliens to a dangerous cultist who destroyed families. Raël saw his home base rapidly becoming hostile, so he relocated to Quebec. There was a strong Raëlian following there, and the stories from France didn't follow him. In fact, he successfully gained access to American media. Profiles appeared in the *San Jose Mercury News*, the *Miami Herald*, and even the *New York Times*. The tone was invariably mocking, but it didn't matter. The publicity increased Raëlism membership, which rose to nearly forty thousand at the time, and many of his devotees donated 1 percent of their salaries to Raël. Meanwhile, he traveled with teams of bodyguards and lawyers, living a life of luxury.

LYING BEFORE CONGRESS?

The 1990s have to be seen as the golden age of Raëlism—if one were Raël, of course. Some Japanese and European Raëlians sponsored a race car for him, and he raced professionally for the next six years. His best finish was third place in a GT1 at Lime Rock Park, in Lakeville, Connecticut, but usually he finished out of the money toward the back of the pack.

But even in Montreal, he couldn't escape controversy. His 1997 book, *The True Face of God*, included a passage that recommended parents teach their children about sexuality. "We have to explain to them how to use it in order to get pleasure." This was widely interpreted as encouragement for pedophilia, a stance that outraged critics. A woman known publicly as Corinne F. told a French TV news program that her teenage daughter's boyfriend had reported she was being sexually assaulted by her father, a recent convert to Raëlism, who confessed right away to the crime. The ease of his admission showed that he felt his behavior was justified in some way.

In response, Raël went on a public relations offensive, issuing numerous statements and giving interviews that categorically denied Raëlism endorsed pedophilia in any way, affirming that it is "not the role of parents to initiate children into sex"—despite the fact that this was the exact opposite of what he'd written in his latest book. He claimed that he'd only meant young people shouldn't feel guilty about masturbation.

But this contretemps did not make Raël steer his movement away from sexual freedom. They had now established a bracelet system for their meditation sessions and seminars, signifying whether one was straight, gay, monogamous, or polyamorous. They also indicated if one was underage, although soon no one in this category would be allowed to attend these sessions. During this same time frame, in the late 1990s, Raël gave a Raëlian baptism—meaning the DNA was telepathically beamed to a nearby Elohim spaceship—to a new follower: Sophie de Niverville. At the time, Sophie was fifteen. Raël and Sophie were married the very next year, when she turned sixteen. The brazenness of Raël marrying a girl of this age during a public firestorm on the same topic is stunning.

As the controversy roiled, Raëlians targeted the Catholic Church, jumping on the systemic child abuse perpetrated by the clergy as a way to gloss over their own negative publicity. They pounded home the message without any subtlety: the Catholic Church victimized children and Raëlism did not. This is a classic example of deflection: Raël found a bigger villain than his own group and went on the attack. The Raëlians wanted to appear as if they were coming to the aid of victimized children in the hope that no one would examine their own activities too closely.

But this was not Raëlism's only controversy. The early 2000s saw a global debate on the ethics of human cloning. President Bill Clinton sought to ban research on it within the United States, and his successor, George W. Bush, continued that push. Because Raëlism claimed to have developed a method of cloning human beings through their scientific research branch, Clonaid, Raël appeared before a congressional committee on March 28, 2001.

He and Dr. Brigitte Boisselier, the chief scientist at Clonaid, claimed that they had already begun to implement cloning technology. While other experts pushed strenuously for a ban, Raël and Boisselier defended their supposed breakthrough, claiming that human cloning carried enormous health benefits and could prolong life. Raël even claimed to be going ahead with the cloning of a recently deceased infant at the grieving parents' request. This was a stunningly heartless lie—promising heartbroken individuals that he could bring back their child and repeating the outlandish assurance as a scientific certainty before Congress, all in an effort to drum up more business for his profitable sham. Still, Raël stayed on message, carefully feeding his audience. He said nothing about being cloned during his visit to Yahweh's home planet, only focusing on health care, never mentioning anything about UFOs or sensual meditation or his half brother Jesus.

That same year French television reported that, over dinner with his childhood friend Roland Chevaleyre, Claude Vorilhon had been asked if he'd been lying about the Elohim. According to Roland, his response was, "Yes, I lied. I can tell you that I lied. But you knew that already." It was a damning admission, but not as surprising as what followed. Roland was, at the time, recovering from a divorce, and Vorilhon suggested that Roland spend the night with the girl who'd accompanied Claude—a young woman who was clearly under his spell. When the story broke, Raël sued his old friend, and because he couldn't prove that he hadn't lied—possessing no evidence of any of his encounters with the Elohim—he lost and had to pay court costs and damages.

Despite this setback, Raël continued to push his claims of cloning. According to the *Washington Post*, Clonaid was charging people $200,000 for its services. In 2002, Dr. Boisselier called a press conference to announce that they had successfully cloned a girl named Eve. Even though the name was a little too obvious, and Boisselier offered no evidence, no progress reports, and no photos, the story was picked up by news outlets from CNN to the *Guardian*, which presented Clonaid's claims alongside interviews with scientists calling the entire announcement a fraud. The Vatican joined in, denouncing the claim as "the expression of a brutal mentality that lacks any kind of human and ethical consideration."[1]

These preposterous pronouncements of scientific success invited investigations from the press. This was when the *Daily Mail* of London interviewed Vorilhon's now ex-wife Marie-Paul, and she reported his sex addictions, his flagrant infidelity, and his cruel behavior. Marie-Paul held nothing back, calling him abusive. She also revealed that she'd finally been able to reconnect with her children, now in their twenties and who had freed themselves from their father's influence. While their daughter, Aurore, has very much stayed away from the media, their son, Ramuel, gave a rare interview on French television in 2003 and noted that even if Raël had made everything up, he'd acted out of love and compassion.

THE HAREM OF THE SEX CULT

In the early 2000s, Raël created a high-priority mission to establish a select order. It began with a group of 165 women, all selected by Raël to act as missionaries. They welcomed new recruits and attended to his personal needs. This was the order of the White Angels. Above them was an even more exclusive group: the Pink Angels, six of the most beautiful Raëlian women chosen from among his followers. They were auditioned in casting call–like fashion, with headshots and interviews. Once selected, the Pink Angels took a vow of what might be called Raëlian celibacy. They were not allowed to have sex with any men in order to keep them pure for the Elohim, as when the aliens finally arrived on Earth, the Pink Angels would be there to sexually please them. The Pink Angels were, however, allowed to have sex with each other and with Raël, since his real father was Yahweh—a rather convenient arrangement for the cult leader.

While Raël promoted sex within his organization, he also used it to bring new peers into the fold. Several former members have acknowledged they were recruited by strippers and sex workers. He even created a group called "Raël's Girls," who worked in the sex trade but were also Raëlians. Supposedly this sex-positive group was formed to help industry workers take pride in their profession. But he was really using these young women to prey on impressionable new followers.

People seek the services of a sex worker for a variety of reasons, one of which is addiction. According to Dr. Joe Kort, the founder of the Center for Relationship and Sexual Health, sex addicts are likely to also suffer from other disorders, including substance abuse, borderline personality disorder, and depression. They crave a sense of comfort and belonging, making them more susceptible to the machinations of a cult, the desire for a place where they can belong. Raël was capitalizing on the weakness of one oppressed group to help him prey on other marginalized people, all in an effort to grow his numbers.

Another example of this kind of carnival barker opportunism can be seen in Raël's reaction to the Iraq War in March 2003. Raël pounced on the chance to join the anti-war protests prevalent at the time, luring more people into Raëlism by having female members appear topless in public. While this may have garnered some cheers from some of the male protesters, it's still another example of Raël objectifying women. This stunt was a salacious way for Raël to stay in the headlines and potentially attract members of the anti-war movement.

He returned to this publicity spectacle in 2007, attempting to go viral on social media by creating a Raëlism-themed day in line with frivolous holidays like National Hot Dog Day or National Best Friends Day. Raël tried to create a groundswell for a National Go Topless Day, but there was no official recognition for this "holiday" outside his group. He claimed this movement was designed to restore women's rights to enjoy the same unquestioned ability of men to parade around topless.

Once again, Raël sexualized and objectified women with this idea. But even more galling, he tried to hide behind a facade of women's rights to do so. And the charade continues to this day: GoTopless.org is a half-hearted website that promotes "Women's Equality Day" and shows a "boob map" listing all the planned parades purportedly taking place worldwide. There are links to merchandise and recommended reading (books by Raël) and a Donate button beneath the question "Would you like to support the cause?" It's an apparent ghost site that seems to be updated about once a year.

THE INTERNET EXPOSES AN ORDINARY BOOMER

Building an embassy to welcome the Elohim to Earth was supposed to be a central mission of the Raëlian movement. According to the promises made to Raël, once this embassy was built, the Elohim would reveal themselves to all of humanity. But the lack of progress toward this goal since 1973 is remarkable: no land has been purchased, and not a single brick has been placed toward what was supposed to be the most important unifying mission of the movement.

Raël's journey began in the 1970s long before the dawn of the Information Age. He must have felt confident then that nobody would ever find the real sources for some of his most outrageous claims. But the internet changed all of that. First, his writings came under additional scrutiny from the sci-fi community, who accused him of plagiarism. One example came from a 1953 book called *The Flying Saucers Have Landed* by Desmond Leslie and George Adamski. In it the authors describe a UFO, shaped just like the one that Raël describes, landing in front of him and transporting a small gray creature in a one-piece bodysuit. And it's not just those details. In 1969 the French author Jean Sendy published a book whose later English edition, titled *Those Gods Who Made Heaven & Earth: The Novel of the Bible*, connected the

Bible to the theory of ancient astronauts. In a specific example, Sendy wrote that the Elohim were aliens misidentified as gods by primitive people, in a work that was published seven years before Raël's.

With the massive amount of information disseminated online, it was getting harder for Raël to maintain complete control over what his followers knew about his story. In 2010 a group called Raëlianleaks brought to light some harsh accusations about Raëlism. Around this time, Raël claimed membership of approximately 85,000 members worldwide. But Raëlianleaks secured internal documents showing global membership realistically to be around 15,000 to 20,000.

It's hard to pinpoint exact membership throughout the years, but today there are social media barometers to measure membership. Raël's Facebook page is liked by only 7,500 people, and on YouTube, RaëlTV has 5,000 subscribers—hardly the numbers of a worldwide phenomenon. There's no doubt Raël has been able to gather people to his movement; however, his allure seems to be waning as the years go by.

Raëlism today appears to be a shadow of its former glory as more cracks in the armor have appeared. A group of former Raëlians claim to have had his DNA tested, which he was "careless" with due to his many affairs. The results showed the genes of an ordinary man with no trace of anything otherworldly. It's unclear if the test findings ever reached Raël, as he never responded to this group's accusations. But they acknowledge the word that he is likely most afraid of: "ordinary."

The future of Raëlism is murky. Before the outbreak of Covid-19, the Raëlians were based in Las Vegas. They held cellular transmissions, or "baptisms," four times a year at a nearby mountain range, which they claim gave them the clearest reception to any nearby Elohim spaceship. Pre-pandemic reports of their retreats spoke of a small, disorganized group with no real hope of expansion. It hardly sounds like a movement that's been around for over forty years; more like one that's barely able to get off the ground, so to speak.

Now in his seventies, Raël is estranged from his two children and does not have a ready-made successor. Dr. Brigitte Boisselier, the CEO of Clonaid and a Raëlian bishop, may be a likely candidate, but nothing has been confirmed. It's also possible Raël doesn't care about someone taking his place. Raëlism has always been about one thing: its leader's own gratification. As long as Raël was receiving adoration—especially from a constantly rotating cast of sexual partners—his mission here on Earth was being accomplished.

In June 2017, Raël posted on Facebook about his ex-wife Sophie de Niverville living with another man. Considering his position as the leader of a sex cult that embraces open relationships, it was a pathetic performance. He opined, without providing support, that she was bipolar, had been unfriended, and that her DNA transmission to the Elohim had been canceled. After all the lovers, all the fame, and adulation from his followers, Raël ironically was portraying himself as another aging man complaining on social media about a younger, pretty ex who wanted nothing more to do with him.

SADISM

ROCH THÉRIAULT
AND THE ANT HILL KIDS

The Ant Hill Kids, a doomsday cult that set up communes in remote parts of Canada during the 1970s and '80s, began as utopian isolationists preaching purity and a healthy lifestyle. But they ended their existence as a horrifying example of sadism spinning out of control. It is hard to determine which is more unbelievable: the cruelty of its cult leader Roch Thériault or the passivity of his victims, who tolerated his barbarity and heartlessness for years. Alone with his followers in the wilderness, Thériault, a handsome French Canadian with the gift of salesmanship, perpetrated atrocities on his multiple wives, murdering one in a torturous home surgery and then defiling her corpse. He brutalized his many children in acts so cruel that one mother left an infant to die in the snow rather than submit her child to Thériault. Finally committed to prison after amputating a spouse's arm, he still commanded such intense loyalty that he fathered three more children while in prison during conjugal visits with three separate wives. But his ungodly charisma had no effect on his fellow prisoners, and he met his fate at the age of sixty-three from a cellmate armed with a contraband knife.

THE MALIGNANT NARCISSIST

Nearly every cult leader can be classified as a narcissist. But narcissistic personality disorder can include such a wide range of behaviors that, in extreme cases, certain individuals appear to be different creatures altogether. Marshall Applewhite (who we'll learn more about later in this book) was, by most accounts, a kindly figure who inspired the kind of unquestioning devotion that gave him the power to lead thirty-eight people to their deaths. But no one—especially not those who knew him personally—would ever describe Roch Thériault as kindly.

Thériault was brutal, ingeniously cruel, callous, and unemotional. Again and again, he showed a taste for violence that overrode any natural human instincts, mutilating his own children and showing a depraved indifference to the pain he caused. The psychological disorder that he almost certainly suffered from has a classification all its own: malignant narcissism, which is supercharged with elements of antisocial, paranoid, and sadistic personality disorders. The malignant narcissist exceeds the garden-variety narcissist in the Hare Psychopathy Checklist because of their remorseless use of others, reactive anger, and impulsive violence. But unlike Adolfo de Jesús Constanzo, Thériault did not spend a childhood training for his violent future by ritually killing animals and learning that the pain of others might serve his own dark purpose. Thériault seems to have been inspired by the sheer love of seeing the pain of others. His unrepentant sadism rose to the level of "joyful cruelty," a description that led the psychologist M. Scott Peck to suggest "evil" as a useful diagnostic term.

Thériault was born on May 16, 1947, in Saguenay, Quebec, an industrial town on the Saguenay River. His father, Hyacinthe Thériault, a housepainter, soon moved south for employment to Thetford Mines, Quebec, one of the world's primary sources for asbestos. Perhaps because he recognized that psychologists—believing mistreatment breeds mistreatment—often search for evidence of childhood abuse among the most abusive, Roch Thériault enjoyed telling people that he himself had suffered terrible violence as a boy. He found that this story helped him get what he wanted, from both the women he tried to seduce and from the court-appointed psychologists he hoped would exonerate him. He told one of his wives, Gisèle (née Lafrance), that his father badly injured him by punching him in the stomach. At other times he claimed that his father pushed him down the stairs somewhere between the ages of nine and twelve. (He was plagued by stomach ulcers as a man and attributed this condition to the violence he professed to have endured, although blunt force trauma is almost never cited as a cause.)

Thériault peddled his history of abuse to account for his most inexcusable acts, including one recitation in a letter addressed to the sister of the woman he'd brutally murdered. "I am from a family in which I was mistreated and beaten worse than a dog from the age of two until fourteen, when my father, having beaten me, threw me out of the house and told me never to set foot in it again," he wrote. But Thériault was never kicked out of his home. He was a studious and talented student who loved to read and, by his own account, spend time outdoors. Although, in his abject apologies as an adult, Thériault frequently depicted his father as a violent alcoholic, neighbors and friends don't remember him that way. His father denied beating his son, but he admitted, "I punished him when he needed it." Corporal punishment was common in those days, and Thériault, who was a gifted liar and blamed his siblings whenever he was at fault, seemed to have provided his father opportunities for such discipline. Still, one neighbor did recall that Hyacinthe and his sons would play a game called "Bone," in which they sat around the kitchen table in their heavy work boots, kicking each other in the legs until someone gave in.

Did Thériault suffer more than any number of children from strict homes of that era? Or was he callous and unemotional from the start, a common condition in psychopaths? According to Kent A. Kiehl, a psychologist and the author of *The Psychopath Whisperer: The Science of Those Without Conscience*, in such children the limbic system, the part of the brain devoted to processing emotions, is underdeveloped from the start. They may have an inactive amygdala, the brain's fear center, and so they don't recognize distress or fear in themselves or others, predisposing them to committing acts of criminal violence. They may even understand emotions intellectually, but because they don't feel them, it can give them a heightened ability to manipulate others. Their heart rates don't rise when they inflict pain. Instead, extreme emotions like terror, surrender, and distress only serve to make them curious.

People with this level of psychopathy also exhibit an inability to control themselves, which makes them prone, later in life, to pursuing things like sex, drugs, and alcohol to excess, searching for any kind of excitement that can create a spark within, that can substitute for the palette of emotions that they don't normally experience. Their lack of fear combined with their inability to understand the boundaries of acceptable behavior create a combustible mix that causes them to seek gratification from the fear they inspire and, fueled by substance abuse, enjoy creating situations when they can terrify and do harm.

Is this what led Roch Thériault to torture, castrate, mutilate, dismember, murder, and defile his followers in the remote Canadian wilderness? It's hard to determine now. But the circumstances of his childhood, according to his family and his neighbors, don't offer anything remotely proportional to the horrors he seemed to enjoy inflicting on others. One could speculate that he'd always been predisposed to find pleasure in pain.

THE BIRTH OF A SELF-TAUGHT DOCTOR

Thériault stood out at school and his teachers found him intelligent, creative, and diligent—a promising student at the top of his class. He taught himself English, which was useful and also allowed him to show off how much smarter he was than his French-speaking family. But his parents were working-class, and like all his siblings Thériault discontinued formal studies after the seventh grade, the last level offered at the local school. Rather than travel to nearby towns and continue his education, he remained at home, cutting lawns and picking up work to help support the family.

He continued to further himself by reading the Bible, one of the few books on hand, and, based on his adult ability to preach eloquently and at length, he appears to have read his scripture deeply. His family belonged to a Catholic faction, the Pilgrims of Saint Michael, which was popular in Quebec in the aftermath of the Great Depression. The group blended a socially conservative stance with a type of economic populism known as social credit, promoting redistribution of profits to working people. If it had ever been put into practice, it would have been akin to the universal basic income proposal that candidate Andrew Yang promoted in the 2020 Democratic primaries.

The Pilgrims of Saint Michael were also known as the White Berets, because they went door-to-door wearing such headgear, handing out promotional literature and trying to gain followers by selling people on the values of social credit. The highly visible hats made the followers stand out, especially when Monsieur Thériault took his son and the rest of his siblings with him to march around the neighborhood campaigning for les Bérets-blancs and seeking donations.

Thériault's friends made fun of this public participation, a crushing blow to his precarious sense of self-esteem. Narcissists, despite their inflated sense of self, are obsessed with gaining the approval of others and can't tolerate being teased. Thériault loathed being forced to make this commitment with his father and, as a result, grew to resent Catholicism in the bargain. He could not separate the faith of his parents from the sense that his friends and neighbors were laughing at the Thériault family as they paraded around town for the White Berets.

But as much as this situation tormented him, he still gained valuable experience finagling the approval of the strangers he faced in a notoriously difficult brand of salesmanship. Later in life, Thériault became remarkably adept at this cold-call style of persuasion, and it's difficult not to wonder, for all his distaste for les Bérets-blancs, if he still profited from the trying experience.

After leaving school in 1961, Thériault performed odd jobs for pocket money and spent his time at dance halls. Now, instead of demonstrating his superiority by gaining top marks, he found that he was able to exercise another peculiar advantage. As Paul Kaihla and Ross Laver recount in *Savage Messiah: The Shocking Story of Cult Leader Rock [sic] Thériault and the Women Who Loved Him*, their book on Thériault and the Ant Hill Kids, Roch would later write, "Since my childhood, I have always believed I was different, not your average Joe. This was not only a mental impression but also an anatomical one." He became convinced that his large endowment set him apart and contributed to the enviable sexual prowess he claimed for himself. Even without considering this, he was tall and good-looking, with intense blue eyes shaded by heavy brooding brows. He could talk about anything and soon gained a following among the women in his small mining town.

After spending his teenage years circulating among the ladies he talked up in the local dance halls, the now twenty-year-old Thériault tried his hand at a conventional lifestyle, marrying the seventeen-year-old Francine Grenier in 1967. He built a home about half a mile from his parents—not really something that a child who stated he'd been kicked out of his house at fourteen would think to do. Still, Thériault and Francine didn't remain there for long, moving within a year to Montreal, where he found work as a chimney inspector. Alcohol came into his life, but he was a happy drunk. The couple seemed content. In January 1969, they welcomed their first son, Roch-Sylvain, then a second, François, in April 1971.

But while Francine was still pregnant with François, Thériault took a sudden turn for the worse, complaining of the severe stomach pains that would plague him for the rest of his life. Doctors diagnosed him with peptic ulcers, a condition now effectively treated with pills to control acid secretion. But back in 1971 he was forced to endure a vagotomy, a type of surgery that has since been nearly discontinued and that involves cutting the vagus nerve, the single longest nerve system in the body, where it passed through the stomach. At the time, the role of the vagus nerve was poorly understood, but now it is known to have a profound effect on the body's parasympathetic nervous system, which governs the calming rest-and-repair instinct—the opposite of the sympathetic nervous system, which governs the stress response known as the fight-or-flight instinct.

Did this unsuccessful surgery contribute to the radical mood shift that Francine noticed in the immediate aftermath of the procedure—the one that turned her husband into an increasingly abusive presence? When the doctors excised a considerable portion of his stomach, did Thériault also lose a key element in controlling his metabolism and temper? After a second operation in the fall of 1971, he spent months vomiting, racked with unbearable pain. He later learned that, as a result of the botched surgery, he now had a condition called dumping syndrome, which handicapped his digestion. Food was moving directly from the stomach to the small intestine without giving his body time to properly absorb any nutrients. Today, the condition affects only about 15 percent of patients who undergo gastric bypass surgery, and it can usually be resolved with straightforward adjustments to the diet. Only those who don't stick to the specialized diet suffer horrible symptoms, including weariness, vomiting, and stomach pain—the very same afflictions that began to plague Thériault.

The chronic pain affected his mental health. He changed from a happy-go-lucky family man into a person consumed by agony and dark obsessions. Thériault's savant-like ability to quickly absorb complex information had always fueled his general reading. But now he channeled these skills into a fixation on medical textbooks, reading them from cover to cover and lecturing his friends at length about human anatomy and dumping syndrome. Francine later cited the surgery as the turning point in their previously decent marriage, transforming Thériault from a loving husband who doted on his wife and child to an obsessive preoccupied only with himself. On top of that, his homeschooling left him with a dangerous overconfidence in his abilities to practice medicine.

Chronic pain, medical obsession, and drinking to self-medicate all played a role in Thériault's subsequent unraveling. He quit his job,

forcing the growing family to return to Thetford Mines. He began telling people that his insides were now plastic and he was going to die.
When he wasn't going on about his health, he fixated on Francine and
her appearance. Suddenly, after years of insisting that she wear long
skirts to keep other men from looking at her, he reversed himself and
wanted her to wear short skirts that showed off her legs.

These seemingly arbitrary impulses to control Francine and
enforce his will were early warning signs of the abusive tendencies that
would soon overwhelm their marriage and then his entire existence.
This sudden interest in her clothing wasn't the only evidence of a new
and troublesome sexual fixation. He began to talk about starting a
nudist colony and even asked his in-laws if he could use a section of
their land for that very purpose. This was the first appearance of his
urge to create an alternate world where he would be the sole person in
charge. And this original unfulfilled impulse seemed to have been the
simplest and most primal expression of such an urge, since membership in a nudist colony would have allowed him to parade his anatomical advantages around the clock.

SALESMAN TURNED PROPHET

Back in Thetford Mines, Thériault, who appears to have inherited a
practical facility from his father that served him well both as a trades-
man and later as a survivalist, got permission to start a woodshop on
his parents' land. At first the new business prospered. He cut down
trees and turned the timber into furniture and wooden utensils. When
some neighbors grew angry with the local permitting process for new
construction, Thériault seemed to memorize the entire municipal
code, turning around and arguing on their behalf, pointing out inconsistencies in the laws that his hostile neighbors could actually exploit.
His success as an advocate helped him get elected to the city council in 1975. He'd also joined a local Catholic social organization, the
Aramis Club, that helped fund charity events and local dances, and

was appointed chief of the initiation committee . . . until his constant stream of inappropriate ideas—the desire for club members to wear outfits adorned with a picture of Satan on the back, for instance—forced his membership to be revoked. He ran into a similar fate on the city council, which he rarely attended. The few times he did, he bullied fellow board members who argued against his unsound and fiscally irresponsible building proposals. They soon ran him out as well.

Meanwhile, his marriage wasn't faring any better than his attempts at civic participation. As he wasted his time on far-off affairs that he disguised as "business trips," the revenue from his furniture business dwindled and the couple was forced to turn to other fields to keep their finances afloat. Francine took a job as a waitress, and Thériault started ferrying his carpentry work to larger nearby towns. Soon, Francine came to realize that her husband was spending less time selling than he was meeting women and taking them back to his hotel. One of the clues: he'd return from his trips convinced that his stomach medications were interfering with his sexual performance. On the doctor's recommendation, he stopped taking his medicine, and went back to drinking to moderate the pain. Soon after that change, in 1976, Francine divorced him and left with their two children.

What took his mind off the collapse of his marriage and his business? An attractive twenty-six-year-old named Gisèle Lafrance, and a new outlet for his obsessiveness. He'd met Gisèle, as Francine suspected, at a Holiday Inn dance while on the road. Not long after, she'd rented a place in Thetford Mines and he was spending his weekends there with her, even introducing her to his sons. At the same time, after he was kicked out of the Aramis Club, his personal faith took another turn: he decided to become a Seventh-day Adventist and began walking around town in a monk's robe. The first person he converted to the faith was Gisèle, starting a pattern of mixing sex and evangelism that he would continue to pursue while he was a free man.

Seventh-day Adventism appealed to Thériault for many of the same reasons it appealed to David Koresh (we'll learn more about him on p. 231): the structure made room for individual inspiration, and that kind of validation could be used by the unscrupulous as a stepping-stone to godlike power over others. The denomination did not specifically encourage living prophets, but it was historically receptive to their ideas. However, before Thériault could exploit Seventh-day Adventism as a path to personal dominion over others, he connected to its strict dietary rules from Leviticus and its general focus on health, which he embraced with a convert's zeal. Pastor Pierre Zita recognized this enthusiasm and sent him out to draw in others who might be moved by such a transformation and join the faith.

Once again, Thériault was able to exercise his salesmanship ability to a remarkable degree. Before long, he had established himself as a leading figure in both the church and the local organic-food movement, two groups with a great deal of overlap. Thériault could point to his own health as an example of the wonders that the faith could provide: he quit drinking and adopted a healthy, vegetarian lifestyle in the belief that Judgment Day and the Second Coming were imminent. His pitches brought in dozens of new members.

By the summer of 1977, Pierre Zita was deploying Thériault to new pastures, trying to draw converts from French Catholics in the nearby town of Plessisville. As he had before, Thériault recruited young parishioners, including a man named Jacques Fiset, and three women who were friends of his: nineteen-year-old Chantal Labrie, eighteen-year-old Francine Laflamme, and twenty-one-year-old Solange Boilard. This success made Thériault realize that he wanted to be the one to lead this surge in membership. It would take nearly a year for him to put his plan into action, but within a matter of months he was plotting ways to set up his own breakaway congregation.

One key to his success in sales: Thériault was adept at spotting weaknesses he could exploit. Solange Boilard was a bright and rebellious young woman with an unhappy home life. She loathed her father, an alcoholic who abused everyone in the family, leaving her susceptible to what is known as an intergenerational cycle of violence—a pattern beginning with the parents and continuing when their children grow up and fall into their own spirals of similar relationships, either as victims or abusers. Whether or not Thériault was a recipient of abuse himself, he was quick to recognize this fragility in others.

Unlike Solange, Chantal Labrie had a happy home life. She was a daydreamer with loving and protective parents. Still, she was prone to moodiness and possible depression. And Francine Laflamme was outgoing but insecure about her appearance. Male cult leaders often take advantage of young women's self-doubt to make them feel loved, beautiful, and special. And Thériault had an intense charisma that he used to charm anyone he came into contact with.

It wasn't long before he was inviting Jacques, Solange, Chantal, and Francine to camp out at Gisèle's apartment during the weekends, where they could listen to his long, rambling speeches about the imminent end of the world. One of the most consequential steps a cult leader can take is to isolate his followers using such a method. This is one of Robert Jay Lifton's eight principles of thought reform: milieu control. Keeping everyone at Gisèle's place was just the first of many maneuvers Thériault employed to cut his followers off from others and reinforce the group dynamic.

It turned out to be a productive summer for Thériault, who soon added six more members to the core: Nicole Ruel, a young woman haunted by the death of her mother, met him and quickly moved into Gisèle's apartment. Twenty-four-year-old Claude Ouelette, who had hopes of attending optician school, soon became a regular at Thériault's Bible sessions. Then two of Francine's friends from high school began showing up: an eighteen-year-old identified in accounts only as "Marise" and twenty-year-old Josée Pelletier. After that, at a seminar retreat for Seventh-day Adventists near Lake Rosseau, Thériault recruited two more pretty young converts: Gabrielle Lavallée and her friend Yolande Guinnebert, two French Canadian members of the resort staff.

By autumn of 1977, Thériault convinced his new recruits to drop out of college and help him prepare vegetarian meals for his programs to quit smoking. Soon the new collective was clearing several thousand dollars a week by soliciting donations for the Seventh-day Adventists, which Thériault pocketed for himself. He'd not yet laid a hand on his followers, but he was already shamelessly exploiting them, turning them into a profitable labor force.

September brought two new members: twenty-four-year-old construction worker Jacques Giguere and his wife, twenty-three-year-old cake factory worker Maryse Grenier. Jacques Giguere was seduced by Thériault's speeches about living a simpler life, but Maryse was simply following the man she loved. She remained aloof from others in the group and was the only woman who never fell prey to Thériault's sexual allure.

Once the parents of Thériault's followers realized that their children had never reported to university that fall, they tried rescuing them from a person they viewed, quite correctly, as a dangerous con man. Chantal's parents were especially insistent, rushing their daughter to a psychologist who could help extricate her from Thériault's clutches. Chantal agreed to a one-month stay at a psychiatric hospital.

The lesson Thériault drew from Chantal's sudden exit was that his followers had not been sufficiently isolated. He needed to remove them completely from outside influences, especially parents or therapists who wanted to interfere with his plans. That explains why, in October 1977, he rented a two-story building in Sainte-Marie-de-Beauce, about an hour's drive from Thetford Mines. Thériault then dropped by the hospital and sweet-talked Chantal into rejoining the group, and they eventually drove together to their new collective home.

Thériault's followers began passing out flyers to bring in people to the smoking-cessation programs they ran in their new headquarters, dubbed the Healthy Living Clinic. Francine's friends, Josée and Marise, quit school to permanently join the group and work at Thériault's clinic even as their leader began to increase his control over his followers, making them all wear long robes and give up their worldly possessions.

While many seemed to love the family atmosphere, Gisèle was starting to feel like an afterthought. All the new female followers seemed to be in love with her boyfriend. But, she reminded him, *she* was the one he was actually sleeping with. In what turned out to be his final concession to conventional morality, Thériault agreed to marry Gisèle on January 8, 1978. But he never took his vows seriously. There was no honeymoon, and group activities resumed exactly as before. Although Gisele soon became pregnant with their first child, Thériault no longer seemed interested in her. She threatened to leave, and physical violence followed.

THE ANT HILL KIDS

The residents of Sainte-Marie-de-Beauce were beginning to grow suspicious of Roch Thériault. He wasn't paying his bills. And apart from this first incident of abuse against Gisèle, which the townspeople knew nothing about, the rumors of his behavior were growing more disturbing. In March 1978, he convinced a leukemia patient named Geraldine Gagné Auclair to leave the hospital, promising that he could cure her with grape juice. But no miracle cure was forthcoming, and Geraldine died soon after coming under his care. Thériault quickly supplied his followers with a favorable interpretation of the tragedy, telling them that his kiss had returned Geraldine to life, but then he recognized God's will and committed her soul to the afterlife.

The police couldn't find a reason to hold Thériault responsible for Geraldine's death, but they kept watch over him and his Healthy Living Clinic. And while Thériault may have intended his story about his mystical kiss as a demonstration of his spiritual power, what it clearly shows is that he was seducing a vulnerable woman with a terminal illness—treating her as a sexual object—with complete disregard for her tenuous hold on life. This would not be the last example of such callousness.

When the Seventh-day Adventists, troubled by his shady proselytizing and ragtag band of devotees, expelled him from the organization in the spring of 1978, Thériault began to realize that, between the church, the police, his creditors in town, and the immediate families of the people living with him, he was attracting too much scrutiny. If he wanted to maintain control over his followers and continue to operate under the radar, he had to isolate them even further. So, early on June 5, 1978, he loaded more than a dozen followers into a truck, a bus, and a car, and the caravan left Sainte-Marie-de-Beauce forever. When parents filed missing person reports, the authorities searched Thériault's former whereabouts. All they found was an abandoned bag containing the ID cards of everyone who'd disappeared.

Now they were all out in the wilderness, in a place so remote, they didn't even need identification. And there was no one to stand between Thériault and his faithful. There was only one thing that he was missing: a religion he could call his own. A month into their wandering, on July 6, 1978, he announced that doomsday would arrive in a few short months—on February 17 of the following year. This was not an inventive strategy. Multiple prophets in the Seventh-day Adventist tradition had predicted the end times. In fact, the faith was founded in the aftermath of one such failed event, known thereafter as the Great Disappointment.

Thériault added a few new touches to make this pending calamity all his own. He claimed that great hailstorms would destroy the Earth and only he and his followers would be spared, because God had made Thériault his personal prophet. Until the end, they were all to lead peaceful lives in the wilderness. Once the world collapsed, they would begin rebuilding society.

Thériault and his followers soon began looking for the ideal place to set up camp and wait. They found a clearing about thirteen and a half miles from the town of Saint-Jogues, in a remote portion of Quebec's Gaspé Peninsula. That far from civilization, Thériault's followers would have almost no contact with anyone outside the cult. He'd successfully segregated them, a necessary step for asserting his control, calling their new home "Eternal Mountain." By endowing it with an aura of holiness, Thériault was trying to cast his exploitation in a mystical light.

In fact, as expected, it took much work just to survive. Thériault made his crew of mostly college-age kids cut down trees, dig a well, and build a log cabin from scratch. He himself didn't lift a finger, so everyone but him was constantly exhausted. They were so productive that he came up with a nickname: the Ant Hill Kids. This was another technique designed to break their will. Working recruits to the point of collapse, then waking them early to start again, was the entire point of military basic training, and Thériault had hit upon his own wilderness version of the classic reprogramming technique. Facing the specter of doomsday, he convinced them of the need to save their rations and skip necessary sleep. Sheer exhaustion made them reliant on him for even the most basic decisions.

While they were building their encampment, Thériault was busy renaming them according to the Bible. Gisèle became Esther, Solange was now Rachel, and Gabrielle was Thirsta. He was Moses, the prophet and giver of laws. But that wasn't the end of it. Whenever they did have a break, he made them confess their secrets, stripping them of privacy and exposing their weaknesses. He reminded them that the society they'd left behind was evil—all of it, including their families. He renamed their new community the "World of the Dead."

Roch Thériault was establishing his own versions of every technique that cult leaders use: setting the group in opposition to society; enforcing public confessions to expose vulnerability; isolating the group physically; and alienating them from their families. In this world that now ran entirely on his say-so, he realized there was no need for him to remain faithful to Gisèle.

But in a psychological twist, he made it all seem like her idea. When Gisèle told him that the other girls were growing lonely, he began sleeping with them as if he were performing a kindness at her request. It wasn't long before he made the bonds between him and each of the women sacred, using his authority as a prophet to marry every one of them. He cited the biblical example of King David, who had many wives, even more than the eight mentioned by name. Perhaps he wanted to equal King David's twenty children as well: soon he'd impregnated all the women in the World of the Dead except for Maryse, who had no interest in him and remained faithful to her husband, Jacques.

Amid the hardships of life in the woods, Thériault soon abandoned the healthy lifestyle he'd followed as a Seventh-day Adventist. He made his followers trudge into Saint-Jogues, the nearest town, to buy junk food and alcohol. He began beating with a wooden club anyone who angered him. Thériault also began to formulate one of the most alienating principles of his doomsday cult: his three biological children would be considered the chosen, but any progeny who were not his—like Jacques and Maryse's daughter, Jeziel, and their new infant son, Samuel—were to be treated like slaves or animals.

Meanwhile, worried parents had banded together and convinced the authorities to apprehend Thériault and bring him to Quebec City—a seven-hour drive—for psychological evaluation. One psychiatrist believed that he suffered from schizophrenia. Still, the deviously persuasive Thériault managed to convince the medical professional that he was harmless—a scenario that would be repeated. Some criminal behavior or act of violence, some suspicion of atrocity, would result in an investigation of Thériault, but then he'd manage to fool a court-appointed official with his intelligent, affable demeanor.

In fact, by this point Thériault had already begun brutalizing his followers for insubordination, forcing them to write letters of ritual debasement to their "Papy" for perceived offenses, like sneaking extra food. ("It is this fault which causes my plumpness," one letter says. "I do not want to be a fat and plump servant. That is too ugly next to the man you are.") It might seem comical in another context, but for the Ant Hill Kids, the penalties for crossing some often-arbitrary line could be swift, and disproportionate to the act. In the fall of 1978, in a similar food-related incident, Thériault broke two of Maryse's ribs, because the starving, pregnant mother hadn't asked his permission before eating two pancakes. When Maryse considered leaving, Thériault bullied Jacques into cutting off one of her toes as punishment.

MOSES GOES TO PRISON

February 17, 1979, the day of Thériault's prophesied apocalypse, came and went, and the world was spared, with Thériault stating that God's understanding of time was so different from humanity's that naturally there had been a mix-up. For some reason his followers accepted this ludicrous explanation, probably because by now he'd broken their willpower so effectively that he could have told them anything. When Jacques Fiset briefly fled in April 1979, he still refused to say anything negative about Thériault to reporters.

Chantal's parents continued to try to save their daughter, and once they had figured out the cult's location through fleeting contact with her, they made another desperate attempt. Just a few days after Jacques Fiset's newspaper interview appeared in print—his depiction making them sound like a church group on an extended holiday—police took both Chantal and Thériault away for psychiatric evaluations.

He was once again able to trick psychiatrists into giving him a clean bill of health. Chantal also failed to excite their suspicion. But in reality Thériault continued to descend into utter brutality. His most frequent target was Samuel, Maryse and Jacques's infant son. At Thériault's direction, Jacques would "punish" his child for crying by rolling the naked infant in the snow.

Thériault, who gave himself more liberty to move between the encampment and town than he allowed his followers, arranged for the sons from his first marriage with Francine to visit him in the wilderness. When twelve-year-old Roch-Sylvain and ten-year-old François finally arrived in March 1981, Thériault had his followers throw a celebration to welcome them. During the party, a new follower, a mentally ill young man named Guy Veer, couldn't bear the sound of the now two-year-old Samuel's crying and harshly beat the toddler. But instead of getting the child to a hospital, Thériault responded to the immediate concern—the child wasn't passing urine—by operating on the toddler's genitals with a razor blade, forcing Samuel to drink two ounces of pure ethanol as an anesthetic before the procedure. Samuel died that same night and his mother, Maryse, already traumatized from beatings and depleted from starvation and lack of sleep, didn't even react when she heard the news, but just kept doing her chores. Thériault instructed his followers to tell anyone who asked that Samuel had been trampled by a horse, an excuse that reflects the extent of the damage inflicted on the boy.

The rest of the cult was equally numb. No one spoke a word of blame. So Thériault decided to accuse someone else. In fall 1981, Thériault put Guy Veer on trial. Although everyone else thought Veer was blameless owing to his mental health issues, Thériault convinced them that Veer needed to be castrated as punishment for his crime. He made Veer lie down on a kitchen table, removing the man's testicles with a razor blade. Veer, meanwhile, was a willing participant, even believing Thériault's line that the castration would help with his frequent headaches. But this still didn't satisfy Thériault—or perhaps he sensed that the murder of a child required more retribution than had been exacted. So he began performing mock executions of Guy Veer, a campaign of terror that led the man to run away and confess to the police about Samuel's death. Although he was not mentally competent to fully explain Thériault's true role in the death of the child, Veer gave them enough to arrest the cult leader. On December 19, 1981, Roch Thériault was charged with being criminally responsible for Samuel's death and sentenced to two years in prison.

But even forcible separation couldn't break the hold he had on his followers. They left the wilderness and moved sixteen miles south to a house in New Carlisle just to be near the prison. The ties within the cult were growing more complex, as many of the women now had children with Thériault and several more gave birth during his prison term. At one point in the previous years, he had presided over the marriage of Solange Boilard and fellow cult member Claude Ouelette. Then he made Solange his concubine anyway, and she bore him three children between 1980 and 1986. Still, while Thériault was locked up, she tried to leave, but Gisèle lured her back, promising to let Solange be Thériault's primary wife upon his return. Her decision to stay would end up costing her life.

RITUAL MURDER IN THE WOODS

Thériault finished his prison sentence in February 1984, and within two months he'd convinced his loyalists to abandon city life and return with him to the bush, this time nine hundred miles to the west of Eternal Mountain and a hundred miles northeast of Toronto, in the English-speaking province of Ontario—a wooded property thirteen miles outside of Kinmount, population 500, on the outskirts of an even smaller town called Burnt River, population 250. There, it was not just the wilderness that contributed to their isolation but language as well. All his followers were French Canadian, and only Thériault could speak fluent English. They were more dependent on him than ever.

The move—and the increased remoteness it imposed on the group—inaugurated an era of even greater violence. Thériault imposed many classic cult strategies of total control, such as creating seemingly arbitrary rules that kept the Ant Hill Kids in a state of near-constant fear that they were not living up to his standards. This atmosphere of terror was interrupted by periods of sexual depravity that provided some relief if only because they seemed to set him at ease.

Back in the wilderness, Thériault again observed while his followers built the new housing and other structures the cult required. The Ant Hill Kids were becoming proficient carpenters by this point, and their log cabin dwellings and barns and storage sheds had a rough-hewn solidity that was typical of rural communes from the frontier days. But the size of the group was growing, because the women kept giving birth to more of Thériault's children. ("Roch was always telling us that it had to be that way because he was like Abraham in the Bible," Gabrielle Lavallée later recalled. "He had to have many wives and children to keep his tribe going.") Whenever there wasn't enough food, Thériault made his followers steal from the stores in Kinmount—crimes that ended in January 1985 when they were caught shoplifting.

Yet, for all the remoteness, Thériault still kept up with the outside world enough to be drawn to news of Alex Joseph, the likable Libertarian mayor of Big Water, Utah, who lived openly with eight wives in a form of plural marriage. That seemed to inspire Thériault, who made at least three trips to visit Alex Joseph during the 1980s. As part of the journey, Joseph held a lighthearted ceremony and presented Thériault with a gold crown, naming him king of the Israelites. Upon the cult leader's return to the Canadian wilderness, he took to wearing long robes and his crown, behaving as if he were indeed royalty.

Despite his newfound hubris, he still had to feed his children. He came up with the idea of opening a roadside farm stand, to be manned by his followers, who would sell fresh produce. Surprisingly, the farm stand did well, and he expanded the operation to a bakery dubbed the "Ant Hill Kids," after his hardworking group. He borrowed baking equipment, and for a few years the cult brought in real money.

But even with this conventional success, Thériault was still wrestling with his own demons while inflicting pain and depravity on others. He started drinking again. He took two or more wives to bed with him at a time and had them compete in having orgasms. He staged gladiatorial combats that lasted for hours as he awarded points for blows landed. He threw elaborate group orgies and urinated in the participants' mouths. He whipped people or beat them with the blunt side of an axe. At one point he performed an adult circumcision on Jacques Fiset, or at least sentenced him to one, ordering the group to cut off the tip of Jacques's penis.

Judging from the remorseful letters written by his followers, it's clear that he had everyone terrified of his power, whether it was spiritual or physical, or a combination of both. Solange/Rachel wrote to him ("Good day Moses, my Master"), apologizing for a fit of anger "exercised through you," as she put it, as if the abuse Thériault inflicted happened only when he was possessed by "a powerful spirit," and the poor man was merely a vessel for a heavenly vengeance. "I really believe that what you did doesn't come from you," she wrote, "but from someone much higher." Things were so twisted that she was somehow apologizing to Thériault after he threw a knife at her, shot at her with a rifle, and otherwise inflicted some unspecified harm on "Mamy."

From a reasonable person's perspective, the violence of these unmotivated acts of sadism are hard to fathom. Why did none of his followers leave? Had he worked them so far beyond the point of exhaustion that they no longer had the will to go? Did they fear the immediate threat of bodily harm? Did they still believe Thériault when he said that he was a prophet of God and that if they abandoned him the Lord would strike them dead? Or maybe they could recognize that the pace and scale of violence were increasing and, in their helplessness, they prayed that the day would soon come when he would once again attract the attention of the authorities and they would finally intervene, this time for good.

The death of little Samuel, which the group did register with the local authorities, had certainly captured the attention of social workers, who were now on the lookout for evidence that Thériault was mistreating his children. Their suspicions only grew when, on January 26, 1985, Gabrielle left her infant son out in the cold overnight, considering exposure to the Canadian midwinter preferable to handing the child over to the cult leader for one of his punishments. The baby perished, but despite such obvious fatal mistreatment, the coroner listed the cause of death as sudden infant death syndrome.

This second death caused the social workers to double their efforts. They consulted with the nonprofit group Council on Mind Abuse, which confirmed that Thériault was indeed leading a cult. Thériault now seemed to buckle under the official watch, blowing up at a social worker who came to visit the cult's children that March. By

June, Thériault's drinking increased, and he would tell his loyalists that doomsday had finally arrived. He made fake distress calls to passing aircraft on a ham radio.

Visiting social workers interpreted the passivity of the children as evidence of potential abuse. But no matter how obvious it felt to them, they failed to gather enough tangible proof to warrant removing them en masse—until Maryse finally left the cult in October 1985, taking along her young sons, Jeziel and Thomas. Through their subsequent interviews with her, they learned of sustained and horrific abuse, both sexual and physical. Thériault would commit such heinous acts as suspending children from trees by nailing them by their clothing to the trunks and urging his followers to stone them for punishment, then calling it off just before anyone threw a rock. He would throw infants when he grew angry, or drop them in the lake. When they cried, he crushed their fingers to make them stop. He would hold two babies over the fire at once, forcing his followers to plead for their lives. He never did burn the children, but he was violently unpredictable, and all of them knew that he was capable of extreme cruelty. He made the children watch the adults during their orgies and encouraged his own kids to abuse animals. On December 6, 1985, the social workers, with the help of the Ontario Provincial Police, finally raided the commune and took away all thirteen children.

One might think the authorities finally had enough evidence to return Thériault to prison. Instead, he was able to play upon the sensibilities of the assigned child psychologist, who he believed would, as a fellow French Canadian, share his experience of mistreatment at the hands of the English-speaking majority. The psychologist not only exonerated Thériault but expressed admiration for the work he'd done in bringing the children back to a state of nature. Court documents show that Thériault was painted the victim of a prejudiced society, and it was recommended that the court reunite the children with their extended family.

Fortunately, the judge reprimanded all concerned and on October 27, 1987, ruled that the children should be permanently removed from the cult. But even though Thériault confessed to police in August 1986 that he had hurt his wives and children, Assistant Crown Attorney Alex Smith decided not to prosecute the case against him. Amazingly, Thériault remained a free man, and over the next two years, nine more children would be born to his followers. All of them became wards of the state within days of their birth.

With the children gone, the behavior of the adult Ant Hill Kids deteriorated into a cycle of orgies and violence, and Thériault grew even more dangerously unstable. He used his hold over them—the spiritual and physical terror that he exercised to keep them in his thrall—to perform even more unspeakably sadistic acts. He burned the skin off several cultists with a welding torch. He struck one of his pregnant wives in the stomach so hard that she suffered a miscarriage. He used common pliers to yank teeth out of the mouths of his followers seemingly on a whim. He punched them, stabbed them, shot at them. On different occasions he forced Claude Ouelette to eat human feces and a dead mouse. Part of the horrific cycle seemed to involve Thériault collapsing in tears, seeking forgiveness, and begging God to stop commanding him to commit such depraved acts. His followers, who persisted in their belief that he was either himself divine or speaking on behalf of God, never seemed to learn and forgave him every time.

By 1988 the physical cost of this lifestyle—the lack of sleep, the shortage of food, the constant vigilance and fear of abuse—was beginning to show in the poor health of Thériault's followers. But he showed no mercy. Reacting to some minor transgression that he spotted in Claude Ouelette, Thériault punished him by wrapping a rubber band around his testicles, which proceeded to swell and turn orange. When Ouelette complained, Thériault cut open his scrotum, removed a single testicle, and cauterized the wound with a hot iron.

Solange Boilard, in particular, was betraying the stress. One might think that Thériault would have some sympathy for a person experiencing severe stomach pain. Instead, he once again intensified the torture with an improvised medical procedure, announcing that he was going to operate on her liver. The room was paralyzed into silence, each follower afraid to speak out and attract his attention.

He began by giving Solange an enema consisting of molasses, oil, and water, then cut open her stomach and ripped out her intestines with his bare hands, flooding the abdominal cavity with the digestive acids that eventually caused her death. No one moved to stop him. At one point he decided to perform a crude intubation and forced several of his loyalists to stick a tube down her throat. He gave Gabrielle Lavallée a needle and thread and told her to sew up Solange, who spent the night writhing on the floor until she inevitably passed away the next morning.

It goes without saying that Roch Thériault truly seemed possessed by an uncontrollable madness. After burying Solange, he became convinced that he could raise her from the dead; he forced his disciples to exhume her, cut open her skull, and join him in ejaculating onto her decaying brain. He then cut out some of her ribs and wore them like a necklace, convinced that one day he would, like Adam, give birth to Solange by biblical means. For their own sake as much as for Solange, his followers cremated her corpse, hoping to bring an end to his desecrations at long last.

LIVE BY THE KNIFE

The year 1988 passed with no official reaction from the outside world to Solange's disappearance. Even when social workers noticed her absence and received an unsatisfactory response, police still failed to open a formal investigation. It took Thériault's terrifying mutilation of Gabrielle in the summer of 1989 to finally get the Ontario Provincial Police involved again.

Ever since Gabrielle had joined the group, Thériault seemed to single her out. At one point he pulled out eight of her teeth in an attempt to cure her toothache. But on July 29, 1989, he committed an act of torture that would finally bring his entire cult crashing down around him. Using another method of savage overkill, he attempted to cure a stiffness she had complained about in her finger by impaling her right hand with a hunting knife and pinning it to the kitchen table. He left her there for more than an hour as she bled profusely and tried desperately to avoid passing out from the pain, fearing that Thériault would kill her as he had done to Solange the moment she lost consciousness.

Finally, he freed her by severing her arm between the shoulder and elbow with a box cutter.

Gabrielle survived the mutilation and ran away to a women's shelter, but Jacques Fiset—the man who'd had the tip of his penis removed at Thériault's insistence—located her and convinced her to return. Back at the encampment, on the night of August 11, 1989, Thériault made his followers hold Gabrielle down, then heated a driveshaft with an acetylene torch and applied it to the stump of her arm. Three days later she ran away again, back to the women's shelter, and finally was taken to a hospital.

Police questioned Gabrielle about her injury, but she couldn't bring herself to confess the true nature of Thériault's crime and said he'd had her arm removed after she'd been pinned down in a car accident.

There was enough inconsistency in her account that police decided to go after Thériault. On August 19, they arrived to search the compound, only to find that everyone had vanished. Gabrielle's dismemberment had proven to be the last straw for most of his followers, who finally found the courage to abandon him for good. Thériault was now on the run, joined only by Jacques, Nicole, and Chantal. They managed to evade capture for almost two months while living in a makeshift camouflaged hut right near the compound. He was finally apprehended on October 6, 1989. Only after he was in custody could Gisèle bring herself to confess the full truth regarding Solange's death, enabling authorities to formally charge him with murder.

By December 18, a judge ordered Roch Thériault to be held for trial on second-degree murder charges. Even facing such grave allegations, he was still able to dupe psychiatrists into thinking he was a good person. Court documents from December 1991 reveal that doctors described him as "a very bright, inquisitive, and sensitive man" with "considerable knowledge" of medicine and suggested that Thériault's issues stemmed from being "an extraordinary person in an ordinary world."

But the court believed otherwise, and on January 18, 1993, Thériault was sentenced to ten years to life in prison with the possibility of parole for good behavior. After surviving a decade of torture and mutilation, most of his followers, like Gabrielle and Gisèle, managed to free themselves from his control. Gabrielle received much-needed therapy and began to recognize the dangerous psychological techniques Thériault had used to manipulate his victims. She later published a memoir in French called *L'alliance de la brebis* (*The Alliance of the Sheep*).

Thériault's eldest sons also published a memoir about the nightmare they had lived through. But most of Thériault's victims disappeared into anonymity, seeking refuge with friends and family as they struggled to move on with their lives. Many of them have been given monetary assistance by the Criminal Injuries Compensation Board in Ontario, which offers financial help to the victims of violent crimes.

But some of Thériault's followers never freed themselves from his control. Francine, Chantal, and Nicole rented homes close to his prison to be near him, continuing to visit and having his children. They even opened a bakery together, using the skills they'd honed during the Ant Hill Kids era. The business venture was successful until its patrons learned that the women running the charming little boulangerie were the wives of a deranged murderer who were still hoping to be reunited with him after his release.

And while Thériault was able to charm psychiatrists and keep several of his followers under his thumb, there was one group he wasn't able to sway: his fellow prison inmates. In April 1993, Thériault was transferred to Kingston Penitentiary for his own protection: even among other stone-cold killers, his horrific crimes set him apart as repellent and inhuman.

His charm offensive couldn't save him. On February 23, 2011, prison video shows Thériault's cellmate, Matthew Gerrard MacDonald, stabbing him in the neck with a shiv. MacDonald then walked up to the guards with the murder weapon and said, "That piece of shit is down on the range. Here's the knife. I've sliced him up."

Roch Thériault's life was over, but his case remains deeply disturbing due to the extreme violence he perpetrated and the power he was able to exert, sometimes so mesmerizing that some who escaped had a change of heart and returned to him of their own free will. It is difficult to perceive what kind of an influence he still maintains over the survivors even after his death or if those who followed him—or grew up in the shadow of such brutality—will ever escape the horror he inspired.

MEGALOMANIA

DAVID KORESH AND
THE BRANCH DAVIDIANS

David Koresh, who predicted his own death in a blaze of glory, steered his cult, the Branch Davidians, into a bloody showdown with the federal government of the United States, one that played out daily in the media. For fifty-one days his small band of believers held off the FBI, who'd surrounded their compound outside Waco, Texas. The intensity of the final confrontation on April 19, 1993—with seventy-six Branch Davidians dead, twenty-one of them under the age of sixteen—made "Waco" a buzzword in survivalist circles, convincing prepper groups that if the government was ready to attack its citizens with that much force, then they needed even more firepower to either withstand or overcome such an attack. Within the Mount Carmel compound, Koresh had kept massive stockpiles of weapons that included machine guns and grenades. And he practiced a flagrant brand of polygamy: he considered every woman in the compound his wife, even children as young as eleven. But like so many cult leaders who call themselves messengers of God, he seemed to prefer death rather than giving up his claim to divine authority or admitting that he was merely human. In the final accounting, his own end-days prophecy came true, at least the part about him personally: while his compound burned around him, he died from a gunshot wound to the head—likely from one of his own followers.

ONE HUNDRED AND FIFTY YEARS
OF FAILED PROPHECIES

Beware the passionate believers following a charismatic leader who promises that the end is near. It's a volatile proposal, turning death into a blessing, a fate to be welcomed, maybe even encouraged, because death would not be the end for true believers but the first step toward entering a paradise reserved exclusively for them. This was the mindset for many inside Mount Carmel, the Branch Davidian compound in Axtell, Texas, some twelve miles outside Waco. Even today, after the bloody maelstrom of April 1993, there are still survivors of this faith who consider the prophecies of their leader David Koresh to be divine.

These Branch Davidians living communally in Mount Carmel were a splinter group three times removed from the original Seventh-day Adventists founded in 1863. Those original members believed that the Second Coming of Christ—the "advent" referred to in their name—was imminent. But even this foundational belief was descended from a failed prophecy, one by William Miller, who foretold that Christ would come again on October 22, 1844. Both that movement and day are commemorated as the "Great Disappointment." But in those years before the American Civil War—a period of social reform and religious upheaval—the remnants of the Millerites rallied and revised their beliefs, saying instead that that October day opened a period of "investigative judgment," when the faith and deeds of true believers would be judged by God and Christ.

But nowhere did this new faith, founded on the Great Disappointment, say when this period of probation would end. The true believers already prized divine revelation, which, as a tenet of their faith, they could point to within recent history. They also believed in the imminent arrival of a decisive hour when, through their faith and good efforts on Earth, they would be led into the heavenly tabernacle. Although this day of judgment was not tied to any specific future date in the secular calendar, the sense that it was coming soon endured, a belief that added urgency to their faith.

These two beliefs—in divine messengers of flesh and blood and a pending final judgment—made followers especially susceptible to charismatic leaders like David Koresh. As a rule, Seventh-day Adventists and their splinter groups are receptive to prophets and feel bound by their faith to at least hear someone out if they claim to have been anointed by God. In fact, today, at the entrance to the Mount Carmel compound, which is still legally Branch Davidian property, there are a pair of commemorative walls, each about waist-high and built of individual slabs inscribed with the names of the eighty-two dead (six perishing in the initial raid on February 28, 1993, which began the siege, and seventy-six others on April 19). A headstone set atop one of these walls lists the "Seven Shepherds of the Advent Movement." Those names trace the legacy of revelations starting with Ellen G. White, who founded the Seventh-day Adventist movement during the Civil War, to Vernon Wayne Howell, the birth name of David Koresh and founder of the "Davidian Branch Davidians of the Seventh-day Adventist Movement."

The tragedy of Waco—the most fatal confrontation with the FBI in US history—grew out of 150 years of prophecy, anticipation, and revelation. These are the ingredients that made it possible for a charismatic leader to build his fervent following. Koresh took advantage of appetites already present and part of the faith and, step by step, transformed the remnants of a splinter group prone to infighting into a passionate core awaiting the Apocalypse together.

Just before the raid, about a hundred students of Koresh lived at Mount Carmel. It was a multiracial and multiethnic group: forty-five members were Black, and the cult also included citizens from the United Kingdom, Australia, and Canada. In contemporary accounts of the raid, the group was known as the Branch Davidians, but by 1993 they called themselves "Students of the Seven Seals," as they believed Koresh had been anointed by God to interpret the biblical seven seals found in the book of Revelation. They were so focused on the heaven he promised that they were willing to overlook the fact that he had sex with preteen children. They said nothing when he violently abused the babies who were born of these encounters. They ignored all these despicable acts because they believed that only Koresh could open the seven seals and usher in the End of Days. They turned a blind eye to his outrageous behavior because they concluded those end times were at hand. And for Koresh and eighty-one of his followers, it came in a blaze of fire.

THE UNWANTED CHILD HAS VISIONS

The man who became notorious for holding off the United States government for nearly two months was born on August 17, 1959, in Houston, Texas, to Bonnie Sue Clark (age fifteen) and Bobby Wayne Howell (age nineteen). Before Vernon was even born, Bobby Wayne took off with another woman. Perhaps Bonnie Sue hoped that he would return, because she gave her boy the last two names of his absentee father.

Bonnie Sue was an indifferent parent who went to California when Vernon Wayne was only four years old, leaving him behind with his grandmother, Earline, and a mentally ill aunt, Beverly. When Bonnie Sue returned three years later, she was in the company of Roy Haldeman, a violent alcoholic. These two extremes of parental behavior—abuse and abandonment—were not promising signs for Vernon's future mental fitness. On a psychological level, neglect on this scale in the earliest formative years can leave a child with no healthy model for forming affiliative bonds—and with no pattern for intimacy and no memory of this important primary connection, these children find it difficult to connect as adults. Instead, they manipulate others, exciting affection and then reenacting the abandonment they suffered themselves, as if to punish anyone foolish enough to feel love. And physical abuse, especially in someone already starved for affection, can leave one with lifelong symptoms of post-traumatic stress.

After such childhood trauma, what prompted the adult Vernon to start a cult, convince scores of people that he was God incarnate, and ultimately lead them to a fiery death? Troubling signs were certainly apparent in him from early on. The boy struggled at his Seventh-day Adventist school, the Dallas Junior Academy. He was diagnosed as dyslexic and pulled from regular classes for special instruction. Once again Vernon was being forcibly separated from the opportunity to make meaningful connections with others. It's entirely possible that this kind of exile, repeatedly enacted, was beginning to make him think in some perverse way that he'd been singled out. Perhaps he wanted to exert power over the people from whom he'd been exiled.

One can see why he might contemplate such fantasies of total control. When he did manage to get back with his peers on the playground, he was teased and bullied. Vernon also alleged that a group of older boys tried to rape him when he was eight years old. When his mother came back, she took him to a new home in Dallas over his strenuous protests; there, he joined her church: the Seventh-day Adventists. The youth, who hated being picked on, began to lift weights and grow proud of his body.

The Seventh-day Adventists set great store by the gift of prophecy, and the founder of the religion, Ellen G. White, wrote reams of pages translating her prophetic dreams. This appealed to Vernon, and perhaps because his dyslexia made traditional academic achievement nearly impossible, he dedicated himself to committing to memory vast sections of the Bible—especially the poetic and mysterious prophecies in Revelation, which are filled with symbolism, numbers, and references to other biblical passages and ancient prophets. Vernon was drawn to this dark material, with its allusions to great power unleashed upon a sinful world.

After school, he spent countless hours studying the Bible and praying. Is it possible that if he'd put some of that fervor into his schoolwork, he might have made it past high school? It's difficult to say. Many dyslexics trail their peers in academic studies. But these signs of unusual religious zealotry were accompanied by evidence of troubling neurological and psychological problems. On March 4, 1993, during the compound siege, as part of the negotiations with the FBI, Koresh stated, "People . . . say God talks to them. Well, I had that problem too, you know, but my problem began as a child." He went on to describe an experience he had around 1970 at the age of twelve: "One night . . . I was confronted, praying towards, you know, the northern part of our universe. And there was a very beautiful star—like an explosion in the universe. And this star . . . this is just part of my growing up. And I told my mama about it and she says, well—go to sleep and it will go away."

These childhood experiences may have been ecstatic hallucinations, which can be caused by temporal lobe seizures. In an interview with John Hockenberry for the World Science Festival, the neurologist Oliver Sacks described such hallucinations as "a sudden sense of bliss or rapture and feeling that one has been transported to heaven. . . . There is nearly always some mystical or religious or sexual bent to ecstatic hallucinations."[1] It's only conjecture, but many psychologists, including Sacks, have written about the role of ecstatic seizures in religion. The theory is that the visions of some of the most influential religious figures, from Paul in the Bible to Joan of Arc to early Seventh-day Adventist Ellen G. White, may have possibly been caused by temporal lobe epilepsy. This is not meant to discredit religious experiences in general, or to compare Vernon Wayne to figures in history or in the Bible; it is only meant to offer current speculation connecting the association of temporal lobe epilepsy with claims of mystical experience.

SEX AND REVELATIONS AND ROCK AND ROLL

Vernon claims that he dropped out of high school in the ninth grade during the early 1970s, although Garland High School outside Dallas notes that he finished tenth grade and attended sporadically for two years after that. He tried picking up odd jobs and handyman work. Since he'd been spending time practicing guitar in addition to memorizing the Bible, he also auditioned for local bands. His junior high friend, Larry MacDonald, remembers doing typical teenage activities—messing around with music, drinking beer, getting high. When it came to girls, though, "Vern was kind of a quiet guy, but when he wanted to, he could turn it on as if stepping out on stage. The guy could be magnetic."

With his guitar skills improving, he joined some small acts that brought him more attention. He had his first sexual experiences at eighteen with a teenager named Linda, whom he later referred to as "jailbait"—a prominent theme in Vernon's sexual history. He described her as very beautiful and later told FBI negotiators that she seemed older than her age. But because of his fervent religious beliefs, he felt conflicted about sex and stayed away from her. He must not have gone very far, because Linda tracked him down, telling him first that she was pregnant (even as Vernon had claimed he was sterile) and that she'd had an abortion. The turmoil appeared to rekindle their affection for each other, and Vernon ended up moving in with Linda at her father's house.

His behavior during this time reveals a confused sense of both personal and religious ethics. On the one hand, he had no qualms about abortion or living with a sexual partner outside of marriage. In contrast, for religious reasons, the couple refused to use condoms when they had sex, which verified that Vernon was not in fact sterile, as Linda once again became pregnant. At this point, her father, revealing a similarly confused sense of priorities, kicked Vernon out of his house.

Vernon wondered: Why was Linda's father permitting his teenage daughter to engage in premarital sex, but once she became pregnant, he was forbidden from ever seeing her again? This time, Linda carried the pregnancy to term, but her father refused to let Vernon be a part of the child's life. Little else is known about Linda; her father seems to have successfully erased her connection to the future David Koresh. But one of the reasons Vernon may have had no say in the matter could have been that Linda truly was underage.

It's impossible to tell now whether this young parent at age twenty really did want to be part of a family, but Vernon's response to being refused any kind of visitation rights was to dive deeper into religion, consulting with any pastor he could find about his own interpretations of scripture. His mother, Bonnie Sue, recalled, "He had made a diagram of the big-breasted woman that's talked about in Revelation and in Genesis. It didn't go over very well."

Soon Vernon was taking his permissive interpretations of the Bible in another direction when he took a romantic interest in a pastor's daughter at the Seventh-day Adventist church he was attending in Tyler, Texas. He prayed to God about his attraction to the fifteen-year-old Sandy Berlin and then told her father, L. Hartley Berlin, that when he emerged from prayer, he'd found his Bible open to Isaiah 34:16: "None of these will be missing, not one will lack her mate." Vernon read this as a personal message from God that he should be with the young woman. Or, as he put it: "God told me I could have your daughter."

The pastor did not share this interpretation of holy scripture, and when Vernon persisted, he was ousted from the congregation. This would be the first, but not the last, time that Vernon claimed God had told him he was supposed to be with a particular woman. Despite his initial lack of success, he must have realized that he had hit upon a valuable strategy.

While he was getting this first taste of manipulating Bible readings for his own questionable reasons, Vernon was also indulging his other passion. Around 1980, after being expelled from the church, twenty-one-year-old Vernon moved to LA to pursue a music career. He even recorded a few songs that were eventually released in 1994 when Sandy Berlin, whom he'd kept in touch with and considered his longtime girlfriend, passed the music along to a record company. He wasn't the first musician to react to sexual rejection by cutting an album, or even the first cult leader to try to channel a desperate need for attention into a recording career. But just like Charles Manson, Vernon discovered there was no great demand for a thin-voiced singer who overestimated his own charm.

GOD TELLS VERNON TO MARRY A TEENAGER

Vernon's experience with the Seventh-day Adventists had made him aware of the historical yearning among its believers for a flesh-and-blood prophet. He also knew from the book of Revelation that if the end was at hand—and with the new millennium approaching, many now believed it was—then there must be a prophet here on Earth to speak God's message. Vernon's mother, Bonnie Sue, told him she'd heard of such a person. So, in 1981, he set out for the Branch Davidian compound of Mount Carmel, twelve miles outside Waco, Texas.

The Branch Davidians remained loyal to many of the ideas of Seventh-day Adventism, and, through a series of prophets, could trace their lineage straight back to Ellen G. White. In 1929 a group led by Victor Houteff broke off from the Seventh-day Adventists and became the Davidian Seventh-day Adventists, believing that descendants of the biblical king David would return to rule over Palestine. They established the compound at Mount Carmel in 1935.

Then, in the 1960s, the Davidian Seventh-day Adventists splintered again, the new heirs to Mount Carmel calling themselves the Branch Davidians. Initially led by Benjamin Roden, this group believed the Apocalypse was imminent, and that the biblical events describing its run-up were already happening. They lived with a high level of excitement about the possibility of eternal life, and no small amount of fear over the end of everything on Earth. They were an evangelical denomination attempting to build their congregation to save souls.

When Ben Roden died, his widow, Lois, took over, declaring she'd had a vision—a prophecy about the feminine Holy Spirit. She was in power when Vernon arrived at Mount Carmel. On his first visit in 1981, he heard the sixty-one-year-old Lois preach. Her message resonated with his own ideas, and he quickly became her right-hand man, traveling with her to recruit new followers. Some people thought that they were married, and it is widely believed they were in a relationship.

Vernon told Lois that the Holy Spirit would shine upon them and he would make Lois pregnant with the Chosen One. He cited biblical precedents for children born of older parents: John the Baptist's father was ninety-nine and his mother eighty-eight when he was born; and Abraham's wife, Sarah, was ninety when she gave birth to Isaac. This was the first public glimpse of Vernon's narcissism, imagining himself as selected by God to procreate with a woman in her sixties—the incarnation of the feminine Holy Spirit, the maternal counterpart to God the Father.

In 1983, Lois designated Vernon as her successor, and he began preaching to the group, beginning with a talk at Passover that he called "The Serpent's Root." It was a skill he started honing way back in junior high school—memorizing scripture—and he'd become very adept at weaving his citations and interpretations into speeches on the fly. This capacity of his to talk extemporaneously from and about the Bible deeply impressed other Branch Davidians, who knew that his formal education had ended in early high school. They came to view the ability of this untutored man to recite from and speak about the Holy Scripture for hours on end as a sign that he was truly touched by God. And the Branch Davidians weren't bothered by the age difference between him and Lois. But as Vernon gained their attention, he began working to wrest power away from her, convincing the Davidians that she had lost the "spirit of prophecy" and going so far as to burn a portion of the group's publishing building so that Lois's magazine, *SHEkinah*, which explored the feminine nature of the divine, could no longer be printed.

By 1984, Vernon, who was now certain that he had adherents within the group, abandoned his relationship with Lois, and his next move revealed just how much power he'd actually accumulated. It was also the turning point when he departed from reasonable standards of behavior, having come to believe that his growing status as a prophet gave him control over the faithful. At the age of twenty-four he announced that God had told him to marry fourteen-year-old Rachel Jones, the child of two Branch Davidians.

Fourteen was below the legal age to marry in Texas without parental consent, but Rachel's parents believed in Vernon and his message. And he knew just how to deliver the news, expressing the right number of reservations concerning God's will but stressing his own desire to follow the word of the Lord. Her father dutifully went to the Waco courthouse and signed on the dotted line so his teenage daughter could marry Vernon. Her parents believed in something bigger than common law and their own moral compass: they believed in Vernon Howell.

SPIRITUAL BATTLEGROUND

By befriending Lois Roden and gaining a powerful base within the Branch Davidians, Vernon had made at least one enemy: her son George, who understandably believed that he had a prior claim to lead the Mount Carmel congregation. George was an unstable and often violent man who already felt passed over when his mother took control of the compound after his father's death. But now, upon witnessing Vernon's steady rise in the hearts of the faithful, George focused his frustration on this interloper. In 1985, with his mother growing feeble, George finally asserted his control and ran Vernon and his followers out of the congregation.

Vernon—along with the majority of the Branch Davidians who were now loyal to him, including his teenage wife and her family— moved ninety miles east, to Palestine, Texas. The conditions there were primitive, and most of the congregation lived like homesteaders, in plywood lean-tos through the stifling heat of summer, listening to Vernon's Bible study sessions, which could stretch on for hours.

Not long after the move to Palestine, Vernon took two more spiritual wives, making him officially a polygamist. In 1986 he married Karen Doyle, age fourteen, and Michele Jones, age twelve. Pedophilia is clinically defined as an attraction to prepubescent children; Vernon's declared purpose in having multiple wives was for these girls to bear his children, so he was actually engaging in hebephilia, which is sexual attraction to minors in the earliest stages of puberty. But no matter how one officially labeled it, it was clearly sexual abuse.

In 1986, Lois Roden died, which put George in charge of Mount Carmel. Without his mother to guide him, George flailed in the pulpit, which pushed even more followers to Vernon. Roden rebranded Mount Carmel as "Rodenville," and in a videotaped tour of the property he toted a semiautomatic rifle and betrayed an almost criminal obsession with the rival pastor. "It's basically a holy jihad, Khomeini versus Israel, that's what Vernon Howell has with me," he said.

Meanwhile, Vernon was venturing out on recruiting trips to Seventh-day Adventist communities in California, Canada, England, Australia, and Israel. He was slim and handsome and soft-spoken, with an easy approachability. He established common ground with nearly anyone he met, often by playing up his musical talent, and he seemed to know how to immediately seduce those who showed an interest. As with so many who have narcissistic personality disorder, Vernon understood how to reflect a person's interests and concerns right back to them so they felt seen and relevant. He used his attention like a spotlight, and for as long as he trained his attention on them, his followers felt uniquely favored.

Vernon's core group grew in part because he continued marrying more women. In his second wave of matrimonies, the spouses were slightly older: Robyn Bunds, seventeen; Nicole Gent, sixteen; and Dana Okimoto, twenty. He told these women that he was carrying God's seed and they had been specifically selected to carry His child.

While this cult of personality grew around Vernon, Mount Carmel under George Roden was turning into a ghost town. In a misguided attempt to restore what he saw as his rightful place as the head of the Branch Davidian movement, George challenged Vernon to a bizarre spiritual showdown. George exhumed Anna Hughes, who'd been buried for twenty years in the Mount Carmel community graveyard, and set her up on an altar at the compound's chapel in an open casket draped with the flag of Israel—one of the core symbols of the

Branch Davidians. And in a gesture that showed just how mentally unstable George Roden had become, he challenged Vernon to see which of the two could raise this woman from the dead.

Neither man succeeded, and it's not clear how many even showed up for this macabre contest. Vernon claimed that he hoped to get photographic evidence of the body Roden had dug up. But that pretext fails to explain why he and seven members of his breakaway sect arrived at Mount Carmel after dark with five semiautomatic assault rifles, two rifles, two 12-gauge shotguns, and nearly four hundred rounds of ammunition. Roden apparently had only an Uzi submachine gun, and in the ensuing battle, as he hid behind a tree that was riddled with bullets, Roden suffered a minor injury on his hand and fled the scene.

Following the shootout, Vernon and the followers who'd joined him on the raid were brought up on charges of attempted murder. After a two-week trial in a Waco court, they were all acquitted, with Vernon's case ending in a mistrial. Vernon's fourth wife, Robyn Bunds, later said that seeing him weep during court proceedings touched her heart. It drew her closer to him, the only man she'd ever seen cry.

A few months later, George Roden was arrested on an unrelated attempted murder charge. Now, with no one at the helm of Mount Carmel, the compound's finances fell into disarray. By 1988, Vernon had gotten the money together to pay the back taxes on the land. With this final step, he was now in possession of the entire Mount Carmel compound, and his ascent to the leadership of the Branch Davidians was complete.

George Roden, on the other hand, had been completely dispossessed of both the land and the position that he considered his birthright, and suffered a sharp mental decline as a result. He managed to stay out of jail for a while, but in 1989 he began imagining that Vernon had hired his roommate to murder him and he took action, shooting and killing an innocent man. Roden was found not guilty by reason of insanity and sent to the Big Spring State Hospital, three hundred miles to the west, outside Odessa, Texas. Ironically, George outlived his sworn rival by a number of years but never regained his sanity. In 1997, at sixty years of age, he was found dead of a heart attack on the grounds of Big Springs.

THE NEW LIGHT

Megalomania is not a recognized condition in the official handbook of the American Psychiatric Association, the *Diagnostic and Statistical Manual of Mental Disorders* (*DSM*), but it is mentioned frequently in the literature as if it were a synonym for narcissistic personality disorder, or NPD. In a sense, and in the case of Vernon Howell, the difference between NPD and megalomania is simply one of scale. The narcissist is plagued by a grandiose sense of self-importance, and the megalomaniac not only tells people that he is the son of God but convinces an entire band of believers to go along with this assertion and carry out his commandments. The narcissist requires excessive admiration, and the megalomaniac believes that he is entitled to impregnate all the women in his sect so that they may bear the children of God.

After his group moved back into Mount Carmel, Vernon began to assume all the trappings and entitlements of the prophets who'd preceded him. It's important to note that he was not inventing the tradition of prophets but merely taking advantage of the existing one. There were already strains in Seventh-day Adventism that were receptive to revelations from God. Even in periods when there was no prophet of God on Earth to point to, when nobody was seen to be directly speaking the word of God to His people, they still held the belief that such a person could arrive at any time and deliver the holy word.

This gave the faithful a constant undercurrent of excitement. It was especially true among sects like the Branch Davidians, who could trace their lineage in part by following the "Spirit of Prophecy" all the way back to founder Ellen G. White. While the established central church, governed by a general conference, divisions, and local unions, consider the gift of prophecy one of their "28 Fundamental Beliefs," it mostly viewed the Gift of Prophecy as something reserved for the teachings of Ellen G. White. But the Branch Davidians believed that the gift had passed as a living tradition from Victor Houteff to Benjamin Roden, to Lois Roden, and finally to Vernon Wayne Howell. This tradition of prophets directly connected to God was a central element of their faith. And it drove believers, who now had direct access to God's representative on Earth, to extreme behaviors. They felt inspired to obey the Lord's word made flesh among them, which made it easy to arm themselves and raid a rival compound or stand by prayerfully while their prophet led a Bible study session for fifteen hours straight.

It also seemingly enabled them to stand by and say nothing on the night of August 5, 1989, when Vernon delivered the message that fundamentally changed the nature of their sect. He called his revelation the "New Light," and it was a bombshell. He was in California at the time, in a group house in Pomona belonging to one of the West Coast members of the Davidians. (Victor Houteff had his own revelation in California, so there was a sizable contingent of Davidians who still lived there.) According to one former member who bore witness that evening, Vernon interrupted what had already been four hours of Bible study and looked up at the ceiling as if he were listening to something. Then he promptly annulled all the marriages of his followers.

From that point on, all the women in the group were his to choose from. He was their perfect mate and entitled to 140 wives, he told them, and he had the right—the heavenly duty—to have children with all these women because they needed many in preparation for their rule in paradise. The men—instantly the former husbands of these women—would be given their perfect mates, too, but this would be in heaven, as Eve had been made from Adam, out of their own ribs. Until then, the men would be celibate and give up their earthly wives to Vernon, and they would now be part of God's Army. This was a key moment in the transformation of the Branch Davidians, when they seemed to transform without warning into a sex-crazed cult of personality dedicated to the worship of a mortal man who was nothing more than a master polygamist and statutory rapist.

Prior to setting out this new doctrine, Vernon legally changed his first name to David, after the Bible's King David and also what Victor Houteff referred to when he established the Davidian Seventh-day Adventists in 1934. Vernon added "Koresh" to his name after the Persian king Cyrus, called Koresh in Hebrew and the "anointed one" by the prophet Isaiah.

It's challenging to fathom now why anyone would want to associate themselves with such a person. Here was a man, one who was already preying on underage women, granting himself permission to take any of his female followers as a sexual partner. Yet it's clear from the FBI tapes, made during the long hours of negotiation, that Koresh himself interpreted what he and his followers believed to be convincing evidence—written in the Bible—that this behavior was decreed by God.

One can see now how quickly this revelation would lead to the events of April 19, 1993. But the Davidians were blinded to such a reality. Koresh had convinced them that he was the Lamb of God and that he had the power to open the seven seals described in Revelation. He was the one who would sit upon the throne in the new kingdom surrounded by the twenty-four elders as described in Revelation 4:4. Koresh, apparently, could be mesmerizing when it came to the Bible; he'd convinced the Branch Davidians that those twenty-four elders would all be his children. In fact, they were the children that it was now his duty to bring into this world—not just with one of his wives, but with any of the women within their group as decreed by God.

Koresh's fourth wife, Robyn Bunds, who'd already borne him a son, was at the Pomona house when he revealed his "New Light" teaching. In fact, her parents were the legal owners of the property. After she'd left the group, Robyn said that in the early days she'd been entranced by the notion that one of Koresh's wives would give birth to the Messiah. "It was like a beauty contest. All of us battling against each other to be this woman that God thinks is the greatest. It was like a fairy tale," Bunds later told reporters at the *Waco Tribune-Herald*. "Back then I was still dreamy-eyed. I wasn't into reality."

The new edict created much tension. Koresh chastised the male followers who were reluctant to give up their wives. He separated the men and women so that they would come together only during Bible study, all under his watchful eye. To prove his point, he once told a woman to lift her skirt and show the men her underwear. He then asked if any of them felt aroused. They all raised their hands. Koresh said that proved his point: inevitably men would want to have sex with women, and that was why they had to be kept apart.

But Robyn Bunds had never liked sharing Koresh with other women, and between having her son and maturing on her own she realized the entire situation was ridiculous. When Koresh started sleeping with Robyn's own mother, that was the final straw, and she left the Branch Davidians. In retaliation, Koresh kidnapped their son, hoping to take him back to the Waco compound. When law enforcement insisted he return the boy, Koresh dropped his son off at the local police station and left California.

Even after leaving the cult, Robyn Bunds felt Koresh hadn't always been so bad until his revelation. She noted, "He has totally changed. He was really nice. He was humble. He was very well mannered. Over the years, though, he's lost a lot of those qualities. He's become this obnoxious, foul-mouthed, pushy person because of the power he has over these people."

BEWARE THE WHORE OF BABYLON

The Harvard neurologist Evan Murray has looked at the symptoms of psychosis in historical religious figures. It's a provocative, deadpan discussion of the potential psychotic disorders of such luminaries as Abraham, Moses, Jesus, and Saint Paul. In a summary discussion of the limits of his analysis, he makes an interesting side observation: those with psychosis and psychopathology cannot always be separated from the sane based on a failure to communicate or function in society. He argues that David Koresh—who clearly suffered from paranoid, grandiose, messianic delusions, coupled with behavior on the psychotic spectrum—still was able to successfully attract adherents and form intense social bonds. In simpler terms, Koresh's brand of madness didn't keep people from liking him and enjoying his company.

There is a possibility that Koresh, who often explained that he received his insights on the Bible from his visions, may not have been fabricating this explanation and that he suffered from temporal lobe seizures associated with Geschwind syndrome. This disorder is typified by such traits as excessive talking, compulsive writing, hyper-religiosity or morality, and an enhanced mental life in general. And these symptoms slowly increase over time. This description would fit Koresh: he could lead Bible study sessions that would last for nineteen hours and write his prophecies for days at a stretch. And while the syndrome often goes along with depressed sexual desire, in some cases it can be connected with hypersexuality, which would seem to be the case with Koresh.

He once told a follower about a vision from 1985, during a visit to Israel: "While I was standing on Mount Zion, I met up with these angels, these presences made of pure light. They were warriors surrounding the Merkabah, the heavenly throne, riding on fiery horses, armed with flaming swords. They only allow those who can reveal the Seals into the higher realm, into those innumerable worlds that exist alongside our own." Koresh explained that he had been taken up by the angels to meet God and given the key to the scriptures. "I knew then it was my destiny to unlock the Seals and open the way for our community," he said.

Oliver Sacks, the neurologist and author, wrote of the temporal lobe seizures: "Such epileptic hallucinations bear a considerable resemblance to the command hallucinations of psychosis, even though the epileptic patient may have no psychiatric history. It takes a strong and skeptical person to resist such hallucinations and to refuse them either credence or obedience, especially if they have a revelatory or epiphanic quality, and seem to point to a special and perhaps exalted destiny."[2] It's rather clear that David Koresh was not that strong and skeptical. His own neediness, after a childhood of neglect and abuse, made these visions impossible to resist.

When these alleged visions combined with what seems to have been a particularly virulent form of narcissistic personality disorder that gave Koresh the tools to exploit his believers and the callousness to ignore the consequences of his actions, all the elements of the coming disaster fell into place. But to create a tragedy on the scale of Waco, it took several other intensifying factors.

Koresh was always looking for signs of the coming apocalypse. He was especially taken by the far-right conspiracy theories referred to as the "New World Order," which theorized that a cabal of super-capitalists, cosmopolitan elites, and shadowy figures wanted to dissolve nation-states and attempt to take away freedoms, establishing a rule based on their principles.

These theories gained a foothold among fundamentalists and members of the militia movement, and it led to growing distrust of government in general. Literature about the New World Order could be found at gun shows, and in the late 1980s and early '90s it began to attract a following among conspiracy theorists who thought they could spot these operations in all sorts of fringe phenomena (UFOs, the lost continent of Atlantis) and crackpot scenarios (Kennedy assassination theories, satanic rituals). This was catnip to David Koresh, who conceived the notion that he and the other Branch Davidians were supposed to go to Israel to fight on its behalf against the United Nations.

But in 1991, once the United States went to war in the Persian Gulf, Koresh shifted to the belief that the US government was the Babylon that was spoken about in Revelation ("Babylon the Great, the Mother of Harlots and Abominations of the Earth"). This was not a leap for many Seventh-day Adventists. Keeping with Ellen G. White's teachings in *The Great Controversy*, written in 1858, they already believed that Revelation predicted a false church that had power over the kings of the Earth. Koresh was merely updating her prophecy to the present day.

Soon after he started toying with these ideas, he became convinced that there would be a final clash. And in this coming apocalypse, Koresh—as the one who could open the seven seals, as the scripture revealed—would play a leading role. He told the Branch Davidians that this great battle would take place exactly where God had put them: there in Texas. The Branch Davidians began to stockpile supplies, including food, weapons, ammunition, and propane, preparing for war as a religious obligation. They were energized by Koresh's Bible study sessions. This is why Revelation, with its vivid poetic imagery, is so central to self-anointed prophets like Koresh: the Apocalypse is always at hand, eternal life is at stake, and all its evocative imagery is open to interpretation.

Their new focus gave the Branch Davidians a justification to attend gun shows. In fact, they entered the side business of buying and selling weapons, modifying them for profit and their own personal stockpile. They formed an on-site gun shop, the Mag Bag, in 1990, allowing them to traffic in weapons and parts. Koresh and followers Paul Fatta and Michael Schroeder traveled to gun shows all over Texas and used their now-profitable business venture to raise money in support of the Branch Davidians. It was both a revenue stream and a wise course for the spiritual warriors, who believed the attack of Babylon was imminent. Koresh adopted the view, common in New World Order types, that the government was getting ready to confiscate citizens' guns. He told his followers that they needed to be armed to protect themselves from authoritarian rule.

This is where paranoid prophecies became self-fulfilling: In the summer of 1992, a UPS driver had a damaged package for delivery to the Mount Carmel compound. Inside the box were firearms and empty grenade casings, which, in the right hands, could be converted into live ordnance. He followed company policy and reported this potentially illegal weapons trafficking to the authorities.

The intel about the growing arsenal marked the beginning of the end for David Koresh and the Branch Davidians. Very soon the pressure on them began to mount. In January 1993 the Bureau of Alcohol, Tobacco and Firearms (ATF), the government agency in charge of policing the illegal use and trafficking of weapons, among other duties, sent undercover agents to live next door to Mount Carmel. One survivor of the Waco raid later claimed that Koresh knew from the start that their new neighbors were Feds. He even welcomed them at Bible study. Koresh's attitude was that maybe these guys were in the area because of their job, but his message from God might reach them. He actually thought he could convert the agents—a mindset that proved to be fatal overconfidence.

THE PROPHET CARRIES A GLOCK

The new interest from the ATF seemed to confirm the already strong suspicions in the group that they were regarded as outsiders and that the government was an enemy of their cause, and Koresh fed this narrative. Now events seemed to confirm his prophecy that the final battle was at hand, that Babylon, in the form of the US government, was ready to attack.

After the New Light revelation, some reasonable followers like Robyn Bunds had fled the Branch Davidians for saner places, but on the day of the ATF raid—February 28, 1993—there were, by some estimates, nearly a hundred Branch Davidians on the grounds at Mount Carmel, all prepared for confrontation. This went beyond just viewing violent war movies as part of their training, as Koresh had mandated in 1990.

Koresh's twenty top lieutenants and personal bodyguards—known as the "Mighty Men," after the biblical warriors who protected King David—were well versed in the use of AK-47s and M16s. The Mighty Men were, in turn, responsible for training other cult members, including children, how to shoot to kill. The highest-ranking Mighty Men were Douglas Wayne Martin, forty-two, and Steve Schneider, forty-eight. Martin was Koresh's most trusted advisor and one of the most surprising members of his cult. He and his wife, Sheila, had seven children, a few of them adults, one severely disabled. At least four lived with their parents at Mount Carmel. Martin was college educated, a Harvard-trained lawyer who'd previously taught at North Carolina Central University in Durham.

While living a rugged life with no running water out at Mount Carmel, Martin practiced law in town, turning all his earnings over to Koresh. He was well-known to county judges and even close friends with a Waco City councilman, who spoke of him as a congenial lunch mate. A conscientious lawyer, Martin actually managed to send money out of the compound during the standoff with the FBI in order to compensate clients he could no longer represent. According to the *Washington Post*, "Gary Coker, a Waco lawyer who had represented members of the cult, also spoke to Martin before the FBI cut the telephone lines. He said Martin seemed 'almost calm' and described him as a kind man and particularly devoted father."[3]

Steve Schneider, on the other hand, was quite the opposite—a top lieutenant with a temper who could be possessed by intense rage at unpredictable moments. His wife was one of the first women Koresh claimed after his 1989 New Light revelation, becoming Judy Schneider Koresh. As angry as her husband was about the dissolution of his marriage, he remained fiercely loyal to Koresh. He told federal negotiators that his leader had "powers that we are not aware of, and for us to even challenge him, we're making a big mistake." Schneider had some college education and hoped to become a minister before he fell in with David Koresh. He managed one of the group's businesses, the music production outfit Messiah Cyrus Productions, which recorded Koresh's music, including songs like "Mad Man in Waco," and released it in the local community.

Two of the Mighty Men were also musicians: Michael Schroeder and David Thibodeau, both drummers. Steve Schneider had met

Schroeder and his wife, Kathy, in the late 1980s and told them about David Koresh. Soon, Michael and Kathy Schroeder drove cross-country for a visit to hear Koresh preach and liked the experience. In 1989 they loaded their children into a beat-up van and took off for Mount Carmel to join the group. Michael's mother said the van was so run-down, she didn't know if they'd make it. Somehow she knew she'd never see her son again.

Michael and Kathy were seekers, and Koresh's message spoke to them, even though the rules he imposed were harsh. Kathy was pregnant at the time, but they were still separated upon arrival, under the New Light doctrine. Koresh had boots on the ground in Australia and California and used his followers' homes as impromptu operating bases as needed. He sent Michael to one of those spots in California to help recruit more "soldiers for God," and Michael didn't meet his newborn son until six months after his birth. Once Michael returned to Texas, he frequently slept at an auto shop where he worked. Like other husbands, he primarily saw his wife during Bible study, under the watchful eyes of Koresh.

Koresh didn't want the Branch Davidian men to spend time with their children. The parent-child bond was a direct threat to his control. But Kathy arranged secret visits so Michael could see his son. Like Martin and Schneider, many Davidians had jobs in the community and turned their wages over to Koresh, although gun dealing proved to be their most profitable enterprise.

David Koresh was starting to feel pressure coming from the outside world. He knew his views and his practices, particularly polygamy and having sex with children as young as eleven, were considered criminal activity. In February 1992, a full year before the ATF raid, the Texas Department of Health and Human Services and two sheriff's deputies paid the Mount Carmel compound a visit to investigate claims arising from a custody battle—namely, that Koresh was sexually abusing young girls. The investigation, which yielded nothing because no one in the group would speak a word against him, amplified Koresh's belief that he would be martyred for his cause. But he wasn't planning to go down without a fight: he was prepared for armed conflict and always kept a Glock near him, even when he slept.

THE MIGHTY MEN TAKE ARMS

That same year a couple of the Mighty Men were said to have traveled to California to pick up a machine-gun conversion kit from the Bundses' Pomona house. The Bundses, who found the kit after the Branch Davidians cleared out, saved it in the garage in case David Koresh ever came back for it. Even though Robyn and her mother had left the group, they couldn't entirely escape Koresh's hold. In a way, it seemed that they were still protecting him. If they'd really cut all ties, they might have just gotten rid of the illegal weapon, but Koresh had enough power over the family that they quietly stored his property.

The ATF's 1993 raid warrant states that when the UPS driver went to Mount Carmel to deliver packages, "he saw several manned observation posts and believed that the observers were armed." One of their employees reported talking to a young boy around eight years old. "The child said that he could not wait to grow up and be a man. When Joyce Sparks of Child Protective Services asked him why he was in such a hurry to grow up, he replied that when he grew up he would get a 'long gun' just like all the other men there."

Although the principal motivation for the ATF's raid of Mount Carmel was the suspected possession of illegal weapons, the warrant cites multiple sources alleging sexual abuse. Some of the information was firsthand, based on suspicious behavior observed the year before and prompted by a visit stemming from Robyn Bunds, who'd told police that Koresh "has regular sexual relations with young girls there. The girls' ages are from 11 years old to adulthood." At times Koresh seemed unabashedly proud of his crimes. Marc Breault, a former Branch Davidian who testified against Koresh in a custody battle, said he was once asked by Koresh who he thought the favorite wife really was. Breault guessed Koresh's first and only legal wife,

Rachel. But Koresh told him that it was Rachel's sister. "Can you believe it, Marc?" he said. "She's been with me since she was 12 years old!"

One of the ATF's undercover agents was Robert Rodriguez, who began visiting the group ostensibly to hear Koresh's teachings, but really trying to get more information on the group's armory. David Thibodeau, who survived the initial raid and the final confrontation, later claimed that Koresh knew Rodriguez was undercover from the start and still welcomed him onto the land and into Bible study sessions. It didn't take divine prophecy to see they were being watched; the compound was under surveillance by helicopter, and the frequent flights tipped Koresh off.

During the weeks that Rodriguez spent at the compound, he befriended the leader. In conversations with the FBI during the siege, Koresh said that Rodriguez was a good guy and that he loved him. Despite such closeness, Rodriguez couldn't confirm that the Branch Davidians actually had illegal weapons. But he had verified that the Mount Carmel complex nevertheless had a substantial arsenal, as well as the ability to convert semiautomatic weapons to automatic. That meant that the ATF had probable cause for a search. Army documents later revealed suspicions that the ATF may have knowingly lied in its application for a warrant, claiming that there was an on-site meth lab, one of the few circumstances that would have allowed them to get additional tactical training for the raid from the military.

On February 25, 1993, the United States District Court for the Western District of Texas issued warrants for the arrest of David Koresh and a search of the compound. Agents were authorized to seek out heavy artillery as well as homemade grenades and bomb-making materials, along with assault rifles and the items needed to convert them to be fully automatic.

In a lawsuit filed after the April siege by surviving Branch Davidians, a Texas Ranger testified that "about 300 assault rifles and pistols were found in the charred remains of the Branch Davidian compound hours after the structure burned to the ground"—a substantial weapons cache. The expectation of heavily armed resistance was a major factor in what happened during the ATF raid.

On February 28, the ATF prepared to serve a "no-knock warrant" to Mount Carmel, whereby agents didn't have to announce themselves before sweeping in to execute their search, giving them the element of surprise. But in the preceding days, more than a hundred agents and support staff flooded into Waco to prepare for the compound search, filling local motels. The press picked up on the large federal presence and prepared their own coverage teams. And on the morning of the raid, a reporter from KWTX-TV got lost on the way to Mount Carmel and asked a local postman for assistance. It turned out the postman knew somebody who lived on the compound: his brother-in-law, David Koresh.

Undercover agent Robert Rodriguez was at the compound, studying, when Koresh got the heads-up call and Rodriguez realized his cover was blown. Yet there was no friction between the men. Koresh wasn't panicked; he was happy to let Rodriguez leave. In some ways Koresh was pleased with the news: the confrontation he'd predicted was about to happen.

The Mighty Men and others in the Branch Davidians' fighting force sprang into action, donning the black armored clothing that had been sewn by their former wives. A federal affidavit later claimed that Douglas Wayne Martin wore a necklace of hand grenades. The women and children went into hiding, although at least one woman, a former police officer, took part in the firefight. She was one of the six Branch Davidians who died that morning.

Rodriguez notified the ATF that the Branch Davidians knew what was coming. The federal agents' plan was predicated on a surprise visit; however, instead of postponing the operation, ATF leadership determined that they would forge ahead with the raid. They wanted to rush in, hopeful that the Branch Davidians wouldn't have time to get ready—an incredibly foolish decision in retrospect. The Davidians were fortified by a sizable compound. There were dozens of vehicles on-site, including buses. The buildings were arranged in a tight rectangular formation with a large pool along the back left side and included tactically significant structures like a water tower and a watchtower. There were group living quarters, Koresh's living quarters, a gym used for storage, and multiple concrete bunkers. Breaching the Mount Carmel compound wouldn't be a simple task.

At 9:30 a.m. the ATF tried to execute their warrants. One hundred agents climbed aboard two cattle trailers and hid under large tarps. There were helicopters overhead with gunmen. But communication among the ATF crew was shoddy. Some had been fully briefed on the number of weapons in the compound, while others had no clue. There's still a debate that's impossible to settle about which side fired the first shot, but the massive gun battle that followed lasted over two hours. Survivor Kathy Schroeder said in an interview, "I saw the cattle trucks pull up out front and the men coming out. They're all in black and they have guns. Then I heard shots and I ducked down." Kathy and her kids pulled everything out from under the bed in order to hide. Bullets pierced the water jugs in the room, and the liquid drained on the floor. The kids were crying, but the shooting lasted so long that one of them actually fell asleep under the bed.

During the firefight, Koresh called 911 and announced, "This is David Koresh. We're being shot all up out here." But the call that seemed to start as a legitimate emergency call ended with what FBI negotiators came to call "Bible babble," with Koresh talking about the seven seals. In between, he recounted the casualties on his side with a remarkable lack of emotion. Here was a man—a father many times over—who seemed to project neither empathy nor remorse. Then, suddenly, he got excited: "I've been teaching this for four years! We knew you were coming and everything!" He wasn't talking about the fact that he'd been tipped off; he was boasting about his own ability to read the signs in Revelation, which had informed him years earlier that the government was targeting him. He wanted everyone to know that he'd not only predicted this event, and preached about it to his followers, but that he'd even taken steps to ensure that the Branch Davidians were prepared for the confrontation he had foretold.

One of the sources of fascination in diving deeply into the lives of cult leaders is that they represent an unthinkable extreme of human behavior. Maybe, when we're looking at their childhoods, we can see the forces that shaped them into monsters, and it's possible to feel pity: Charles Manson watching the mother he loved hauled away by the police; Adolfo de Jesús Constanzo living in shame, trying to reserve a small corner of order in a home filled with squalor; and Vernon Wayne Howell, now David Koresh, abandoned, beaten, dyslexic, plagued by visions, trying to find something in life that would help him fit in.

But here we have a different moment, no less typical in the lives of cult leaders—a critical turning point when there is still a choice, even with fate closing in, to avoid the bloodshed and turn away from a disaster of their own making. But over and over, the cult leaders see what's coming and they cannot or will not change course. This is the moment when they are at their darkest and most extreme, when they move ahead with violence, overriding even their own survival instinct, because this is who they are.

For cult leaders like David Koresh, there seemed to be no turning back. From that point on, he only grew increasingly committed to the destiny he had set in motion, coming alive, making impulsive decisions, ignoring the danger, inspiring his followers, writing manically in his book of prophecies. He knew that death was coming for him and everyone else, but it didn't matter to him as much as all the mayhem and violence arriving exactly as he'd concluded, for the world to see.

Koresh, as a sexual predator of minors and preteens, didn't really need prophetic vision to guess that the government would come after him one day. But his followers had stopped thinking of him in those terms long before that. Instead, the raid and the subsequent siege only increased their loyalty. They now believed that Koresh had been right all along; here was the war he'd spoken of, and that would mean he'd been correct about everything. And if the Apocalypse was looming right outside the compound, they clearly didn't want to leave his side and give up eternal life. This was a case of cognitive dissonance in action: the Branch Davidians reacted to the clear evidence stacked against them—their leader was a violent man, a polygamist, and a pedophile; the government had them surrounded; this could not end well—and turned that into evidence of the opposite. They felt that they were right to believe heaven was at hand and that David Koresh was the messenger foretold in Revelation.

But the US government wasn't faring much better. The ATF had been caught off guard by the strength of the resistance they encountered—quite a blunder, since their warrant authorized them to look for a large cache of weapons and explosives. The ATF's actions that day showed they were both poorly prepared and grossly over-confident. The gunfight lasted more than two hours, and by the end of it the government was running out of ammunition—an indication that they had underestimated the risk involved, evidence of their own lack of fire discipline, or both. Nor had they thought to arrive with emergency medical services. The hasty decision to rush in when they knew they were expected; the poor communication within their own forces; the insufficient coordination among law enforcement agencies; the limited ammunition; and the lack of on-site emergency services all added up to a nightmare for the ATF. Within hours the FBI took over the operation.

The FBI brokered a successful cease-fire, and the ATF agents were able to go in and clear out their casualties. The local police encouraged David Koresh to accept medical assistance for the Branch Davidians, but Koresh said none of them were hurt seriously enough and they didn't want any help. He didn't reveal that the Branch Davidians had already lost six people and he himself was wounded in his left wrist and hip. One of his injured followers later told negotiators via phone that she didn't want to come out for treatment; she'd rather die standing up for their cause.

ALL EYES ON WACO

The standoff that would go on for fifty-one days had begun. The negotiations were primarily between leading Branch Davidians Koresh, Martin, and Schroeder; Lieutenant Larry Lynch of the McLennan County Sheriff's Office; and the ATF's Jim Cavanaugh. Meanwhile, the FBI set up operations and strategized. Koresh was allowed to broadcast his religious teachings on a Dallas radio station and also do a phone interview with CNN. Twenty-four-hour cable news was still a relatively new medium in 1993. Still, more than 50 million households had cable TV access, compared to fewer than 20 million a decade before. Almost overnight the Branch Davidians had gone from fringe group to lead item on news broadcasts all over the world. For David Koresh, this was either a dream or possibly a temporal lobe seizure come true.

On March 1, the day after the raid, President Bill Clinton was updated. He agreed with FBI director William Sessions's approach: string out the negotiations with Koresh in the hope of arriving at a peaceful solution. As the day dragged on, ten children were sent out of the compound, along with a small number of adults, including two elderly women. Kathy Schroeder later told the *Tampa Bay Times*, "None of the children really wanted to leave. But David said children under the age of 12 are not accountable. It was David's decision for them to leave. It was different for me. Even if we had died, we would all die and be eternally together. I thought, 'I'm sending my kids out to Babylon,' to a world full of evil."[4]

Hours after the cease-fire began, Kathy Schroeder heard shots fired out in a field. She had a premonition that it was her husband, Michael, being killed by the FBI while trying to return to the compound. She was right: his body would lie on the ground between the two sides for four days before it was removed.

By 5:00 p.m. local time on March 1, the FBI had full command of the situation. David Koresh, meanwhile, had grown agitated that armored vehicles had taken up closer tactical positions and that the compound's phone lines were disabled except for the open line to the negotiators.

The FBI, mindful of the Jonestown massacre fifteen years earlier, wanted assurances that Koresh and his group weren't planning a mass suicide, especially with so many children still inside the compound. He assured them that the Branch Davidians had nothing of the sort in mind. Talks continued into the early hours of March 3, when Koresh promised to surrender after a tape of his religious teachings was broadcast on national television. Again, his priorities did not include the safety of the Branch Davidians; his sole concern was exposure for his ideas.

At 1:30 p.m., his tape was aired nationally on the Christian Broadcasting Network. However, by 6:00 p.m., Koresh had reneged on the FBI deal, saying God had told him to stay put. This put the Feds in a tough spot. They were well versed in dealing with hostage negotiations, but this situation was unique: nobody had a gun to anyone's head. These hostages were captive to an ideology. And not only that, the Branch Davidians believed they had more to fear from the FBI than from David Koresh. If everything went up in flames, as Koresh had been preaching for years, they were guaranteed eternal life. But if they left the compound, they'd be thrown into the Lake of Fire with other nonbelievers—a big disincentive to come out.

David Koresh seemed to enjoy his new audience. And the FBI got a firsthand experience of his stamina with interpreting the Bible. March 3 passed with relentless religious instruction. Negotiators learned how he'd been anointed to unlock the seven seals. According to survivors, Koresh also told his followers that they were now in the midst of the fifth seal, when they would be martyred in a moment of great persecution. They were ready to die and then wait for the other martyrs before living forever in the new kingdom to be ushered in after the full cycle of seals was complete.

Koresh also described his gunshot wounds, saying, "I've tried to sit up, which I can't do, and also my hip . . . being shot's a dramatic thing. It shocks the body and plus . . . it cracked or went through or did something at the top part of my hip bone because it hit me from the side in my belly, headed over and hit the hip and then went around and out kind of like towards my rear."[5]

None of this slowed him down, though. On March 4, he spent nearly eight hours on the phone with negotiators. On the FBI side, tensions were running high. Tear gas was floated as an option, but that had never been deployed on children before, especially in the large quantities being proposed.

On March 5, nine-year-old Heather Jones left the compound with a note from her mother pinned to her jacket. It said that once the children had left the compound, the adults would die. The message confirmed that the biggest worry for the FBI was also part of the conversation within the compound. Koresh and Schneider repeatedly denied to the government that the group had plans for mass suicide, but the FBI didn't trust them, especially since some of those who'd left the cult before the standoff reported that Koresh constantly preached about how they'd all have to die for him. And the recounting to psychologists from the released children led them to believe mass suicide was possible.

This likelihood seemed like a disaster in the making. There were still dozens of children behind the compound walls. The FBI already knew that the Branch Davidians had plenty of weapons and ammunition, as well as enough food to last about a year. From March 6 to 8, conversation went nowhere. The FBI delivered milk for the children, and Koresh sent out a videotape of children saying they were happy, pointing out a number of his own children, including his oldest son, eight-year-old Cyrus, by his first teenage wife, Rachel.

On March 9, the FBI cut the power to Mount Carmel and continued to rearrange the armored vehicles into more threatening positions around the compound. This enraged Koresh and Schneider, who didn't know that all the movement was a sign of fraying tensions between FBI negotiators and the tactical team. On the FBI side, the sight of Mighty Men putting plywood covers over the compound windows with cutouts for gun barrels was not perceived as a good-faith measure either. Koresh refused to talk until power was restored, a cat-and-mouse game that was a consistent feature of negotiations throughout the siege.

March 10 and 11 came and went with little progress. President Clinton's attorney general, Janet Reno, the first woman to serve in that position, was sworn in on March 12 and brought up to speed on the situation. That same day Kathy Schroeder exited the compound, once again reassuring the FBI that there were no plans for mass suicide. Years later she told Susan Aschoff of the *Tampa Bay Times* that the reason she'd left was that she'd been caught smoking. Koresh said her "reckless disregard for God's law was going to cause the whole group to be held back."[6]

The FBI began using torture techniques to force a surrender. The power was deliberately cut during a cold snap. They pointed bright lights inside the compound to interrupt sleep and played music at a high volume, which included the screams of dying rabbits. Two more men left the compound, with another seven adults to follow in the days ahead. One of them, Rita Riddle, said that she'd seen federal forces flipping the bird from their tanks and mooning the Branch Davidians. That behavior made the group feel even more righteous. Who were these crude men who had no respect for God?

One can only speculate what it felt like inside the compound. Were the followers panicked? Glorying in the heavenly fate they believed awaited them? Were the children upset? The FBI teams were certainly showing signs of stress. The negotiators still thought a peaceful resolution was possible, but more aggressive tactical options were gaining ground. On March 23 another adult, British national Livingstone Fagan, left the compound and was arrested. In an interview with Cole Moreton of the *Telegraph* twenty years after the siege, Fagan, still a believer, admitted, "I didn't want to go, but I was asked to do so by David. In the event that we were all killed, there needed to be some voices outside to tell the story from our point of view."[7]

From March 29 to 31 a representative from Attorney General Janet Reno met with FBI officials about the infighting among the Feds.

And Koresh was allowed to talk to his lawyers for the first time. Soon after, he agreed that his followers would all come out following Passover, one of the most important holidays to the Branch Davidians. On April 4, in conversation with his lawyers, he repeated this pledge. They observed Passover on the fifth . . . but by the seventh Koresh was again refusing to name an exit date. The idea of tear gas was again now in play, the multiple instances of Koresh's broken promises contributing to the situation.

The saga of the standoff in Waco is remarkable in the history of cults because there is so much raw data publicly available. Koresh does not sound like a brilliant biblical interpreter so much as a man with command of a few images supplemented with claims of prophetic visions that are actually more convincing than his analysis of the scriptures. Here's an example of one of those conversations, edited for length and clarity:[8]

> **Koresh:** *And so there's only one acid test for anybody that claims to be enlightened in regard to the knowledge of God—show me the Seals— and if they can't then they have to wait until somebody can.*
>
> **FBI:** *David? How did you get to the point where you can interpret the Seals?*
>
> **Koresh:** *Well—in 1985 I was in Israel. And there was these Russian cosmonauts that were—the reason I'm telling you about this is cause we got two witnesses to this. The Russian cosmonauts gave the report that they saw seven angelic beings flying towards earth with the wings the size of a jumbo jet. Okay. So what happened was in 1985 when I was in Israel I met up with those people. Seriously.*
>
> **FBI:** *You met up with who? The two cosmonauts?*
>
> **Koresh:** *No. No. No. See—the Russian cosmonauts were in their space station.*
>
> **FBI:** *Right.*
>
> **Koresh:** *And they radioed down to their headquarters. They were terrified.*
>
> **FBI:** *Right. I can understand.*
>
> **Koresh:** *That they saw seven angelic beings moving towards the earth.*

FBI: *Okay. And you met these seven angelic beings.*

Koresh: *Exactly.*

FBI: *Where?*

Koresh: *In Israel.*

FBI: *Yeah. But where in Israel?*

Koresh: *On Mount Zion.*

FBI: *Oh. Okay.*

Koresh: *Okay. Let me tell you something. It's awesome. Angels don't really have wings. But what they have is called a Merkhavah.*

FBI: *A what?*

Koresh: *A Merkhavah.*

FBI: *Which is?*

Koresh: *It's a—it's a spaceship.*

FBI: *A spaceship?*

Koresh: *It's a vehicle. It—it travels by light. The refraction of light—*

FBI: *Oh, okay.*

Koresh: *You know how the rainbow and all that?*

On April 9, Good Friday and forty-one days into the standoff, David Koresh sent four letters to the FBI. One said, "The heavens are calling you to judgment." So of course the FBI enlisted psychological experts to analyze the evidence. Their verdict: they considered Koresh to be in a highly paranoid state and possibly psychotic. They also agreed that he had no intention of coming out. It's important to remember that Koresh was still healing from a serious gunshot wound. Even if the bullet had exited his body, he continued to run the risk of infection and was likely experiencing significant pain up until the end.

THE FLAMES AWAIT

Easter Sunday passed on April 11 with no surrender. Passover ended on April 13 with a similar lack of progress. But on April 14, David Koresh relayed the news that he was furiously writing his interpretation of the seven seals in Revelation. He promised that when the manuscript was complete, he would come out. Two days later he informed the FBI that he had gotten as far as the first seal, which gave them a rough estimate of how long they'd have to wait: twelve more days at his current pace. On the fiftieth day of the standoff, the Branch Davidians climbed a tower that the FBI had told them was off-limits because it could be used as a shooting turret. They held up their children for the Feds to see. It was a tense moment: the government didn't know if they were asking for mercy on the children or using them as human shields to cover an aggressive first move in the hostilities. The Davidians, who understood that they were always under surveillance, held up a sign that read: "The Flames Await. Isaiah 13."

An hour before sunrise the next day, April 19, the assigned FBI negotiator told the Branch Davidians over a loudspeaker that the standoff was coming to an end: tear gas was about to be deployed and they were all under arrest. At 6:01 a.m., the FBI used two combat engineering vehicles to knock holes high in the wooden building and inserted tear gas into the compound through spray nozzles attached to a boom. The FBI knew that the Davidians were equipped with gas masks, but even those begin to lose their effectiveness after about eight hours. The latest strategy was to increase the pressure by degrees.

The FBI was listening via devices smuggled into the compound early in the siege, hidden inside supplies like suture kits or coolers of milk for the children. They heard people within the compound talking about pouring gas in various areas, and then the Davidians planning to shoot at the Feds. The FBI held their fire but continued to smash through the walls with the booms of their combat vehicles, filling the interior with more tear gas. By 9:30 a.m., one of the vehicles had created a hole low in the building that was large enough for people to escape.

At 11:00 a.m., the situation seemed to be going well for the FBI, but forty-five minutes later one of the compound's back walls collapsed.

Just after noon, several fires began erupting within the Mount Carmel compound. Behind the scenes, the FBI scrambled to get fire trucks dispatched, but they were way out at the staging area. The Feds called for Koresh to surrender and lead the Branch Davidians to safety. Nine members exited the compound and were promptly arrested, including David Thibodeau. They were the last to leave—and the only ones to survive what came next.

Soon after this small band of Branch Davidians had been taken away from the building, the sound of gunfire came from inside the compound. Since it didn't seem to be directed at the FBI, the Feds came to believe that those inside the building were either committing suicide or killing each other. After the massive fire was extinguished, seventy-six Branch Davidians were found dead. Twenty-two children had been hiding in a concrete bunker with the few remaining women. They all perished when the structure collapsed on them. Some died immediately from blunt trauma; others later from smoke inhalation. All remains were partial, and what was found was charred beyond recognition. Any identification in the autopsy reports has been listed as speculative, based on limited available dental records or DNA samples. The children ranged in age from less than a year to thirteen years old. Two of the dead were only hours old, likely born during the attack when the traumatic nature of the unfolding events triggered delivery. Four of the children were Wayne Martin's. DNA testing proved that fourteen of them, including the two newborns, were David Koresh's biological children.

Seven teenagers between the ages of fourteen and nineteen were dead. The adults who stayed behind were an international crowd: twenty-three were Americans; twenty were British, mostly of Jamaican origin; there were single representatives from Canada, Israel, Australia, and New Zealand. Twenty people, including six children, had gunshot wounds, and a three-year-old was stabbed—likely mercy killings once the fire threatened to overwhelm them.

David Koresh died alongside Steve Schneider, both from fatal gunshot wounds. The order of the two deaths couldn't be determined, but the consensus is that Schneider first shot Koresh in the head and then committed suicide.

One of the lingering controversies in the months and years that followed focused on determining the person or agency responsible for igniting the fires that consumed the Mount Carmel compound. There were tapes from eleven listening devices secretly planted in the compound. The FBI monitored these devices but claimed there was generally too much background noise to make out anything. Long after the event, enhancement of the tapes seemed to indicate that the Branch Davidians within the compound were pouring fuel in the hallways and reminding each other, per Koresh's instructions, to light it only "when they first come in with the tank, right as they're coming in."

But the FBI did act in real time on information gained from the devices. At 7:40 a.m., an hour and forty minutes after the combat vehicles began breaching the walls, FBI headquarters learned that Koresh was telling people inside not to fire "until the last minute." The FBI tactical commander on-site gave the go-ahead for his team to use military tear gas rounds, a step that had not been okayed in the operating plan because launching the rounds could trigger fires. In the middle of all this, the devices picked up Schneider stating, "The manuscript is almost complete."

When the FBI conferred some three and a half hours into the operation, wondering why no one had emerged from the compound, they were told that the listening devices suggested a large number of Davidians had hidden in a concrete bunker below the tower and that the tear gas wouldn't reach them there. About ninety minutes later a combat vehicle rammed an area of the tower, collapsing the roof. Later, they knocked out the last working surveillance device, but not before hearing chatter about lighting torches and whether it was time yet to ignite the fires. Just after noon, the hostage rescue team monitoring the situation, waiting to help anyone who emerged, reported seeing a figure pouring something and then appearing to light a fire. Minutes later, FBI aircraft, using infrared cameras, reported the first fire.

The circumstances on both sides were utterly tumultuous. The phone calls with Schneider and Koresh were no longer an option; sometime shortly after Sage's 5:59 a.m. call, a CEV accidentally severed the phone line. The reporting from one agency to another was confused, and the agencies on hand seemed to be working against each other, or independently, as much as they were coordinating their efforts. There was plenty of blame to spread around, but later investigations ultimately cleared the federal government of culpability for the fires. David Koresh was held responsible for all the deaths that day, and the Branch Davidians were equally determined to be at fault for failing to comply with daily orders to leave the compound.

But these verdicts did not convince New World Order conspiracy theorists and anti-government militia types. In the aftermath of the tragedy, "Remember Waco" became a rallying cry, quite literally a call to arms among far-right groups bent on stockpiling weapons against the possibility of future government attacks. On the second anniversary of the Waco fires, domestic terrorists Timothy McVeigh and Terry Nichols detonated a truck full of explosives in front of the Alfred P. Murrah Federal Building in Oklahoma City in a misguided attempt to exact revenge for what they considered government overreach at the Mount Carmel compound. One hundred and sixty-eight people died, mostly federal employees, including young children attending the on-site daycare center. Many of the same FBI agents who'd worked at the Waco standoff also investigated this new horrific crime.

Years later Kathy Schroeder said, "I never really wanted to be there." But she figured if David Koresh was a real prophet, she would go to heaven, and if he wasn't, then her blood would be on his hands. For her, that seemed like a calculated risk to take. Another mother who'd left the compound early in the standoff mentioned Koresh twenty-four times during an hour-long interview. She never spoke of her husband or children, all of whom would later die in the fire. Koresh's power was nothing short of intoxicating to many.

Survivor Livingstone Fagan was sitting in jail when the fire broke out. His children had come out of the compound before him, but he watched on the prison TV the blaze that would kill his wife and mother. He served fourteen years for voluntary manslaughter and a weapons offense. His kids were raised by a brother back in the UK. In his view, the voices on the enhanced recordings were "orchestrated" and "fake, manufactured." In his *Telegraph* interview twenty-five years later, he related that he didn't recognize any of the voices. He still believes the end that David Koresh predicted is coming soon: "The timing of it remains in God's hands. We were told to watch as events unfolded."[9]

Many survivors of the Branch Davidians hold an annual gathering on April 19, but not at Mount Carmel; it's too painful for them to return there. The site is still legally owned by the group. There are few traces of the buildings on the compound site today. Inside the visitors' center, a banner that says "Waco: The Prophecy Fulfilled" is surrounded by photos of the "Seven Shepherds of the Advent Movement," including David Koresh and Ellen G. White. Walking the grounds, it's nearly impossible to tell where the fire took place without a map. The land on the flat Texas field where the compound once stood is paler in some places, and here and there on the level earth it's possible to imagine the general outline of a floor plan. But the heat is unrelenting in this part of Texas, and the grass growing over the plot of ground where the seventy-six believers were consumed by fire that April day has blanched in the sun.

SADISM

KEITH RANIERE AND NXIVM

Keith Raniere stands out in any list of cult leaders, not because he's more depraved than his peers, but because his cult is the most contemporary. NXIVM grew in plain sight, from its founding as an "Executive Success Program" during the tail end of the Clinton administration to Raniere's final sentencing on racketeering and sex trafficking charges just days before the 2020 election. From the beginning he capitalized on a run-of-the-mill business format—multilevel marketing—to attract women. His followers included the daughters of a liquor magnate, the costar of a popular cable TV series, and a journeyman voice-over artist, who joined a self-help program and wound up part of a harem of sex partners. But even this level of perversity might have gone unnoticed if Raniere had not created a special group within NXIVM, an inner circle of sex slaves branded with his initials and forced into submission with their ultimate "master." When word of the branding reached the *New York Times*, the whole pyramid scheme toppled, and Keith Raniere, captured by Federales after fleeing to Mexico, landed in jail with a 160-year sentence.

LADIES' MAN

From his first breath, Keith Raniere was drawn to vulnerable women. The attraction began in Brooklyn, New York, where he was born in 1960. Psychologists dating from Sigmund Freud through modern times note that a boy's relationship with his mother is the primary source of many lifelong behavioral patterns. And young Keith's experience taking care of his mother, an alcoholic dance teacher with a heart condition,[1] provided him with aptitudes he relied on for the rest of his life. One of the key principles in NXIVM, the self-help program that he would later come to found, involved getting people to face their own emotional trauma, partly because discovering such vulnerable spots was his gift. As his self-help program grew into a cult of personality, he became even more skillful at exploiting these discoveries, often sadistically, for his own profit and twisted pleasure.

As Raniere would later explain to women he was cultivating, his mother, Vera, drank often and alone, except for the presence of her young son. He claimed he had to take care of her constantly, something Suzanna Andrews of *Vanity Fair* discovered through interviews with the women who knew him best.[2] His father, James, an advertising executive, refuted his son's account, although he divorced his wife when Keith was eight. According to James, Vera may have imbibed more than she should, but never enough that it became a problem.

Despite these differences, all accounts agree that the parents provided their only child with a good education. Just about the time their marriage started falling apart in the late 1960s, Vera and James realized that the boy might be intellectually advanced and had him tested.[3] The results confirmed that he was gifted. Barbara Bouchey, one of Raniere's longtime girlfriends, told Josh Bloch on his CBC/Radio-Canada podcast "Uncover: Escaping NXIVM" that Raniere's father said, "It was almost like a switch went off. And suddenly overnight he turned into like Jesus Christ, superior and better than everyone, like he was a deity."[4] Researchers Eddie Brummelman, Brad J. Bushman, and their colleagues, in a study on the development of narcissistic personality disorder, found that "when children are seen by their parents as being more special . . . than other children, they may internalize the view that they are superior individuals, a view that is at the core of narcissism."[5] This seemed to apply to young Keith Raniere, who began to believe that he was better than everyone else.

It wasn't long before his new, arrogant attitude showed up in his behavior at school. In an interview with *Epoch Times* reporter Bowen Xiao, a former classmate identified only as "L.M.," who attended the same Waldorf school as Keith, said, "He was always bragging about how smart he was, how much better at math. He walked around like he was a miniature professor. . . .

"He had a really gentle voice and gentle approach," L.M. continued. "It was deceptive. It could draw you in."[6] These displays of arrogance could have been by-products of the boy's belief in his intellectual superiority. He might have also been acting out at school in response to trouble at home.[7] After his parents' separation, Keith lived with his mother and her drinking escalated. According to Barbara Bouchey in her interview with Josh Bloch, Keith Raniere "learned to become a nocturnal person because of his mother. He kept watch over her at night, because that was when she would sometimes combine taking medicine and drugs and alcohol."[8]

Perhaps it was this unhealthy dynamic that caused Keith to escalate his antagonistic behavior at school. By the time he was around ten, he was no longer satisfied with just bragging. He began taunting, even torturing, his classmates. L.M. recounted a disturbing story that she referred to as the "bottle incident." One day she was sitting on the bus next to Keith when she let slip a closely guarded secret about her sister. Initially, L.M. didn't worry. After all, they were all friends, so she didn't think he would try to use the information against her. But later that same day Raniere approached L.M. and said, "You know, it's like I have this little bottle of poison I can hold over your head."[9]

Confused, L.M. asked him what he meant and he explained, "Well, I don't know. I just don't think your parents or your sister would be very happy if I told them."

L.M. couldn't figure out what he wanted. It wasn't as if he was demanding anything. It wasn't blackmail. It just seemed like he enjoyed having the power to threaten her with something. And he didn't stop there. He'd call her sometimes, entirely out of the blue, and say the same two words: "Little bottles." Just that, repeatedly, like a private signal that he would use his knowledge against her. He continued to harass L.M. until she finally broke down and told her mother. Only after she intervened did the relentless phone calls come to an end.

Apparently he also had another side that emerged when he took care of his own mother late into the night. He began to reveal a softer aspect of his personality as he entered his teenage years. As Bouchey told Josh Bloch, Vera had a front-row seat to her son's new way of interacting with the girls in his class. What she overheard worried her, so much so that one night she called her ex-husband in a panic. Bouchey recalled James telling her that "dozens of young girls were calling the house and [Vera] was overhearing his conversations with them where he was telling every single woman, every single girl the same thing: 'You're the special one. You're the important one in my life and I love you.' And she says, 'And he's saying this to different girls.'" Since they couldn't all be special to him, she came to the conclusion that her son was a liar, and a skillful one.

Robert Hare's psychopathy checklist includes pathological lying, manipulativeness, and a grandiose sense of self, all emerging traits in this young high schooler. The arrogant behavior after learning his IQ test results suggested an inflated sense of self. The "little bottles" incident hinted at his taste for power games. And his lies to dozens of teenage girls proved his capacity for deceitfulness. In retrospect, these troubling signs stand out, and—although it would've been premature to brand thirteen-year-old Keith as a psychopath at that point—they only grew more pronounced into adulthood.

In 1984, at the age of twenty-four, Raniere was still seducing teenage girls. According to James M. Odato and Jennifer Gish of the *Albany Times Union,* that was when he met fifteen-year-old Gina Melita in a community theater troupe in Troy, New York. Raniere made a pass at her, running his hands over her face and legs during a trip with some friends from the theater. Gina didn't have the life experience to be disturbed by an adult man putting the moves on her. In fact, according to Odato and Gish, "she thought it was cool to be with an older, smart guy. . . ."[10] The two started dating, going to local arcades and playing video games. (In fact, Raniere would allegedly later take his title as the leader of NXIVM from the 1980s arcade game *Vanguard.*) But Raniere wasn't hanging out with Gina so they could only indulge in age-appropriate activities: he wanted something far more adult. Shortly after they started seeing each other, he had sex with Gina in a dark room, the door dead bolted.[11]

The experience was painful; Gina was shocked by how much it hurt.[12] Despite her discomfort, Keith insisted they do it again. Raniere continued hounding her for sex, even though the age of consent in New York State was seventeen and he was committing statutory rape. Feeling there was something wrong with the relationship,[13] Gina broke things off. Raniere suggested that the two continue having sex anyway. As she told Gish and Odato, that was when she realized that he didn't care about her at all.[14]

Around this time, Raniere started working at Amway.[15] According to Eric J. Roode, a work friend who spoke with Josh Bloch for his podcast, Raniere began talking about founding a company of his own that mirrored Amway's multilevel marketing structure. It was also during this time that the first seeds of Raniere's cult following were planted. He started holding court at his town house in Clifton Park, New York. He led long philosophical sessions, transforming them into a sort of hippie hangout. Dozens of young women showed up at the house to listen to him talk.

In addition to vague dreams about improving on Amway's structure, Raniere also discussed the human potential movement, which sought to bring about positive change by unlocking untapped resources hidden in each individual. Cynics have seen this movement as a tellingly self-involved one, allowing people to imagine they're improving global conditions by concentrating exclusively on their own betterment. But Raniere felt no such hesitation, perhaps because it was this topic that most appealed to the women who were listening. With his gentle voice and his seemingly rapt attention, he told any number present that he saw great potential in *them*. According to one of his friends from that time, Raniere often encouraged them at these sessions "to fulfill whatever their gifts and talents might be."[16]

Soon the people attending his hangouts began to see Keith Raniere as a sort of guru. Before long, he started to discuss how he might formalize this mix of elements, marrying his goals of founding a multilevel marketing organization of his own with his desires to help people fulfill their potential. Eventually, a consensus was reached: everybody agreed that Keith should take another IQ test. It's likely they believed that doing so would bolster his credibility, allowing him to start the business of his dreams.[17] So, in 1987, according to Irene Gardner Keeney in the *Albany Times Union*, twenty-seven-year-old Raniere took a forty-eight-question IQ test sponsored by the Mega Society[18] and got forty-six answers right. This put his IQ at an enviable 178.[19] For comparison's sake, it's believed Albert Einstein had an IQ of 160. Armed with his new genius ranking, Raniere began marketing himself as "smarter" than the man who developed the theory of relativity.

But even that wasn't enough. He soon began claiming that he had an IQ in the stratospheric 240 range.[20] Although no one now can reconstruct how this happened, Raniere and his new high score was included in the Australian edition of the *Guinness Book of World Records*, which billed him as the man with the highest IQ on Earth.[21] The local Albany newspapers covered the unexpected discovery of a genius within their midst, calling him a "one in ten million" intellect.[22] It didn't seem to matter to the reporters that the test supposedly proving Keith's intelligence was of the untimed, take-home variety. Nor did anyone bother to check the supposed genius's college credentials.

If they had done so, it would have been discovered that Keith Raniere graduated from Rensselaer Polytechnic Institute with a GPA of 2.26.[23]

But in 1988, none of those facts surfaced. Now twenty-eight, Keith Raniere tirelessly publicized the Mega Society test results and his inclusion in the *Guinness Book of World Records* to brand himself as the "Smartest Man in the World." This was the moniker that helped him establish the first of his predatory enterprises two years later: a brand-new company he called Consumers' Buyline, Inc., or CBI. Like Amway, CBI was a multilevel marketing company promising to deliver deep discounts on household products to its members. Like other MLMs before it, it also spoke of members' financial incentives for recruiting new affiliates. It did well for a few years, saving its members money on bulk orders of household items, like a Costco without the big-box buildings.

The outreach for new members was powered by Raniere's ability to sell both the concept and his own exceptional status. But from the beginning, Raniere also used his road show for more nefarious purposes. CBI behaved more like a Ponzi scheme, designed to move membership fees up the ladder to corporate headquarters. It also drew in women he could exploit. Consumers' Buyline was the first of many companies that he ran, but each one seemed to give him greater access to vulnerable women, leading to toxic and increasingly sadistic relationships.

1991: TONI NATALIE

In 1991, when Toni Natalie was thirty-three and married, she met Keith Raniere at a promotional seminar in Rochester, New York, for Consumers' Buyline. Toni's husband, Rusty, whose tanning bed business was in trouble, had wanted them to check out the membership seminar. "He's a triple-major graduate from Rensselaer Polytechnic Institute," Rusty said. "He's a pianist, cyclist, an East Coast judo champion. And he wants to save the world." Toni's first impression:

the guy was actually short and a bit of a blowhard, dubiously claiming to have an IQ of 240. But once he began to pitch, Toni's reservations faded away.

After the presentation, Toni approached Keith Raniere and, as she recounted in her memoir, *The Program: Inside the Mind of Keith Raniere and the Rise and Fall of NXIVM*, she asked him, "You have a 240 IQ. Why are you not curing cancer or changing the world, making it a better place?"[24] Raniere replied, "I *am* changing the world. I *am* making the world a better place. Don't you want to come along?"[25] Toni signed up and within a few months became one of CBI's best salespersons. By the summer of 1991, she and her husband were so successful at selling CBI memberships that Raniere awarded them with the company's top regional prize, which came with a $16,000 bonus. Raniere wanted Toni to move to Albany to work for CBI full-time and said so repeatedly in phone calls. Toni countered with commitments to her son, her husband, their home. Raniere again behaved as if he had a higher calling, telling her, "I feel like you're meant to help me change the world."

She reminded him that she was married and had never finished high school. He replied that there were different types of intelligence, and hers was emotional. After this pitch, she and Rusty decided to make the three-and-a-half-hour drive to Clifton Park to see the business for themselves. The CBI building was uninspiring, but the offices told a different story. In 1991, personal computers were still not standard business equipment, but there were dozens of CBI employees tapping away at multiple terminals.

She was also pleasantly surprised to see more women than men employed. One had even brought her daughter along, a twelve-year-old with braces. Toni watched the girl thumbing through an algebra textbook. Keith Raniere was even taking time to tutor her in math. On that initial tour, Toni was impressed that the CEO would devote part of his day to mentor a young math student. Years later she'd learn that "mentorship" didn't explain the dynamic between a thirty-one-year-old and a tween. According to court documents, by 1991 Keith

Raniere had been raping the child for an entire year, grooming her by offering instruction in algebra and Latin. In private, what he really taught her was how to "hug the way adults do, pelvis to pelvis." Then he took her virginity.[26] According to subsequent reporting in the *Albany Times Union*, Raniere continued sexually assaulting the girl, "not only in his townhouse but in empty offices, in an elevator and in a broom closet at the plaza that housed Consumers' Buyline. . . ."[27]

After the visit to the CBI headquarters, Raniere began calling Toni constantly, trying to convince her to relocate. Rusty was amused by the frequency of his calls, but he wasn't threatened; after all, Keith Raniere was no beauty contest winner. But Raniere made up for that with his evidently boundless capacity for listening. It seemed to Toni that no had ever paid her such close attention. So she talked, confiding in this stranger that her husband hadn't made love to her for two years. She admitted her insecurities about being a high school dropout. She even trusted him enough to share that she'd been sexually abused when she was four years old.[28]

Raniere would later dub his method of soothing a person's emotional triggers as "integration." But with Toni Natalie he was still working out the kinks. She initially refused him—until a few months later, when her husband's tanning bed business finally went belly-up and she asked Keith Raniere for financial help. He claimed he couldn't sign off on any loans unless she met with his business manager, George Weiss, so Toni had to make the pilgrimage once more to CBI headquarters in Clifton Park.

This time she discovered what so many others who got close to him would: that he was far less than he seemed. She met Raniere at his house, and it was filthy: there were trash cans overflowing with garbage, dishes with congealed food stacked in the sink, clothes strewn all over the floors like a teenager's bedroom. Apparently, the Smartest Man in the World didn't know how to maintain a clean living space. The second thing she noticed were his residential companions. He still lived with his college ex-girlfriend, Karen Unterreiner, and two more had joined her: Pam Cafritz (who happened to be the daughter of influential DC socialites) and Kristin Keeffe. The setup felt odd—a successful executive living with three women as if they were all university roommates.

Raniere took her to meet with George Weiss, just as he'd promised. But instead of agreeing to a loan, he offered Toni a job running a new skin care business that he wanted to add on to CBI. While the salary would be generous enough for her to pay off her husband's debt, there was a massive catch: she would have to relocate to Clifton Park. Even though he'd asked her to move several times before, Natalie was now tempted by the money, and she felt her husband and son could be convinced to join her, as it was all for the best. But she would also be cut off from her brother, friends, and business contacts back home. She promised to consider the offer. With the meeting over, Raniere asked to accompany her back to her hotel.

He followed Toni to her small room at the Best Western . . . and soon it became apparent that this was the real reason she'd been invited to Clifton Park. In their isolated state, Keith Raniere executed what came to be his signature strategy: breaking down a vulnerable woman under the guise of expressing compassion, keeping her talking for somewhere between twelve or thirteen hours, asking her to tell him about the sexual abuse she'd suffered as a child. So she did: she was four when a relative first assaulted her, and it continued for years. But every time after she recounted a painful memory, Raniere had another question. She begged for a break, to close her eyes. He assured Toni that he wanted to ease her pain. Then he'd ask her to tell him the story again, from the top. She eventually broke down, crying and exhausted.

At the sight of her tears, Raniere told her that he could help her, if she'd only move to Clifton Park and take the job. Feeling defeated, she finally gave in, more for relief by that point than because she wanted to. It's not surprising that she buckled under Raniere's not-so-subtle and sustained psychological assault. In a series of studies, the researchers Pam Lowe, Cathy Humphreys, and Simon J. Williams found a "connection between sleep deprivation and the establishment of a regime of power and control by one person over another" and that "[s]leep deprivation was clearly a direct strategy of abuse used by perpetrators . . . [to undermine] the mental and physical resilience of women."[29] Even though Keith Raniere wasn't physically abusing her, his emotional manipulation and relentlessness were just as harmful. Toni fell for it, taking his control strategies for compassion.

Over the next five months, Toni Natalie began working full-time for CBI, traveling with Raniere whenever he gave seminars about the life-changing virtues of the company. On one of these trips, he told Toni that he was in love with her. She was flattered that the Smartest Man in the World could fall for her, a high school dropout. She divorced Rusty and left with her son, convincing herself that it was a necessary change a long time coming.

In the spring of 1992, Raniere's roommate Kristin Keeffe helped Toni find a house so close that Raniere could walk from his backyard into hers—and he immediately took advantage of this proximity. The first night in her new home, he came over and they had sex. Unlike Rusty, who hadn't touched her in so long, Raniere was insatiable. After years of being ignored, Toni felt restored by this evidence of her desirability.

Keith Raniere also told her repeatedly that he loved her, that she completed him, and that she was special. But the next morning in the parking lot of CBI, still basking in the afterglow, Toni leaned over and kissed Raniere on the cheek, and he instantly pushed her away, saying they had to hide their relationship or people would think she'd slept her way into her job. After all, he said, that seemed a more likely explanation, given the fact that she was just a high school dropout.

His words felt like a physical slap. In private, Raniere had said that her lack of official credentials didn't matter. But once she felt secure in his affection, he easily shifted into a cold, brusque manner, like a manager during a bad performance review. From that point on, Raniere insisted that their romantic entanglement remain a secret.

And things weren't much better at the company itself. On May 21, 1992, the *Albany Times Union* published an exposé describing Consumers' Buyline as a pyramid scheme and detailing investigations into CBI by authorities in New York and Maine and ongoing legal action by the Arkansas attorney general.[30]

Keith Raniere responded to this report as if it were a personal attack, the kind of reaction that, according to psychoanalyst Heinz Kohut, revealed his weakness in a sequence he described as "narcissistic rage." Raniere labeled the journalists liars and the state attorney general vindictive. He recorded a five-minute message to CBI employees trumpeting his high ethical standards. And at first they believed him. But this show of support didn't satisfy Raniere, who became increasingly paranoid, accusing the government of spying on him, opening his mail, and tapping his phones.[31]

He was even more erratic outside the office. He took to letting himself into Toni Natalie's house at all hours of the night, shaking her awake to demand what he called "physical comfort." She grew fed up with his outbursts, his odd mixture of sexual demands, and his ongoing refusal to acknowledge their relationship in public. She threatened to leave him, but Raniere convinced her to take him back, first by agreeing to recognize her in public, then by moving in with her and her son. A few months before, she might have been thrilled, but she couldn't shake the feeling that she was making a huge mistake.

On the surface it looked as though she'd made the right decision. After CBI eventually collapsed under the weight of multiple lawsuits in the mid-nineties, Keith Raniere and Toni Natalie started a successful new business, National Health Network, selling nutritional supplements at a 30 percent discount. They bought a beautiful home in Waterford, New York, where they were raising her son, Michael, together.

But after three years Toni finally admitted to herself that there was something very wrong with Keith Raniere. For starters, he refused to do any chores. He just sat around the house and expected Toni to wait on him hand and foot. Secondly, he was practically nocturnal, staying up at all hours of the night and sleeping through the day. And unlike her ex-husband, he was demanding sex every single day. If she showed no interest, he forced himself upon her. She took to barricading herself in her closet just to get away from him.

She felt trapped, with no one to talk to about Raniere's violent and manipulative behavior—until she met Nancy Salzman, who'd showed up for their nutritional supplement business looking to treat severe constipation. After Toni prescribed her a cocktail of supplements that resolved the issue, Salzman wanted to return the favor, offering treatment in her own area of expertise. At the time, as Toni Natalie told Katie Heaney at The Cut, Salzman was billing herself as the world's number two expert in neurolinguistic programming, behaving as if this entirely imaginary qualification entitled her to work as a therapist.[32] She seemed to have had some success with this ruse, convincing executives from such companies as Con Edison and American Express to pay her for regular consulting work. Likewise taken in by Salzman's credentials, Toni agreed to meet with her. At their first session, she told Salzman about trying to understand Raniere's erratic behavior and his refusal to maintain normal sleeping hours, although she left out his constant sexual assaults. In response, Salzman smiled and said, "Oh, that's easy. I can help you. He's a sociopath."[33]

Then Salzman recommended regular therapy sessions. But, strangely, by their next session Salzman had changed her tune. There was no more talk of Raniere's psychopathic behavior. Instead, she told Toni that her intimacy issues were a result of the sexual abuse she'd suffered as a child. That was very strange, because Toni had never said a word about her childhood trauma. Still, she was so grateful that someone was recognizing her predicament that it didn't occur to her to question where Nancy Salzman had gotten the information or why she'd completely reversed her opinion on Keith Raniere. Had she dug deeper, she might have realized that this change of heart came from Raniere himself.

By the time she sat down with Salzman for her second session, Raniere had already gotten his hooks into her. After Natalie's initial meeting, Salzman had violated therapist-patient confidentiality and told Raniere about it. He then booked his *own* session with the neurolinguistic programmer. Three more sessions quickly followed, and by the time Toni put all the pieces together, it was too late. She was already being gaslit by a woman pretending to be her therapist.

Meanwhile, Raniere and Salzman had started to draw up plans for a new company, but this time the product was going to be something very valuable and almost undefinable. As Natalie wrote in her book, "Keith had decided that saving consumers money was too pedestrian for his singular genius—and too fraught with legal minefields. Life coaching, executive success, and self-improvement hokum . . . that was the way to go."[34] Like Consumers' Buyline before it, Raniere decided his new venture—Executive Success Programs, or ESP— would also have a multilevel marketing structure. However, this time, instead of having members shill household products, they'd be selling self-improvement "technology." This so-called scientific coursework would be similar to the neurolinguistic programming that Nancy Salzman offered her corporate clients.

While the two were laying the groundwork for Executive Success Programs, Raniere's relationship with Toni Natalie began to unravel. One afternoon in April 1999, the two had a blowout argument over a new sweater she'd asked him not to put in the dryer the one time she'd convinced him to help with the laundry. When he did, and the sweater shrank, he refused to accept responsibility, yelling at her to admit she was wrong, and then, when she wouldn't, demanded she beg for "reinstatement." He even sent her a breakup letter with a photocopy of Milton's *Paradise Lost*, pointing out the places where her behavior precisely mimicked that of Lucifer rebelling against God. The fight highlighted the issues she had with him their entire relationship: Raniere was dismissive, egotistical, and cruel. She left him for good at last, and he retaliated by leveling a number of spurious lawsuits, with no success, and kept harassing her for years, having his devotees break into her house, steal her mail, and call the local utility companies to shut off her phone service and electricity.

But despite this ongoing vindictiveness, Keith Raniere finally moved on. He had a different business scheme in mind and a brand-new woman to partner with: Nancy Salzman. With her input, Raniere launched ESP . . . and over the years, the business shifted almost imperceptibly from the multilevel marketing model that he was so familiar with—"Because Keith is," as Natalie told The Cut, "at heart, a frustrated Amway salesman"—into the sadomasochistic cult NXIVM.

1999: NANCY SALZMAN

Almost from their first meeting, Salzman and Raniere began devising self-improvement technology. They filled notebooks with fuzzy terms like "rational inquiry," which to them meant something like logical consistency or high-functioning insight, although in practice it really meant skills one could only acquire in Executive Success Programs seminars costing $7,500 or more. Another big term was "Explorations of Meaning," or "EMs"—intense encounter sessions in which a person would be directed to explore negative experiences and to reintegrate and lighten the weight of that mental burden. Another key concept involved identifying "disintegrations": those mental dysfunctions acquired in life that held back the individual but could be treated and resolved through more costly intensive sessions. Raniere would later claim that his Executive Success Programs could help people become Oscar-winning actresses, Olympic medal athletes, and successful entrepreneurs, although he never named any real-life examples among ESP graduates.

From the beginning, ESP attracted smart, capable people with plenty of spare cash and who'd come to a personal crossroads looking for the kind of knowledge that Raniere and Salzman seemed to possess. ESP promised "more" in vague terms: more success, more happiness, more certainty that the committed Espian (their term for themselves) was on the right path. The Espians were sincere in their eagerness to improve. And because the cost of the self-improvement intensives was so prohibitively high, that meant that anyone who signed up was likely to meet other people just as smart and successful as they were—the kind who would confirm that they had joined a self-selecting elite. Keith Raniere had effectively monetized the mutual admiration society.

From the beginning, Raniere and Salzman wanted to build a financial colossus based on vague promises and hefty enrollment fees. But almost unconsciously they also instituted a second dynamic involving a strict hierarchy that, over the years, turned into a perverse mechanism for the expression of dominance. It started innocently enough, with a ranking system (Raniere had been inspired by Scientology's eight levels of Operating Thetan) made visible to everyone enrolled in ESP, and later NXIVM, by sashes that Espians were expected to wear around their necks. The sash system determined where a person stood in the hierarchy. Beginners wore white, followed by yellow, orange, green, blue, and purple. Gold was reserved for Nancy Salzman, and only Keith Raniere had attained the level of an "Ethereal," which meant he supposedly had no color—although his sash appeared to others as white. Moving up the color ranks cost money in fees or recruitments, and the prices were steep. Green cost about $1 million; blue, around $5 million. Eventually, sexual services to Raniere became part of the calculation; the only three purples were his girlfriends—or, in the case of Toni Natalie, his ex-girlfriend. On top of this visual hierarchy, students were expected to refer to Nancy Salzman as "Prefect" and Keith Raniere as "Vanguard."

To move from one color to the next, a student had to first earn four stripes on the sash they currently possessed. This was another studied variation of Scientology, which offers a graduated path they term the "bridge to clear." The ESP/NXIVM version offered the stripe path to ethereal. The sash rankings also provided a relative measure of advancement within the group. Students always knew where they stood in relation to each other, an important distinction, since more rules governed how a lower-ranked student was to interact with a higher one. First, there was the special handshake. Normal handshakes occur on a lateral plane, with hands at equal height, but an

Espian had to put their hand beneath that of a higher-ranked student. An Espian was also supposed to stand for a student of higher ranking to show respect, and to bow to one another and to Vanguard.[35]

All of Raniere's mandated rituals and insignias of rank played a very important role. According to Namkje Koudenburg, a social psychologist from the University of Gronigen in the Netherlands, and her colleagues, "a sense of 'us' can emerge in the background of specific actions that individuals perform together."[36] By giving Espians this uniform system of dressing and interacting with each other, Raniere crafted a new group identity.

Espians also learned that the world was divided into two groups: parasites and producers. And while all human beings were born parasitic, dependent on others for their survival, some humans remained in this stunted state, perennially feeding off the success of others to sustain themselves. On the other side of the equation were the self-sufficient producers—those who were independent and driven enough to earn their success. As Vanguard, the man with the ethereal sash, Keith Raniere held himself up as the ultimate producer.

If students wanted to leave behind their parasitic state, they would have to throw themselves wholeheartedly into ESP's curriculum. During EM sessions, a coach would take a student through an analysis of a thought or behavior to find the root cause of the student's negative emotional responses. Once the origin was located, usually in a childhood memory or some other formative experience, the coach would help the student diminish the power of the moment by asking them targeted questions. In this way, Explorations of Meaning were very similar to Scientology's auditing sessions.

ESP promised that with enough Explorations of Meaning, students would destroy the ultimate cause of the negative emotions holding them back from success. In other words, EMs would give them effective producer-like "mindsets." The more people who achieved this mindset, the better the world would be. To help increase the number of producers, Raniere strongly encouraged his students to recruit.

In fact, recruitment, with its measurable increase in revenue, not self-improvement through Explorations of Meaning, was the principal mechanism for white sashes to move up the Stripe Path.

Perhaps no one was a more effective recruiter than the Prefect herself. "There is probably no discovery since writing as important for humankind as Mr. Raniere's technology," Nancy Salzman wrote in one ESP brochure. In 1999 she encouraged her daughters, nineteen-year-old Michelle[37] and twenty-two-year-old Lauren,[38] to try the classes. According to court testimony, as recounted by EJ Dickson in *Rolling Stone*, a few years after joining ESP, Lauren began a sexual relationship with Keith Raniere.[39] It's unclear whether her mother was immediately aware of this, maybe because she, too, was soon having sex with Raniere. After pulling her family members into ESP, the Prefect moved on to recruiting her friends, convincing her acquaintance Barbara Bouchey in 2000 to join the group. At the time she took her first workshop, as Bouchey later wrote, "I was, at age forty, managing $90 million, grossing $900,000 annually, with a client minimum of $1 million, and I had $1.5 million in savings."[40] Despite her enviable success, Bouchey, like so many of ESP's early recruits, was going through a difficult time, as her second marriage was falling apart. She also soon fell for Keith Raniere, lent him money, signed papers that he misrepresented, and soon lost her entire life savings, covering margin calls on bad bets in commodity trades that Raniere had made her a cosignatory to. She wasn't able to recoup anywhere close to that amount until years later, when she began to manage the multimillions in inheritance money belonging to two of NXIVM's star recruits, Sara and Clare Bronfman, both equal heirs to the Seagram liquor fortune and who also both became sexually involved with Keith Raniere.

2002: DANIELA

In early 2002, sixteen-year-old Daniela's [last name withheld] parents, Hector and Adriana, wealthy Mexican nationals and recent converts to the Espian path, gifted their daughter with an ESP class—a sixteen-day intensive. They hoped that she might get something from the teachings that had resonated with them. Daniela was set to attend an exclusive boarding school in Switzerland and had dreams of going to Harvard and studying medicine. But during the intensive, according to reports filed by CNN investigators Emanuella Grinberg and Sonia Moghe, Daniela was taught a mathematical equation that supposedly demonstrated that the world was going to end in ten to fifteen years. By the end of her session, she'd come to believe that her ambitions were pointless because the only way to change the world was through ESP.[41]

When Lauren Salzman, under constant pressure by her mother to recruit new members, asked Daniela to give up the rest of her formal education and be tutored by Vanguard instead, she agreed.[42] But when Daniela arrived in Albany, Keith Raniere didn't do much tutoring. In fact, he ignored her, according to later testimony in court, so she wound up cleaning the offices just to stay busy.[43] Raniere finally began to focus his attention on her a year later—but he had no intention of tutoring her then either. Instead, the forty-two-year-old kissed the teenage Daniela, floated the idea of having sex, and then admitted that she was too young.

But a few days after she turned eighteen, he changed his mind about their twenty-five-year age difference and performed oral sex on Daniela in an empty office and on a dirty mattress.[44] According to Toni Natalie's book *The Program*, Daniela spent the next couple of years "doing data entry, cleaning houses of high-ranking Espians, and performing oral sex on command for Vanguard."[45] Despite these frequent sexual encounters with Raniere, Daniela described herself in later court testimony as "kind of asexual" until her mid-twenties, when she discovered that she had feelings for Ben Myers, a man closer to her age who worked in ESP's IT department. On a night when a group of Espians had gotten together to watch *Star Trek*, Daniela and Myers were left alone, and she discovered that sitting close to him brought up intense feelings that she liked. At a second group event, the two kissed. When she told Raniere about this wondrous new feeling of falling in love, he reacted in ways that a reasonable person would not associate with the so-called Smartest Man in the World: he flew into a rage, locking himself in the bathroom and refusing to come out, telling her that he had a mystical union with his sex partners and that when they did something wrong it caused him physical pain.

In the aftermath of her confession, Raniere saw to it that Daniela, now twenty-four, was confined to a room in her family home, and convinced her parents—who took Keith Raniere for the ethereal being that the ESP hierarchy said he was—to help enforce his punishment, limiting and later eliminating her access to phones, iPads, money, immigration papers, and the outside world. Daniela's own family became her jailers. She was allowed to have pens and paper, though, if only to write him letters explaining her faults. She was told she had to "restore and intensify" her sexual feelings to Raniere, and he sent her emails asking for explicit details of what she and Ben had actually done with each other. As Sarah Berman reported for Vice, he inquired: "Did he touch you on your vagina inside your clothes or was it outside your clothes?" In another, he demanded, "I need to be your WHOLE life. This is the only way."[46]

In her isolation, she later told the court, Daniela grew so lonely and upset that she started obsessively scratching her arms. Raniere had a fetish for thin women, and one of the conditions that was placed upon her, if she wanted to regain her freedom, was that she had to get her weight below a hundred pounds. If she deviated from her weight-loss regimen—if she ate a little extra or had sugar in her coffee—she was accused of "pride." It became a standard complaint: any assertion of will contrary to Raniere's wishes was evidence of this so-called flaw. She had nothing to do, so she imagined every step that she would take just to go to a nearby Walmart, everything she'd see on the way, what music they'd play inside the store. Her door was never locked but she had no money, no working papers, no passport. Her only visitor was Lauren Salzman, she informed the court, who was cruel and gave her updates on the ever-changing steps Daniela would have to take to get back in Raniere's good graces. She wrote him love letters one day and the next day she pleaded with him to set her free. She gave them all to Salzman for her to pass along. Keith Raniere never even opened them.

He kept Daniela imprisoned in her own home for two years, during which time she collected cleaning supplies, hoping to end her life. She knew that if she left without resolving her "ethical breach," her parents would abandon her.[47] Finally, she couldn't take it any longer and walked out of her confinement to confront the only Ethereal. When Keith Raniere saw her, he ran away, dodging through the crowd of "Nxians" in his attempts to hide. Before she could confront him, a gang of lower-level sashes grabbed her. Her father and another advanced-level Nxian drove Daniela back to Mexico and left her on her own.[48]

Her freedom was bittersweet. Raniere still was using both of Daniela's sisters—the older Mariana and the younger Camila—as sexual partners. Because he didn't use birth control, arguing that it interfered with the spiritual benefits that accrued to his partners, both of them got pregnant and had abortions. According to prosecutors, Raniere referred to Daniela's youngest sibling as "Virgin Camila,"[49] or "VC," because he began a sexual relationship with her in 2005 when she was only fifteen years old. On top of that, she worked as a maid for Nancy Salzman. None of this qualified her for special treatment. Raniere also harassed the teenager to get her weight down to below a hundred pounds and pressured her to "find other virgins" on Tinder for him to have sex with.[50]

WhatsApp messages between the two also suggest that Camila might have been Keith Raniere's first slave. In 2015 he pushed the now twenty-five-year-old Camila to find one of her own, texting, "I think it would be good for you to own a slave for me that you could groom and use as a tool to pleasure me."[51] In another he asked Camila if she'd agree to take a brand. The young woman responded with horror: "What do you mean, branded like cattle?" He sent back a flippant reply, texting, "Don't you want to burn for me?"[52] Camila did not, and she never had to suffer the pain of having Raniere's initials branded on her skin.[53]

2002: THE BRONFMAN SISTERS,
SARA AND CLARE

Despite Keith Raniere's regular psychotic breaks and his habit of turning juveniles into sexual prey, ESP still had a respectable public face in its first decade of existence, enough to lure in Sara Bronfman, the billionaire heiress to the Seagram liquor empire. In 2002, twenty-five-year-old Sara's four-month marriage to Irish jockey Ronan Clarke was on the rocks,[54] a failure that sent the usually bubbly party girl on a search for answers. When a family friend, Susan White, recommended ESP, Sara decided to give self-improvement classes a try. Like many in their twenties, Sara had a checkered relationship with possible careers. She had left NYU, opened a skydiving business in Turks and Caicos, spent time with the European horsey set, and partied in Belgium, which was where she first heard about the organization. She took an intensive in Mexico City, where Keith Raniere had a following among the wealthy (allegedly including Emiliano, the son of former Mexican president Carlos Salinas de Gortari, and Ana Cristina, the daughter of then president Vicente Fox Quesada). She responded to ESP classes immediately, so much so that she encouraged her sister, Clare, to give it a try.[55]

The siblings were a study in opposites: Sara was the effervescent blond socialite, and Clare was the driven dark-haired Olympic hopeful. Sara traveled around the world chasing a variety of passions she quickly discarded; Clare was a Grand Prix–winning equestrienne. According to Suzanna Andrews, who wrote about the Bronfmans for *Vanity Fair*, Clare "had a defiant air about her. . . . She would tell people that she had decided to spend the rest of her life with horses, because she didn't like human beings."[56]

Keith Raniere targeted them both, as they were equally and wildly rich. Their father, Edgar Bronfman, had an estimated net worth of $2.6 billion, and both of his daughters boasted trust fund balances in the nine figures.[57] Early on in their time with ESP, Raniere convened a series of one-on-one meetings with the recalcitrant Clare.[58] There is no record or court testimony about what they discussed during these private sessions, but by the end of them Clare was just as enthusiastic about ESP as her sister. In fact, according to several former members of the group, Clare had fallen in love with Raniere.[59]

With both of them on his hook, forty-three-year-old Keith Raniere was ready to reel in the Bronfman family. In 2003 he pushed Sara and Clare to set up a meeting with their father. This was a difficult ask. After Edgar's divorce from their mother, who was his second wife (or third, but his second marriage was annulled), the siblings had spent the bulk of their childhood living apart from the Bronfman riches and iso-lated from their half siblings from Edgar's first marriage. They hadn't grown up in New York society like Edgar Bronfman's older children, nor had they attended fancy private schools. And while they did have access to impressive trust funds of their own, they had their own issues with their father, who'd been almost completely absent from their lives during childhood.

The sisters therefore hesitated when Raniere asked them to reach out to the senior Bronfman. But when they did, they found Edgar eager to fix his strained relationship with his daughters. He signed up for one of ESP's specially designed VIP solo sessions, taught by Nancy Salzman herself, for $10,000. And at first Bronfman loved the classes. He began flying Salzman out to his estate in Virginia so she could give him one-on-one ESP therapy sessions.[60]

Now Raniere could count a billionaire among his clientele and a membership of 3,700, who all paid for expensive intensives, many with surprising regularity. Unfortunately, this level of success came with a downside: the taxman could come calling at any minute. According to Toni Natalie, the profits of ESP were large enough that Raniere began strategizing how to avoid paying taxes on his sudden wealth. He divided ESP's ventures among an array of separate entities, folding them all into an umbrella corporation. The structure would insulate him from direct ownership but allow him to live off the income he generated. Keith Raniere called his new venture NXIVM.[61]

At about this time, Raniere received yet another piece of news he considered fortunate: *Forbes* magazine wanted to do a feature article on him. He eagerly cooperated with the publication, believing that the national exposure would usher in an even greater level of success. But he was dead wrong. Michael Freedman of *Forbes* did careful research, discovering a number of NXIVM apostates like Toni Natalie who weren't afraid to describe the inner workings of program. As Freedman wrote:

> His teachings are mysterious, filled with self-serving and impenetrable jargon about ethics and values, and defined by a blind-ambition ethos akin to that of the driven characters in an Ayn Rand novel. His shtick: Make your own self-interest paramount, don't be motivated by what other people want and avoid "parasites" (his label for people who need help); only by doing this can you be true to yourself and truly "ethical." The flip side, of course, is that this worldview discredits virtues like charity, teamwork and compassion—but maybe we just don't get it.[62]

The article was a disaster of such magnitude that it threatened his relationship with Clare Bronfman, putting the whole NXIVM empire at stake. By this point Raniere was juggling intense sexual and emotional relationships with multiple women. But in his excitement about the *Forbes* profile, he failed to adequately manage Clare's feelings. Toni Natalie indicated that Clare had always been overshadowed by her prettier older sister. NXIVM was supposed to be different. In this arena, Clare felt she deserved to be placed in the forefront. After all, she'd given up her dreams of being a champion equestrian to focus on the group full-time.[63] But it seemed to Clare that Raniere and Salzman were making a bigger fuss over her sibling with the *Forbes* journalist.[64] In fact, the article ended with a quote from Sara. "I don't know how much you know about my family," she told Freedman, "but, coming from a family where I've never had to earn anything before in my life,

[it] was a very, very moving experience for me to be awarded this yellow sash. It was the first thing that I had earned on just my merits."[65]

Feeling overlooked and underappreciated, Clare decided to retaliate and called her father, telling him that Keith had borrowed $2 million from her (something she later denied to *Forbes* when the magazine got in touch with her to confirm the loan). Edgar Bronfman now realized that Raniere was not the ethical guru he presented himself to be but just a con man out to take money from his daughters. He had his own comment for the *Forbes* piece: "I think it's a cult."[66]

Instead of addressing the parts of the article that called his own behavior into question, Raniere homed in on Edgar's quote. He targeted Clare, furious that she had disclosed the information to her father. After the article went public, both Clare and Sara stopped talking to Edgar, most likely at Raniere's urging. But that still wasn't enough. As he did with Daniela, Raniere accused Clare of committing an "ethical breach" of violating NXIVM's mission statement. And Clare, desperate to get back into his good graces, turned over the management of her assets to fellow NXIVM member Barbara Bouchey, as did Sara.

Bouchey was a successful financial planner with the skills to manage their accounts. But she failed to disclose that she, too, was sleeping with Keith Raniere. Perhaps this conflict of interest had something to do with the fact that Bouchey didn't raise any alarms when Raniere convinced the girls to start spending their money at a startling rate. They paid $1 million to refurbish Nancy Salzman's mansion, $1.7 million for NXIVM's headquarters in Albany, New York, and $2.3 million for a nearby NXIVM horse farm. They also purchased a private jet and made it available to NXIVM's higher-ups, as well as donated an astronomical $20 million to a NXIVM-controlled foundation.

On top of all this, Clare underwrote Raniere's many legal battles against parties he saw as enemies. She initiated litigation when anyone defected from NXIVM, as well as bullied critics of the program with threats of expensive lawsuits. She funded "opposition research" on his enemies, dossiers of extensive, sometimes incriminating information on everyone from local politicians to Toni Natalie.[67] But Keith Raniere still wasn't satisfied. In early 2005 he told the Bronfman sisters that he'd devised an ingenious mathematical formula that would allow him to make millions in the commodities market. And since he was supposedly the Smartest Man in the World, they allowed him to make such trades with their funds.

What followed was a financial bloodbath. He burned through $65 million on extreme, badly thought-out commodity trades.[68] When Clare and Sara Bronfman finally asked him about these losses, he claimed that their father had acted in cahoots with the commodities clearing firm to steal the girls' funds. Edgar Bronfman was the root cause of these massive losses, not Keith Raniere, and both women believed him.

According to Robert Hare's checklist, psychopaths have a persistent need for stimulation, poor behavioral controls, and impulsivity.[69] These three factors help to explain why there's often a correlation between psychopathy and gambling addictions.[70] And there's another trait on Hare's list that psychopaths share: they're known to live parasitic lifestyles.[71] They also feel virtually no compunction about lying or saying anything that gets them what they want. Compare Keith Raniere's behavior (living off the trust funds of his followers) to the ESP program, which cautioned that the world was made up of producers and parasites. Raniere taught Nxians that he was a perfect case study of the producer, but his behavior was clearly parasitic. He had sex, both consensual and nonconsensual, with multiple women in his inner circle; he demanded elaborate proof of devotion; he blew through millions—first of Bouchey's money, then of the Bronfmans'. Despite the predatory nature of his actions, the female members of NXIVM were so in thrall to Keith Raniere that they couldn't see him for the taker he really was. In fact, even after Raniere received multiple life sentences for his role in NXIVM, Clare Bronfman still would not disavow him, writing the judge in her own sentencing, "Many people, including most of my own family, believe I should disavow Keith and Nxivm, and that I have not is hard for them to understand and accept. However, for me, Nxivm and Keith greatly changed my life for the better."[72]

2003: KRISTIN SNYDER

When Raniere began to expand NXIVM's offerings, he created one program—JNESS—that promised female empowerment through a movement that "facilitate[d] an ongoing exploration of what it means to be a woman." It accomplished this fuzzy goal through eleven-day intensives at a cost of $5,000. Apparently, quite a number of victims fell for this pitch, including one Alaska native, Kristin Snyder, who began acting strangely during the intensives, interrupting the classes with bizarre statements unrelated to the conversations on the floor. During the intensive, she stopped sleeping because she'd come to believe that Keith Raniere didn't sleep, either, and she wanted to emulate him. At some point she called her parents and claimed responsibility for the *Columbia* space shuttle explosion.[73]

After days of this erratic behavior, one of ESP's proctors came to a decision. They wouldn't try to remedy Snyder's outbursts or integrate her negative emotional responses through their supposedly patented Exploration of Meaning technology. They simply ordered her to go away. According to the Alaska State Police, Snyder paddled a kayak into the middle of Resurrection Bay, one hundred miles south of Anchorage, and, although she was an expert in the sport, she presumably drowned. Police discovered a suicide note on the seat of her Toyota Tacoma parked near her departure point at Miller's Landing, near Seward. In it she wrote, "I attended a course called Executive Success Programs . . . [M]y emotional center of the brain was killed/turned off. I still have feeling in my external skin, but my internal organs are rotting. Please contact my parents . . . if you find me or this note. I am sorry life, I didn't know I was already dead."[74] Her overturned kayak did wash up onshore, but Snyder's body was never discovered—an understandable outcome, since Resurrection Bay can be as deep as 970 feet in some places.

The suicide note is evidence that she was in extreme emotional crisis if not suffering from clinical psychosis. Extreme sleep deprivation may have been a contributing factor. According to researchers Flavie Waters, Vivian Chiu, and their colleagues, prolonged sleep deprivation can cause "psychotic symptoms . . . from simple visual/somato-sensory misperceptions to hallucinations and delusions, ending in a condition resembling acute psychosis."[75] And lack of sleep may well have exacerbated any existing conditions. But a twenty-eight-year-old woman who took the same ESP course in Mexico also suffered a mental breakdown, and there was no evidence of sleep deprivation in her case. This suggests that there may well have been destabilizing factors built into ESP's curriculum that caused both episodes. After all, ESP's Explorations of Meaning made students hyper-focused on their most negative emotions and memories to rid them of their power (despite the fact that no research has ever pointed to the success or failure of such treatment). It could well be that this course had the opposite effect in a small but not insignificant number of Nxians, as the hyper-focusing brought negative emotions painfully to the surface, forcing a reckoning that could turn emotional pain into a psychotic episode.

But if there was something dangerous about ESP's methodology, Keith Raniere didn't care to root it out. According to Toni Natalie, Raniere claimed that Kristin Snyder faked her suicide because she was involved in a drug-smuggling ring, a conspiracy theory that had no basis in fact.[76] Instead, it's another example of behavior typical of malignant narcissists, who, when threatened, not only lie more often and on a grander scale but also intimidate and attack, all in an attempt to reaffirm their own grandiose vision of themselves. In fact, this pattern of behavior is so predictable that it has a name in the cult recovery literature: narcissistic abuse syndrome.

2010: ALLISON MACK

Around NXIVM headquarters, the tragic incidents in Mexico and Alaska did not dampen the enthusiasm for the JNESS program. In fact, the sessions claiming to be NXIVM's "women's movement" only grew in number and popularity. Three years after Kristin Snyder's disappearance, many of the highest-ranked NXIVM members turned out for a JNESS session in an otherwise unremarkable hotel conference room in Vancouver, Canada: Sara and Clare Bronfman had flown in on their private jet, and Nancy Salzman and her daughter Lauren were both scheduled to be in attendance. This was not a coincidence. Keith Raniere had picked his shrewdest members to participate. They were all there for one person, who'd been convinced to come (in other words, recruited) by Kristin Kreuk, who'd taken the same course not long before. Kreuk was reportedly bringing Allison Mack, her costar in the hit CW TV series *Smallville*, which followed the adventures of a young Clark Kent in his high school years, and the actress had just won a Teen Choice Award for Best Sidekick.

Raniere had sent in his A team to "love-bomb" Mack with the aim of bringing her into the fold on a more permanent basis. The upper echelons of NXIVM were filled primarily with accomplished women. Nancy Salzman helped shape the entire program and the Bronfman sisters funded much of the operation. Quite apart from their personal recruiting skills, their presence in the highest ranks was a primary draw for other powerful women taking their first intensives. NXIVM's teachings were, from a feminist perspective, almost Neanderthal— Salzman "talked about how women have been raised to be monogamous and how men's general nature is to be more polygamous, to spread their seed," Susan Dones, a member at the time, later told the *Hollywood Reporter*.[77] But regardless of the teachings, Raniere hoped that a popular celebrity spokesperson would lure more Hollywood types: he was hoping that Allison Mack could do for him what Tom Cruise did for Scientology, and create a lucrative West Coast revenue stream for his New York–based group.

Lauren sat next to Mack through the entire intensive, eating meals with her and gossiping, and by the end of the session the two were acting like best friends. The Bronfmans invited Mack to fly back to New York with them to visit NXIVM headquarters and meet Keith Raniere in person, which she did, staying for weeks and diving deep into the program. Soon after she arrived, Mack had the chance to be part of "Vanguard Week," or "V-Week," originally a business conference meant to promote NXIVM that had, by 2006, morphed into a ten-day celebration of Keith Raniere's birth. During V-Week, Nxians from all over the United States, Europe, Canada, and Mexico descended on the compound in Clifton Park.

Filmmaker Mark Vicente, a former Nxian, likened the proceedings to "a summer camp for adults where you had all these things you could choose from that you wanted to do. Drumming, dancing, singing, [even] poetry."[78] It was all meant as a tribute to Raniere, recognizing him as the creator of a philosophical movement. His veneration wasn't restricted to V-Week; it had become part of nearly every facet of Nxian life, especially among the group's female members.

Raniere played volleyball at the compound almost daily, and when he did, rows of women would wait for him on the sidelines. As soon as there was a break between plays, they'd rush him as if he were a rock star, asking him their deep, pressing questions.[79] This level of adulation helps explain why Raniere, despite claiming to be celibate, was able to continue multiple sexual relationships with female students. According to an FBI report, by the early 2000s he had between fifteen and twenty sexual partners at any one time.[80] Maybe Allison Mack couldn't see any of this. But what was impossible to miss was the rampant deification of Vanguard.

According to social psychologist Robert Zajonc, nearly everyone is vulnerable to a phenomenon called the exposure effect. Zajonc found that the more a person is exposed to an object or idea, the more likely they are to believe it.[81] Early on in Allison Mack's introduction to NXIVM, she saw Keith Raniere being celebrated as an enlightened being during V-Week and mobbed like one of the Beatles after his volleyball games. As a result of such exposure, it's possible Mack, too, began to view Raniere in the same light.

But there were other reasons Mack could have been vulnerable to a savior figure like Keith Raniere. She was a former child actor who'd been working in film and TV since the age of seven, got her part in *Smallville* at eighteen, and never had a chance to go to college. By twenty-four, she'd spent nearly her entire life in showbiz, and as her fellow child star Christine Lakin told the *Hollywood Reporter*, "she was so hungry for something bigger, some kind of sign [that would show] the purpose and meaning of life."[82]

Allison Mack wasn't the only notable actor drawn to NXIVM. Grace Park of *Hawaii Five-O* and Nicki Clyne of *Battlestar Galactica* were both reported to be members. Certain professional traits in acting could possibly have left individuals vulnerable to NXIVM. Everyone in the performing arts faces rejection, either directly via auditions or indirectly when a role they have lobbied for goes to someone else. They constantly face negative reactions, at both ends of the job, from competing for a part to sometimes bad reviews. Confronting this takes bravery, persistence. To survive, every actor must learn how to negotiate cognitive dissonance. This survival mechanism—the ability to reconcile inconsistencies between closely held beliefs (*I'm good at this*) and objective reality (*Nobody out there thinks I'm good at this*)—is practically a job requirement. Such constant assaults to a sense of self-worth might explain the attraction of NXIVM to Hollywood types like Allison Mack: they came in with a hunger for a more stable form of acceptance and support. It might also explain why, later on, Mack continued to believe in Keith Raniere and his program despite mounting evidence of legal jeopardy.

But setting aside the unique psychology of actors, all women who signed up for JNESS were searching for self-empowerment. This was a paradox that Raniere could exploit, since their presence at the sessions exposed their current lack of power and self-esteem. This insecurity made them easy marks for indoctrination. And Mack quickly internalized the NXIVM focus on negative emotions. In a 2007 blog she wrote, "I have a tendency to say I am stupid. I [have become] very comfortable chalking things up to the fact that I don't have a proper education."[83] In essence, the JNESS philosophy was reinforcing her own habitually low opinion of herself.

But once Allison Mack joined NXIVM, she became an effective advocate for the organization and one of its top recruiters. She

preached to friends and family members about Keith Raniere's bril-
liance and NXIVM's unparalleled ethics.[84] She constantly tried to
bring in her fellow actors as well. According to Scott Johnson and
Rebecca Sun, writing in the *Hollywood Reporter*, Mack attempted to
recruit Grammy-winning singer Kelly Clarkson and *7th Heaven* actress
Beverley Mitchell. Her campaign to bring in *Harry Potter* film actress
Emma Watson took place on Twitter, with Mack imploring her to
come try NXIVM's "unique human development and women's movement."[85]

After a few years, her feverish involvement with NXIVM began
to take a toll on her health. According to Susan Dones, who bumped
into the actress at a Vancouver yoga studio, by 2010 it was clear that
Mack had started a sexual relationship with Raniere, because she'd
already acquired the "gray pallor that was common to Keith's women,
as they all [started] to get a little sickly."[86] Raniere fetishized unnatu-
rally skinny women and manipulated them into extreme weight loss.
As a result, his girls began to take on a similar frightening look: as they
dropped the pounds, their heads began to appear too big for their
bodies, until they started to look like bobbleheads.[87]

2008: THE NXIVM NINE

By 2008, Barbara Bouchey had been a member of NXIVM for nine
years and she'd been sexually active with Keith Raniere nearly the
entire time, as well as deeply involved in the financial side of the operation. With that insider perspective, she'd developed serious reservations about how NXIVM was being run. She wasn't alone. Eight other
women shared similar concerns, including fellow upper-level Nxian
Susan Dones. Sensing strength in numbers, the nine women confronted Vanguard. In an article for Frank Parlato's website, devoted
to investigations of NXIVM and Keith Raniere, Susan Dones ran
through their main points. She called him out for his sexual exploitation of female students, for borrowing large amounts of cash from

members, for laundering money, and for his refusal to pay state or federal taxes.[88]

In their face-to-face meeting in Albany, Raniere was simultaneously condescending, dismissive, and threatening in a frighteningly mild way. The conversation was filmed and Dones later posted a section on YouTube. In the video, Dones and Bouchey sit at one end of a couch and Raniere sits on the other, close enough to reach out occasionally and touch the women for emphasis or to silence them. In the recorded portion of the encounter, Keith Raniere speaks in vague and complicated sentences whose meaning, like his quiet voice, is almost indecipherable. In response to specific complaints, he tells the two women that they don't have the data to understand the true reality of the situation.[89] Nor do they have "experience of leadership or the experience of preserving people's lives," although what exactly he means by that is not clear. At that point, one of the women, whose face is blurred, reminds Raniere that he can't really take credit for leadership in business, either, since his company, Consumers' Buyline, "[fell] apart within a few years." This accurate synopsis of his failure with CBI causes a flicker in his calm demeanor. "That's not—" he says sharply, then catches himself before his emotions can get the better of him. In the next bit of conversation, he almost completely escapes meaning: "Well," he notes, "here's the thing. I've been shot at because of my beliefs. I've had to make choices: Should I have bodyguards, should I have them armed or not? I've had people killed because of my beliefs, and because of their beliefs and because of things that I've said. And I'm leading an organization and it's doing something very good, you might say. You know, this is an old Christian adage, 'The brighter the light, the more the bugs.' So I think what we have is a very bright light." Like someone putting on airs to prove their erudition, he mispronounces the word "adage" so that it rhymes with "mirage."

Despite bringing up their worries frankly and in person, the nine women did not get the response they'd hoped for, or any at all. Raniere refused to address their complaints or admit any wrongdoing. Fed up, all of them defected. It was the largest intentional exodus of upper-level members Raniere had suffered to date, and it came soon after one of NXIVM's greatest triumphs, when Sara Bronfman, through her contacts with Buddhist monk Tenzin Dhonden, convinced the Dalai Lama himself to visit Albany and appear onstage with the Bronfman sisters and give a talk on "Compassionate Ethics in Difficult Times."

Early in his preamble, the Dalai Lama pointed to the sisters to thank them, and he waved to the "respected teachers and I think leaders" in the front row: Keith Raniere and Nancy Salzman. In the wake of the mass defections, the aura of holiness that Raniere had hoped to claim by association—at one point in the evening, the Dalai Lama placed a white sash around Raniere's neck—had disappeared, and all those present could talk about were the Nxians' departure and the circulating rumors of malfeasance. Raniere, thanks to Clare Bronfman's money, took Susan Dones to court, and in every case, with Dones acting as her own attorney, she defeated the high-priced lawyers who were meant to intimidate her.

2017: SARAH EDMONDSON

After the defection of the "NXIVM Nine," the suspicions of mismanagement at NXIVM headquarters started to spread, even though questioning Keith Raniere face-to-face was grounds for being written up for an "ethical breach." The complaints that Dones and Bouchey had lodged publicly—about financial improprieties and increasingly more reckless tax fraud—were starting to worry managers at NXIVM's satellite locations, in Vancouver, Mexico, and New York City. Given the pall that it cast, sensible people would not have considered it a favorable time to start an entirely new Ponzi scheme built on a hierarchy of sex slaves, with Vanguard as the ultimate "Grand Master" at the top. Keith Raniere envisioned such a system of thousands under his control, maybe even someday including an elected politician. In typical half-baked fashion, Raniere named the group Dominus Obsequious Sororium, which was reportedly intended to be Latin for "Master over Slave Women" but is in fact gibberish—a mix of false cognates, mistaken vocabulary, and misspelled Latin that translates to something more like "Eagery Master of Sisterses." But people were so inured to nonsense acronyms like JNESS or pseudo–brand names like NXIVM that nobody dared to call out Raniere's schoolboy mistake. Instead, the new group grew by word of mouth as exclusive invitation-only, usually referred to only by its initials, DOS, like the 1980s Microsoft operating system.

The name was hardly the most ill-conceived part. The top-line recruiters, like Lauren Salzman and Allison Mack, completely avoided any mention of its sexual nature to prospective initiates, instead promoting it to select NXIVM members (already eager to rise in the ranking system) as a "top-secret women's group." That's how Lauren Salzman spoke of it to Sarah Edmondson when she began recruiting her in 2016. "How committed are you to your growth?" Salzman said when she first brought it up. In *Scarred: The True Story of How I Escaped NXIVM, the Cult That Bound My Life*, Edmondson recorded her response, one she now considers dangerously naïve: "Whatever it takes, obviously."

Edmondson was a veteran Hollywood actor and voice-over specialist with decades of film and TV credits and a deep contact list among entertainers in the United States and Canada. She was considered one of NXIVM's top recruiters, mostly through the Vancouver outpost, whose classes she organized and often led herself. And Lauren Salzman was a close friend, the godmother of Edmondson's son, and the officiant at her wedding to fellow Nxian Anthony Ames, a former Brown University quarterback. Edmondson trusted Salzman implicitly.

Still, she was rattled by the preconditions for admission, something Salzman referred to as "collateral"—videos she had to record that falsely accused her parents and husband of committing atrocious acts. But because she did not believe that her closest friend in the program would steer her wrong, she agreed to take a vow of obedience, to keep her membership a secret from her husband—"It's a private choice you're making about your growth," Salzman explained—and, even more bizarrely, to call her friend "Master." The honorific was little more than a formality, Salzman said, dismissing it with a joke: "It's not like you're going to live in a cage or anything."[90]

The levity set Edmondson's nerves at ease. In addition, like several of the other DOS recruits, Edmondson had already internalized the principles set forth in JNESS: that women were weak, flaky, and lacking in follow-through. She enjoyed the thought of being part of a sisterhood who would help her become the strongest, most ideal version of herself. But once she handed over her collateral, Lauren Salzman changed. Edmondson was required to answer texts from her Master within sixty seconds no matter the hour. Lauren also badgered Edmondson to recruit her own slaves so that she, too, could become a Master.

There were warning signs right from the start: a sudden change of tone, a new thread of condescension in Salzman's requests that belied her earlier assurances that the title "Master" was nothing more than a formality. Salzman seemed to dispense with the humanizing touches of friendship now that she had the ability to order Edmondson to do things. But despite the alarming developments, Edmondson was also cowed by the collateral her friend held over her head.[91] That was why, a few months after joining DOS, when Salzman invited Edmondson to fly to Albany for an initiation ceremony that would formalize their new relationship, she agreed. According to *Scarred*, on March 9, 2017, Edmondson and four other women were blindfolded and led by Lauren Salzman into a house. Although Salzman refused to tell them their location, Edmondson peeked out of her blindfold and recognized the surroundings: Allison Mack's residence, although the actress was nowhere in sight.

Salzman then led the women into another room and told them to take off their blindfolds and strip down to their underwear. Edmondson recognized the other women from events over the years at NXIVM. She also noticed that the room boasted a large massage table. Salzman had said that part of the initiation ceremony would involve getting a dime-sized tattoo of a symbol that represented the four elements.

Edmondson had never gotten a tattoo and certainly didn't want one now. When she raised these reservations earlier, Salzman had replied in typical Nxian fashion, framing her resistance as an obstacle to be overcome. "What do you make it mean?" Salzman asked. "What if it stands for your character and your strength as symbolized on your body?" Edmondson swallowed her objections at the time. And when Danielle Roberts—a longtime Nxian and a doctor—entered the room, she felt marginally reassured: at least a medical professional would be there to administer the tattoos.

This feeling drained away when Salzman pulled down her jeans and showed the women the area around her pelvis, where she already had the mark they were about to receive. It horrified Edmondson. It wasn't a tattoo but a brand, a raised and still-raw scar, "like a hunk of meat hanging from . . . the most delicate place on her body."[92] She wanted nothing of the sort done to her, but she couldn't leave. Salzman still had her collateral, the horrible things she'd said about her parents, her husband. And judging from Salzman's unsettling new edge, Edmondson now believed that Salzman might actually use it.

So she put on the face mask they told her to wear for hygienic reasons. She helped hold down the legs of the first slave, as instructed, while Dr. Danielle Roberts dragged a cauterizing pen across the woman's skin. The process took forty-five minutes while everyone in the room had to listen to the screams of pain. When it was her own turn, Edmondson climbed up on the table and lay down. At Lauren's prompting, she said the words, "Master, would you brand me? It would be an honor."[93] Then she tried her best to lie still as Dr. Roberts directed the burning-hot cauterizer across her skin.

A few weeks later, as the brand began to heal, Edmondson was better able to make out the design. She didn't see any symbol for the four elements. Instead, she saw four letters. First an *A.M.*, then a *K.R.* Keith Raniere's and Allison Mack's initials had been burned into her skin forever.

At that point Edmondson stopped feeling powerless and she grew furious. Despite the claims that DOS was all-female, she now felt certain that Keith Raniere was involved. The directives about collateral and the unnecessary and painful branding came from him: they literally had his signature. To confide her suspicions, she turned to Mark Vicente, the filmmaker, who'd recruited her into NXIVM more than a decade earlier. Both he and his wife had already decided to leave. Hoping to find an ally, she spoke with him on the phone.

Vicente had similar suspicions. He told Edmondson that he was disturbed about what was happening to the young women in Albany. "There's like some alternative Stripe Path," he told her. "And Allison Mack is at the top."

Women in the group were being blackmailed into sleeping with Raniere.[94] One had to take a photo to prove that she'd done it and was told beforehand, "You have permission to enjoy it." Vicente's revelation showed the twisted logic behind NXIVM's organizational structure: every division of NXIVM operated in a vacuum, with one never knowing what another was up to. Even though Vicente and Edmondson were both upper-level Nxians, they each only had bits and pieces of the puzzle that was DOS.

Edmondson realized that she'd been brought in to be part of this. Since she weighed more than 110 pounds, she doubted that she'd been chosen to service Keith Raniere. But she was one of the best salespeople in the program, and in fact Nancy Salzman had picked out ideal prospects for her to start recruiting. Everyone whom Salzman pointed out on the Vancouver center's Facebook page were all extremely attractive. Edmondson was revolted and immediately decided to go to the FBI, collateral or not.

For an hour, she laid out to federal authorities what had been done to her and others, filling them in on her twelve years in NXIVM and the latest twist: the predatory nightmare of DOS. Then, according to Barry Meier of the *New York Times*, "Ms. Edmondson filed a complaint with the New York State Department of Health against Danielle Roberts, a licensed osteopath, a follower of Mr. Raniere, who performed the branding . . ."[95]

Next, Edmondson took her story to the media. First she contacted Frank Parlato, a blogger who'd once been hired by Keith Raniere to dig up dirt on NXIVM's enemies. In the process, Parlato had grown horrified by what he discovered about Raniere, starting with the millions of dollars from the Bronfman sisters' trust that Raniere had lost on spectacularly bad commodity trades. When Raniere heard that Parlato was asking the Bronfman sisters about their financial losses, he fired him and maybe even took him to court, which so incensed the journalist that he began relentlessly digging up even more dirt. In 2017, when Edmondson told Parlato that Keith Raniere had graduated from bilking heiresses to outright mutilation, he jumped at the chance to publish the story so he could watch his nemesis burn.

Parlato's report was the first to reveal the existence of a group within NXIVM that was practicing the branding of women. The news did cause some people to quit, but the bulk of NXIVM members stayed, turning on Edmondson instead, labeling her a "weak woman having a tantrum."[96] The law enforcement response was similarly disappointing. So far, nothing had come of her allegations. As a result, Edmondson ramped up her efforts.

Nxians dismissed Parlato as a disgruntled ex-employee, but it was much harder to write off the *New York Times*. On October 17, 2017, reporter Barry Meier published a front-page story, "Inside a Secretive Group Where Women Are Branded." After that, coverage in mainstream media outlets exploded. ABC's *20/20* covered the story, interviewing Mark Vicente, Toni Natalie, and Sarah Edmondson.[97] Vice ran a profile of Frank Parlato.[98] *Dynasty* actress Catherine Oxenberg went on Megyn Kelly's morning show and told the world that she feared her daughter, India, had become a branded DOS slave.[99] The national attention finally spurred the FBI to formally open a criminal investigation into NXIVM, calling Sarah Edmondson back in for a full two and a half days of detailed questioning.[100]

2019: THE PYRAMID COLLAPSES

Once Keith Raniere was notified that women were being interviewed by federal law enforcement about their membership in DOS, he fled to a gated community in Puerto Vallarta, Mexico, where a stay in one of the villas could cost upward of $10,000 a week. Five DOS women, so-called top-line slaves, including Allison Mack and Lauren Salzman, flew there to stay with him, where they planned a "recommitment ceremony" that reportedly involved all the women engaging in a simultaneous sex act. In later court testimony, Lauren Salzman recalled thinking at the time, *There has to be a way that I can grow that isn't this. I have no way of growing except a group blow job.*[101]

Fortunately for Salzman and the others, the "ceremony" never came to pass. On March 25, 2018, Mexican Federales broke into the now fifty-eight-year-old Keith Raniere's Pacific getaway while Salzman was downstairs making smoothies. As the authorities stormed the building, Salzman raced to the bedroom upstairs to protect Raniere or help him hide. As the Federales banged on the door and finally broke in, Salzman crouched down to the floor.[102] "The whole time I kept thinking they could just shoot in this door, thinking really legitimately, 'I could get shot right now,'" Salzman later recalled in court. Meanwhile, Raniere hid in the closet. When the officers finally entered, Salzman instinctively called out Vanguard's name, betraying his whereabouts. "I chose what I believed we had been training for this entire time. I chose love," she said in court. "It never occurred to me that I would choose Keith and Keith would also choose Keith."

Soon after his capture, the Mexican authorities extradited Raniere back to New York. There, he faced charges for "racketeering, forced labor conspiracy, wire fraud conspiracy, and sex trafficking."[103] Federal authorities believed Raniere—not Allison Mack, as he later tried to say in court—had created DOS. They accused him of coercing women into having sex with him and then branding them with his initials. But even though they were building the case that he'd been the mastermind behind the formation of the group, subsequent cases proved that he wouldn't have been able to build DOS without the persuasive powers of his crew of accomplices; as a result, similar charges were filed against Clare Bronfman, Lauren Salzman, Nancy Salzman, Allison Mack, and NXIVM bookkeeper Kathy Russell.

On April 2, 2019, Lauren Salzman pleaded guilty to one count of racketeering and admitted to her part in holding Daniela captive for two years. In court, she expressed her remorse, stating, "I'm very sorry for my poor decision-making and decisions that result[ed] in the harm to others and not [just the] victims in this case but to hundreds of members of our community and their friends and families as well."[104]

On April 8, former CW actress Allison Mack pleaded guilty to one count of racketeering conspiracy and one count of racketeering. In court, she admitted to forcing women to give the "embarrassing information and photographs" that were known as "collateral" in group parlance so that they'd submit to Keith Raniere's demands.[105] She was sentenced to three years in prison and fined $20,000.

Prefect Nancy Salzman, billionaire heiress Clare Bronfman, and bookkeeper Kathy Russell also pleaded guilty to crimes connected with NXIVM. In court, Bronfman expressed her remorse, but the judge viewed this as couched in a continued belief in Keith Raniere. As a result, he sentenced her to eighty-one months in jail, exceeding what was requested by the prosecution.

In February 2022, Nancy Salzman began serving her three-and-a-half-year sentence in a federal prison in Alderson, West Virginia, for racketeering conspiracy. Lauren Salzman and Kathy Russell both avoided prison time, serving five years and two years of probation, respectively, along with community service.

On May 7, 2019, a little over a year after his capture, Keith Raniere finally appeared in Federal District Court in Brooklyn. Toni Natalie followed the proceedings from across the courtroom. During her previous opportunity to speak with Raniere, he'd predicted that the next time they met, Natalie would be either dead or in jail. As fate would have it, the opposite was the case: Natalie was the one walking free and it was now Raniere who was facing hard time behind bars.

In her opening statement, assistant prosecutor Tanya Hajjar said, "The defendant said that he was a mentor, but he was a predator. He targeted young girls, selecting some for special attention, but this was an excuse. He offered to mentor them to teach them and that was an excuse to groom them for sex."[106]

Marc Agnifilo, Keith Raniere's attorney, gave an opening statement in which he compared his client to William Churchill vowing to defend Great Britain after the evacuation of Dunkirk, and claimed that all of Raniere's actions were done in good faith. He characterized DOS "as a sisterhood" formed so that members could "make their lives better." He also pointed out that more than 17,000 people had taken NXIVM courses and many of them received something wonderful out of it.[107]

But Agnifilo's characterization didn't hold up in trial. Over the course of a grueling three-day testimony, Lauren Salzman took the jury through her relationship with "Vanguard" Keith Raniere. She told them how he promised her a baby, then left her with nothing. Lauren also tried to explain the depth of her feelings for him, saying, "He was my master. My most important person. I looked up to him. I wanted to be like him."[108]

Salzman told the jury how her love for Raniere led her to restricting her diet, sending him up-close pictures of her vagina three times a week, and helping him craft a misogynistic rulebook for DOS.[109] And she admitted that the worst thing she had done at his behest was aid in his imprisonment of Daniela years earlier. When the young woman begged Salzman for her immigration papers so she could return to Mexico, Salzman denied the request, believing that, by doing so, she would be viewed as a responsible parent by Raniere and he would give her the baby he'd long promised her.[110]

The defense then called Daniela to the stand. She confirmed that Keith Raniere had indeed imprisoned her for two years. While there was no lock on the door, her room was a cage in all but name because her parents were staunch Nxians. Raniere had told them that their

daughter had committed an "ethical breach" and that her confinement was meant to cure her of excessive pride, when in fact he took
her freedom because she'd shown an interest in another man.

An actress identified only by her first name, Nicole, who had been
recruited into DOS by Allison Mack, told the jury about her harrowing experience of being bound to a table and having an unknown
person perform oral sex on her.[111] Sylvie, an aspiring equestrian, burst
into tears as she recounted being coerced into seducing Raniere.[112] Yet
despite all the horrific accounts of Raniere's behavior from the prosecution's many witnesses, defense attorney Marc Agnifilo insisted that
all of the guru's relationships were entirely consensual.[113]

On June 19, 2019, after six weeks of testimony, the jury returned
with a unanimous verdict: guilty on all seven counts, including racketeering, forced labor, and sex trafficking.[114] Toni Natalie mockingly
wore a striped "jail" shirt as the verdicts were read. More than a year
later, on October 27, 2020, Keith Raniere was sentenced to 120 years
in prison and fined $1.75 million. In a statement he read before the
victims, he maintained his innocence and claimed that many of the
witnesses had lied, but still claimed to be "deeply sorry" for the pain
and anger that he had incited. "Where I am is caused by me," he said,
in an oddly grandiose expression of remorse. "This is all my doing."

On January 21, 2021, Raniere was transferred from the Metropolitan Detention Center in Brooklyn to a maximum-security federal
penitentiary in Tucson, Arizona. This facility offers a sex-offender
management program, so he will likely spend the remainder of his life
in the company of convicts such as Larry Nassar, the serial rapist and
child abuser who was once the team doctor for USA Gymnastics and
is now serving concurrent sentences of 60, 125, and 175 years. Sex
offenders make up 70 to 80 percent of the population in the Tucson
prison, where Keith Raniere has been forced to relinquish the name
"Vanguard." He is known by the new title that he so richly deserves:
Federal Prisoner #57005-177.[115]

ESCAPE

CREDONIA MWERINDE AND THE MOVEMENT FOR THE RESTORATION OF THE TEN COMMANDMENTS OF GOD

For much of her life, most likely by design, Credonia Mwerinde eluded attention. Born in the remote rural southwest of Uganda, she scrupulously avoided the limelight even as she built one of the harshest and most successful doomsday cults in history, the Movement for the Restoration of the Ten Commandments of God. She preferred money to the spotlight and was brutal in its pursuit: her followers gave the Movement all of their earthly goods, then lived in holy servitude; her henchmen terrorized anyone who stood in her way. But after the apocalypse she prophesied failed to appear three successive times (in 1992, 1995, and 1999), Movement members began deserting her. Sensing the end was near, she ordered systematic exterminations at each of her compounds, then gathered more than five hundred loyal adherents in a wood-frame building, locked them in, and set the structure and its occupants on fire. She escaped with the Movement's funds and has never been seen again.

HOLY VISIONS AND MASS MURDER

Credonia Mwerinde lays claim to one of the highest body counts of all infamous cult leaders. On March 17, 2000, within the grounds of the Movement for the Restoration of the Ten Commandments of God's central compound, Ishayuriro-rya-Maria, or Mary's Place of Rescue, she led more than five hundred of her followers into a wooden building that they called an ark and had been lined with sixty-eight jerry cans of gasoline. Then Mwerinde, the cult's high priestess, known to initiates as the Programmer, stepped outside, sliding a wooden bolt across the door of the ark. Knowing that there was no escape, she set the extremely flammable building ablaze. The resulting fire was so intense that local pathologists at first believed the heads of the faithful had exploded, although it's more likely that their skulls became brittle as the bodies were consumed and falling rafters shattered their fragile remains, the structure disintegrating around and on top of them.

But later it was discovered that this horrific event was not the only mass extermination Mwerinde could take credit for. Soon after the first conflagration, investigators unearthed mass graves at three other Movement compounds scattered throughout the Kanungu District. These recovered bodies showed signs of strangulation, stab wounds, and poisoning. They'd already begun to decompose, making the authorities believe that the murders had been committed in haste, at least a week before the fire at Mary's Place of Rescue. Following this gruesome discovery, Mwerinde could lay claim to more than 1,075 followers dead by her command.

How did this woman, born in 1952 to Paul and Farazia Kashaku, in an idyllic corner of Uganda near the Bwindi Impenetrable Forest, come to make such a bloody mark on the history of her country? She did not grow up without resources. Her family had landholdings, pineapple groves and sugarcane fields, cash crops in a lush part of the country. But Mwerinde seems to have had ambitions of her own. She learned to brew banana beer, inserted herself into the home life of a local bar owner, then took over the running of the place. She used this template several times: insinuating herself into a family, bringing the man of the house under her spell, then turning his wealth and resources to her own purposes. She took control and then moved on.

In 1989, after the collapse of her bar business, Mwerinde set her sights on a religious movement in the deeply Catholic country-side, using one of the few paths to power available to a woman: she claimed that the Virgin Mary had appeared to her, a phenomenon known as a Marian apparition. The Church seemed to offer safety, a stable income freely given by the faithful, a power structure that she could exploit with impunity, and moral cover for any crimes she might commit. Although we have no way of knowing how much was planned at the outset, Mwerinde again brought her skills to the attention of a powerful man: Joseph Kibwetere, a wealthy landowner and the founder of a Catholic school, Nyakazinga Secondary School, built on his own extensive holdings in Rwashamaire. He became the public face of the Movement, while she ran it all as the power behind the throne, unsung by choice, a preference that earned her the nickname the "Programmer."

Over the next ten years, Mwerinde would use her alleged direct contact with the Virgin Mary to build the Movement of the Restoration of the Ten Commandments of God into a highly profitable religious enterprise funded by the generous donations of followers who promised to give up all earthly possessions and follow the orders of the Programmer. Her adherents built compounds, farmed the land, and hired themselves out as a skilled and unskilled local labor force, working all the while for next to nothing for her Holy Commandments. These followers recruited still more citizens from among their own families and friends. Some of the most favored even became enforcers, exacting revenge on those who dared to defect, even at times committing murder in Mwerinde's name, since, as the Programmer assured her inner circle, the Virgin Mary had told her that members of the Movement had permission to kill.

How much wealth Mwerinde was able to amass, how she converted these earthly riches into a fortune she could take with her, and how exactly she managed her final escape are crucial questions that remain a mystery. It was only after the mass murder that the world beyond her small corner of Uganda learned of the Movement, and by that time she had vanished—the only known architect of a brutal doomsday cult to escape death, elude punishment, and disappear without a trace.

BRUTAL AMBITIONS IN A VIOLENT COUNTRY

It is horrible to say that Mwerinde's deeds, heartless as they were, did not necessarily stand out against Uganda's extensive history of factional violence, religious wars, colonial exploitation, and economic pillage. From the earliest point of contact with Arab traders and European colonial forces, a series of conflicts, based partly on faith and partly on financial interest, racked the countryside. Although little is known for certain about local history prior to when explorers and missionaries began to arrive en masse in the nineteenth century, traditions suggest the many kingdoms that would one day be colonized within the future Uganda had solid political institutions of their own.

Political power was always supported by spiritual authority. Numerous clans within the kingdoms worshipped a creator god, known by various names, including Katonda, Kazooba, and Ruhanga, along with a variety of lesser local gods and spirits. Clan leaders, called the *emandwa*, formed local cults favoring their own grouping of gods from this vast mythology. Starting in the mid-nineteenth century, these clans and their cultures found themselves challenged by the missionaries of Europe and the Middle East. Islam arrived first and then, in 1877, Anglican missionaries arrived in the company of the British East Africa Company, who were themselves following Arab traders up the Nile River to its origin in Jinja, Uganda, on the shores of Lake Victoria. Two years later, in 1879, the Anglicans were followed by a second wave of French Catholic missionaries. As trade agreements were signed among the tribes and the colonial powers, ostensibly religious wars sprang up, first between Muslims and Christians, then between Protestants and Catholics. These clashes often threated to turn into bloodbaths, especially if one side had been supplied with advanced Western weaponry, as sometimes happened.

The chaos of these overlapping conflicts led to the establishment of the British Protectorate in 1894, which was aimed less at pacifying the country than at minimizing the economic losses due to violence. The protectorate ran the country until colonial rule ended in 1962, when the newly liberated nation replaced the governor of the British Protectorate with Apollo Milton Obote. The new prime minister (and later president) was aided in his consolidation of power by the highest-ranking African national in the British forces, the ruthless Idi Amin Dada. Amin had helped the British put down the Mau rebellion in Kenya and aided in the elimination of the rebel threat in Somalia.

Obote made an uneasy alliance with his bloodthirsty chief of military operations. He knew that Amin had turned a simple assignment— to control cattle rustlers in Nairobi—into a brutal terror campaign, with Amin's forces torturing the rustlers to death and in some cases burying them alive. Nevertheless, Obote made Amin the head of his armed forces and collaborated with him in establishing profitable smuggling operations.

Later, in the political maneuverings that followed the discovery of Amin's misappropriation of $350,000 worth of gold and ivory he'd received from Congolese rebels in exchange for arms, Mutesa II, the king of Buganda, who'd been set up by the British to share power with Obote, complained bitterly of this thievery, but Amin and Obote chased him from the country and consolidated their hold on power. Obote's reign, which was itself known for its brutality, ended when Amin seized control in 1971.

Idi Amin, with six wives and as many as thirty mistresses scattered about the countryside, was originally hailed as a charismatic liberator of his nation. His benevolence seemed to increase when he allowed Mutesa to return from exile and pardoned Obote's political prisoners.

But while he was grabbing headlines for his mercy, he quietly set up killer squads to murder soldiers from the Acholi and Lango tribes thought to be loyal to Obote. Soon he began picking battles with little regard for their economic impact. He expelled wealthy Asians and Israelis from the country, even though they ran many of the companies, plantations, and construction projects powering the nation's economy.

Amin's killer squads didn't cease operations after he consolidated his hold on power. Instead they increased their activity, committing ethnic cleansing, eliminating political rivals, and assassinating competitors to his business interests and journalists who dared to investigate his crimes. Estimates of the dead range from 300,000 to 500,000. Amin himself claimed to have eaten human flesh. Uganda's reputation plummeted after he allowed Palestinian hijackers of an Air France Airbus to land at Entebbe Airport; nearly all the hostages were rescued in a daring and successful raid by Israeli forces. But despite this defeat on an international scale, Amin gave himself increasingly grander titles—His Excellency President for Life, Field Marshal Al Hadji Doctor Idi Amin, VC, DSO, MC, CBE, Lord of all the Beasts of the Earth and Fishes of the Sea, and Conqueror of the British Empire in Africa in General and Uganda in Particular—and some say he descended into madness caused by untreated syphilis. Large portions of his troops fled to Tanzania, then collaborated with Tanzanian forces to eventually rout Amin and, in April 1979, permanently remove him from power.

This ouster was followed by a decade of unchecked civil war in the country. From 1980 to 1986, the Ugandan government—once again under Milton Obote and now backed by the United States—fought against factions of the National Resistance Army, who in turn were backed by Libya and Saudi Arabia. The rebels won, installing Yoweri Museveni as president, where he remains to this day. His reign, too, has been marred by human rights abuses and violent bush wars, especially in the north, where Joseph Kony has led the Lord's Resistance Army.

Kony is a brutal and fearsome warlord, until recently hunted by international agencies who blame him for massacres, sexual violations, mutilations, and systematic theft. But in many ways his claim to lead arose from the same spiritual impulse, the same supposedly divine origin, as Credonia Mwerinde's. He says he was called to be a mouthpiece of God, blessed with spiritual powers, visited by divine forces. He even says that he is fighting on behalf of the Ten Commandments, as the Movement for the Restoration of the Ten Commandments of God claimed to do. Despite these quasi-spiritual beginnings, Kony is notorious throughout the world for his cruelty, raiding villages, and turning boys into child soldiers and girls into sex slaves.

One can't really confirm what the early life of Credonia Mwerinde was like, but many of the traits that she displayed—especially violence cloaking itself in the guise of holiness, as well as her lust for wealth achieved by exploitation—were features of normalcy in Uganda when she came of age. Viewed on its own, her behavior stands out for its exceptional ruthlessness, but in a country whose history has been soaked in bloodshed, her cruelty had plenty of precedents.

A FIERY TEMPER

In 1952, Credonia Mwerinde was born in Kanungu, the rural town that later gave the district its name. Her parents were Paul and Farazia Kashaku, and it's only known that they were landowners by deduction, since Mwerinde later managed to wrest control of the family lands from her brothers and sisters. Very little is known about her childhood. One can only assume that she had extensive schooling in the Catholic Church, given her knowledgeable manipulation of matters of faith later in life. What is known is that she did not conform to her family's idea of good behavior or fit into the mold of a pious Catholic girl. She was quick to anger and, once she grew up, promiscuous.

None of this is unusual for a young person raised in a strict religious community. Rebellion is a natural response to a cloistered upbringing, where parents and teachers are constantly imposing order. Once a child from this environment grows old enough to explore life free of guidance, there's a good chance they'll start testing out all those forbidden behaviors. But when Mwerinde strayed, her parents urged her back to the Church. Religion, the missionaries promised, was designed to save their souls.

In her early twenties Mwerinde hit the first known stumbling block when she fell in love with a local health officer. Perhaps she thought she'd found a way out of the strict home life that she'd known until then. But the man allegedly jilted her, or at least Mwerinde felt that she had been set aside. Her reaction was violent: she broke into the man's house and set his belongings aflame.

This is the first example of Mwerinde's lifelong obsession with fire. The tendency to commit arson is one of the three elements of what is known as the Macdonald triad, activities that are said to be predictive of later predatory behavior, a precursor of sociopathy. (The other two factors are cruelty to animals, considered a rehearsal for murder, and bedwetting, which is not violent in itself but, when it appears in conjunction with the other two habits, strengthens the prediction.) Many believe that these behaviors are an early sign of homicidal tendencies.

It must have struck her family and the local authorities in the same way, because Mwerinde was shipped off to a mental ward. But she was not accurately diagnosed in any meaningful way. After some months passed, she was simply labeled "mentally disturbed" and sent packing. That experience clearly didn't help Mwerinde establish a direction in life, as she never again turned to psychology for help in sorting out her inner demons. As designations go, "mentally disturbed" is far from useful. While the term "borderline personality disorder" is still vague, merely an umbrella term for more difficult-to-diagnose disorders, the general profile seems to fit Mwerinde: unstable emotions that lead to impulsive or dangerous behavior patterns. There can be intense periods of anger spiraling into anxiety or depression. This begins a destructive cycle, with behavior and emotion feeding off one another.

There were signs of sociopathy as well. With her self-centered focus, Mwerinde seemed prone to making dramatic and violent decisions. Many sociopaths exhibit narcissism, craving attention and putting their own well-being over that of anyone else in their lives. If slighted—as Mwerinde was by this officer—sociopaths may take it as an earth-shattering event and respond in kind. Whatever the case might have been, it was also a tragic one. There was no way Mwerinde could have ever been properly diagnosed at the time, not even in the United States. After a failed attempt at a pure Catholic upbringing and a trip to the mental hospital, many around Mwerinde began looking down on her.

BREWING UP TROUBLE

Mwerinde decided to take control of her fate using her natural charisma and ability to tempt others to join her in darker or riskier pursuits. During this time—the early 1980s—Uganda had fallen under the control of the brutal Idi Amin Dada, and the country's economy and infrastructure were entering a tailspin. Mwerinde needed a safe harbor, and she found temporary refuge by joining forces with Eric Mazima, another Kanungu local, in a common-law marriage, convincing him to evict his second wife from her home and to invest money in a Kanungu bar that Mwerinde would run. This is one fact that emerges in multiple accounts of Mwerinde's early life: her skill as a brewer of banana beer, an East African staple.

But apparently, though busy running her bar, she found enough time to nurture her violent streak. One unverifiable story can be found in a letter to a member of Mwerinde's family, warning them that the writer believed she had committed murder. The details are scant but frightening. One night Mwerinde lured upstairs a weary traveler who came into her bar. In the morning the regular crew stopped by for an early drink of Mwerinde's locally famed banana beer and found her scrubbing what seemed to be blood from the concrete floor. Credonia appeared unfazed by their presence and asked what the drunkards might like from her menu.

This is another indication of Mwerinde's sociopathic streak: whenever she was caught in a risky situation, her response would be to smile or joke, an almost playful defense mechanism. Somewhere around the time of the alleged murder, in March 1981, she decided to use her charms to infiltrate God's kingdom. While the date comes from Mwerinde's later writings and clearly can't be trusted, this is when she supposedly encountered her first Marian apparition. The Virgin Mary told Mwerinde to repent for her sins and return to the flock she had abandoned. Whether or not Mwerinde believed this sighting actually had occurred, it was during the next decade, as Idi Amin's unstable dictatorship fell to pieces and the country slid into civil war, that she decided she was worthy of sainthood.

Maybe as Mwerinde witnessed the country descending into chaos around her, and seeing the rising fortunes of various warlords, she thought that she could also claw her way to legitimacy, power, and widespread influence. Soon after her supposed encounter with divinity, Mwerinde began playing up her promiscuous image, starting a rumor that she was a sex worker as well as a bartender. While it's possible the claim is based on some truth, her husband, Mazima, refuted it. But it didn't matter, as Mazima wasn't her husband for long. The sex work, real or imagined, could be early evidence of her new career path: Mwerinde wanted to be seen as a modern-day Mary Magdalene, so she tried to appear as deeply engaged in sin as possible. Her redemption was on the horizon. This was Mwerinde's craftiest move yet, the first evidence of the master narrative that she created while exercising control over the Movement.

In 1989, Credonia's bar went belly-up and her marriage fell apart, just as Yoweri Museveni was consolidating his power and routing Joseph Kony in the north. But Mwerinde already had a new plan. June 14, 1989, marked the occasion of Mwerinde's second Marian apparition. It was during this vision, in a cave outside Kanungu, that Mary delivered unto Mwerinde the words that would become the opening salvo of the Movement's text: "A Timely Message from Heaven." The mission was made clear to her: the day was coming for the sinners of humanity to repent, and they needed a leader to show them the way. And the Blessed Mother had tasked Credonia Mwerinde with seeking a partner in this endeavor.

A WEALTHY MAN TO SHARE HER VISION

Joseph Kibwetere was a Ugandan Catholic and twenty years Mwerinde's senior. By his nation's standards, he was a wealthy landowner from a pious family. Religious leaders gave the Kibweteres preferential treatment on both counts. Joseph saw himself as a born leader. Above the poorer class from birth, he envisioned a grand future, leading the faithful into the truth, and assured of the prosperity the Church told him he deserved.

In 1960 he married a woman named Theresa and worked as an assistant supervisor to his area's Catholic school system. As Joseph's stature grew, so did his inheritance: his family continued to acquire large swaths of land. Soon he worked his way up to be the overseer for the district government's agricultural and construction projects. But when he tried to take the next step in what he thought of as his inevitable rise—political office—he lost the nomination. He didn't take kindly to this defeat, like many who are not used to having the rights of their privilege questioned. He staged a hasty retreat, back to the land his family owned in Rwashamaire. Now the lord of several large properties, hundreds of cattle, and a prosperous mill, he could cover up for his failure to enter a true position of power in the government. Much like Mwerinde, Joseph Kibwetere decided that if power wouldn't come to him one way, he would retreat to the original source of it in his life: religion.

Kibwetere funded the construction of a new Catholic school, called Nyakazinga Secondary. He taught at his own school, as both headmaster and professor of religion. Like his own upbringing, the doctrine was strict. This should have satisfied all the conditions for Kibwetere's drive in life. It wasn't a large-scale congregation, but it made him the most well-respected man in the community. It also gave him a direct line of access to young minds. Kibwetere lived to influence people, and there is no easier target than children. Orthodox religious schools offer a particular opportunity to not only teach but truly mold.

The Church gave Kibwetere the influence and funds to build the school. In turn, his institution supplied the Church with eager new congregants who would eventually become either lifetime members and donors or even friars, nuns, and priests. While running this school, a greater change came over Kibwetere's psychology. He became more of a proselytizer, seeking power, and religion—in particular its mythmaking—could grant him what he wanted. And Mwerinde recognized this strategy with its virtuous circle—his respect growing as he built up his religious school, the Church sending him students, the school sending the students back well tutored in the faith. It's likely that Mwerinde had also heard about Kibwetere for another reason: on April 25, 1984, he claimed to have had his own Marian apparition.

It certainly could be useful to a man running a Catholic school to have a blessing from the Virgin Mary. Mwerinde likely noticed the effect this had on the locals, who didn't seem to seek much proof of his claim to a holy vision. They seemed to welcome the idea, as if it had been something granted to all of them. If the Virgin Mary had blessed Kibwetere, she had vicariously done so for the entire community. It was as Kibwetere had always noted: they were a chosen people, just like the Israelites of the past.

But as the years passed, he wondered if he had acquired enough prestige. And just as this crisis in his faith took hold, Credonia Mwerinde came to him, with two women, cousins or sisters from her own family. Mwerinde told him that the Virgin Mary had told them to seek out Kibwetere, and they backed up her claim. This was just the jolt that Kibwetere needed: now there was no doubting that the Blessed Mother had chosen him for a reason.

Mwerinde stood before him, requesting his help in a divine mission. But one thing quickly became apparent: Mwerinde held all the power. Kibwetere was a respected and wealthy community leader; yet he was brought to his knees before this stranger redeemed by her own apparition. He was intelligent but clearly didn't have the spark necessary to truly make himself known in the world. He was a staid bureaucrat without a real bureaucracy. Mwerinde, on the other hand, radiated religious charisma. She had long since unburdened herself of any self-doubts, even those buried the deepest.

And from that day forward, Kibwetere became Mwerinde's first true convert, apart from members of her own family. Nineteen eighty-nine was the year that the Movement for the Restoration of the Ten Commandments of God was truly born. Mwerinde buoyed Kibwetere's belief in his Marian apparition and even gave him her own interpretation: the Virgin Mary had singled him out to be the leader of a new Catholic population in Uganda, a chosen people there in their homeland. She was molding his desires to fit her own needs. Kibwetere had become the student now, and he was all too willing to submit behind the scenes if it meant fulfilling a greater destiny.

Women had far less influence in Ugandan society than men. Mwerinde's acquisition of Kibwetere's loyalty could be considered her first and most unlikely miracle. She had made someone who considered himself the highest authority submit to her as an even higher one. She even made him believe it was all his own idea. Kibwetere's son Juvenal Rugambwa explained it as such: "The next thing we knew, she was in our house and they had decided to start their cult here. Soon, she was beating us all. My father was in awe of her and would do anything she said."

And how did Mwerinde plan to build her new religion? She told Kibwetere that their movement would be formed in the same way Christ had constructed his own. Property would be relinquished, and wealth would be sacrificed for the mission. Kibwetere began selling his excess properties off, a necessary exchange. He finally realized, working through his own warped internal logic, that true power didn't need a link through physical property, because true power was spiritual. He sold his mill's equipment and pulled his children out of the very school he had built. Strict homeschooling, under Mwerinde's watch, would be the new order of business from then on.

The foundation was laid. Mwerinde would be the Programmer, the one who instituted the rules and set the course of the Movement. Kibwetere would be the figurehead, soon bestowed with the title of bishop. But if they were to define themselves as a legitimate Catholic enterprise, they needed some real authority figures: clergy. Later accounts from the Movement's holy text state that Kibwetere was led north by the Virgin, who told him to seek out a religious devotee known as Scholastica Kamagara. In reality, Scholastica was just someone Kibwetere's wife, Theresa, already knew: a vocal figure in the diocese of central Mbarara District. She had family connections, and there was one man in particular who seemed perfect, someone else frustrated by his own ambition and who would complete the Movement's construction . . . sending them hurtling toward their collectively imagined doomsday revelation.

A CAPTAIN FOR THE ARK

Status, security, and continuity were important in Uganda, partly because all of them were in such short supply. Throughout the upheaval of the civil war, the institutions of the Catholic Church provided refuge and an authority that was above the fray, and the priests in charge knew this. As Professor Bernard Atuhaire writes in his book about the Movement, *The Uganda Cult Tragedy: A Private Investigation*, "Religious teaching, as a product of missionary work, has always portrayed priesthood in a mystified fashion to the extent that the claimed infallibility of the Pope is generally believed to be shared by the clan of priests and the religious."[1] Priests enforced this hierarchy over the years, establishing themselves as arbiters of society—capable of dealing out punishments and blessings in equal measure. Respect was their currency.

Which is why the soft-spoken Father Dominic Kataribaabo stood out so much. He wasn't one who wielded his spiritual authority with a heavy hand. Genial and articulate, Dominic seemed to fit much better into the archetype of the gentle priest. He was rector of the Kitabi Seminary in the Bushenyi District of western Uganda, directly west of the central Mbarara District, from the late 1970s to the early 1980s. A surrogate father for many of his students, Father Dominic won his followers through compassion instead of strict discipline.

The best example of this emerges through his relationship with pupil Joseph Kasapuraari. Father Dominic saw something in this quiet young man that reminded him of himself. Every year, within the seminary, there were elections for student leadership roles. Kasapuraari sought such a position but knew he didn't have the personality to carry the vote. Still, when Dominic announced the various winners, he took a dramatic beat and in a surprised voice told the seminary that Kasapuraari had won a place in the student government. Was rigging the election deliberate kindness or a tool to earn loyal devotion? Religion was so entwined in these men's lives that the difference between an act of generosity and one of ambition is hard to distinguish. That's the danger in investing religious institutions with such power in society. But to Joseph Kasapuraari, ambition or generosity was a distinction without a difference, and Dominic's actions earned Kasapuraari's eternal gratitude.

With such followers at his back, Father Dominic saw to it that in the Rugazi Parish he would be seen as a true holy man and humble follower of God. This pleased him, because underneath the gentle exterior the holy man shared a condition with Joseph Kibwetere and Mwerinde: the lust for something more in this life on Earth. One account, recorded in Professor Atuhaire's history, tells of Dominic forcing the seminary workers to spend countless hours digging through the swamp behind Kitabi—all because he found one stone that shone with glittering elements. Common phrases from his weekly self-help sessions with his students rang with worldly and ambitious statements like "You are not cheap," "Always aim high," and "If you want peace, prepare for war." Value, for Father Dominic, was not limited to faith in God; it was equally rooted in oneself. He taught his charges to strive for an idealized, libertarian self-sufficiency.

But as seen with Kibwetere and Mwerinde, unrealized ambition can be dangerous fuel. Father Dominic was greedy for advancement. Within the Mbarara Diocese as a whole, those of the Rugazi Parish were known for their feelings of superiority, seeing themselves as the true leaders of the area's religious destiny. Standouts from the Rugazi Parish had historically received influential positions within the dioceses of Uganda, such as treasurer, editor of the Church's newspaper, and the coveted title of vicar general.

Father Dominic always fancied himself a shoo-in for the role of bishop in the nearby Kasese Diocese. But this illusion was soon shattered when another holy man was selected for that honor, and Dominic was to remain in his small seminary. Many in the Church believed Dominic politicked too much, trying to gain local support on his own behalf, and there were those who saw a potential usurper beneath his quiet demeanor.

Then, at his lowest point, a friend came to save Father Dominic Kataribaabo: his old student Joseph Kasapuraari, who was the son of none other than Scholastica Kamagara, the woman Kibwetere had been directed to either by the Virgin Mary or by his wife, Theresa. Scholastica and John Kamagara, Joseph's father, were fiercely devoted people. They'd wanted to become a nun and priest, respectively, but for some reason were never able to achieve such status. Joseph had always been molded to be their own religious warrior; John and Scholastica saw in their son a chance to redeem their failure. They made sure he attended mass every day and pushed him in his own ambitions at the Kitabi Seminary.

When Father Dominic's frustrations became known to Joseph, Scholastica relayed this information to Theresa Kibwetere. In this way, Theresa became aware that an ordained authority of the Catholic Church was wavering in his faith. Dominic, Joseph, and his parents were all desirable candidates for conversion in Mwerinde's eyes—highly educated, prominent in the Catholic world, and, most importantly, a tight-knit group. This would soon emerge as Mwerinde's dominant strategy for recruitment—aiming to enlist full families and even entire neighborhoods in one mass conversion, the most efficient way to build a workable infrastructure for what would soon become the Movement for the Restoration of the Ten Commandments of God.

In the growing Movement, Father Dominic's ambitions aligned with those of Mwerinde and Kibwetere. If the Catholic Church did not want to give him higher power, he would seize it for himself. And as a bonus, he would prove them wrong. From the beginning, the Movement never branded itself as anything separate from Catholicism. They did not market themselves as a rebel group—just a circle of devotees concerned that the Church had gone off track and seeing themselves as the chosen few who could save it.

Joseph Kasapuraari and his parents joined the Movement as apostles, and the enterprise gained momentum. And Mwerinde made sure that Dominic was rewarded by appointing him as vicar general. The Church had not given him the honors he felt he deserved, but Mwerinde was offering him the chance to achieve everything he felt was rightfully his.

However, before more conversions could begin in earnest, a text was needed. While the Bible was still canonized by the Movement, their narrative was based on the idea that the Virgin Mary returned to Earth with a new directive from on high. A religious text is the foundation of any such development. It contains the rules, it is the law, it is the culture. It needs to communicate the grand mission in the clearest possible way. As a result, Mwerinde needed to finalize a version of "A Timely Message from Heaven."

Here's a sample quote from the text itself that seems to speak in the voice of a vengeful God: "There will be great tribulation upon all the people, such that has never been experienced by any person since the creation of the world. People will be absent-minded and will develop a spirit of independence from God in their deeds, and this spirit will displease the Creator. He will in reaction release to the world chastisements that will include the shedding of blood in many countries . . ."[2]

In other words, the apocalypse was coming. God was enraged at humanity, and it would take a last-ditch effort by the Virgin Mary and Christ himself to halt the Creator's wrath. Mwerinde and her followers were the final line of defense here for believers on Earth and the Movement was the last chance for salvation. And to increase the sense of urgency within the fold, all their actions now were part of a race against the clock: the Virgin and her Son had tasked the Movement with redeeming as many as possible before the end times.

And that event seemed right around the corner. As the civil war tore Uganda apart throughout the 1980s, its citizens felt vulnerable and desperate for something to sustain their frustrated hope. Time was running out. On top of the war consuming their country, the new millennium was looming. Against the irrational fear and paranoia, the Movement for the Restoration of the Ten Commandments of God could provide what the Catholic Church could not: an ark and a vessel to heaven. Unfortunately for those who hoped to board this vessel, it was actually taking them closer to a grisly end.

USING FAMILY TO BUILD A CULT

Elections followed the fall of Idi Amin Dada in 1979. But when Yoweri Museveni lost to Milton Obote, recently returned from exile, Museveni declared the process a sham. He formed the National Resistance Army and took up arms against the Obote government's Uganda National Liberation Army and a rebel group known as the Uganda National Rescue Front. The result was the Ugandan Civil War, also known as the Ugandan Bush War, a guerrilla conflict that raged across the country from 1981 to 1986.

Even when the National Resistance Army won and Museveni assumed the presidency in 1986, the divisions in the country remained raw. Both sides had committed atrocities, some even rivaling Idi Amin's brutality. Uganda still hadn't found the stability it had been searching for since independence in 1962. In the face of this persistent instability, there was a profound longing for hope, security, and spiritual certainty. This made the country the perfect breeding ground for an apocalyptic theology.

On the ground in local communities, status held the keys to safety and prosperity. But access to status was controlled by those who were the gatekeepers to education, and in the region where the Movement was born and elsewhere, this was under the authority of the Catholic Church. Although the emerging high society of Uganda paid lip service to the value of education, the newly wealthy didn't want to offer the poor any real entrée to power, so they cut off all avenues to intellectual achievement and upward mobility. Credonia Mwerinde and Joseph Kibwetere saw that the only way they could rise through the ranks was by acquiring religious influence—and by promising it to others.

With Kibwetere in place as the bishop of the Movement and Father Dominic Kataribaabo now installed as the vicar general, Mwerinde had both the power structure of her movement and the template for all later conversions. Ugandan communities were made up of close groups, a tapestry of villages and interrelated families. Once the weak points of entry could be identified, the Movement would be able to spread quickly. Atuhaire writes, "The propagation of the messages took on a chain approach. Right after the immediate family and friends, followed relatives and their friends."

It was a distribution system as well as a marketing scheme. First, one member of the family would hear of the Movement and be convinced to join. Religious fervor would convince those closest to them to follow their lead. Neighbors would then see families moving en masse to live in compounds of the Movement. Soon, everyone in a particular village knew about the Movement, and any curious neighbors who showed interest would soon be descended upon by recruiters.

And Mwerinde made sure the Movement appeared as accepting as possible to outsiders. As she wrote in "A Timely Message from Heaven," the main text of the Movement for the Restoration of the Ten Commandments: "Our Lord Jesus Christ . . . said: 'I died on the cross and shed my blood for everybody that has breath; be it a Protestant or a Catholic, be it a Muslim or a pagan who never embraced any religion, or whatever belief one embraces provided he is alive, let him hear these messages.'"

Passages from "A Timely Message from Heaven" were distributed in many ways. First, they would be quoted verbally around town. Next, they would run in local papers. This had precedents, as the Roman Catholic Church often published notices, prayers, and religious messages in newspapers. Local authorities and citizens were accustomed to seeing religious texts printed alongside the news and community notices. Finally, "A Timely Message from Heaven" would hit the local airwaves, beamed out around southwestern Uganda, helped along by Father Dominic's and Joseph Kibwetere's connections to broadcast stations.

Although reliable records of membership levels are scarce, it's clear that by 1993 the Movement had gained a sizable following. It was awarded legal status to trade as a nongovernment organization by Ugandan authorities. This allowed them to set up official posts in towns that were less than accepting of their beliefs. Because of their apparent legitimacy, they gained new followers.

All of this was intentional. Mwerinde, who grew up under the heavy mantle of expectations imposed by the Church, understood the influence of peer pressure and community expectations on the devoted. When potential followers balked at recruitment and claimed they could exercise good faith outside of the Movement, they were told that the world was too full of sin and that the new commandments of the Virgin Mary could not be followed unless this was done within the Movement itself. They were compelled to join or else their sins would prove too heavy, and their prayers wouldn't be enough. They had to enlist or they'd be on the wrong side of the apocalypse.

Once recruits were inside the fold, they soon found that all exit routes were closed. When someone tried to back out of the Movement, Mwerinde gathered their loyal family members and granted them temporary leave so that they could return to their hometowns, where they would physically prevent the would-be defector from entering their former home. The importance of family in Uganda cannot be overstated, and by abandoning the Movement, a person ran the risk of becoming homeless. Often, they simply returned to the Movement just so they would have a place to live.

There was another factor that greatly contributed to membership in the Movement: the AIDS epidemic that grew in strength in the late 1980s and early 1990s. A passage was added to the circulated excerpts of "A Timely Message from Heaven" that contained a direct reference: "The chastisement He released for that Commandment the world calls it AIDS disease: but from the Lord, it is a punishment. 'I will not give them any medicine, its medicine will only be to repent and restore my Ten Commandments. Those who will do that will be forgiven, and they will even be given medicine. I will only take away that punishment from them when they all repent, when they cry out to me and restore my Commandments.'" Allegedly, AIDS was a sign of the coming apocalypse and a problem that only the Movement could solve—and a marketing opportunity that helped recruiters bring more converts into its various complexes across southwestern Uganda into a new world of silence and unspeakable cruelty.

LIFE IN THE COMPOUNDS

The Movement controlled several satellite trading posts and inter-village housing units, but the bulk of the membership lived in four massive compounds that served as the centers for the Movement's operations. Ibumbiro-rya-Maria, or Mary's Place of Molding, was located on Kibwetere's land in Rwashamaire, just outside Kagamba in the Ntungamo District. Itakiro-rya-Maria, or Mary's Place of Confession, was built near the town of Mitooma, the capital of the Mitooma

District. Then there was Igabiro-rya-Maria, or Mary's Place of Giving, in Rugazi Parish. This was built on Father Dominic's land, outside his old seminary, a sizable chunk of farmable real estate that Dominic won over for the Movement. It was the most central of all the compounds, as it sat near the Trans-African Highway.

Finally, there was Ishayuriro-rya-Maria, or Mary's Place of Rescue. This compound sat in the secluded foothills of Kanungu, near Mwerinde's birthplace. After her parents passed away, Mwerinde took possession of the land and designated her mother and father as the "Grandparents of the Believers," building the altar of Mary's Place of Rescue right above their tombs. Although Paul and Farazia Mwerinde had no real connection to the Movement, they became its icons, the Abraham and Sarah of the Movement's first generation.

These huge complexes were funded through the donations of the members and maintained by their labor. Once a potential recruit decided to commit, they were required to give up all material possessions, which were handed straight over to the Movement's leaders. The wealthy were told to follow the Bible's admonition to sell all they had and devote their lives to the Movement. The poor had a higher price to pay: with little land or things of value to hand over, they were forced to write out a list of their sins and then fined for their wrongdoings.

Mwerinde's teachings, as communicated by Kibwetere, made it clear that the Movement expected followers to lead something close to a life of poverty. "We have presented you with the picture of Jesus and Mary," he explained. "We have not given you presents such as cattle, money, or cars, because we are poor in body, but we are rich in spirit and in everything that leads to eternal life."

Behind the scenes, the leaders lived by very different rules. For example, Joseph Kasapuraari entrusted his belongings to other higher-status friends outside of the Movement. These two sets of rules didn't bother the converts, as they were taught that the leaders had already been spared.

New trainees still needed to earn their places. The first task they were assigned was listening to the complete tapes of "A Timely Message from Heaven," the words supposedly dictated directly from the Virgin Mary to Mwerinde and Kibwetere. They'd only been teased with snippets during recruitment, and now they were trusted with the full version, a demonstration that their decision to join the Movement was already paying off. The message was then laid out: The world had rejected the Ten Commandments and given itself over to Satan. God was ready to wipe out humanity, but the Virgin Mary and Jesus Christ had earned mankind one last chance.

Credonia's embellishments promised a spectacular apocalypse on the horizon. Different countries, she explained, would pay in different ways. In an excerpt from "A Timely Message from Heaven," it's stated that:

> Russia will have the pest of locusts of various types. Mozambique will be destroyed by its own machinery. Japan will have rain for as long as our Father wants. France, your laziness will not permit you to endure the chastisements that will be inflicted upon you until you are destroyed in lamentation.

These prophecies would all come to pass if the Ten Commandments were not restored worldwide. Mwerinde clearly knew the book of Revelation. Like that final book of the New Testament, "A Timely Message from Heaven" wasn't overruling the Bible; it was a sequel—with blockbuster special effects slated for the climax.

The Movement didn't promise to save the world; they wanted to gather enough true believers to begin a new one. The time between the present and the coming apocalypse was designated as the "sieve" (a revealing choice of nomenclature, since a sieve is what is sometimes used to pan for gold). The sieve would end, according to their belief, sometime before the year 2000, when the chastisements would rain down upon the Earth, to be followed by three days of darkness.

This was where the Movement compounds came into the picture. There would be fortified arks, filled with food and other supplies, to sustain the believers during the end times. The trainees were told that they had just bought their way into refuge, safe from the destruction of the world.

After memorizing Mwerinde's version of the apocalypse, trainees would then turn to the Virgin's messages to Kibwetere, whose visions were meant to govern daily life and ritual within the Movement compounds. Four-sevenths of the average day was to be spent in prayer. Two-sevenths would be dedicated to work. Only one-seventh of the day was allocated for rest. Of course, for the able-bodied, work was usually pushed beyond its daily allocation and could include anything from constructing the compound's many buildings, working the fields for crops to feed every member, to digging wells, caring for livestock, and maintaining the facilities. In this way, the leaders made each compound a self-sustaining unit.

There was even a school opened at Mary's Place of Giving, on Dominic Kataribaabo's land. Children attended the school day in, day out, their lives consumed by the Movement. They were kept away from family members and told that their new family was the Movement and that its mission was their entire existence. This must have been an incredible strain. Children can be resilient, but patterns instilled during their impressionable early years become difficult to root out later on. Mwerinde and the leaders counted on this. Maintaining a hold on their membership would only get easier if the next generation had no attachment to material goods or any knowledge of reality outside the compound.

Within the community at large, all familial connections were cut off. Followers were stripped of their birth names. All unmarried girls and boys were sisters and brothers, and all married women and men were aunts and uncles. Older members had their own titles. Civil marriages and parenthood were not recognized. Individual identity no longer mattered; only the Movement was the priority.

Speech was discouraged except for prayer or during occasional town hall meetings, where members were allowed to air grievances with others before a council of leaders. Sign language and writing were the only viable means of communicating. When visitors came to a Movement compound, only leaders or those selected by them were allowed to break the silence and talk. It gave the outward appearance of a highly obedient and dedicated population.

This cult was at its most powerful and cohesive between 1993 and 1995. Trainees who could sustain themselves in this lifestyle looked forward to "learning process" sessions that could lead to their full certification in the Movement. From 8:00 a.m. to 4:00 p.m., the trainees would fast and face lectures from *entumwa*, who were also known as the apostles of the leaders. Earlier in the Movement's operation, the apostles were known to be violent, literally beating the demons out of trainees. But here the *entumwa* would pray over every member before the end of each session.

Whenever sessions took place in a compound when Kibwetere was present, the bishop himself would preside. Such a visible presence led Kibwetere, rather than Credonia Mwerinde, to become the face of the Movement. This was all part of their plan, though: Mwerinde might have been controlling the minds of the followers, but only a male presence could command the fear and respect needed to sell their program to the masses. These learning process sessions went on for five consecutive weeks. Afterward the apostles selected those they felt were ready for full-time Movement service, and their training was then completed. From that point on, they would be known as *abatende-kwa*, or disciples.

But even the disciples knew the ladder of leadership remained steep, and perhaps inaccessible. *Abebembezi* was the name given to the highest leadership. Beyond the all-powerful Bishop Kibwetere and the influential Vicar General Dominic, there were all the family members descended from the Grandparents of the Believers: Credonia Mwerinde, the Programmer; her niece Ursula, the Loudspeaker of Saint Maria Goretti and the Angels; Credonia's sister, Angelina, the Dress of the Virgin Mary; and her brother Henry, the Building of Saint Joseph.[3]

Titles like these are what distinguished the highest levels of command from the rank-and-file disciples. The family of Father Joseph

Kasapuraari were known as visionaries. His mother, Scholastica, an influential counselor to Credonia, called herself Heaven's Loudspeaker, claiming the ability to funnel the voices of saints and angels at will. Then there was a shadowy figure known only as Bampata. Handpicked by Mwerinde, he led the intelligence wing of the leadership council. He and his workers monitored every disciple and every trainee, sending agents out to villages for recruiting and spying on the family of members who still held out against the Movement's influence.

Apart from Kibwetere and Dominic, most of these leaders were either relatives of Mwerinde and the original apostles or high-status individuals from the so-called sinful world. They were the most useful members of the Movement as agents for expansion, gathering regularly in meetings with the heads of planning. The agenda they discussed was always kept secret from the rest of the Movement. However, a key piece of information became available from a high-profile defector, Father Paul Ikazire, who left after 1993 when there was no apocalypse yet in sight. According to this former member of *abebembezi*, soon before his departure, Mwerinde told the other leaders she had received new word from heaven: the Movement had been permitted to kill if necessary.

DISAPPEARING IS NOT ESCAPE

In 1993, murder, even one inexplicably ordered by none other than the Virgin Mary herself, seemed like a remote possibility, an unimaginable extreme. The Movement had just reached its peak level of status, thanks to the talents of Vicar General Dominic Kataribaabo. Pope John Paul II had arrived in Uganda on a pastoral visit, and Dominic was able to gain an audience on behalf of the Movement.

Dominic presented the pope with a clarified mission statement for the Movement, and he allegedly gave it his blessing. In reality, the pontiff most likely waved a kindly hand in blessing over the petitioner. But the facts held little weight here. For the disciples in the Movement, this recognition meant everything: their mission had been blessed by God's highest authority on Earth.

The vicar general was invaluable to Mwerinde in this way. He was the Movement's chief fundraiser, skilled at convincing local bureaucrats and authorities to donate money and provide protection. Local commissioners in the districts where the Movement compounds were built were often paid off in food, praise, and service from the disciples.

Again, the speed at which Mwerinde built the Movement was remarkable. After only five years the leaders claimed the Movement had as many as three thousand members. But the cracks soon began to show.

The first troubles arose from the very creation myth of the Movement itself. The entire theology depended on the apocalypse, and at first the leaders stated it would be 1992. When the end failed to arrive, the date was revised to 1995, and once again the apocalypse was a no-show. The third version, slated for December 31, 1999, inspired skepticism in the more educated. The apostles could only say that this was a "heaven-based" decision.

Next came the consolidation of the compounds. Mary's Place of Molding was lost when Kibwetere's own family rebelled against him and took back the land—and by 1998 even Kibwetere's wife, Theresa, could no longer tolerate his ambitions. After the defection of Father Paul Ikaire, the leaders decided that Dominic's land at Mary's Place of Giving was too valuable to lose if there were a mass defection in response. They sold off the farmable property at a high profit.

Many full-time disciples permanently relocated to Mary's Place of Rescue in Kanungu, Mwerinde's secluded homeland. Small factions were kept at the other open compounds and trading villages to maintain the illusion of stability. Defectors who survived these final years tell of increasingly hostile grievance sessions between disciples and apostles. When certain disciples spoke up against the leadership, questioning everything from handing over their property to the various postponements of the apocalypse, the apostles would casually and dismissively quiet them down.

Soon those same disciples began to disappear. The apostles said that the Virgin Mary had taken the believers early for their strength of faith. Then, in 1998, the school at Mary's Place of Giving was shut down after a government investigation showed abuse had taken place within its walls. The remaining children who attended were shuttled off to Mary's Place of Refuge before further inquiries could be conducted.

It's possible that the vicar general paid off some authorities to help contain any fallout from the school shutdown and limit any follow-up investigations. But that wasn't the worst setback. Joseph Kibwetere was hospitalized and diagnosed with bipolar disorder. However, he refused medication that might stabilize him and left the health-care facility. He was never seen outside a Movement compound again.

By the time the sun rose on January 1, 2000, it was clear that God's vengeance against humanity had been mild, even undetectable.

Movement member Andrew Tumusiime, one of the few who survived the final days, spoke of threats to Mwerinde's safety as a result. The disciples were growing restless. As the year 2000 advanced, the Movement engaged in strange activities. Bampata, Mwerinde's chief of intelligence, was sent out across southwestern Uganda with his unit of enforcers to round up disciples who had scattered to the outposts or even abandoned the cause.

Some of these agents tried to trick defectors into coming back, telling them loved ones in the Movement had fallen ill. Sometimes Bampata tried the more direct route of kidnapping. He even went to his own children's school and attempted to remove them from class, perhaps as a way to show deserters that he, too, was heeding Mwerinde's call and gathering his family. When the teachers stopped him, he dumped a sack of cash in their arms but ended up leaving without them. His children would never see him again.

An invitation was sent out from Mary's Place of Refuge, inviting local authorities in the Movement's pocket and family members of disciples alike to a celebration taking place on March 18, 2000. This was a final trick on Mwerinde's part, an effort to disguise the preparations for the actual event on the horizon, the spectacular apocalypse that was finally going to arrive.

On the morning of March 17, at Mary's Place of Refuge, the disciples were told that the end of the sieve had finally arrived. Soon the sinful would be visited with the chastisements that God had prepared for them. There is no one alive to recount exactly what promises Mwerinde made, but the disciples were marched into the arks they had built themselves, singing while the exits were sealed behind them.

The remaining leaders promised that they were being kept inside for their own safety. No one was to venture out during the three days of darkness. But within the arks, the days of darkness did not last long, the structures having been doused in flammable liquid and set aflame, burning as if the end times had truly arrived.

More than five hundred people were killed. No one had predicted that the Movement would slowly build up to this moment. Mainstream media outlets, especially in the West, were clueless as to the existence of the Movement for the Restoration of the Ten Commandments. But as investigators branched out to the other compounds and strongholds of the Movement, a more dire portrait came into focus. First, at Dominic Kataribaabo's compound, Mary's Place of Giving, they found more than 155 additional bodies. At the other Movement sites, similar grisly discoveries were made: more than 400 victims.

Later, reports came in describing how Father Joseph Kasapuraari had traveled around, buying up quantities of battery acid, almost certainly the poison used to eliminate the disciples at the other sites. In total, at least 1,055 people were killed in the Movement's final weeks, making it the deadliest cult in the history of the modern world.

Investigators never got very far. Some who came across the Kanungu fire as it began also reported seeing a truck fleeing the scene, with glimpses of Credonia Mwerinde riding in the back. There were later rumors of a Ugandan search team in the north country following sightings of Joseph Kibwetere. These reports didn't turn up a trace of either elusive figure, but it's almost certain that at least Mwerinde escaped, since she was the prime architect of the destruction.

A closer search of Mary's Place of Rescue revealed six more bodies buried beneath the leader headquarters. It could have been any of the *abebembezi*. One body, wearing the collar of a holy man, was assumed to be the vicar general himself, Dominic Kataribaabo, or possibly Kasapuraari or one of the other holy men who went over to the Movement.

The rest of the investigation failed to produce any convincing leads. The search for Credonia Mwerinde, Joseph Kibwetere, and other surviving leaders of the Movement went completely cold. After the Movement school was shut down in 1998, the central Ugandan government in Kampala began to get an idea of the true nature of the organization. If Kampala officials had launched an inquiry into the Movement earlier, local commissioners and government figures— the very ones whom Dominic Kataribaabo had cultivated with timely contributions—could not have helped the Movement's leaders avoid criminal charges. The local authorities might have actually begun exerting pressure on the *abebembezi*, especially the troika of Kibwetere, Dominic, and Mwerinde.

Add that pressure from outside to the tensions already growing inside the cult, and Credonia Mwerinde knew she was in trouble. And she could have easily convinced many of her fellow leaders of this. The Movement had been designed to grow quickly, to gain influence for *abebembezi*, and to satisfy certain darker urges for control. But no thought had been given to anything beyond this impulse to expand and amass followers and wealth. After it proved impossible to sustain the myths of the Marian apparitions, everything began to fall apart.

As an economic enterprise, the Movement depended on attracting converts who would give everything they owned to support expansion. But as a religious organization it relied on the most extreme leaps of faith, vows of poverty and silence, separation from family, belief in the sinfulness of the world, and the blessed protection of God and the Virgin Mary, whose actual representatives appeared in the flesh and walked among them.

Details are scarce as to which collapsed first: the economic model or the spiritual one. But Credonia Mwerinde, like so many cult leaders before her—such as Charles Manson and Jim Jones—discovered that her charisma was only effective when building the foundational deception that fueled the cult's growth. When it came to untangling that web of lies, all of them proved impotent. Being a cult leader is a dangerous game, but judging from historical accounts, once one discovers the knack for it, it's hard to stop the manipulations that give ultimate power over this life and the next until it's far too late.

Making the decision that it's better to incinerate more than five hundred people than admit a mistake may not be the textbook definition of "narcissism," but this heinous act more than clearly demonstrates both a sense of entitlement and a lack of empathy, two key characteristics of the personality disorder. But this is not what sets Credonia Mwerinde apart from her confederates.

Where Mwerinde's story diverges from others is in her escape, that final tantalizing report of hitching a ride out of the burning compound and riding off into obscurity. It is tempting to speculate that she laughed off mass murder the same way she could look up from scrubbing blood off the floor to banter with clients looking for a quick morning shot of her banana beer. But that vision doesn't align with the reality of life in Uganda or the Democratic Republic of the Congo, which is just across the border and her most likely avenue of escape. Even if she somehow managed to turn the illiquid assets of the cult— mostly land and real estate—into something to be carried deep into the bush, how long could she, a woman alone, defend herself from potential attacks, let alone protect any remaining loyal henchmen elsewhere after the depravity of the cult was exposed?

Credonia Mwerinde has only escaped from history. The forests into which she disappeared hid rebel forces, fierce warlords constantly on the lookout for possible financial gain or the opportunity to indulge in violence or lust. Even if she could elude detection by herself or with a small cadre of supporters, the fact that she was never heard from again lends credibility to the theory that her ultimate fate lay in the jungle. No one—not even Credonia Mwerinde herself—could escape the unimaginable horrors she had committed.

DENIAL OF REALITY

MARSHALL APPLEWHITE AND HEAVEN'S GATE

Over three consecutive days in March 1997, in Rancho Santa Fe, California, Marshall Applewhite led a band of thirty-eight followers to their deaths. On the final day the wide-eyed mastermind of Heaven's Gate joined his recruits in taking a mixture of phenobarbital, applesauce, and vodka so he, too, could "exit his vehicle"—or, as the rest of the world would see it, take his own life. It was the largest mass suicide in US history. The numerous followers, who ranged in age from twenty-five to seventy-two, believed what Applewhite had told them: that they were beaming up to a spaceship traveling behind Comet Hale-Bopp to join a "kingdom level above human," a heaven-like civilization of advanced beings who were somewhere between aliens and angels. After the suicides, final video recordings of each of the followers, called "exit statements," surfaced. They showed a group of believers in complete agreement, calm, modest, even excited about their upcoming big event—a willful denial of reality with almost no parallel in history. The fact that Marshall Applewhite could orchestrate a deception like this with so many people is both a tragedy and a master class in mind control.

THE COLLECTOR OF SOULS

Sometime in the early 1970s, Marshall Herff Applewhite and Bonnie Lu Nettles developed a quasi-religion—a start-up they called Heaven's Gate, whipped together from elements of popular science fiction, Applewhite's childhood Presbyterianism, and Nettles's psychic hodgepodge of New Age spirituality. The basic premise was simple: they claimed exclusive knowledge of The Evolutionary Level Above Human (TELAH), a superior intelligence that unenlightened people could glimpse only occasionally when UFOs appeared in the night sky. The two of them knew how to travel to this level, they said, and could even bring along a select few willing to prove themselves ready to accept their teachings.

The tenets of this new religion were outlandish and unverifiable. They were also vague enough that the two could always tinker with the formula, reinventing core beliefs as they went along. As their group grew in number, attracting as many as two hundred members at its peak, the two founders—known by such nursery school nicknames as "Bo and Peep" or "Do and Ti"—never changed the welcoming soft-sell approach that endeared them to newcomers. They presented themselves as celestial angels placed on Earth by God to redeem humanity and who knew that their rules were sometimes strict, but they were also understanding, and anyone who took up their nomadic lifestyle was always free to leave at any time.

This appearance of kindness and acceptance belied the tight grip they maintained on their followers and the control they exerted over the smallest aspects of everyday life. There were daily schedules that laid out who peeled the vegetables, who shared rooms, who drove whom to work. There was a mandated circumference for pancakes. They had diets that went to extremes: all pasta or all veggies or three weeks of nothing but water, lemon juice, cayenne pepper, and maple syrup. They all wore the same clothing that they traded regularly (down to their underwear) so that no one would become attached to an outfit or an appearance or a sense of their own individuality. They did things together, like watch *Star Trek* and *The X-Files* or go to the restaurant chain Marie Callender's for their final meal. They had their own vocabulary: groups of people rooming together were "Star Clusters"; periods of enforced silence were called "tomb time"; the people who weren't part of the group were Luciferians or just "Lucis."

The concept of "brainwashing," first put forward in the 1950s to try to understand how so many American POWs came to cooperate with their Chinese and North Korean captors, was later reapplied in the 1970s to explain the scores of seemingly good, college-age American youths taken in by the likes of Charles Manson and the Symbionese Liberation Army. Some of those who studied cults, like Margaret Thaler Singer, the author of *Cults in Our Midst: The Continuing Fight Against Their Hidden Menace*, often testified in court about the operation of these principles as they applied to specific individuals. As a legal defense, it failed to convince juries, and although the term "brainwashing" did make it into the *Diagnostic and Statistical Manual of Mental Disorders, Fifth Edition (DSM-5)*, which serves as the handbook for psychiatrists, the idea behind it has fallen into disfavor in therapeutic circles as well. Both the law and psychiatry depend on free will.

But Robert Jay Lifton, who was among the first wave of psychiatrists to treat those American POWs, has framed a broad point-by-point argument about how the captors achieved that level of mind control. His term for it—"thought reform"—emphasizes the gradual nature of the process. And nearly every one of the principles of thought reform that he outlines—milieu control, mystical manipulation, confession, self-sanctification through purity, loaded language, the aura of sacred science, dispensed existence—can be seen in action with the Heaven's Gate cult.

Time after time, lonely and vulnerable people would spot the printed flyers that the group posted around whatever town they were passing through—

UFO's
- Why they are here.
- Who they have come for.
- When they will leave.

—and then, on a whim, they would drop in on Applewhite's public lectures. Almost before they knew it, they'd completely upended their lives, cutting all ties with family, giving everything they had to the group. They moved into the Heaven's Gate compound and started living by the cult's intricate rules. Many of those who killed themselves in 1997 had been with the group for twenty years or more. Their sense of belonging, of bonding with a sect that believed in exactly what they did, extended all the way to their final breaths on Earth.

Those who joined Heaven's Gate had a particular kind of profile. On one level they seemed to represent a cross section of the United States. They came from many states and were of different ages and professions. But most of those who committed to the outlandish beliefs and rigorous daily rituals of Heaven's Gate over the long term had suffered serious loss or abandonment. There was the oysterman who'd lost his business, his marriage, and his brother before turning to drugs. There was the foster child who'd watched her best friend drown; the unemployed bus driver who couldn't get over his mother's death; the free spirit who mourned her infertility. These were wayward souls who longed for something that everyday life could not provide. Many were highly intelligent. "Most people don't try to make things more complicated than they are," said an ex-girlfriend of one of the victims. "These people were so smart they thought the world must be more complicated."[1]

These traits were found repeatedly in the obituaries and memorials of the Heaven's Gate dead. They were too clever for their own good. They were heartbroken. They'd lost their families. They didn't fit in with college or their old jobs or relationships. They left everything behind. They were friendly. They were weird. They were distant. It's all a strange collection of characteristics. Maybe not surprisingly, there's one thing that all these traits had in common: they all described Marshall Herff Applewhite, the mastermind of the Heaven's Gate cult.

THE HOLY MISFIT

Marshall Herff Applewhite Jr. was born on May 17, 1931, in Spur, Texas—one of the hardest-hit parts of the country during one of the roughest stretches of the Great Depression. Applewhite's father and namesake was an itinerant preacher, good at founding churches in one Texas town after another but bad at keeping a job there once he did. The family—the preacher and his wife, their two older daughters, and their two sons—Marshall and a younger brother with a severe intellectual handicap whom they later committed to a state-operated home—were constantly on the move. This didn't make them stand out: given the local Dust Bowl conditions, many down on their luck were on the road looking for work. But this nomadic lifestyle did shape Marshall's childhood, instilling in him a lifelong distrust of settling in any one place.

Marshall's sister Louise, who became the spokesperson for the surviving Applewhites after the mass suicide, described her younger brother as a smart, outgoing, handsome child who loved to sing. His natural extroversion helped him make friends wherever the family landed, but with his father uprooting the brood so often, Marshall failed to form the strong personal bonds that came from enduring friendships. Such relationships in early childhood have been associated with the ability to empathize. Similar connections in the teenage years, so crucial in the social lives of adolescents, have in turn been associated with the ability to thrive during adulthood. As with so many cult leaders who died suddenly or violently, any diagnosis of psychological disturbance is purely speculative. But Marshall Applewhite did seem to exhibit the classic aftereffects of his itinerant childhood, even reproducing this rootlessness when he had the chance to lead his own families (both his traditional family and his cult family). Like his father, he constantly moved the Heaven's Gate group from one place to the next, keeping them free from long-term attachments, presenting instability as a spiritual challenge that would prepare his followers to ascend to the next level.

In his boyhood, this upheaval left Marshall with only one outlet for lasting connection: religion. He was always his father's best parishioner and the star of the choir, with a soprano range that grew into a lovely baritone. Floyd Chapman, the president of Corpus Christi Electric Company, and who cofounded the Parkway Presbyterian Church along with Marshall Sr., remembers the father as a very personable and good organizer who quickly built church membership. Louise says her brother took after her father: Marshall Jr., she said, "was always a born leader and very charismatic. He could get people to believe anything."[2]

He graduated from Corpus Christi High School in 1948 and enrolled in Austin College in Sherman, Texas, sixty-five miles north of Dallas, with his own dreams of becoming a minister. He began his studies as a philosophy major and became an active member of several campus organizations. His freshman-year roommate, John Alexander, says that "Herff," as he was known back then, was a joiner with a magnetic personality who signed up for the a cappella choir, the judiciary council, and the campus association of prospective Presbyterian ministers.

Applewhite graduated in 1952 and then met his wife, Ann Pearce, and enrolled in Union Presbyterian Seminary in Richmond, Virginia, to study theology. But he soon found that the prospect of leading a congregation could not compete with his lifelong love of music, and before the end of his first semester at seminary he dropped out and moved with Ann to Gastonia, North Carolina, in order to be the music director at the First Presbyterian Church. The newlyweds brought two children into the world but again pulled up stakes when Marshall was drafted into the Army in 1954.

They spent the next two years in Salzburg, Austria, and then White Sands, New Mexico, where Marshall served as an instructor in the Signal Corps. He received an honorable discharge in 1956 and subsequently enrolled in the University of Colorado, getting a master's degree in music with a focus on musical theater, playing the leads in *South Pacific* and *Oklahoma!* Charles Byers, a former professor who was close with Applewhite during his days at the university, described him as "happy-go-lucky" and "popular with students."

After Colorado, Applewhite began his own life as a troubadour, taking any job that was vaguely connected to music. He tried his hand performing in New York, wanting to break into the opera, but by 1960 he realized his talents and good looks made him better suited for the theater. Yet, despite auditioning for one production after another, he failed to catch on as a stage actor, so in 1961 he packed up his young family to take a job at the University of Alabama.

He lasted four years there as an assistant professor of music and as choral director, until he was fired in 1965 for a reason that came as a shock to his family: he'd been having an affair with a male student. This side of his identity—his recurring struggles with his own homosexual attractions—came to figure prominently in coverage of the mass suicide, as people sought a clue, some hidden motivation, for the senseless loss of life. It's easy to see how his sexual identity could be considered in conflict with both his traditional religious upbringing and his own hopes for a career within the church. But Applewhite was hardly the only person struggling with sexual identity in the early days of the Gay Liberation movement, and it's hard to imagine how this fairly commonplace internal struggle, as tortured as it could be personally, could have somehow contributed to his leading thirty-eight people to their deaths.

Sexuality was clearly a highly charged issue for Applewhite, but the focus on it as a key factor in the tragedy probably says more about the culture wars in the late 1990s than it does about the Heaven's Gate cult itself. Religious figures as diverse as Reverend Pat Robertson of the 700 Club and Troy Perry, the founder of the gay-friendly Universal Fellowship of Metropolitan Community Churches, both pointed to this same incident as they sought to comprehend the mass suicide. Robertson promoted the idea that "offbeat sexuality," as a guest on his TV show put it, was nearly always a part of the slanted spirituality of cults, while Perry saw the workings of "one man's denial and repression of his God-given sexuality, and, on a greater level, society's rejection of and hostility toward gay men and lesbians."[3]

Applewhite's issues with sexuality were no doubt profound, even extreme, as one could later see from the heavy prohibitions his cult placed on sexual relations of any sort. He wanted his followers to overcome so-called earthly desires in preparation for their ascension to the next level above humanity. He had strict edicts about "no sex, no human-level relationships, no socializing,"[4] although this was put in place more as a social control: Applewhite didn't want his people finding meaning in life outside of their dependence on him.

His eventual commitment to celibacy was total: sometime before the mass suicide, he and six of his male followers had themselves medically castrated as a first step in emptying their "containers" of the earthly desires that they had renounced. Some have theorized that castration brought them closer to their androgynous ideal, the form they believed they would assume when they reached the next level. In one of the most bizarre confessional moments in the videotaped interviews before their "final exits," one follower even pointed to his own castration and the general euphoria he felt in its aftermath as a key step in his preparation for suicide. "I can't tell you how free that has made me feel," he said. "I can't see that this next step that I'm prepared to take, and I'm looking forward to taking, is anything more than a clinical operation."[5]

As the "divine leader" of Heaven's Gate, Applewhite was so fixated on creating an alternate reality—and controlling the lives of the people willing to accept it—that it's doubtful he spent much time considering the role that sexuality may have played in his transformation from choral director into suicidal cult leader. But what *is* certain is that Applewhite's affair in 1965 with a male student tore his family apart. After his dismissal from the University of Alabama, he moved to Houston, but by 1968 a trial separation from Ann became permanent: she filed for divorce and won full custody of the children.

For a brief period Applewhite seemed to flourish on his own. In Houston he found a position teaching music at the University of St. Thomas, a small, private Catholic college. He also became the choral director of an Episcopal church and sang fifteen roles with the Houston Grand Opera.

Many acquaintances from this era remember Applewhite as a well-dressed, charismatic figure who enjoyed being the center of attention and was exceedingly generous and endlessly social. But despite his presence in Houston society, in private Applewhite had begun to unravel. He missed seeing his children and was having trouble balancing an apparent double life, squiring one woman after another to public events and then living with an openly gay lover in Houston's Montrose section. To add to the confusion, he also was pursuing a serious relationship with the daughter of a wealthy Houston family who disapproved of their relationship and made threats on his life.

It is challenging from half a century away to tell what came first: Applewhite's hectic and apparently conflicted sexual pursuits or his mental breakdown. University president Father Thomas Braden remembers Applewhite showing signs of dissociation: "He was behaving somewhat oddly at the time. Just talking to him, he would mention things that had no connection to the thing he said before." Patsy Swayze, a fellow member of a Houston theater group and the mother of the actor Patrick Swayze, told the *New York Times* that she remembered him suddenly acting strangely, becoming the source of gossip among the cast and crew for "talking about UFOs and preaching this strange religion."

Very little is known about Applewhite's medical history, and much of what has been disclosed is secondhand, fragmentary, and contradictory. But this same sketchiness makes him an alluring subject to scholars, who find that he easily fits into their own pet theories. This is one reason that cult leaders make such good case studies: because the gruesome facts of their biographies are both widely known and easy to connect to a psychological disorder. For example, Susan Raine, a sociologist at MacEwan University in Edmonton, Alberta, points to the collision of Applewhite's intense religious upbringing and his experiment with an openly gay life as a source of painful internal conflict. She argues that this inner struggle, which dominated his life for years, made him experience his own body as a battleground, leading to the onset of paranoid schizophrenia. Such a diagnosis is consistent with his claim to hearing voices that he interpreted as divine, since auditory hallucinations are one of the hallmarks of the condition.

It is impossible to confirm this diagnosis, but the theory is plausible. Schizophrenia, which affects more than 1 percent of the population, is by no means rare. And the diagnosis could explain Applewhite's claims to celestial visitations and contact with otherworldly beings. It also fits with another well-known behavior: his highly regimented daily schedules for everyone in Heaven's Gate—the strict diets, the carefully regulated behavior—were all consistent with treatment protocols aimed at controlling the occurrence of schizophrenic episodes. In other words, by constantly tinkering with the rules for even the most minor daily activities, Applewhite may have been creating an elaborate self-care program designed to both stave off the occurrence of his breaks with reality and minimize the severity of such episodes. That he prescribed this regimen for everyone in his cult is not surprising, either: whatever other conditions they may have, nearly every cult leader suffers from narcissistic personality disorder to some degree.

What can be verified is that Applewhite was soon dismissed from his position at the University of St. Thomas as well. He claimed the reason was his emotional problems, although there seems to be an alternate explanation: the University of St. Thomas was the second college to fire him for engaging in an affair with a male student. According to conflicting accounts, the troubled Applewhite then checked himself into a psychiatric hospital to "treat" his homosexual urges, an action that would be viewed as highly controversial today. The precise length of his stay is not known, but it was extended enough for him to form a lasting connection with the nurse who'd help him cofound the group that would lead thirty-nine people, including himself, to their deaths.

THE FATEFUL MEETING

The early 1970s were not kind to Marshall Applewhite. Although he was the one who'd caused his marriage to break up over his sexual dalliances, he still missed his children dreadfully. On top of that, his father, whom he'd always idolized, passed away. Applewhite grew depressed and his finances fell into disrepair. He was forced to borrow money, and his erratic behavior began to alienate him from the well-heeled circles where he'd once been popular.

At just this moment of profound loss and psychological distress, he met Bonnie Lu Nettles, the woman who would change his life. Applewhite sanitized his own history; he didn't seem to believe that extensive treatment for psychiatric disorders was consistent with his status as an ascended being. In his version of events, the two met when Applewhite was teaching a class in children's theater that Bonnie's son was attending. In another account, he was visiting a sick friend when he met Nettles. In a third, Applewhite himself was the patient, under psychiatric observation, and they met because Nettles was the primary nurse in charge of his treatment. And if Applewhite really had checked himself in to be "cured" of homosexuality, it could explain why there are so many alternate explanations. It would also explain why Nettles, who clearly knew exactly where they first met, conspired to obscure the circumstances.

Applewhite's sister, Louise Winant, has put forth still another theory: that her brother, who suffered severe emotional distress in the aftermath of their father's death, had gone into the hospital for cardiac surgery, and while his heart blockage was being resolved, he underwent a near-death experience. Depending on its intensity, such an event can approach the transcendental, leaving a person profoundly altered. Those who claim to have had one describe feelings of levitation or detachment from the body, as if the soul or consciousness ascended above the physical framework. Other sensations include feel-ings of warmth, serenity, security, absolute dissolution, and the pres-ence of a strong, shining light.

Louise was the only one to claim that her brother had had such a potentially life-changing quasi-mystical experience, and since it closely matches that of a paranoid schizophrenic episode, there is the pos-sibility that his sister was told a sanitized or destigmatized version of the truth. But all these variations concur in one respect: sometime in the early 1970s, Marshall Applewhite met Bonnie Lu Nettles, a nurse and amateur astrologer. They were both in their forties, although she was four years his senior. Like Applewhite, she was born into a deeply religious family, then born again in Christ at the age of eleven, and by twenty-two had married a sensible businessman, Joseph Segal Nettles, with whom she soon had four children.

But by the time she met Applewhite, her marriage was dissolving, owing to her unsettling new fixation on New Age spirituality and rein-carnation. Nettles had begun conducting séances in the family living room every Wednesday night, helping neighborhood people contact the spirits of departed loved ones. She'd even come to believe that a nineteenth-century monk she identified as "Brother Francis" was communicating directly with her with instructions about the proper way to live.

At about the time that Applewhite and Nettles met, and appar-ently for just that reason, her straight-arrow husband began divorce proceedings. She began to feel increasingly alienated from her sur-roundings. Her daughter Terrie remembers the mood that settled on their lives. "Mom and I didn't seem to fit in with everyone else," she said to Barry Bearak of the *New York Times* a month after the suicides. "We'd go out and stare into the sky, and we'd swear we had seen a fly-ing saucer. We thought, 'Wouldn't it be fun if it'd just pick us up and take us away.'"

When Nettles first met Applewhite, most likely when he was under her care in the hospital, she was emotionally vulnerable, with a sense that she was losing the intimate ties of the previous twenty years. And there was another reason she was so susceptible to reading more into a chance encounter than it deserved. A fortune-teller she'd consulted in 1972 told her she would meet a tall and mysterious man with white hair and a fair complexion. In her state of distress and growing sense of isolation, she'd filed away this vague prediction as if it were a promise, even a divine prophecy.

Applewhite was in fact tall, with silvery salt-and-pepper hair. And, just like Nettles, he had a habit of mythologizing his own history, so it's unsurprising that in his description of their first encounter the two of them locked eyes immediately in a "shared recognition of esoteric secrets." Soon after that meeting, Nettles created for Applewhite a natal chart—a map of the stars at the moment of his birth that functions like a fingerprint of sorts for astrologers—and gave him his own reading. She told him their charts had an uncanny resemblance, even though they actually shared very few significant alignments, and that their meeting had been foretold to her by extraterrestrials. Applewhite was persuaded that he had a divine assignment to undertake. They became extremely close almost instantly—a codependence founded on their mutual need to be seen as divine and powerful—and both soon concluded that they had already known each other for a long time through past lives.

Susan Raine, who believed that Applewhite was just recovering from his schizophrenic episode at about this time, claims that Nettles "was responsible for reinforcing his emerging delusional beliefs." His older sister Louise Winant told ABC News that meeting Bonnie Nettles was the single event that "completely changed him from a normal person to what he became."

The instant connection between Applewhite and Nettles was the foundational moment in the formation of Heaven's Gate, so it's nigh impossible to separate what's true from what they claimed later in refashioning themselves as celestial beings. Nettles, an intelligent, widely read, confident woman, seems to have led the way in their relationship. First, she created the highly charged atmosphere that turned a chance encounter into a fateful meeting of cosmic proportion, prophesied both by the stars and extraterrestrials. Later she convinced Applewhite that not only were they fated to meet but they were destined to form their own religion.

Her eclectic mix of New Age beliefs resonated with Applewhite, who'd been hit by a series of life crises and had begun to look for answers in nontraditional spirituality, whether in astrology, the writings of desert mystics, or in the literary science fiction of Robert A. Heinlein and Arthur C. Clarke. He even started to tell people that a "presence" he'd run into on a beach in Galveston, Texas, had given him the knowledge of where humanity had come from and where it was going. According to friend and artist Hayes Parker, "It made you laugh to hear it, but Herff was serious. And he didn't seem crazy."

There is an emerging consensus that Marshall Applewhite really was suffering from some type of paranoid disorder. Some have suggested that, in such a state, there may even have been therapeutic value in Nettles's encouragement of Applewhite's notion that he was a kind of emissary of the divine. Robert Jay Lifton, for example, believes that Nettles's influence may have helped prevent further mental deterioration. The two seem to have fed into each other's delusions of grandeur, a dynamic that amplified and validated their most eccentric impulses.[6]

Applewhite and Nettles soon moved in together and for a time ran a New Age bookstore called the Christian Arts Center, specializing in works of spirituality. They later changed the name to Know Place as they expanded their mission and taught classes in mysticism and theosophy. During these months at the end of 1972, Nettles's divorce was finalized. They had consistently claimed that there was no sexual attraction between them—perhaps a relief to Applewhite, who appeared to be tormented by his own desires. What truly united them was their shared mission or delusion, the earliest iterations of what later became Heaven's Gate. Nettles lost custody of her children. Soon the two outgrew—or mismanaged—their first business ventures and decided to abandon Houston, leaving behind the heartaches and humiliations they'd both experienced there in favor of the life that Applewhite knew so well: the road.

OTHERWORLDLY INSPIRATION

On January 1, 1973, Applewhite and Nettles hightailed it to Las Vegas. Along the way, they stayed in campgrounds and cheap hotels. One convenient aspect of their delusions of grandeur was that they believed that as divine beings they were under no obligation to pay for things, so they dropped into restaurants, ordered dinner, stuffed free bread in their pockets, then ran out without paying. In Nevada and the Pacific Northwest, they picked up a series of odd jobs, from draining septic tanks to selling their blood, all while spending any free time toiling on their manifesto. They crisscrossed the United States and Canada, receiving instruction from God for their "overwhelming mission" in the Rogue Valley in Oregon. They wrote letters, as was common practice for people on road trips back then, confessing to a friend, "By social, medical, psychiatric & religious standards we and you have long since lost our sanity."[7]

Eventually, this period saw the two hammering out an outline of their beliefs. The first tenet of their religion was also the foundation of their relationship: Applewhite and Nettles were prophets sent by God to fulfill a divine prophecy. The second core principle was that Applewhite and Nettles had been given higher-level minds than everyone else. The third core principle: Applewhite and Nettles would be killed for their beliefs and subsequently resurrected from the grave and transported onto a spacecraft for all to behold, an event that would be known as the Demonstration. To establish their authority as prophets, they cited the book of Revelation 11:3–5:

And I will grant authority to my two witnesses, and they will prophesy for 1,260 days, clothed in sackcloth.

These are the two olive trees and the two lampstands that stand before the Lord of the earth. And if anyone would harm them, fire pours from their mouth and consumes their foes.

Of course, in their interpretation, Applewhite and Nettles were the two witnesses prophesied in the Bible.

After about a year and a half on the road, they gained their first convert: Sharon Morgan, an acquaintance from Houston who, like many in the 1970s, had come to feel trapped in a troubled marriage. She left her family and joined Applewhite and Nettles on the next phase of their road trip, playing a role in their still-unsuccessful attempts to recruit more followers. Morgan would sidle up to strangers, asking them whether they'd be interested in "talking to two people who can tell you how to leave this planet and take your body with you." But when the three circled through Houston, Morgan's husband threatened to have her committed, as Barry Bearak reported in the *New York Times*. He also brought their two daughters to convince her to come back. Their two-year-old ran up to hug Morgan while the six-year-old stood back, tears flowing from her eyes, and asked, "Will you stay?" In the face of such emotional pressure, Morgan abandoned Applewhite and Nettles.

Morgan's husband accused Applewhite and Nettles of credit card fraud, citing all the charges his wife had rung up during her spiritual joyride. Although the case wasn't pursued, the police did pick the couple up and discovered a warrant for Applewhite's arrest during a routine background check. The car they were currently driving— a Mercury Comet that he had rented nine months before and never returned—had been reported as stolen in Missouri.

Applewhite was remanded to Missouri and, by way of defense, told prosecutors that "a force from beyond the earth has made me keep this car." The judge showed no leniency, and he was sentenced to six months in prison. At this point it seemed as if Applewhite was preparing to face reality and call it quits as a celestial being. He updated his résumé so he could look for a new teaching position. But given the difficulty of applying for jobs from prison, he dedicated the majority of his sentence to reflecting on his approach. He thought about the time he and Nettles had spent with Morgan and considered many of their friend's challenging moral questions, such as claiming a divine mission and then running out on hotel bills. He also began reshaping the primary spiritual principles of his new religion, tossing out theosophy and esoterica in favor of science fiction and a disembodied space-based version of evolution.

This veneer of rationality—the science part of his science fiction—would eventually attract hundreds of followers over the next two decades. Many sampled the religion for a while, then left when its daily routines proved too strenuous, but others saw the appeal and took radical steps, abandoning their families and forfeiting all earthly pleasures in order to join Marshall Applewhite and Bonnie Lu Nettles on their mission. In the "statement of beliefs" penned from his jail cell, Applewhite outlined their new cosmic vision, using the metaphor of a caterpillar to convey one of their central teachings. The idea that a good life leads to heaven, he wrote, is as silly as believing that if a caterpillar "dies a good caterpillar, it will mysteriously awaken in a rose blossom and live there forever with the king butterfly." Instead, he said, people must also go through a chrysalis stage, overcoming their humanness in preparation for life in the Next Level.

A transformation this complete, Applewhite continued, required a teacher. Jesus was one, sent by God in ancient times. But two thousand years later, in 1974, two more—namely he and Nettles—had been sent. Like many self-proclaimed prophets—and con artists—Applewhite predicted that a visible "demonstration" of their truths would come "within months." He wrote the two would be killed and then resurrected in a "cloud of light," just like Jesus. That cloud, he wrote, is what "humans refer to as a UFO."

Many sociologists now view the postwar UFO craze as more reflective of Cold War paranoia than the way it's often presented—as suppressed evidence of actual extraterrestrial visitation. The Swiss psychiatrist Carl Jung interpreted this new fixation on such phenomena as a revision of an ancient archetype. In *Flying Saucers: A Modern Myth of Things Seen in the Sky*, he cited sixteenth-century pamphlets and ancient reports of "fiery discs" flying over Egypt in 1500 BC to point out that UFOs were scarcely a new phenomenon, just a fresh incarnation of a well-established mythological image. Jung wrote in his book: "We have here a golden opportunity to see how a legend is formed, and how in a difficult and dark time for humanity a miraculous tale grows up of an attempted intervention by extra-terrestrial 'heavenly' powers—and this at the very time when human fantasy is seriously considering the possibility of space travel . . ."[8]

As we have seen with Claude Vorilhon, a.k.a. Raël, a cult that mixes UFOs and vaguely religious rituals and concepts can become wildly popular. And Raël's cult was by no means the only example that Marshall Applewhite might have followed closely. In 1955, England's George King founded the Aetherius Society, which combined principles of theosophy and yoga with what he claimed were telepathic messages sent from Venus. And further back, during the 1930s, Arthur Bell started a cult called Mankind United that prospered for many years based on the ideas that a swelling membership would allow a group of esoteric sponsors to come out of hiding, conquer the "Hidden Rulers," and inaugurate a global four-day workweek. It was all Hollywood-style nonsense, but it attracted many followers, in part thanks to the promise that these powerful sponsors had access to an advanced technology that would allow the dead to be resurrected on a distant planet.

Applewhite was able to graft Christian elements onto some of these basic ideas. Many of those who were drawn to his group had grown up in traditionally Christian households but found great appeal in the scientific updates Applewhite and Nettles made to the faith of their upbringings. Michael Conyers, a musician and former Heaven's Gate member from 1975 to 1988, attests that the "message that Marshall Applewhite and Bonnie Nettles had was one that was talking to my Christian heritage, yet in a modern, updated way."[9] One example that appealed to him was Applewhite's explanation that the Virgin Mary, Jesus's mother, had been impregnated on a spacecraft. "Now, as unbelievable as that sounds," Conyers noted, "that was an answer that was better than just plain virgin birth. It was technical. It had physicality to it."[10]

THE GROUP TAKES OFF

Michael Conyers saw Marshall Applewhite and Bonnie Nettles at their very first recruitment meeting in May 1975, a few months after Applewhite's release from jail. The two had sent out flyers to dozens of churches from a hotel room in Ojai, California, using Applewhite's prison writings as their calling card. Among the few who followed up was seventy-two-year-old Clarence Klug, a teacher of metaphysics who arranged for his students to meet them in Los Angeles at the home of Joan Culpepper, a former advertising director and part-time psychic who went by the motto "Weird turns me on."

Conyers said the crowd of about eighty were "mesmerized" by "the UFO Two," who had now updated their pitch: they were extra-terrestrials from another planet called the Next Level, the place traditional Christians had long interpreted as "heaven." They continued in this vein, mixing pseudoscience with pseudo-religion. One minute they were saying that they were building a spacecraft that would take them to the Next Level, and the next minute they claimed to be "the two witnesses" mentioned in Revelation 11:3. Somewhere in their travels they'd invented an evil race of space aliens, known as Luciferians— their version of Satan and his demons—who were keeping people tied to the human level by falsely representing themselves as "God." And they promised that those who followed Applewhite (the Second Coming of Jesus Christ incarnate) and Nettles (somewhat confusingly referred to as the Heavenly Father) would henceforth be set on the path to salvation—or, as they put it, to "a higher evolutionary level."

As living representatives from this elevated plane of existence, Marshall Applewhite and Bonnie Nettles were the only people on Earth who could guide their followers to the Next Level, making potential disciples completely dependent on them. They were now known, respectively, as "Do and Ti"—names Applewhite claimed were meaningless but nevertheless paired the two as foundational principles, like the first two notes in the musical scales. This was a smaller example of one of Lifton's principles of thought reform that Applewhite and Nettles had already started putting into practice: the use of loaded language, or the "thought-terminating cliché." For example, the Two referred to the necessary steps to get to the Next Level as "Human Individual Metamorphosis," or HIM. Attaining this HIM was not easy or cheap; it was heaven, after all. To gain entry, prospective followers had to give up all human attachments, a vague long list of things to be abandoned that included careers, family, friends, sexual relationships, material possessions, and even gender.

They'd also mastered what Lifton calls the aura of sacred science. Using the metaphor of the caterpillar, Applewhite contended that their transformation would be an actual biological change, that they'd become a different species in the Next Level. The language sounded rational and scientific and nonreligious, but it was really childlike in the way that it cast the idea of heaven in the most literal of terms. However, nobody at that first meeting registered this objection, and by the end of their presentation Applewhite and Nettles had approximately two dozen new recruits.

Why did anyone fall for something like this? The neuroscientist Sam Harris thinks that it may have been Applewhite's oddly unblinking gaze that had a mesmerizing effect, since it was clearly not the strength of his science or the persuasiveness of his arguments. "This is not a brilliant person," Harris says on his *Making Sense* podcast. "This is not someone who's bowling you over with his ability to connect ideas or turn phrases."[11] But as the videos show, Applewhite kept his eyes wide and let his gaze bore into the camera. This may have been what Bonnie Nettles's daughter Terrie was referring to when she mentioned "this unbelievable power." As Harris writes in his book *Waking Up: A Guide to Spirituality Without Religion*:

> It is not an accident, therefore, that gurus often show an unusual commitment to maintaining eye contact. In the best case, this behavior emerges from a genuine comfort in the presence of other people and deep interest in their well-being.

Given such a frame of mind, there may simply be no reason to look away. But maintaining eye contact can also become a way of "acting spiritual" and, therefore, an intrusive affectation. There are also people who maintain rigid eye lock not from an attitude of openness and interest or from any attempt to appear open and interested but as an aggressive and narcissistic show of dominance. Psychopaths tend to make exceptionally good eye contact.[12]

Harris points out that in terms of logic or expressiveness or charisma, Applewhite was underwhelming. So there had to have been something else drawing people in, because following his stint in prison, people did start dropping everything to follow "Do and Ti." Several of those who eventually participated in the mass suicide had joined after that first meeting at Culpepper's house. There was nineteen-year-old Lee Ann Fenton, a biology student in college on a scholarship, who connected with their idea of immediate salvation. "I wanted to overcome the human condition in this life, not the next," she said. There was twenty-six-year-old Dick Joslyn, a college graduate and former Navy officer fascinated with the subconscious, who appreciated the Two's simplicity in presentation, which did not have the theatrical touches of other New Age preachers. He sensed that they could offer entry into the depths of the human mind.

A solid core of those who stayed with the group until the very end joined in 1975: David Moore, an angry nineteen-year-old who eventually became an IT specialist and one of the few in the group who could be relied on to secure a job and help support Heaven's Gate wherever they landed; Margaret Ella Richter, a drum majorette with a master's degree in computer science from UCLA whose marriage had recently ended in divorce; Susan Paup, who was haunted by her infertility and joined with her husband, then stayed on after he left. Judith Rowland, a former model and mother of two young children, was recruited by her own mother and left a goodbye note for her husband that said simply, "I went to walk with the Lord." Joyce Skalla, a former beauty contest winner, also left a note for her husband, saying she was "relinquishing" their twin teenage daughters to him.

Since the introduction of no-fault divorce laws in 1967, which permitted marriage dissolution by mutual consent, divorce rates skyrocketed in the United States. However, the finality of these particular departures—the way so many agreed to cut all ties with parents, spouses, and children—was highly unusual. One Heaven's Gate recruit, John Craig, had the kind of profile that made him an attractive candidate for the Colorado House of Representatives. He was six-foot-six, a military school graduate, and a Korean War vet who hunted elk with the governor and went skiing with his six children. He was also one of the leading real estate developers in Colorado and a member in good standing of the Durango Chamber of Commerce. But in the summer of 1975, while his wife and kids were away at a swim meet, he met Applewhite and Nettles at the Denver airport, then soon after signed over power of attorney to his wife and disappeared.

"At the time, the group was saying that a U.F.O. was going to arrive within three or four months and take them away," his daughter told the *New York Times.* "I thought, O.K., when that doesn't happen, he'll come home. But he never did." Two months after Craig's disappearance, he did reach out to his daughter, inviting her to one of the group's meetings at the Denver YMCA. She was not allowed to sit next to her father, and he was not permitted to walk with her alone to the car afterward. As his daughter recalled the encounter, "Dad didn't appear to be a zombie at all. I was looking for drug-induced brainwashing. But he was very articulate, very animated. He was my dad."[13]

The family eventually hired a private investigator to track Craig down. But as the PI discovered, Applewhite and Nettles expertly covered their tracks. And even if a detective could have found him, John Craig had no intention of ever returning home. Under his new name of "Brother Logan," he rose to become the group's key organizer, making himself second-in-command to Applewhite and Nettles. He also became one of Heaven's Gate's most active recruits, helping to print out flyers and renting halls for meetings, where he would greet potential followers at the door. He seemed to have exchanged his prominent position in local Colorado real estate circles for an even more pivotal position as group's de facto chief of staff, the organizer keeping the cult running. He consolidated his leadership role by using his personal wealth to make significant financial contributions to the group.

Word of the so-called UFO Two spread, which boosted recruitment. In late 1975, Applewhite and Nettles held a meeting at a Waldport, Oregon, hotel. Afterward, approximately thirty people in attendance sold off all their worldly possessions, said goodbye to their families, and disappeared with Do and Ti. That incident got Heaven's Gate its first taste of national attention and negative press coverage.

Hurt by this, Applewhite decided to take the group further underground. He and Nettles led their now nearly two-hundred-member crew on a nomadic journey across the country, re-creating his own childhood, in a sense, with his new family. The crew would sleep in tents and sleeping bags in public parks and camping grounds throughout the Rocky Mountains and Texas, often panhandling during the day. At one point a power struggle emerged when a charismatic recruit convinced several followers that it was still possible to indulge in sex and marijuana and yet follow the principles—an appealing level of permissiveness that threatened the authority of Applewhite and Nettles. But the Two quickly ejected the breakaway faction and continued to turn away anyone else who didn't take the practices seriously, until they were down to seventy loyal devotees.

Applewhite and Nettles set up a regimen designed to make adherents completely dependent on them, whether through name changes or by cutting ties to the outside world. Members worked and traveled in pairs. The Two put together people who, by their assessment, were least likely to form attachments, so that each person always had a platonic "check partner," a system that emphasized obedience, enforcing the idea that they, and only they, were the source of truth. After the brief insurrection, Applewhite and Nettles continued to treat close friendships as a threat to cohesion. Applewhite encouraged followers to be like pets in their subordination, meaning their only responsibility was to obey their leaders. He encouraged them to ask themselves, "What would Do do?" whenever faced with a decision.

This new authoritarian setup led to further defections in the new recruits, but those who stayed were fiercely loyal and even found Applewhite's attitude to be laid-back and paternal. He kept people busy, creating arbitrary exercises that tested the ability of followers to perform repetitive tasks, like working in isolation while concentrating on the sound of a tuning fork, designed to keep them focused on the Next Level while ignoring human thoughts. Another activity involved wearing blinders that allowed members to see only what was directly in front of them. The loyalists who endured this monastic regimen were referred to as "the class" and were told to prepare for their "graduation" to the "Kingdom Level Above Human."

One way they kept their focus on the Next Level was through examining the night sky. The group would, in lighter moments, take trips together to any planetariums they came across in their travels. They were told their extraordinary devotion had been rewarded in June 1976, when Nettles claimed that she'd been contacted by extra-terrestrials on the Next Level. The Two gathered the disciples at Medicine Bow National Forest in southeastern Wyoming, promising a visit from a UFO that very evening. Not surprisingly, nothing ever appeared. At daybreak, Nettles apologized to the group, saying, "Well, I feel like I have egg on my face," and informed them that she'd received a message that the visit had been canceled. This may not have been intended as a test of faith, but for those who had sacrificed the most by giving up their children and settled lives, this no-show experience left them with their belief strengthened, which may have been the point all along.

A CELESTIAL BEING EXITS HER VEHICLE

In the late 1970s, the group received a large sum of money, believed to be either the inheritance or donation of a former member. With such financial security, Heaven's Gate was now able to rent or purchase homes whenever they moved from town to town. However, living in local residences surrounded by prying eyes, as opposed to campgrounds far from the entanglements of civilization, made Applewhite more paranoid than ever before. He feared that he, like Jesus, would be assassinated by the government for spreading their gospel, and worried wherever they went that law enforcement would start cracking down on the group's activities or presence. The Two came up with several elaborate security measures as a precaution.

Michael Conyers recalled that they would assign designated people permitted to leave the house for groceries and errands. So while there may have been well over fifteen people living together at any given time, it appeared to neighbors that there were only two or three people coming and going. Usually the unassuming group would be able to remain under the radar for months or even years at a stretch, but once Applewhite suspected that someone in the neighborhood was catching on, the entire group would pick up and move somewhere else—a habit made easier thanks to the group's finances and John Craig's skill negotiating favorable leases. This stringent prohibition against contact with the world at large is precisely what Robert Jay Lifton meant by "milieu control," where communication not just with family and friends but even everyday contact with the world beyond the cult is cut off. These restrictions could even have been presented as a positive, since it allowed for more focused concentration on individual human metamorphosis.

But while the lifestyle for the typical Heaven's Gate follower was growing more regimented, the doctrine it was based on was very much a living document and open to change. Over the years, Applewhite and Nettles made significant alterations in their practices and beliefs. They incorporated more New Age concepts, especially the idea of a "walk-in," a concept popularized in Ruth Montgomery's 1979 book *Strangers Among Us: Enlightened Beings from a World to Come*, which suggested that the original human soul associated with a body could be displaced by a newer one.

In the Heaven's Gate update, a walk-in was not another human soul but an extraterrestrial one from the Next Level, a planet Applewhite and Nettles insisted was not just a real physical place but also the location that earthly religions referred to as heaven. This meant that Marshall Applewhite and Bonnie Nettles were not "Do and Ti"; those personas were Next Level walk-ins now inhabiting the former bodies previously associated with those earthly names. This was a convenient fiction, since it allowed the two of them to erase all connection to their personal biographies and pasts. "Do" had never been fired for having an affair with a male student, and "Ti" had never abandoned her marriage; they were both recent arrivals from outer space.

In some ways, the cash infusion allowed the founders to loosen their rules a little. By 1980 the group's eighty members were permitted to hold jobs, mostly in computers or auto repair. By 1982 they even started to occasionally call their abandoned families. And in 1983, members could schedule short visits with their families on Mother's Day. But this was not a step toward normalization so much as an effort to improve the group's image. Followers were told to tell their families that they were studying computers in a monastery, leaving the impression that they remained part of Heaven's Gate through their own free will.

But the most drastic change to the core beliefs came in 1985, when Bonnie Lu Nettles—Ti, the "Heavenly Father"—passed away and, according to Applewhite, ascended to the Next Level.

From a medical perspective, her death was anticipated well in advance, having lost an eye to cancer in 1983. At that point, the doctor let her know that the disease had begun to spread to the rest of her body.

As a former nurse, Nettles certainly understood the gravity of this diagnosis. Nonetheless, it appears that she continued to maintain the idea that the Two had previously preached: that she and Applewhite, along with their followers, would be lifted in their current physical form by a UFO that would transport them to the Next Level. However, by 1985 the cancer had spread to her liver, and she checked into Parkland Memorial Hospital in Dallas, under the pseudonym Shelly

West. By mid-June, she was dead. This not only left Applewhite with-out the partner who'd helped create this entire enterprise but also as the sole voice of a religion now in crisis.

Applewhite went into a state of depression after Nettles's death, a crisis of faith that he only emerged from thanks to devoted Heaven's Gate loyalists, who reminded him of his mission and helped lift him out of his state of inaction and despondency. But upon facing the very real consequences of Nettles's physical death—she was cremated and her ashes were scattered over a nearby lake—it was clear that he had to revise one of the core principles of his UFO cult. He began telling people that Ti had exhausted the corporeal body she'd left on Earth and that her ascension was a spiritual one. In fact, Do said, she was carried off via a spacecraft en route to the Next Level, where she would enter a new body.

Although this new doctrine was surprisingly similar to one he'd rid-iculed earlier, in which the caterpillar dies and mysteriously reappears in a rose blossom beside the king butterfly, only one person quit as a result of this about-face. For most of them, it strengthened their faith. In fact, the idea fit in surprisingly well with the prior switcheroo that converted Do and Ti from extraterrestrials and recast them as walk-ins. After all, if Ti could walk in, it made sense that she could also walk out.

It may not have been obvious in 1985, but this change ultimately had fatal consequences. Once the group had accepted the idea that their living bodies would not be boarding an actual UFO on a flight to the Next Level—that they would not be taking a charter flight to heaven in human form, as they had all been led to believe—it became necessary to lay out exactly how they *would* arrive at the Next Level. Unfortunately, this transformation laid the theoretical groundwork for the mass suicide that would follow twelve years later. What was once seen as literal was radically revised after Ti died. They soon began talking of the body as a "temporary container." Getting to the Next Level would now take a "final act of metamorphosis" that would include "exiting the vehicles."

THE AWAY TEAM

Nettles's death caused the paranoia-prone Applewhite to become even more suspicious that people were out to kill him. The group went further underground, maintaining such a low profile that outsiders began to assume Heaven's Gate had ceased to exist. By the early 1990s, membership had dwindled to as few as twenty-six members. With their numbers declining, Applewhite redirected the money generated from Higher Source, the group's new business designing websites—the newest tech trend—and paid to broadcast a twelve-part video series via satellite featuring Applewhite preaching his gospel.

In May 1993, Applewhite placed a $30,000 full-page ad in *USA Today* calling the group "Total Overcomers Anonymous" and warning the public of an impending catastrophic judgment that was to befall humanity. As a result of this ad, at least twenty former members rejoined the cult. And more came aboard in 1994 after a second series of video lectures. The group had doubled in size from its low point. Heaven's Gate was gaining a reputation in the emerging internet subculture, and quite a few new followers had been introduced to Do through its website.

But this combination of heightened visibility among early adopters of the World Wide Web and Heaven's Gate's simultaneous public reemergence after years underground brought renewed scrutiny and criticism that Applewhite took to heart. The depression that had taken hold after Nettles's passing grew in force, and he seemed to show signs of exhaustion—understandable from someone who'd spent the previous two decades leading an outlaw band, staying in campgrounds and illegal leases, and managing a rotating core of needy and dependent followers. He complained about his body, which he said was deteriorating. He told people he had cancer (although the autopsy after his death showed no evidence of it). Susan Raine points out that this preoccupation with one's physical self, along with a frequent review of one's accomplishments, is a characteristic of paranoid schizophrenia.

Regarding his body and body of work, Applewhite found reasons to despair.

He began speaking openly of suicide, saying that in order to ascend, everything human, including the body, must be sacrificed. "It may be necessary," he said, "to take things in our own hands." Like the Manson Family, the Narcosatanists, and the Branch Davidians before them, the members of Heaven's Gate were growing increasingly captive to the internal logic of their own beliefs. They had spent years saying that people were "hooked to humanity." Their disciplines—the bizarre diets, the forced confessions of their own sensual urges that they recited in front of the group—seemed designed to help them get past this "mammalian humanity." Now they began to speak of themselves as the "graduating class," eager for their transition to the Next Level.

It's impossible to re-create the thinking within the cult, but Marshall Applewhite may have tried to avoid the horrific fate with an odd detour. In 1995, two Heaven's Gate members signed the visitors' log of a New Mexico architect's workshop, which specialized in energy-efficient, off-the-grid buildings made of rammed earth and recycled materials, such as old tires (the earth is sledgehammered inside the tires, which are then stacked to make the walls) and glass bottles (used as structural and decorative elements in concrete walls). Perhaps they were attracted by the name of the enterprise: Spaceship Earth. They purchased a set of building instructions, and for a few months Heaven's Gate moved to a remote area in New Mexico and began constructing their own "earth ships." Was it an attempt to follow the dictates of their own faith to the letter, by living aboard their own spaceship in a way that avoided mass suicide? Some members complained about the difficulty of the work, perhaps having grown used to living more comfortably with trust fund support. Applewhite listened to their complaints and aborted the experiment, and they moved on.

At about the same time, on one of their astronomy-related field trips to a nearby planetarium, they learned of the celestial approach of a previously uncharted comet. The heavenly body—spotted independently and simultaneously by two amateur astronomers, Alan Hale and Thomas Bopp, and named for them—was unusual for its faint sodium tail, a previously unobserved phenomenon. The bright cosmic event inspired conspiracy theorists, including one who called in to a late-night radio show—*Coast to Coast AM with Art Bell*, which often entertained guests speculating about UFOs—claiming to have spotted a separate, Saturn-like object trailing the comet.

It is believed that Applewhite transfigured some combination of these claims and aberrations into the real-world proof he needed. He used superficially scientific evidence to convince his followers that there was a spaceship trailing Comet Hale-Bopp, that Ti herself was aboard the vessel, and that it was coming to transport them all to the level of existence beyond human. The group took this as a confirmation of everything they had believed in for so long.

In October 1996, six months before the expected path of the comet would come closest to Earth, Heaven's Gate rented a 9,200-square-foot seven-bedroom home in Rancho Santa Fe, California, twenty-five miles north of San Diego. The property was in foreclosure, so the rent was a bargain: $7,000 a month, a cost they were able to cover from the proceeds of their website business. The house was located near the end of a street in a gated community that prized privacy—down to eliminating streetlights that might make unwanted surveillance easier.

Those who were most employable—Margaret Richter and David Moore, both computer adepts, and Susan Paup, a technical writer—continued to hold down jobs. By all reports, as employees, the Heaven's Gate members were punctual and ate bag lunches, which they always took precisely at 12:15 p.m. After the suicides, one employer remembered the odd way they dressed for Southern California: "Long sleeves in the summer, buttoned up all the way to the neck. Dark colors. And their hair was short." Another small-business owner who contracted their web services remembered them as "good, smart, well-intentioned people. And they believed so strongly, they were willing to give their lives for it." They were open enough about their intentions, vaguely mentioning an upcoming big event on their calendar, that at least one employer joked with them about the approach of March 25. He said they talked about the comet so much that he got to looking at his pager whenever they came in, teasing them by remarking, "T minus 18 days and counting."

The group videotaped their exit statements outdoors on the Rancho Santa Fe property, against a lushly green suburban backdrop. On the video, they seem rather excited about the prospect of ascension, chuckling together about being beamed up and seeming to recognize that anyone viewing their statements would misinterpret their deaths as drastic or irrational, and their tone appears solicitous and reassuring. There is no real evidence of second thoughts or hesitation. These final testimonials serve as a document of belief. It is easy to imagine them laughing together around their kitchen table, as they claimed to do. One notices the bad short haircuts, and those who wear glasses seem to have chosen the cheapest and least flattering frames. Most seem to be swimming in their ill-fitted clothes, as if they had borrowed the outfits from much larger people.

As the fateful date approached, they collectively made quiet gestures of withdrawal. One told an employer that he was going to be away on "monastery business"; another gave his boss a bolo tie adorned with an image of an alien that the supervisor had always admired.

The day before the mass suicides, the group went out for a last dinner together—a reservation for thirty-nine. They made it easier for the restaurant, a Marie Callender's, by preordering identical meals: house salad with tomato vinaigrette, turkey potpie, blueberry cheesecake, and iced tea. They went through more lemon wedges in one meal than the restaurant usually used in an entire day. They left a $52 tip on a $351 bill, just shy of 15 percent, all paid in cash.

At their home, they left a binder, a kind of playbook for their intentions, that investigators discovered upon responding to a 911 call left by a group member who didn't reside with the cult. He'd come by to check on them after receiving via FedEx the full video of their exit statements and discovered the bodies. The victims were all clad in black T-shirts and windbreakers with shoulder patches that read: HEAVEN'S GATE AWAY TEAM. On their feet were identical black-and-white Nike Decades, which had been bought in bulk for $14 a pair (and in a macabre twist, now sell for around $5,000 a pair on websites selling vintage items). The group's binder laid out the order of exit: "Fifteen classmates, eight assistants, then fifteen more and eight assistants, then help each other." All but the last two had purple shrouds covering their faces. Each had ingested a fatal combination of phenobarbital, applesauce, and vodka.

There are many theories about what compelled the Heaven's Gate cult members to take their lives. Was it a mass suicide, or one suicide and thirty-eight premeditated murders? Marshall Applewhite's powerful influence didn't seem to account for the clear-eyed exit statements or the testimony of multiple former members that people in Heaven's Gate were free to go anytime. The cult's website remains active, maintained by adherents, and both the exit statements and many of the rambling wide-eyed speeches of Applewhite can be easily accessed online. The website content tries to turn the tables, presenting a statement laying out its position *against* suicide, that "the true meaning of 'suicide' is to turn against the Next Level when it is being offered"; in other words, anybody who isn't taking their own lives with them is truly committing suicide. This is not so much a denial of reality as a reversal of it. Tragically, all thirty-nine of the dead seemed to have endorsed this statement. As one of them noted, "I think everyone in this class wanted something more than this human life had to offer."

ACKNOWLEDGMENTS

Mom: From reading my high school essays to podcast scripts, you have always been there to support me. You never allowed me to settle. From my dreams to my work, you are a constant positive daily force and encourage my full potential. You ensured that my dreams became a reality. Dad: The impact you have had on me is profound. You have been my North Star constantly, guiding me through life. Your positive attitude, drive, and creativity are an ever-present inspiration. Both of you are my superheroes.

The Parcast team: I am grateful to each and every one of you. Your talent and dedication to storytelling are matched only by your enthusiasm for podcasts. I especially want to thank Julian Boireau, Ronald Shapiro, Drew Cole, Carleigh Madden, Vanessa Richardson, Greg Polcyn, and Maggie Admire for helping bring the *Cults* podcast to life.

Cults, the book, would not have been possible without my agents, Ben Davis and Eve Attermann. I would also like to thank my editor, Ed Schlesinger, and Gallery Books for their continued support. And to Kevin Conley: Thank you for your partnership and hard work in coauthoring this book with me.

NOTES

See accompanying bibliography for additional information on sources consulted.

EXPLOITATION: BHAGWAN SHREE RAJNEESH

1. Sanjeev Sabhlok, "A Religious Guru Who *Strongly* Endorses Capitalism," *Sanjeev Sabhlok's blog,* July 26, 2011, https://www.sabhlokcity.com/2011/07/a-religious-guru-who-strongly-endorses-capitalism/.

2. Osho, *Autobiography of a Spiritually Incorrect Mystic* (New York: St. Martin's Press, 2001), 56.

3. Ibid.

4. Amy Cooper, "Screaming Meditation Aims to Help Stress Relief," *Canberra Times,* August 4, 2021, https://www.canberratimes.com.au/story/7370998/shake-it-off-with-screaming-meditation/.

5. Osho, *The Great Challenge* (New Delhi: Diamond Pocket Books, 2003), 30.

6. Sabhlok, "A Religious Guru Who *Strongly* Endorses Capitalism."

7. Hugh B. Urban, *Zorba the Buddha: Sex, Spirituality, and Capitalism in the Global Osho Movement* (Oakland: University of California Press, 2016), 96.

8. Max Weber, *On Charisma and Institution Building: Selected Papers* (Chicago: University of Chicago Press, 1968), 53.

9. Ma Anand Sheela, *Don't Kill Him!: The Story of My Life with Bhagwan Rajneesh* (New Delhi: FiNGERPRINT!, 2012), 139.

10. Ibid., 114.

11. Robert Jay Lifton, *Thought Reform and the Psychology of Totalism: A Study of "Brainwashing" in China* (Chapel Hill: University of North Carolina Press, 1989), 423.

12. Susan J. Palmer, "Charisma and Abdication: A Study of the Leadership of Bhagwan Shree Rajneesh," *Sociological Analysis* 49, no. 2 (July 1, 1988): 126, https://doi.org/10.2307/3711009.

13. Hugh B. Urban, *Zorba the Buddha: Sex, Spirituality, and Capitalism in the Global Osho Movement* (Oakland: University of California Press, 2015), 97.

14. Malcolm McConnell, *Stepping Over: Personal Encounters with Young Extremists* (New York: Reader's Digest Press, 1984), 72.

15. Win McCormack, "Bhagwan's Devious Trap," *New Republic*, April 12, 2018, https://newrepublic.com/article/147905/bhagwans-devious-trap.

16. Sam Wollaston, "Growing Up in the Wild Wild Country Cult: 'You Heard People Having Sex All the Time, Like Baboons,'" *Guardian*, April 24, 2018, https://www.theguardian.com/tv-and-radio/2018/apr/24/wild-wild-country-netflix-cult-sex-noa-maxwell-bhagwan-shree-rajneesh-commune-childhood.

17. Win McCormack, *The Rajneesh Chronicles: The True Story of the Cult That Unleashed the First Act of Bioterrorism on U.S. Soil* (Portland: Tin House Books, 2010), 233.

18. Dashiell Edward Paulson, "The Routinization of Rajneeshpuram: Charisma and Authority in the Rajneesh Movement, 1981–1985," Thesis, University of Oregon, 2015, 31.

19. "L.A. Resident Gets 20 Years for '83 Bombing of Hotel Rahneesh," *Los Angeles Times*, November 10, 1985, https://www.latimes.com/archives/la-xpm-1985-11-10-mn-3387-story.html.

20. Philip Elmer-DeWitt, "America's First Bioterrorism Attack," Time, September 30, 2001, http://content.time.com/time/magazine/article/0,9171,176937,00.html.

21. Marlow Stern, "'Wild Wild Country': Most Shocking Reveals from the Sex Cult's FBI Informant," *Daily Beast*, April 2, 2018, updated April 4, 2018, https://www.thedailybeast.com/wild-wild-country-the-most-shocking-reveals-from-the-sex-cults-fbi-informant.

22. Harry David, "Guru's Dying Words: 'I Am Leaving This Tortured Body,'" UPI, United Press International, January 19, 1990, https://

www.upi.com/Archives/1990/01/19/Gurus-dying-words-I-am-leav
ing-this-tortured-body/2188632725200/.

23. Noa Jones, "I Charged My Sexual Energies at the Osho Meditation
Resort in India," Vice, April 19, 2015, https://www.vice.com/en
/article/xd7qp4/sex-robes-and-gurus-299.

EXPLOITATION:
JIM JONES AND THE PEOPLES TEMPLE

1. James L. Kelley, "'You Don't Know How Hard It Is to Be God': Rev.
Jim Jones' Blueprint for Nurture Failure," Alternative Considerations
of Jonestown & Peoples Temple, Department of Religious Studies at
San Diego State University, October 26, 2017, updated October 17,
2018, https://jonestown.sdsu.edu/?page_id=70768.

PATHOLOGICAL LYING: CLAUDE VORILHON AND RAËLISM

1. "Vatican Slams 'Brutal' Clone Claim," CNN, December 28, 2002,
https://www.cnn.com/2002/HEALTH/12/28/cloning.vatican
/index.html.

MEGALOMANIA: DAVID KORESH
AND THE BRANCH DAVIDIANS

1. World Science Festival, "Hallucinations with Oliver Sacks," YouTube,
December 8, 2014, https://www.youtube.com/watch?v=8T_Xim
Pe4xU.

2. Oliver Sacks, Hallucinations (New York: Vintage Books, 2012), 159–60.

3. Sue Anne Pressley and Mary Jordan, "'Mighty Men' of Cult Enforced
Koresh's Rules," Washington Post, April 22, 1993, https://www.wash
ingtonpost.com/archive/politics/1993/04/22/mighty-men-of-cult
-enforced-koreshs-rules/3fc01c4f-0990-44f7-8d52-a64899271cc7/.

4. Susan Aschoff, "After the 'War' at Waco," Tampa Bay Times, February
28, 2000, updated September 26, 2005, https://www.tampabay.com
/archive/2000/02/28/after-the-war-at-waco/.

5. United States Bureau of Alcohol, Tobacco, and Firearms, and Federal
Bureau of Investigation, "Negotiation Transcript—Tape 25," The Ashes

of Waco, The Wittliff Collections at Texas State University, March 3, 1993, https://digital.library.txstate.edu/handle/10877/1782.

6.   Susan Aschoff, "After the 'War' at Waco."

7.   Cole Moreton, "Waco Siege 20 Years On: The Survivor's Tale," *Telegraph*, March 24, 2013, https://www.telegraph.co.uk/news/religion/9950378/Waco-siege-20-years-on-the-survivors-tale.html.

8.   Mark Swett, "David Koresh and the Waco Davidians: An Ultimate Act of Faith?," Cult Education Institute, March 2002, https://culteducation.com/group/1220-waco-davidians/24283-david-koresh-and-the-waco-davidians-an-ultimate-act-of-faith.html.

9.   Corey Charlton, "25 Years On," The Sun, February 28, 2018, www.thesun.co.uk/news/5672656/british-survivor-waco-cult-david-koresh-still-believes-apocalypse-coming/.

SADISM: KEITH RANIERE AND NXIVM

1.   Suzanna Andrews, "The Heiresses and the Cult," *Vanity Fair*, October 13, 2010, https://www.vanityfair.com/culture/2010/11/bronfman-201011.

2.   Ibid.

3.   CBC, *Uncover: Escaping NXIVM* (podcast), Episode 3: Sex, Money, and Nazis, September 4, 2018 (8:00 mins.).

4.   Ibid., (8:25 mins.).

5.   Lenny Bernstein, "How Parents Create Narcissistic Children," *Washington Post*, March 9, 2015, https://www.washingtonpost.com/news/to-your-health/wp/2015/03/09/how-parents-create-narcissistic-children/.

6.   Bowen Xiao, "EXCLUSIVE: Delving into the Childhood of NXIVM's Leader," *Epoch Times*, May 28, 2018, updated May 30, 2018, https://www.theepochtimes.com/exclusive-delving-into-the-childhood-of-nxivms-leader_2540043.html.

7.   Vanessa Grigoriadis, "Inside Nxivm, the 'Sex Cult' That Preached Empowerment," *New York Times Magazine*, May 30, 2018, https://www.nytimes.com/2018/05/30/magazine/sex-cult-empowerment-nxivm-keith-raniere.html.

8.   CBC, *Uncover: Escaping NXIVM* (podcast), Episode 3: Sex, Money, and Nazis, September 4, 2018 (6:30 mins.).

9.   Xiao, "EXCLUSIVE: Delving into the Childhood of NXIVM's Leader."

10. James M. Odato and Jennifer Gish, "In Raniere's Shadows," *Albany Times Union*, February 18, 2012, updated February 22, 2012, https://www .timesunion.com/local/article/In-Raniere-s-shadows-3341644.php.

11. "NXIVM: Gina Melita's Story," *Albany Times Union*, YouTube, April 22, 2019, https://youtu.be/YWJcMMgXNmw?t=53.

12. Ibid., https://youtu.be/YWJcMMgXNmw?t=58.

13. Ibid., https://youtu.be/YWJcMMgXNmw?t=108.

14. Odato and Gish, "In Raniere's Shadows."

15. Josh Bloch, Kathleen Goldhar, Anita Elash, and Dave Pizer, "The Making of Vanguard," CBCnews, September 12, 2018, https://news interactives.cbc.ca/longform/the-making-of-the-vanguard.

16. CBC, *Uncover: Escaping NXIVM* (podcast), Episode 3: Sex, Money, and Nazis, September 4, 2018 (13:05 mins.).

17. Ibid., (13:40 mins.).

18. Irene Gardner Keeney, "Troy Man Has a Lot on His Mind," *Times Union*, June 26, 1988, https://www.timesunion.com/7dayarchive/arti cle/Troy-man-has-a-lot-on-his-mind-15640272.php.

19. Christopher Ringwald, "Discount Service Target of Probe," *Times Union*, May 12, 1992, https://www.timesunion.com/7dayarchive /article/Discount-service-target-of-probe-15640345.php.

20. Toni Natalie with Chet Hardin, *The Program: Inside the Mind of Keith Raniere and the Rise and Fall of NXIVM* (New York: Grand Central Publishing, 2019), 20.

21. EJ Dickson, "How NXIVM Was the Ultimate Wellness Scam," *Rolling Stone*, October 8, 2019, https://www.rollingstone.com/culture /culture-features/nxivm-keith-raniere-wellness-scam-sex-cult-848439/.

22. Natalie, *The Program*, 19.

23. Barry Meier, "Once Idolized, Guru of Nxivm 'Sex Cult' to Stand Trial Alone," *New York Times*, May 1, 2019, https://www.nytimes.com/2019 /05/01/nyregion/nxivm-keith-raniere-trial.html.

24. Natalie, *The Program*, 21.

25. Ibid.

26. Ibid., 27.

27. Odato and Gish, "In Raniere's Shadows."

28. Natalie, *The Program*, 36.

29. Kimberly Lawson, "Sleep Deprivation Can Be a Weapon in the Hands of an Abusive Partner," Vice, July 9, 2019, https://www.vice.com/en

_us/article/3k3myn/sleep-deprivation-can-be-a-weapon-in-the -hands-of-an-abusive-partner.

30. Natalie, *The Program*, 59.

31. Ibid., 63.

32. Katie Heaney (as told to), "What It Was Like to Date a Cult Leader," The Cut, November 7, 2019, https://www.thecut.com/2019/11 /what-it-was-like-to-date-a-cult-leader.html.

33. Taste of Reality, *Pinkshade* (podcast), Episode 34: "Exclusive: Toni Natalie, Keith Raniere's Ex-Girlfriend, On NXIVM," May 15, 2018 (17:40 mins.), https://radiopublic.com/pink-shade-6rVXLa/s1!76165..

34. Ibid., 84.

35. Michael Freedman, "Cult of Personality," *Forbes*, October 13, 2003, https://www.forbes.com/forbes/2003/1013/088.html#421b130 41853.

36. Namkje Koudenburg, Tom Postmes, Ernestine H. Gordijn, and Aafke van Mourik Broekman, "Uniform and Complementary Social Interaction: Distinct Pathways to Solidarity," *PLoS One* 10, no. 6 (2015), https://doi.org/10.1371/journal.pone.0129061.

37. Brendan J. Lyons, "Guilty Plea Ends Salzman's Long Allegiance to Raniere," *Albany Times Union*, March 15, 2019, updated March 21, 2019, https://www.timesunion.com/news/article/Guilty-plea-of-Salz man-ends-her-long-allegiance-13691433.php.

38. Kate Prengel, "Lauren Salzman: 5 Fast Facts You Need to Know," Heavy, April 2, 2019, https://heavy.com/news/2019/04/lauren-salz man/.

39. EJ Dickson, "'I Was in One Mode: Protect Keith': NXIVM Member Testifies About Naked Meetings, Group Sex, Dungeon Paddlings," *Rolling Stone*, May 21, 2019, https://www.rollingstone.com/culture /culture-features/lauren-salzman-nxivm-sex-slave-keith-raniere-testi mony-trial-836547/.

40. Barbara Bouchey, "Barbara Bouchey Breaks Long Silence and Speaks Out About Commodities Losses and Other Raniere-Bronfman Matters," Frank Report, October 21, 2019, https://frankreport.com/2019 /10/21/barbara-bouchey-breaks-long-silence-and-speaks-out-about -commodities-losses-and-other-raniere-bronfman-matters/.

41. Emanuella Grinberg and Sonia Moghe, "She Says She Dropped Out of School and Left Mexico to Join a Cult," CNN, May 24, 2019,

https://www.cnn.com/2019/05/24/us/nxivm-trial-mexican-witness /index.html.

42. Natalie, *The Program*, 125.

43. Grinberg and Moghe, "She Says She Dropped Out of School."

44. Ibid.

45. Natalie, *The Program*, 126.

46. Sarah Berman, "'I Was Gone from the World and Nobody Noticed': One Woman's Story of Being Trapped by NXIVM," Vice, May 30, 2019, https://www.vice.com/en/article/evy58a/i-was-gone-from-the -world-and-nobody-noticed-one-womans-story-of-being-trapped-by -nxivm.

47. Nicole Chavez and Sonia Moghe, "6 Weeks of Testimony in Nxivm Case Reveal Lurid Details of Alleged Sex Cult, Including Branding Women and Holding Them Captive," CNN, updated June 16, 2019, https://www.cnn.com/2019/06/16/us/nxivm-keith-raniere-trial /index.html.

48. Amanda Ottaway, "Witness in Sex-Cult Trial Says She Was Held Captive for 2 Years," Courthouse News Service, May 31, 2019, https:// www.courthousenews.com/witness-in-sex-cult-trial-says-she-was-held -captive-for-2-years/.

49. Michael Blackmon, "A Former NXIVM 'Cult' Member Says She and Her Two Sisters Had to Have Abortions After Sex with Keith Raniere," BuzzFeed News, May 28, 2019, https://www.buzzfeed news.com/article/michaelblackmon/nxivm-sex-cult-abortion-keith -raniere-sisters.

50. Lisette Voytko, "FBI: Nxivm's Leader Had 'Sex Slave' Cruise Tinder for Him," *Forbes*, June 6, 2019, https://www.forbes.com/sites/lisette voytko/2019/06/06/fbi-nxivms-leader-had-sex-slave-cruise-tinder -for-him/#4993ded93962.

51. Robert Gavin, "Messages Suggest Girl Was 15 When Raniere Relationship Began," *Albany Times Union*, June 5, 2019, updated June 5, 2019, https://www.timesunion.com/news/article/Messages-suggest -Raniere-s-relationship-with-13939595.php.

52. Ibid.

53. Voytko, "FBI: Nxivm's Leader Had 'Sex Slave' Cruise Tinder for Him."

54. Andrews, "The Heiresses and the Cult."

55. Ibid.

56. Ibid.

57. Rozina Sabur, "Seagram Whisky Heiress Clare Bronfman Pleads Guilty to Role in Nxivm 'Sex Cult,'" *Telegraph*, April 20, 2019, https://www.telegraph.co.uk/news/2019/04/20/seagram-whisky-heiress-clare-bronfman-pleads-guilty-role-nxivm/.

58. Barry Maier, "The Journey of the 'Sex Cult' Heiress: From Reluctant Recruit to Criminal Defendant," *New York Times*, August 11, 2018, https://www.nytimes.com/2018/08/11/business/clare-bronfman-nxivm.html.

59. Ibid.

60. Andrews, "The Heiresses and the Cult."

61. Natalie, *The Program*, 147.

62. Freedman, "Cult of Personality."

63. Andrews, "The Heiresses and the Cult."

64. Natalie, *The Program*, 156.

65. Freedman, "Cult of Personality."

66. Ibid.

67. Natalie, *The Program*, 159, in ebook search: "dossier."

68. Andrews, "The Heiresses and the Cult."

69. Kent A. Kiehl and Morris B. Hoffman, "The Criminal Psychopath: History, Neuroscience, Treatment, and Economics," *Jurimetrics* 51 (2011): 374, https://www.ncbi.nlm.nih.gov/pmc/articles/PMC4059069/.

70. Beata Pastwa-Wojciechowska, "The Relationship of Pathological Gambling to Criminality Behavior in a Sample of Polish Male Offenders," *Medical Science Monitor* 17, no. 11 (2011), CR669–75, doi: 10.12659/MSM.882054.

71. Kiehl and Hoffman, "The Criminal Psychopath," 374.

72. Nicole Hong, "Clare Bronfman, Facing Sentencing, Refuses to Disavow 'Sex Cult' Leader," *New York Times*, September 28, 2020, updated October 27, 2020, https://www.nytimes.com/2020/09/28/nyregion/clare-bronfman-keith-raniere-nxivm-sentence.html.

73. Natalie, *The Program*, 128.

74. Ibid., 129.

75. Flavie Waters, Vivian Chiu, Amanda Atkinson, and Jan Dirk Blom, "Severe Sleep Deprivation Causes Hallucinations and a Gradual Progression Toward Psychosis with Increasing Time Awake," *Frontiers in Psychiatry* 9 (July 10, 2018): 303, https://doi.org/10.3389/fpsyt.2018.00303.

76. Natalie, *The Program*, 129.

77. Scott Johnson and Rebecca Sun, "Her Darkest Role: Actress Allison Mack's Descent from 'Smallville' to Sex Cult," *Hollywood Reporter*, May 16, 2018, https://www.hollywoodreporter.com/features/how -smallvilles-allison-mack-went-actress-sex-cult-slaver-1112107.

78. Robert Gavin, "NXIVM Turned Lake George Resort into Annual Raniere Birthday Jamboree," *Albany Times Union*, May 10, 2019, https://www.timesunion.com/news/article/NXIVM-turned-Lake -George-resort-into-annual-13836853.php.

79. *20/20*, S40, E34, "Woman Recalls Being Branded as Part of Joining Secret Society; What Former NXIVM Members Say About Keith Raniere's Attitude Toward Women; How 'Smallville' Actress Became Involved in NXIVM," April 27, 2018, https://abc.com/shows/2020 /episode-guide/2018-04/27-042718-nxivm (~20:00 mins.).

80. Josh Bloch, Kathleen Goldhar, Anita Elash, and Dave Pizer, "The Making of Vanguard: The Story of How NXIVM's Keith Raniere Went from Gifted Child to Self-Help Guru to Accused Sex-Cult Leader," CBC News, CBC Radio-Canada, September 12, 2018, https://news interactives.cbc.ca/longform/the-making-of-the-vanguard.

81. Elizabeth Hopper, "What Is the Mere Exposure Effect in Psychology?: Why We Like Things We've Seen Before," ThoughtCo, updated December 13, 2019, https://www.thoughtco.com/mere-exposure -effect-4777824.

82. Johnson and Sun, "Her Darkest Role: Actress Allison Mack's Descent from 'Smallville' to Sex Cult."

83. Hopper, "What Is the Mere Exposure Effect in Psychology?"

84. Johnson and Sun, "Her Darkest Role."

85. Zack Sharf, "'Smallville' Star Allison Mack Reached Out to Emma Watson About Alleged Sex Cult," IndieWire, April 25, 2018, https:// www.indiewire.com/2018/04/smallville-allison-mack-emma-watson -sex-cult-1201957138/.

86. Taryn Ryder, "How Did Smallville's Allison Mack Get Involved with a Sex Cult in the First Place?," HuffPost, May 18, 2018, https://www .huffpost.com/entry/how-did-smallvilles-allison-mack-get-involved -with-a-sex-cult-in-the-first-place_n_5aff3222e4b0a046186b7fbb.

87. Ibid.

88. Susan Dones, "Susan Dones on the Record: A Detailed and Provoca-

tive Account from an EXpian [*sic*]," Frank Report, October 23, 2017, https://frankreport.com/2017/10/23/susan-dones-on-the-record-the-most-detailed-and-provocative/.

89. Frank Report, "NXIVM Cult Leader Keith Raniere Claims to Have Had People Killed," YouTube, December 6, 2015, https://youtu.be/HuStK6xg-7g?t=212.

90. Sarah Edmondson, *Scarred: The True Story of How I Escaped NXIVM, the Cult That Bound My Life* (San Francisco: Chronicle Prism, 2019).

91. Ibid., 185.

92. Ibid.

93. Ibid.

94. Ibid.

95. Barry Maier, "Inside a Secretive Group Where Women Are Branded," *New York Times*, October 17, 2017, https://www.nytimes.com/2017/10/17/nyregion/nxivm-women-branded-albany.html.

96. Edmondson, *Scarred*.

97. *20/20*, "Woman Recalls Being Branded as Part of Joining Secret Society."

98. Vice News, "The Man Who Blew the Whistle on Alleged Sex Cult Inside NXIVM," YouTube, May 17, 2018, https://www.youtube.com/watch?v=wsoUjimrglE.

99. *Today*, "Actress Catherine Oxenberg Talks About Her Fight to Save Her "Hijacked' Daughter," YouTube, November 2, 2017, https://www.youtube.com/watch?v=Gz9YKhZzzUQ.

100. Edmondson, *Scarred*.

101. Michael Blackmon, "The Founder of an Alleged Sex Cult Hid in a Walk-In Closet When Officials Raided His Mexican Villa to Arrest Him," BuzzFeed News, May 21, 2019, updated May 21, 2019, https://www.buzzfeednews.com/article/michaelblackmon/keith-raniere-closet-arrest-mexico-lauren-salzman.

102. Emily Saul and Lea Eustachewich, "Nxivm Leader Keith Raniere Hid in Closet to Avoid Arrest: Testimony," *New York Post*, May 21, 2019, https://nypost.com/2019/05/21/nxivm-leader-keith-raniere-hid-in-closet-to-avoid-arrest-testimony/.

103. EJ Dickson, "Keith Raniere, Head of NXIVM and Alleged Sex Cult, Found Guilty on All Counts," *Rolling Stone*, June 19, 2019, https://www.rollingstone.com/culture/culture-news/keith-raniere-nxivm-trial-guilty-all-counts-849967/.

104. Amanda Arnold, "NXIVM Member Admits to Enslaving Woman for Two Years," The Cut, April 2, 2019, https://www.thecut.com/2019 /04/nxivm-enslaved-woman-locked-room-lauren-salzman.html.

105. Amanda Arnold, "The Most Disturbing Details from the NXIVM Sex-Cult Case," The Cut, May 7, 2019, https://www.thecut.com/2019/05 /the-most-disturbing-details-from-the-nxivm-sex-cult-case.html.

106. Will Yakowicz, "Nxivm 'Sex Cult' Leader Posed as a Mentor for Women, But Was a Predatory 'Crime Boss,' Prosecutors Say," Forbes, May 7, 2019, https://www.forbes.com/sites/willyakowicz/2019/05 /07/nxivm-sex-cult-leader-posed-as-a-mentor-for-women-but-was-a -predatory-crime-boss-prosecutors-say/.

107. Arnold, "The Most Disturbing Details."

108. Emily Saul and Lea Eustachewich, "Nxivm 'Slave Master' Describes Naked Group Meetings with Leader," New York Post, May 17, 2019, https://nypost.com/2019/05/17/nxivm-slave-master-describes -naked-group-meetings-with-leader/.

109. Sarah Berman, "The NXIVM 'Sex Cult' Story Keeps Getting More Disturbing," Vice, May 20, 2019, https://www.vice.com/en_ca/arti cle/evyb5j/the-nxivm-sex-cult-story-keeps-getting-more-disturbing.

110. EJ Dickson, "'I Was in One Mode: Protect Keith.'"

111. EJ Dickson, "Former Slave Describes Allison Mack's Alleged Abusive, Terrifying Behavior in Detail," Rolling Stone, June 10, 2019, https:// www.rollingstone.com/culture/culture-features/nxivm-trial-allison -mack-sex-slave-nicole-abuse-keith-raniere-845830/.

112. Emily Saul, Lea Eustachewich, and Kate Sheehy, "Nxivm 'Slave' Gives Jurors Look Inside Alleged Sex Cult," New York Post, May 7, 2019, https://nypost.com/2019/05/07/nxivm-slave-gives-jurors-look -inside-alleged-sex-cult/.

113. Chavez and Moghe, "6 Weeks of Testimony in Nxivm Case."

114. Edward Helmore, "Nxivm Trial: Keith Raniere Found Guilty on All Counts in Sex Cult Case," Guardian, June 19, 2019, https://www.the guardian.com/us-news/2019/jun/19/nxivm-trial-keith-raniere-ver dict-guilty-allison-mack.

115. Frank Parlato, "Federal Prisoner #57005-177—a/k/a Keith Alan Raniere a/k/a Vanguard—to Be Arraigned Today; What to Expect," Frank Report, April 13, 2018, https://frankreport.com/2018/04/13 /raniere-to-be-arraigned-today-what-to-expect/.

ESCAPE: CREDONIA MWERINDE
AND THE MOVEMENT FOR THE RESTORATION
OF THE TEN COMMANDMENTS OF GOD

1. Bernard Atuhaire, *The Uganda Cult Tragedy: A Private Investigation* (London: Janus, 2003), xx.

2. Ibid., 6.

3. Ibid., 52.

DENIAL OF REALITY:
MARSHALL APPLEWHITE AND HEAVEN'S GATE

1. Laura Barcella, "Heaven's Gate, 23 Years Later: Remembering 38 People Who Died with Cult Leader," *People*, March 26, 2020, https://people
.com/crime/heavens-gate-22-years-later-remembering-lives-lost/.

2. John Holliman, "Applewhite: From Young Overachiever to Cult Leader," CNN, March 28, 1997, http://www.cnn.com/US/9703/28
/applewhite/index.html.

3. Mubarak Dahir, "Heaven's Scapegoat," *The Advocate*, no. 733, May 13, 1997, 35.

4. Marc Fisher and Sue Ann Pressley, "Crisis of Sexuality Launched Strange Journey," *Washington Post*, March 29, 1997, https://www.wash
ingtonpost.com/archive/politics/1997/03/29/crisis-of-sexuality
-launched-strange-journey/3709d9ff-51ee-4f50-a9cd-a45525d7ad8f/.

5. HeavensGateDatabase, "Student Exit Statements," YouTube, April 9, 2013, https://www.youtube.com/watch?v=wHz9it70TdI.

6. Robert Jay Lifton, Destroying the World to Save It (New York: Henry Holt, 1999), 307.

7. James Brooke, "Former Cultists Warn of Believers Now Adrift," *New York Times*, April 2, 1997, https://archive.nytimes.com/www.nytimes
.com/library/national/0402mass-suicide-recruit.html.

8. C. G. Jung, *Flying Saucers: A Modern Myth of Things Seen in the Skies*, trans. R. F. C. Hull (Abingdon: Routledge Classics, 2002), 11.

9. Jaclyn Anglis, "The Twisted Story of the Heaven's Gate Cult—and Their Tragic Mass Suicide," All That's Interesting, November 14, 2021, updated December 1, 2021, https://allthatsinteresting.com/heavens-gate-cult.

10. Ibid.

11. Sam Harris, *Making Sense* (podcast), Episode 7: "Through the Eyes of

a Cult," March 24, 2015 (10:00 mins.), https://www.samharris.org /podcasts/making-sense-episodes/through-the-eyes-of-a-cult.

12. Sam Harris, *Waking Up: A Guide to Spirituality Without Religion* (New York: Simon & Schuster, 2014) 164.

10. James Brooke, "For Cowboy in Cult, Long Ride into Sunset," *New York Times*, March 31, 1997, https://www.nytimes.com/1997/03/31/us /for-cowboy-in-cult-long-ride-into-sunset.html.

BIBLIOGRAPHY

SHAME: CHARLES MANSON AND THE FAMILY

Bugliosi, Vincent, with Curt Gentry. *Helter Skelter: The True Story of the Manson Murders*. New York: Norton, 1974.

Guinn, Jeff. *Manson: The Life and Times of Charles Manson*. London: Simon & Schuster, 2013.

Heigl, Alex. "The Manson Murders, 45 Years Later." People.com, August 27, 2014. https://people.com/celebrity/manson-family-murders-45-years -later-2/.

Manson, Charles, and Nuel Emmons. *Manson in His Own Words*. New York: Grove Press, 1986.

Ng, Christina. "Charles Manson Denied Parole After Saying He Is a 'Very Dangerous Man.'" ABC News, April 10, 2012. https://abcnews.go .com/US/charles-manson-denied-parole-dangerous-man/story?id =16111128.

People v. Manson, 61 Cal.App.3d 102 (Cal. Ct. App. 1976). https://casetext .com/case/people-v-manson-1.

Sanders, Ed. *The Family*. Berkeley, CA: Da Capo, 2002.

Statman, Alisa, with Brie Tate. *Restless Souls: The Sharon Tate Family's Account of Stardom, the Manson Murders, and a Crusade for Justice*. New York: It Books, 2013.

SHAME: ADOLFO DE JESÚS CONSTANZO
AND THE NARCOSATANISTS

Applebome, Peter. "Drugs, Death and the Occult Meet in Grisly Inquiry at Mexico Border." *New York Times*, April 13, 1989, sec. U.S. https://www.nytimes.com/1989/04/13/us/drugs-death-and-the-occult-meet-in-grisly-inquiry-at-mexico-border.html.

Barber, Nigel. "Why Cults Are Mindless: Mindless Obedience Keeps Religious Cults Together." *Psychology Today*, August 6, 2012. https://www.psychologytoday.com/za/blog/the-human-beast/201208/why-cults-are-mindless.

Bourbon-Galdiano-Montenegro, Carlos Antonio de. *Palo Mayombe: Spirits—Rituals—Spells*. Morrisville, NC: Lulu Press, 2011 (self-published).

Bovsun, Mara. "Spring Break Revelry Turns to Horror as Mexican Druglord Kills University of Texas Student in Sicko Human Sacrifice Voodoo Ritual." *New York Daily News*, March 21, 2015. https://www.nydailynews.com/news/crime/mexican-druglord-kills-college-student-sicko-ritual-article-1.2157613.

Garcia, Guy. "The Believers: Cult Murders in Mexico." *Rolling Stone* (website), June 29, 1989. https://www.rollingstone.com/culture/culture-features/the-believers-cult-murders-in-mexico-53577/.

Giannangelo, Stephen J. *The Psychopathology of Serial Murder: A Theory of Violence*. Westport: Praeger Publishers, 1996.

González-Wippler, Migene. *The Complete Book of Spells, Ceremonies, and Magic*. St. Paul: Llewellyn Publications, 1978.

Gregoire, Carolyne. "The Real Connection Between Ambition and Mental Health." HuffPost, December 16, 2014. https://www.huffpost.com/entry/money-power-mental-health_n_6297946?1418762970=.

Greig, Charlotte. *Evil Serial Killers: In the Minds of Monsters*. London: Arcturus Publishing, 2006.

Mouradian, Vera E. "Abuse in Intimate Relationships: Defining the Multiple Dimensions and Terms." National Violence Against Women Research Center, 2000. https://mainweb-v.musc.edu/vawprevention/research/defining.shtml.

Rakovec-Felser, Zlatka. "Domestic Violence and Abuse in Intimate Relationship from Public Health Perspective." *Health Psychology Research* 2, no. 3 (2014). https://doi.org/10.4081/hpr.2014.1821.

Ramsland, Katherine. *Inside the Minds of Serial Killers: Why They Kill*. Westport, CT: Praeger, 2006.

————. "Merging into Murder: Emotional Investment and Certain Mindsets Can Set Up Moral Meltdown." *Psychology Today*, September 3, 2021. https://www.psychologytoday.com/us/blog/shadow-boxing/202109/merging-murder.

————. "Partners in Crime." *Psychology Today*, July 1, 2014. https://www.psychologytoday.com/us/articles/201407/partners-in-crime.

Schiller, Dane. "Woman Called Priestess of Satanic Cult Says She's Changed: Inmate Has Served 15 Years in Prison in Mexico for Ritual Sacrifices of 13 People." SFGATE, March 28, 2004. https://www.sfgate.com/news/article/Woman-called-priestess-of-satanic-cult-says-she-s-2774267.php.

Singer, Margaret Thaler, and Marsha Emmer Addis. "Cults, Coercion, and Contumely." In *The Mosaic of Contemporary Psychiatry in Perspective*, edited by Anthony Kales, Chester M. Pierce, and Milton Greenblatt. New York: Springer, 1992, 130–42. https://doi.org/10.1007/978-1-4613-9194-4_13.

EXPLOITATION: BHAGWAN SHREE RAJNEESH

Birnstiel, Sheela, and Ma Anand Sheela. *Don't Kill Him: The Story of My Life with Bhagwan Rajneesh*. New Delhi: Fingerprint Publishing, 2013.

Carter, Lewis F. *Charisma and Control in Rajneeshpuram: The Role of Shared Values in the Creation of a Community*. Cambridge, UK: Cambridge University Press, 1990.

Moshakis, Alex. "What Do Near-Death Experiences Mean, and Why Do They Fascinate Us?" *Guardian*, March 7, 2021. https://www.theguardian.com/society/2021/mar/07/the-space-between-life-and-death.

Nagaraj, Anil Kumar Mysore. "Osho—Insights on Sex." *Indian Journal of Psychiatry* 55, supplement 2 (January 2013): S268–272. https://doi.org/10.4103/0019-5545.105549.

Oregon Experience: Rajneeshpuram. Season 7, episode 701. PBS. Aired November 19, 2012. https://www.pbs.org/video/oregon-experience-rajaneeshpuram/.

Osho. *Sex Matters: From Sex to Superconsciousness*. New York: St. Martin's, 2003.

Palmer, Susan J., and Frederick Bird. "Therapy, Charisma and Social Control in the Rajneesh Movement." *Sociology of Religion* 53, Special Issue (June 1, 1992): S71–S85. https://doi.org/10.2307/3711252.

Sarasohn, David. "Antelope's Last Stand." *New Republic*, April 12, 2018. https://newrepublic.com/article/147876/antelopes-last-stand.

Stork, Jane. *Breaking the Spell: My Life as a Rajneeshee, and the Long Journey Back to Freedom*. Sydney: Macmillan Australia, 2009.

Urban, Hugh B. *Zorba the Buddha: Sex, Spirituality, and Capitalism in the Global Osho Movement*. Oakland: University of California Press, 2016.

Way, Maclain, and Chapman Way. *Wild Wild Country*. Netflix docuseries, 2018.

Wright, Charles. *Oranges & Lemmings: The Story Behind Bhagwan Shree Rajneesh*. Richmond, Victoria, Australia: Greenhouse Publications, 1985.

Zaitz, Les. "25 Years After Rajneeshee Commune Collapsed, Truth Spills Out—Part 1 of 5." *Oregonian*, April 14, 2011, updated February 5, 2019. https://www.oregonlive.com/rajneesh/2011/04/part_one_it_was _worse_than_we.html.

EXPLOITATION: JIM JONES AND THE PEOPLES TEMPLE

Bebelaar, Judy, and Ron Cabral. *And Then They Were Gone: Teenagers of Peoples Temple from High School to Jonestown*. Berkeley, CA: Minuteman, 2018.

Mitchell, Dawn, and Michael Jesse. "Retro Indy: Jim Jones and the People's Temple in Indianapolis." *IndyStar*, November 18, 2013, updated November 18, 2019. https://www.indystar.com/story/news/history/retroindy /2013/11/18/peoples-temple/3634925/.

Fondakowski, Leigh. *Stories from Jonestown*. Minneapolis: University of Minnesota Press, 2013.

Gritz, Jennie Rothenberg. "Drinking the Kool-Aid: A Survivor Remembers Jim Jones." *Atlantic*, November 18, 2011. https://www.theatlantic.com /national/archive/2011/11/drinking-the-kool-aid-a-survivor-remembers -jim-jones/248723/.

Guinn, Jeff. *The Road to Jonestown: Jim Jones and Peoples Temple*. Illustrated edition. New York: Simon & Schuster, 2017.

"Jonestown." FBI Records: The Vault. Collection, 1978–1979. https://vault .fbi.gov/jonestown/jonestown.

Kilduff, Marshall, and Phil Tracy, "Inside Peoples Temple," *New West* magazine, August 1, 1977.

Klineman, George, Sherman Butler, and David Conn. *The Cult That Died: The Tragedy of Jim Jones and the Peoples Temple*. New York: Putnam, 1980.

Mahaffie, Michael. *605 Adults 304 Children*. Vimeo.com, 2018. https://vimeo .com/373653092.

Mailman, Erika. "What Happened After Jonestown?" *Rolling Stone*, November 16, 2018. https://www.rollingstone.com/culture/culture-features /jonestown-jim-jones-bodies-memorial-756320/.

Naipaul, Shiva. *Black & White*. London: Hamish Hamilton, 1980.

Reiterman, Tim, with John Jacobs. *Raven: The Untold Story of the Rev. Jim Jones and His People*. New York, Jeremy P. Tarcher/Penguin, 1982.

Scheeres, Julia. *A Thousand Lives: The Untold Story of Hope, Deception, and Survival at Jonestown*. Reprint edition. New York: Free Press, 2011.

PATHOLOGICAL LYING: CLAUDE VORILHON AND RAËLISM

Andersen, Donna. *Red Flags of Love Fraud: 10 Signs You're Dating a Sociopath*. Egg Harbor Township, NJ: Anderly Publishing, 2012.

Bocci, Goali Saedi. "What Is Exotic Beauty? Part II: The Case of Asian Fetish." *Psychology Today*, April 19, 2011. https://www.psychologytoday .com/us/blog/millennial-media/201104/what-is-exotic-beauty-part-ii -the-case-the-asian-fetish.

Chantepie, Emmanuelle. "Raël: Itinéraire d'un gourou en quête d'identités." *Le Journal du dimanche*, January 5, 2003. https://www.prevensectes.me /rev0301.htm#5c.

Clifford, Graham. "Raelian Movement in Ireland: 'Some Think It's a Cult but It's Nothing Like That.'" *Irish Times*, July 28, 2018. https://www .irishtimes.com/life-and-style/people/raelian-movement-in-ireland -some-think-it-s-a-cult-but-it-s-nothing-like-that-1.3575205.

Davis, James D. "Sitting Down with Raëlians, Awaiting Aliens." *South Florida Sun-Sentinel*, September 8, 2001. https://www.sun-sentinel.com/news/fl -xpm-2001-09-08-0109070424-story.html.

"Group Claims Human Cloning Success." *Guardian*, December 27, 2002. https://www.theguardian.com/science/2002/dec/27/genetics.science.

Harris, Nick. "'Experimenting with Life Is What All Parents Do. What's the Difference?'" *Independent*, December 29, 2002. https://www.independent .co.uk/news/science/experimenting-with-life-is-what-all-parents-do -what-s-the-difference-137630.html.

"I Was Married to Clone Cult Leader Raël 15 Years. He Wrecked My Life and Our Children's." *Daily Mail*, January 12, 2003. https://culteduca tion.com/group/1106-raelians/17521-i-was-married-to-clone-cult -leader-rael-15-years-he-wrecked-my-life-and-our-childrens.html.

Kort, Joe. "9 Crucial Facts You Need to Understand About Sex Addiction." *Your Tango*, April 3, 2012. https://www.yourtango.com/experts/dr-joe -kort/sex-addiction-loss-sexual-control-expert.

Le grand échiquier (*The Great Chessboard*). TV series. Aired March 13, 1974. https://www.imdb.com/title/tt9487458/.

McCann, Brigitte. "Get Undressed." *Calgary Sun*, October 13, 2003. https:// www.religionnewsblog.com/4711/get-undressed.

"Narcissistic Personality Disorder." Mayo Clinic, November 18, 2017. https://www.mayoclinic.org/diseases-conditions/narcissistic-personal ity-disorder/symptms-causes/syc-20366662.

Palmer, Susan J. *Aliens Adored: Raël's UFO Religion*. New Brunswick, NJ: Rutgers University Press, 2004.

———. *The New Heretics of France: Minority Religions, la République, and the Government-Sponsored "War on Sects."* New York: Oxford University Press, 2011.

———. "The Real Deal." *Religion in the News* 4, no. 1 (Summer 2011).

Saint-Hilaire, Dominique. Interview by Paul Arcand. TVA. Aired October 30, 2002. YouTube, November 8, 2011. https://www.youtube.com /watch?v=aLcE0RkqAOg.

"Vatican Slams 'Brutal' Clone Claim." CNN, December 28, 2002. https:// www.cnn.com/2002/HEALTH/12/28/cloning.vatican/index.html.

Vorilhon, Claude (Raël). *Accueillir les extra-terrestres* (*Let's Welcome the Extraterrestrials*). Vaduz, Liechtenstein: Fondation Raëlienne, 1979.

———. *Le livre qui dit la vérité* (*The Book Which Tells the Truth*). Brantôme, France: Édition du Message, 1976.

———. *Les extra-terrestres m'ont emmené sur leur planète* (*Extraterrestrials Took Me to Their Planet*). Brantôme, France: Édition du Message, 1977.

———. *The True Face of God*. Vaduz, Liechtenstein: Fondation Raëlienne, 2003.

Weiss, Rick. "Human Cloning's 'Numbers Game.'" *Washington Post*, October 10, 2000. https://www.washingtonpost.com/archive/politics/2000 /10/10/human-clonings-numbers-game/7ed0daa7-3dae-485e-b65a -a540919e314d/.

SADISM:
ROCH THÉRIAULT AND THE ANT HILL KIDS

Bovsun, Mara. "Canadian 'Messiah' Formed Horrifying Doomsday Cult After Ulcer Surgery Left Him with Chronic Pain." *New York Daily News*, February 4, 2018. https://www.nydailynews.com/news/crime/cana dian-messiah-formed-doomsday-cult-ulcer-problems-article-1.3797931.

"Cult Leader Roch Theriault Killed in N.B. Prison." CTVNews, February 27, 2011. https://www.ctvnews.ca/cult-leader-roch-theriault-killed -in-nb-prison-1.612633.

Ford, Laura Grace. *Savage Messiah*. New York: Verso, 2011.

Kaihla, Paul, Ross Laver, Ann McLaughlin, and Barry Came. "The Ant Hill Kids." *Maclean's*, February 8, 1993. https://archive.macleans.ca/article /1993/2/8/the-ant-hill-kids.

McPadden, Mike. "Roch Thériault: The Horrifying Savagery (& Home Surgery) of Canada's Most Violent Cult Leader." ID Crimefeed, September 28, 2017. https://www.investigationdiscovery.com/crimefeed /murder/roch-theriault-the-horrifying-savagery-home-surgery-of-cana das-most-violent-cult-leader.

Palmer, Susan, Martin Geoffroy, and Paul L. Gareau, eds. *The Mystical Geography of Quebec: Catholic Schisms and New Religious Movements*. Cham, Switzerland: Palgrave Macmillan, 2020.

Thompson, Emily G. *Cults Uncovered: True Stories of Mind Control and Murder*. New York: DK Publishing, 2020.

Vandonk, Todd. "Behind the Crimes: Murder, Mutilation, Abuse Part of Life at Ant Hill Kids Commune." Toronto.com, September 10, 2020. https://www.toronto.com/news-story/10148519-behind-the-crimes -murder-mutilation-abuse-part-of-life-at-ant-hill-kids-commune/.

MEGALOMANIA:
DAVID KORESH AND THE BRANCH DAVIDIANS

Activities of Federal Law Enforcement Agencies Toward the Branch Davidians (Part 1). Joint Hearings Before the Subcommittee on Crime of the Committee on the Judiciary, House of Representatives, and the Subcommittee on National Security, International Affairs, and Criminal Justice of the Committee on Government Reform and Oversight, One Hundred Fourth Congress, First Session, July 19, 20, 21, and 24, 1995. Committee on the Judiciary Serial No. 72. Washington, DC: U.S. Government Printing Office, 1996, 221. https://books.google.com/books/about /Activities_of_Federal_Law_Enforcement_Ag.html?id=qisLLk7GO QC&printsec=frontcover&source=kp_read_button&hl=en&newbks =1&newbks_redir=0#v=onepage&q&f=false.

Benson, Eric. "The Branch Davidians: The FBI Agent Who Can't Stop Thinking About Waco." *Texas Monthly*, April 2018. https://www.texas monthly.com/articles/fbi-agent-cant-stop-thinking-waco/.

Gladwell, Malcolm. "Sacred and Profane: How Not to Negotiate with Believers." *New Yorker*, March 24, 2014. https://www.newyorker.com/maga zine/2014/03/31/sacred-and-profane-4.

Mitra, Debkumar. "Following Cult Followings: Why the Crisis Is Omnipresent in India." *Economic Times*, August 27, 2017. https://economictimes .indiatimes.com/blogs/et-commentary/following-cult-followings-why -the-crisis-is-omnipresent-in-india/.

Murray, Evan D., Miles G. Cunningham, and Bruce H. Price. "The Role of Psychotic Disorders in Religious History Considered." *Journal of Neuropsychiatry and Clinical Neurosciences* 24, no. 4 (October 1, 2012). https://doi .org/10.1176/appi.neuropsych.11090214.

Newport, Kenneth G. C. *The Branch Davidians of Waco: The History and Beliefs of an Apocalyptic Sect.* New York: Oxford University Press, 2006.

Thibodeau, David, Leon Whiteson, and Aviva Layton. *Waco: A Survivor's Story.* New York: Hachette Books, 2018.

"Waco Siege." Britannica.com. Accessed January 14, 2020. https://www.bri tannica.com/event/Waco-siege.

Wessinger, Catherine. "The Deaths of 76 Branch Davidians in April 1993 Could Have Been Avoided—So Why Didn't Anyone Care?" The Conversation, April 13, 2018. https://theconversation.com/the-deaths-of -76-branch-davidians-in-april-1993-could-have-been-avoided-so-why -didnt-anyone-care-90816.

SADISM:
KEITH RANIERE AND NXIVM

Andrews, Suzanna. "The Heiresses and the Cult." *Vanity Fair*, October 13, 2010. https://www.vanityfair.com/culture/2010/11/bronfman-201011.

Arnold, Amanda. "NXIVM 'Sex Slave' Gives Harrowing Testimony in

Court." The Cut, May 9, 2019. https://www.thecut.com/2019/05
/nxivm-sex-slave-gives-testimony-in-court-against-raniere.html.

Berman, Sarah. "The NXIVM 'Sex Cult' Story Keeps Getting More Disturbing." Vice, May 30, 2019. https://www.vice.com/en/article/evyb5j
/the-nxivm-sex-cult-story-keeps-getting-more-disturbing.

"Cult of Personality." *Forbes,* October 13, 2003. https://www.forbes.com
/forbes/2003/1013/088.html?sh=483fdd221853.

Dickson, EJ. "How NXIVM Was the Ultimate Wellness Scam." *Rolling Stone*
(website), October 8, 2019. https://www.rollingstone.com/culture/cul
ture-features/nxivm-keith-raniere-wellness-scam-sex-cult-848439/.

Edmondson, Sarah. *Scarred: The True Story of How I Escaped NXIVM, the Cult
That Bound My Life.* San Francisco: Chronicle Prism, 2019.

Grigoriadis, Vanessa. "Inside Nxivm, the 'Sex Cult' That Preached Empowerment." *New York Times Magazine,* May 30, 2018. https://www.nytimes
.com/2018/05/30/magazine/sex-cult-empowerment-nxivm-keith
-raniere.html.

Grinberg, Emanuella, and Sonia Moghe. "She Says She Dropped Out of
School and Left Mexico to Join a Cult." CNN, May 24, 2019. https://
www.cnn.com/2019/05/24/us/nxivm-trial-mexican-witness/index.html.

Heaney, Katie (as told to). "What It Was Like to Date a Cult Leader." The
Cut, November 7, 2019. https://www.thecut.com/2019/11/what-it
-was-like-to-date-a-cult-leader.html.

Johnson, Scott, and Rebecca Sun. "Her Darkest Role: Actress Allison Mack's
Descent from 'Smallville' to Sex Cult." *Hollywood Reporter,* May 16, 2018.
https://www.hollywoodreporter.com/tv/tv-features/how-smallvilles
-allison-mack-went-actress-sex-cult-slaver-1112107/.

Meier, Barry. "Once Idolized, Guru of Nxivm 'Sex Cult' to Stand Trial
Alone." *New York Times,* May 1, 2019. https://www.nytimes.com/2019
/05/01/nyregion/nxivm-keith-raniere-trial.html.

———. "The Journey of the 'Sex Cult' Heiress: From Reluctant Recruit to
Criminal Defendant." *New York Times,* August 11, 2018. https://www
.nytimes.com/2018/08/11/business/clare-bronfman-nxivm.html.

Natalie, Toni, and Chet Hardin. *The Program: Inside the Mind of Keith Raniere
and the Rise and Fall of NXIVM.* New York: Grand Central Publishing,
2019.

"NXIVM: Gina Melita's Story." *Albany Times Union,* YouTube, April 22, 2019.
https://youtu.be/YWJcMMgXNmw?t=53.

Odato, James M. "A Split from NXIVM." *Albany Times Union*, May 10, 2014, updated May 12, 2014. https://www.timesunion.com/local/article /A-split-from-NXIVM-5468731.php.

Odato, James M., and Jennifer Gish. "In Raniere's Shadows." *Albany Times Union*, February 18, 2012, updated February 22, 2012. https://www .timesunion.com/local/article/In-Raniere-s-shadows-3341644.php.

Ringwald, Christopher. "Discount Service Target of Probe Pyramid Scheme Alleged." *Albany Times Union*, May 21, 1992. https://culteducation.com /group/907-nxivm/6023-discount-service-target-of-probe-pyramid -scheme-alleged.html.

Waters, Flavie, Vivian Chiu, Amanda Atkinson, and Jan Dirk Blom. "Severe Sleep Deprivation Causes Hallucinations and a Gradual Progression Toward Psychosis with Increasing Time Awake." *Frontiers in Psychiatry* 9 (July 10, 2018): 303. https://doi.org/10.3389/fpsyt.2018.00303.

Xiao, Bowen. "Delving into the Childhood of NXIVM's Leader." *Epoch Times*, May 28, 2018, updated May 30, 2018. https://www.theepochtimes.com /exclusive-delving-into-the-childhood-of-nxivms-leader_2540043.html.

ESCAPE:
CREDONIA MWERINDE AND THE MOVEMENT FOR THE RESTORATION OF THE TEN COMMANDMENTS OF GOD

Atuhaire, Bernard. *The Uganda Cult Tragedy: A Private Investigation*. London: Janus Publishing, 2003.

Behrend, Heike. "Salvation and Terror in Western Uganda. The Movement for the Restoration of the Ten Commandments of God." *Bulletin des Séances / Mededelingen der Zittingen. Royal Academy of Overseas Sciences* 47, supplement (2001): 77–96. http://www.kaowarsom.be/documents /BULLETINS_MEDEDELINGEN/2001-SUPPLEMENT.pdf.

Borzello, Anna. "The Zealot Who Ran Uganda's Killer Cult." *Guardian*, March 29, 2000. https://www.theguardian.com/world/2000/mar/30/2.

Cauvin, Henri E. "Fateful Meeting Led to Founding of Cult in Uganda." *New York Times*, March 27, 2000. https://www.nytimes.com/2000/03/27 /world/fateful-meeting-led-to-founding-of-cult-in-uganda.html.

Fisher, Ian. "Exploring the Deadly Mystique Surrounding a Uganda Cult." *New York Times*, April 1, 2000. https://archive.nytimes.com/www.nytimes .com/library/world/africa/040200uganda-cult-deaths.html.

"Priestess of Death." *Newsweek*, August 13, 2000. https://www.newsweek
.com/priestess-death-159015.

Reid, Richard J. *A History of Modern Uganda*. Cambridge, UK: Cambridge
University Press, 2017.

Ward, Kevin. "A History of Christianity in Uganda." Dictionary of African Christian Biography. https://dacb.org/histories/uganda-history-christianity/.

Zimdars-Swartz, Sandra L. *Encountering Mary: From La Salette to Medjugorje*.
Princeton, NJ: Princeton University Press, 2014.

DENIAL OF REALITY:
MARSHALL APPLEWHITE AND HEAVEN'S GATE

Bearak, Barry. "Eyes on Glory: Pied Pipers of Heaven's Gate." *New York Times*,
April 28, 1997. https://www.nytimes.com/1997/04/28/us/eyes-on
-glory-pied-pipers-of-heaven-s-gate.html.

Evans, Claire L. "Higher Source: The Immortal Web Design of the Suicide Cult 'Heaven's Gate.'" Vice, April 2, 2014. https://www.vice
.com/en/article/pgapzy/heavens-gate-web-designers-higher-source
-suicide-cult.

Galanter, Marc. *Cults: Faith, Healing, and Coercion*. New York: Oxford University
Press, 1999.

"Heaven's Gate Cult Members Found Dead." History, February 9, 2010,
updated March 24, 2021. https://www.history.com/this-day-in-history
/heavens-gate-cult-members-found-dead.

Lane, Justin E. "UFO Cults." In *Encyclopedia of Sciences and Religions*, edited by
Anne L. C. Runehov and Lluis Oviedo. Dordrecht: Springer Netherlands,
2013, 2317–20. https://doi.org/10.1007/978-1-4020-8265-8_1498.

Lewis, James R., ed. *Encyclopedic Sourcebook of UFO Religions*. Amherst, NY: Pro-
metheus Books, 2003.

Lewis, James R., and Jesper Aagaard Petersen, eds. *Controversial New Religions*.
New York: Oxford University Press, 2004.

Raine, Susan. "Reconceptualising the Human Body: Heaven's Gate and
the Quest for Divine Transformation." *Religion* 35, no. 2 (April 2005):
98–117. https://doi.org/10.1016/j.religion.2005.06.003.

Robinson, Wendy Gale. "Heaven's Gate: The End." *Journal of Computer-
Mediated Communication* 3, no. 3 (December 1, 1997). https://doi.org
/10.1111/j.1083-6101.1997.tb00077.x.

Wessinger, Catherine. *How the Millennium Comes Violently: From Jonestown to Heaven's Gate*. New York: Seven Bridges Press, 2000.

Zeller, Ben. "What the Heaven's Gate Suicides Say about American Culture." The Conversation, March 24, 2017, updated December 4, 2020. http://theconversation.com/what-the-heavens-gate-suicides-say-about-american-culture-74343.